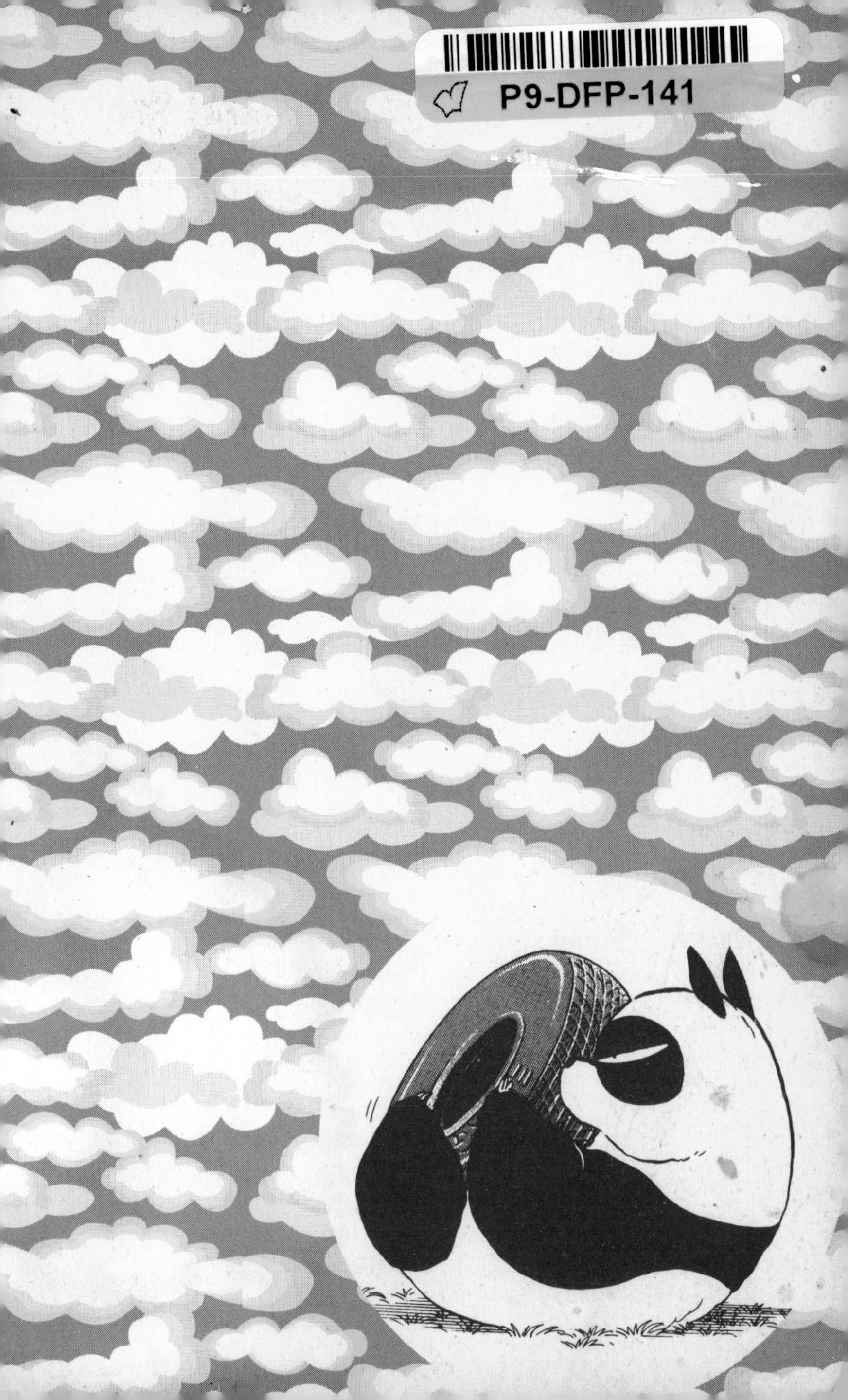

RANMA 1/2

VOL. 3
Action Edition

Story and Art by
RUMIKO TAKAHASHI

English Adaptation/Gerard Jones and Matt Thorn
Touch-Up Art & Lettering/Wayne Truman
Cover Design/Hidemi Sahara
Graphics & Design/Sean Lee
Editors (1st Edition)/Satoru Fujii and Trish Ledoux
Editor (Action Edition)/Julie Davis

Managing Editor/Annette Roman
Editor in Chief/William Flanagan
Dir. of Licensing & Acquisitions/Rika Inouye
VP of Sales & Marketing/Liza Coppola
Sr. VP of Editorial/Hyoe Narita
Publisher/Seiji Horibuchi

RANMA 1/2 is rated "T+" for Older Teens. It may contain violence, language, alcohol or tobacco use, or suggestive situations.

Printed in Canada.

Published by VIZ, LLC
P.O. Box 77010
San Francisco, CA 94107

1st Edition published 1994

Action Edition
10 9 8 7 6 5 4 3 2 1
First printing, June 2003

www.viz.com

store.viz.com

Ranma 1/2™

VOL. 3 **Action Edition**

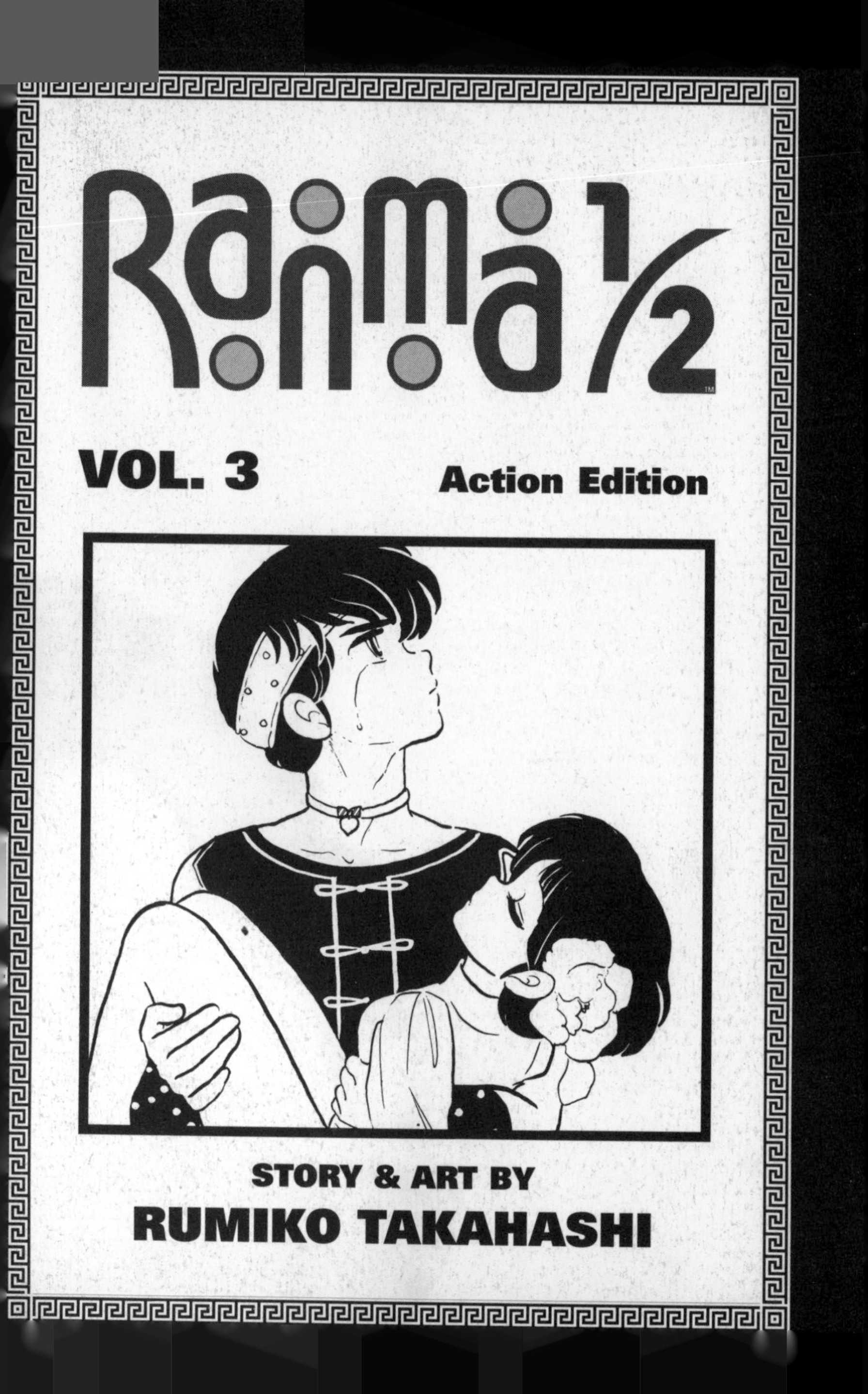

STORY & ART BY

RUMIKO TAKAHASHI

STORY THUS FAR

The Tendos are an average, run-of-the-mill Japanese family—at least on the surface, that is. Soun Tendo is the owner and proprietor of the Tendo Dojo, where "Anything-Goes Martial Arts" is practiced. Like the name says, anything goes, and usually does.

When Soun's old friend Genma Saotome comes to visit, Soun's three lovely young daughters—Akane, Nabiki, and Kasumi—are told that it's time for one of them to become the fiancée of Genma's teenage son, as per an agreement made between the two fathers years ago. Youngest daughter Akane—who says she hates boys—is quickly nominated for bridal duty by her sisters.

Unfortunately, Ranma and his father have suffered a strange accident. While training in China, both plunged into one of many "accursed" springs at the legendary martial arts training ground of Jusenkyo. These springs transform the unlucky dunkee into whoever—or whatever—drowned there hundreds of years ago.

From now on, a splash of cold water turns Ranma's father into a giant panda, and Ranma becomes a beautiful, busty young woman. Hot water reverses the effect...but only until next time.

Ranma and Genma weren't the only ones to take the Jusenkyo plunge—it isn't long before they meet several other members of the "cursed." And although their parents are still determined to see Ranma and Akane marry and carry on the training hall, Ranma seems to have a strange talent for accumulating extra fiancées, and Akane has a few suitors of her own. Will the two ever work out their differences, get rid of all these extra people, or just call the whole thing off? And will Ranma ever get rid of his curse?

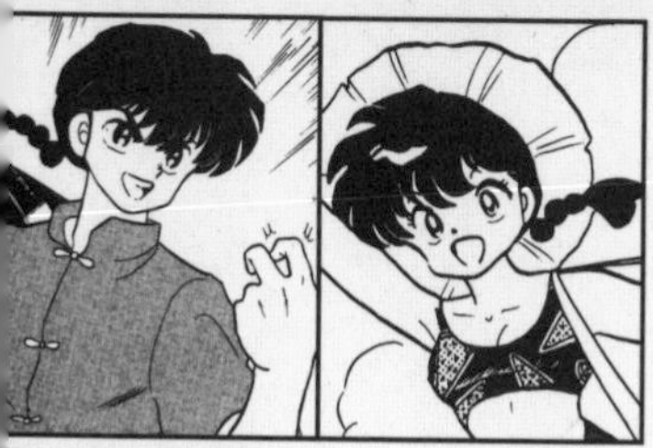

RANMA SAOTOME
Martial artist with far too many finacées, and an ego that won't let him take defeat easily. He changes into a girl when splashed with cold water.

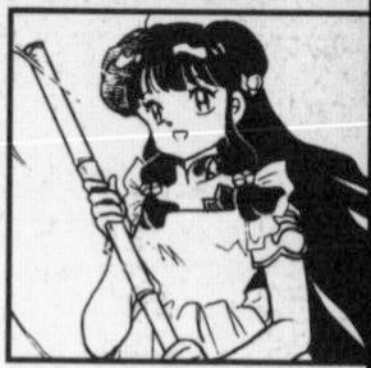

SHAMPOO
An Amazon warrior Ranma met on his travels in China... one who has a serious score to settle.

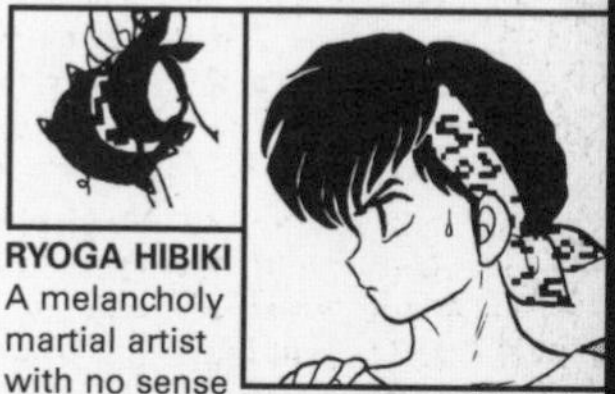

RYOGA HIBIKI
A melancholy martial artist with no sense of direction, a crush on Akane, and a grudge against Ranma. He changes into a small, black pig Akane calls "P-chan."

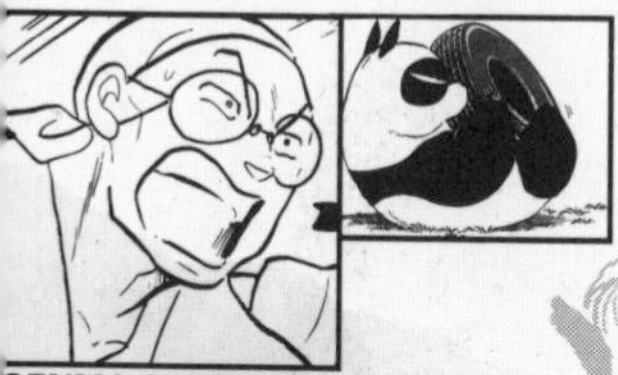

GENMA SAOTOME
Ranma's lazy father, who left his home and wife years ago with his young son to train in the martial arts. He changes into a panda.

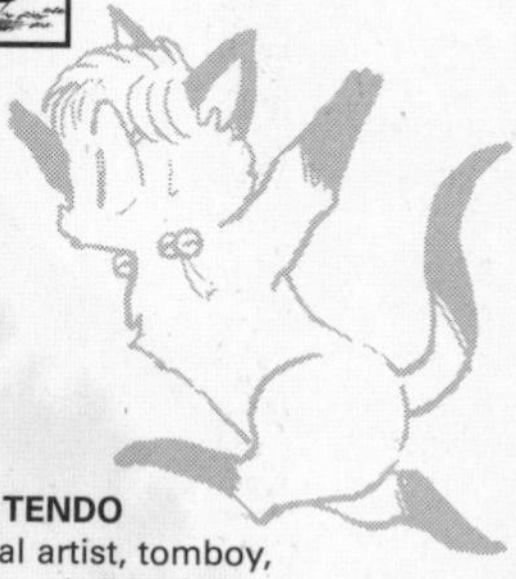

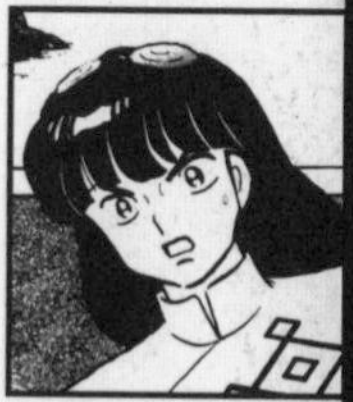

MOUSSE
A nearsighted Chinese martial artist whose specialty is hidden weapons, Mousse has been Shampoo's suitor since childhood.

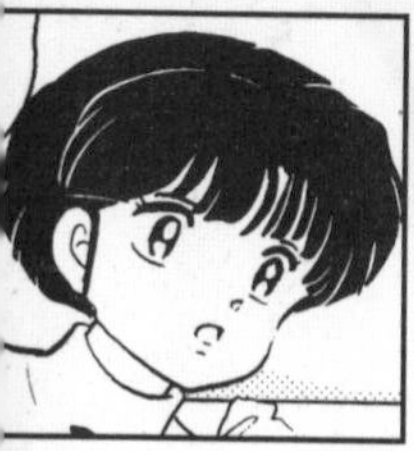

AKANE TENDO
A martial artist, tomboy, and Ranma's fiancée by parental arrangement. She has no clue how much Ryoga likes her, or what relation he has to her pet black pig, P-chan.

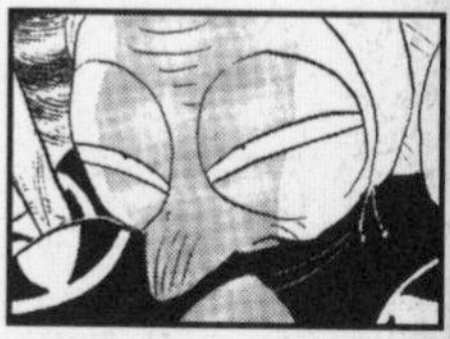

COLOGNE
Great-grandmother to Shampoo who's looking forward to getting a new grandson-in-law in Ranma.

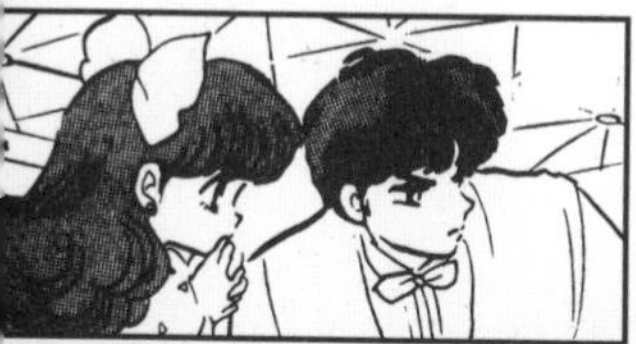

AZUSA SHIRATORI AND MIKADAO SANZENIN
The "Golden Pair" of high school figure skating, this competitive couple have sworn to defeat Ranma and Akane in a skating match with Akane's pet P-chan as the prize!

CONTENTS

Part 1
LIPS AT WAR

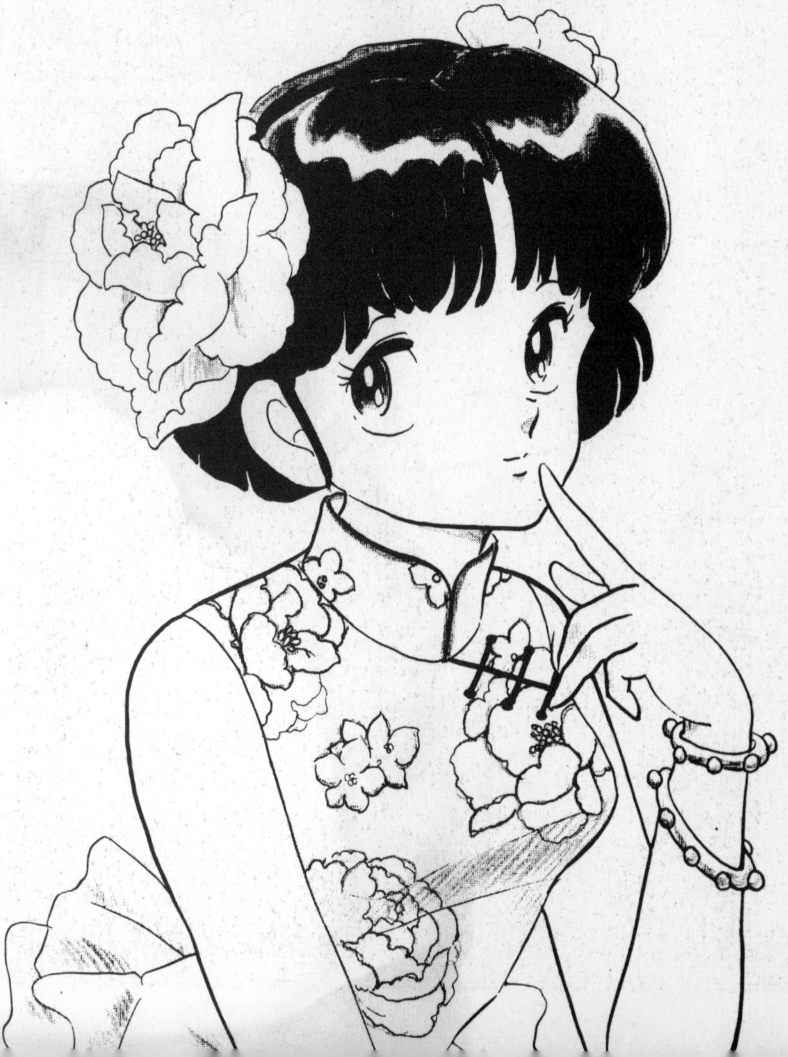

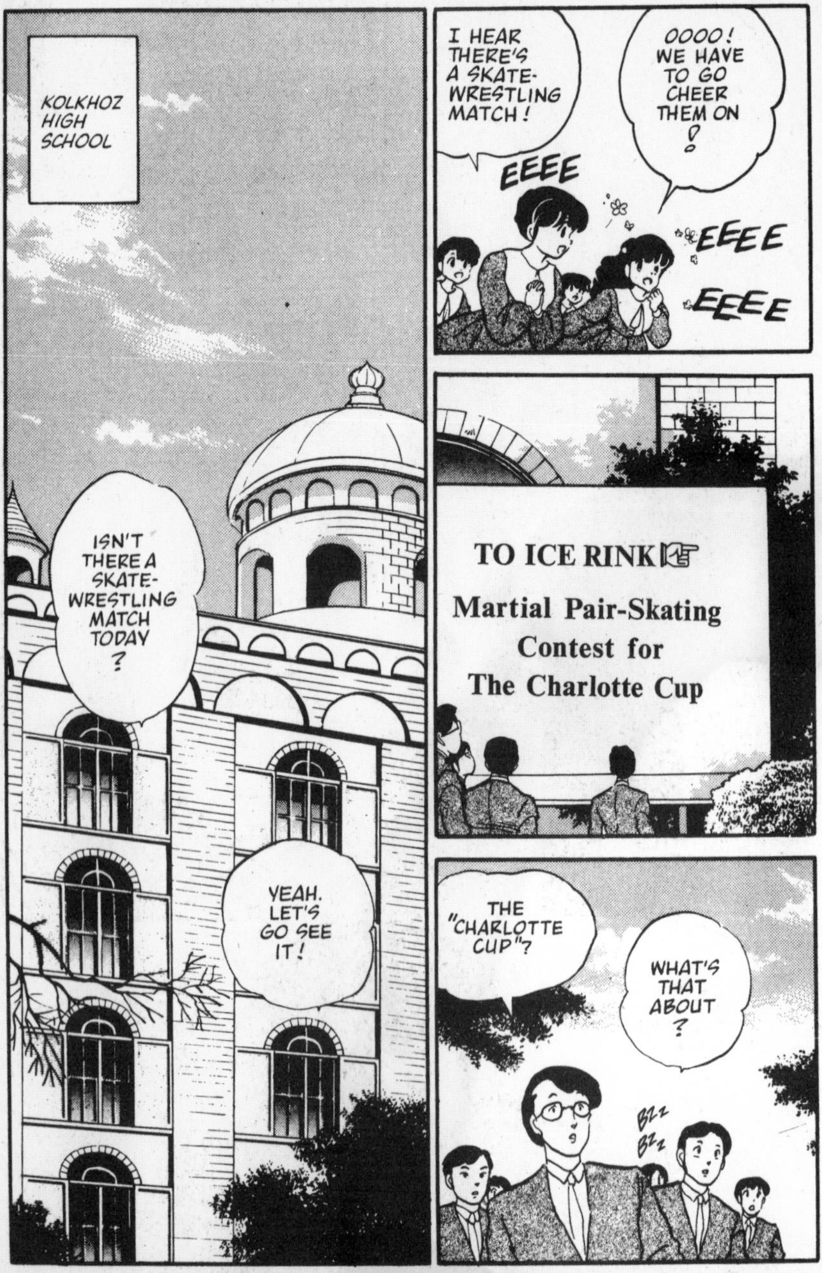
KOLKHOZ HIGH SCHOOL
ISN'T THERE A SKATE-WRESTLING MATCH TODAY ?
YEAH. LET'S GO SEE IT !
I HEAR THERE'S A SKATE-WRESTLING MATCH !
OOOO ! WE HAVE TO GO CHEER THEM ON !
EEEE
EEEE
EEEE
TO ICE RINK
Martial Pair-Skating Contest for The Charlotte Cup
THE "CHARLOTTE CUP"?
WHAT'S THAT ABOUT ?
BZZ BZZ

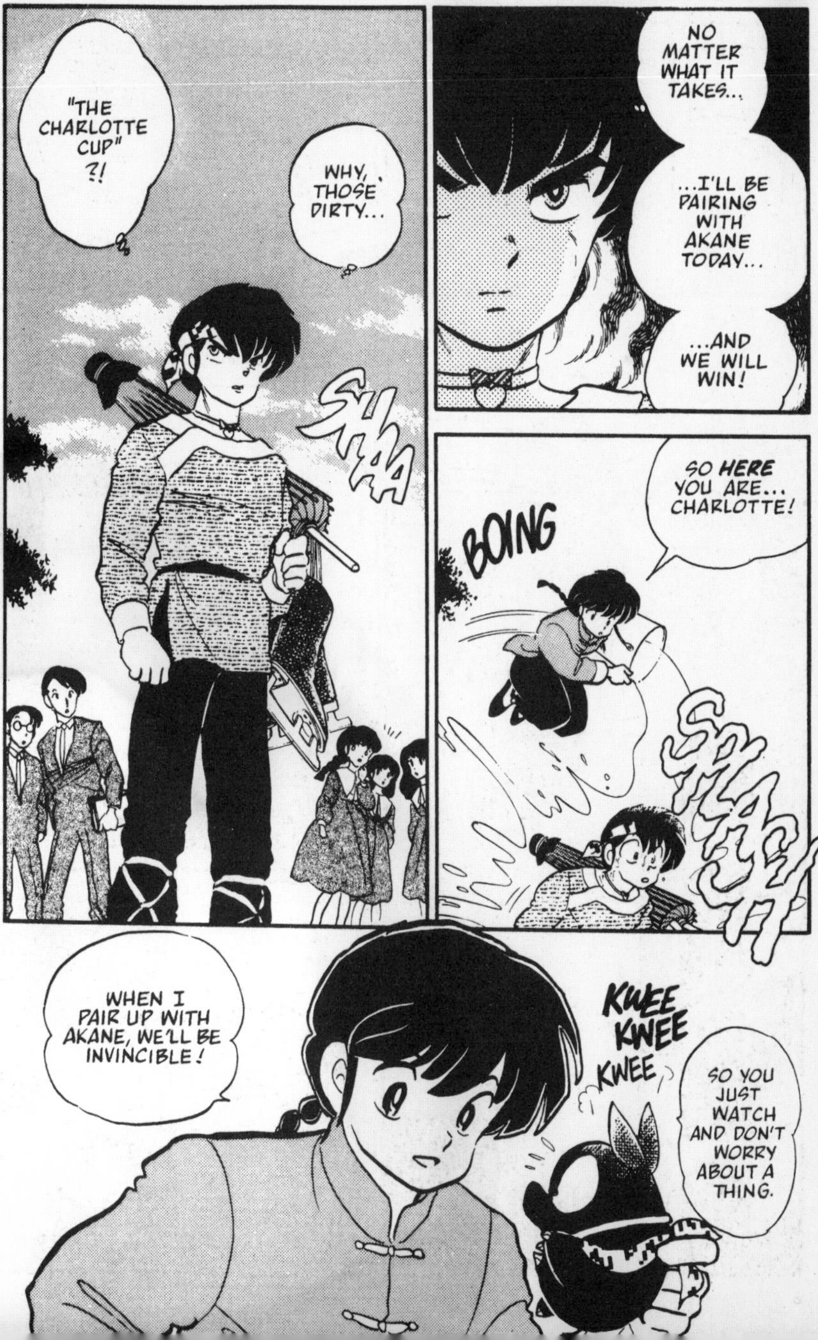
"THE CHARLOTTE CUP" ?!
WHY, THOSE DIRTY...
SHAA
NO MATTER WHAT IT TAKES...
...I'LL BE PAIRING WITH AKANE TODAY...
...AND WE WILL WIN!
BOING
SO **HERE** YOU ARE... CHARLOTTE!
SPLASH!
WHEN I PAIR UP WITH AKANE, WE'LL BE INVINCIBLE!
KWEE KWEE KWEE
SO YOU JUST WATCH AND DON'T WORRY ABOUT A THING.

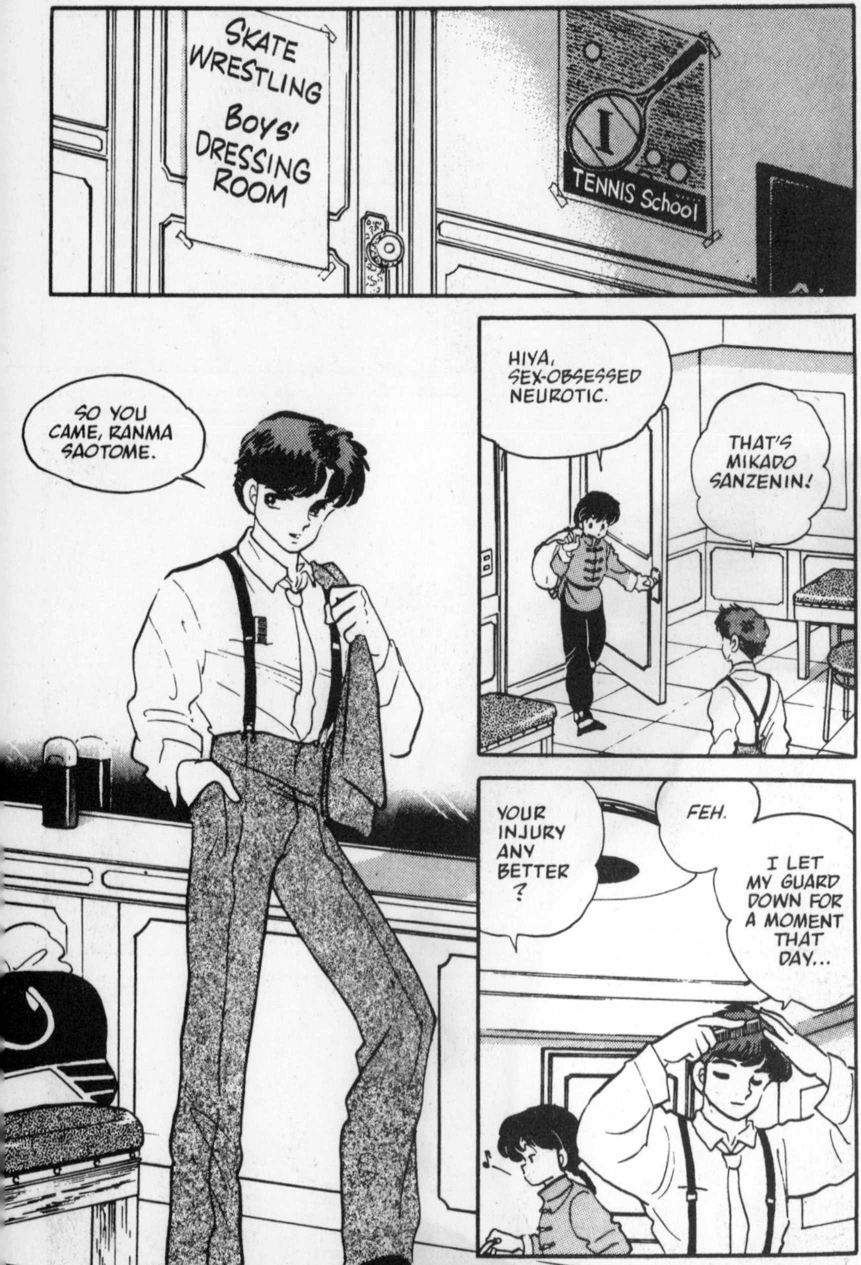
SKATE WRESTLING Boys' DRESSING ROOM
TENNIS School
SO YOU CAME, RANMA SAOTOME.
HIYA, SEX-OBSESSED NEUROTIC.
THAT'S MIKADO SANZENIN!
YOUR INJURY ANY BETTER?
FEH.
I LET MY GUARD DOWN FOR A MOMENT THAT DAY...

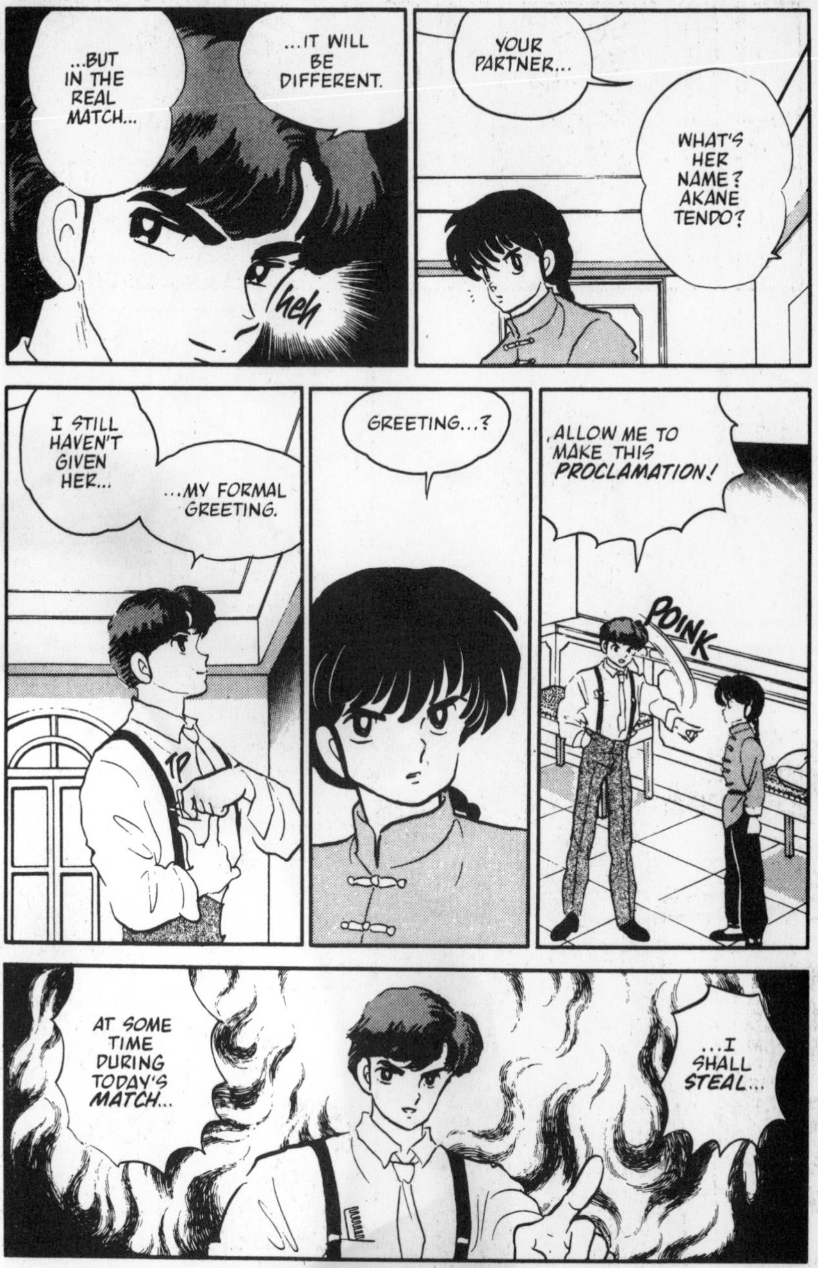
...BUT IN THE REAL MATCH...
...IT WILL BE DIFFERENT.
heh
YOUR PARTNER...
WHAT'S HER NAME? AKANE TENDO?
I STILL HAVEN'T GIVEN HER...
...MY FORMAL GREETING.
TP
GREETING...?
ALLOW ME TO MAKE THIS PROCLAMATION!
POINK
AT SOME TIME DURING TODAY'S MATCH...
...I SHALL STEAL...

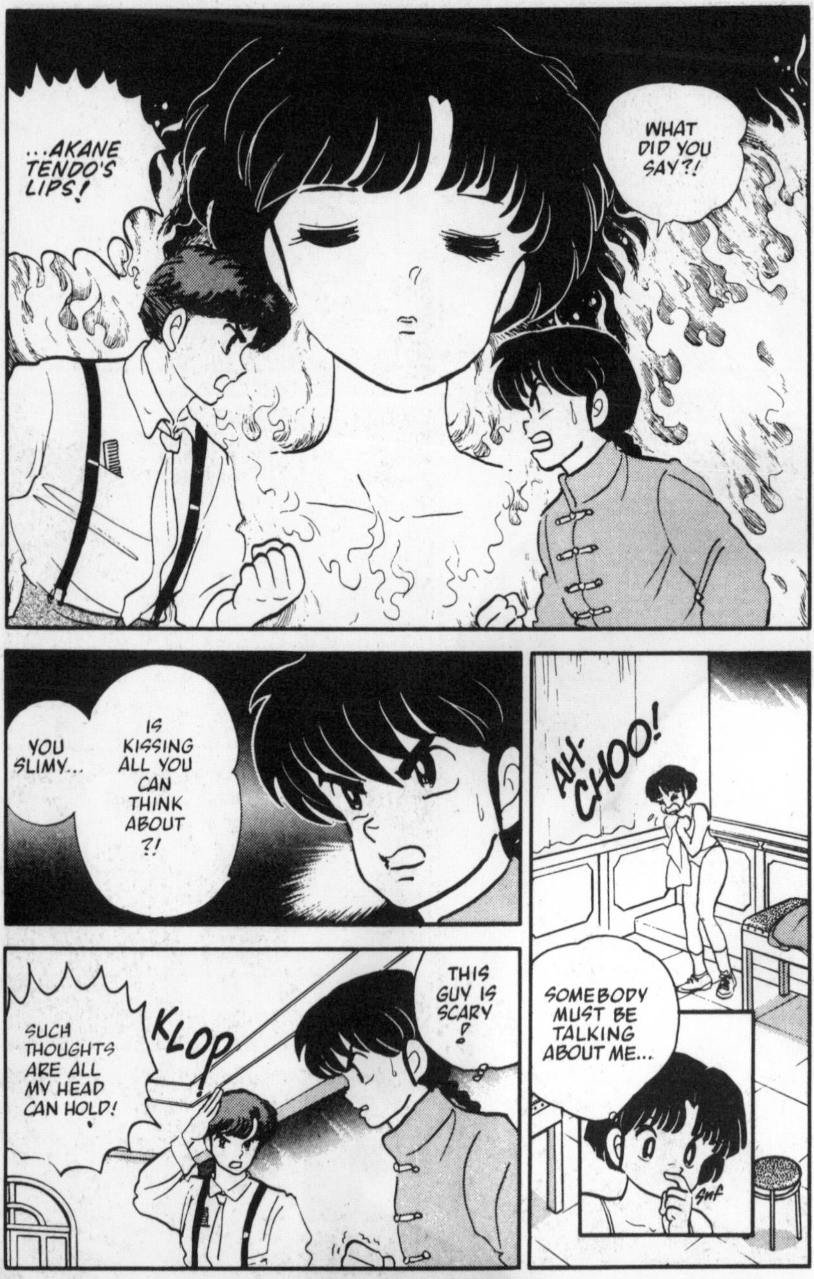
...AKANE TENDO'S LIPS!
WHAT DID YOU SAY?!
YOU SLIMY...
IS KISSING ALL YOU CAN THINK ABOUT ?!
AH-CHOO!
SOMEBODY MUST BE TALKING ABOUT ME...
SNF
SUCH THOUGHTS ARE ALL MY HEAD CAN HOLD!
KLOP
THIS GUY IS SCARY!

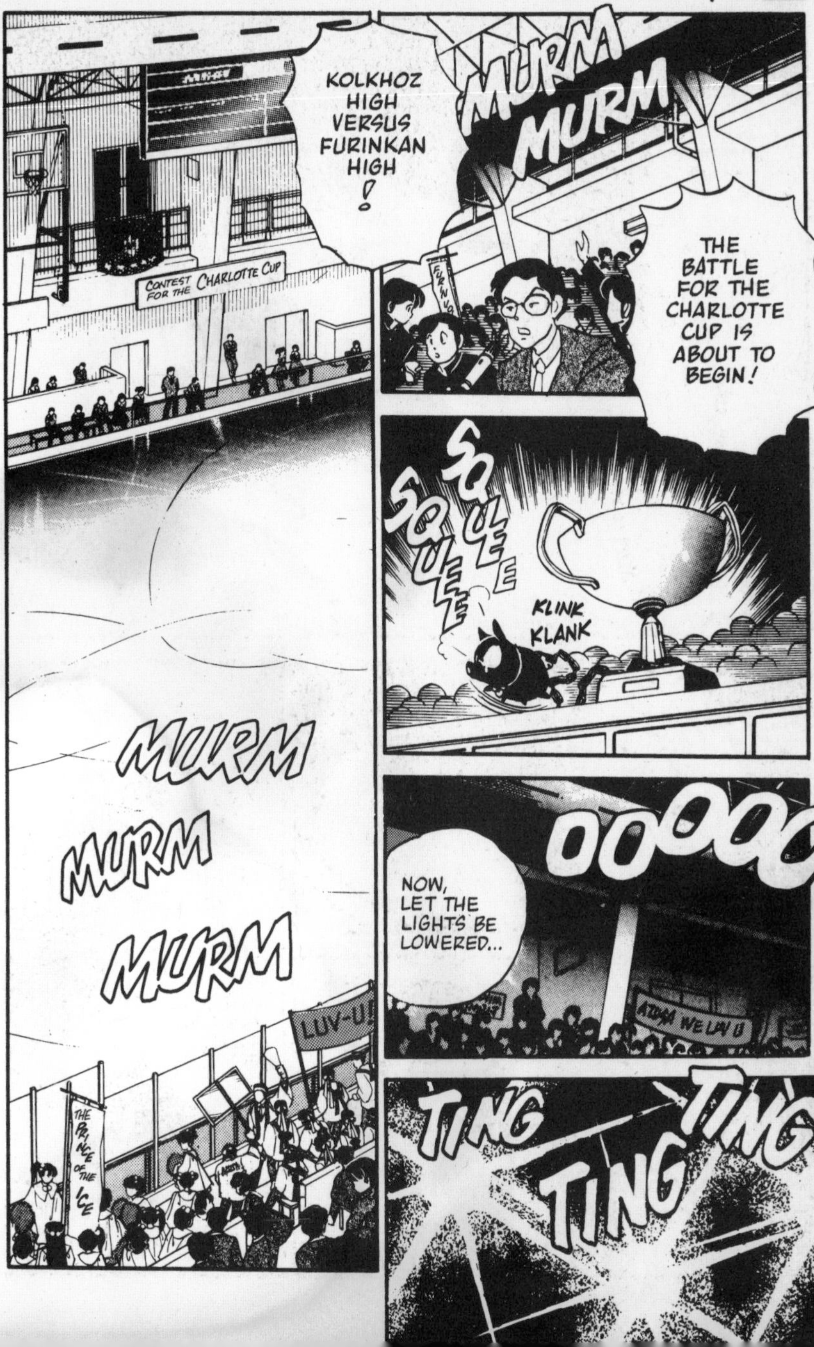
CONTEST FOR THE CHARLOTTE CUP
KOLKHOZ HIGH VERSUS FURINKAN HIGH!
MURM
MURM
MURM
LUV-U!
THE PRINCE OF THE ICE
MURM MURM
THE BATTLE FOR THE CHARLOTTE CUP IS ABOUT TO BEGIN!
SQUEE
SQUEE
KLINK KLANK
OOOOO
NOW, LET THE LIGHTS BE LOWERED...
TING TING TING

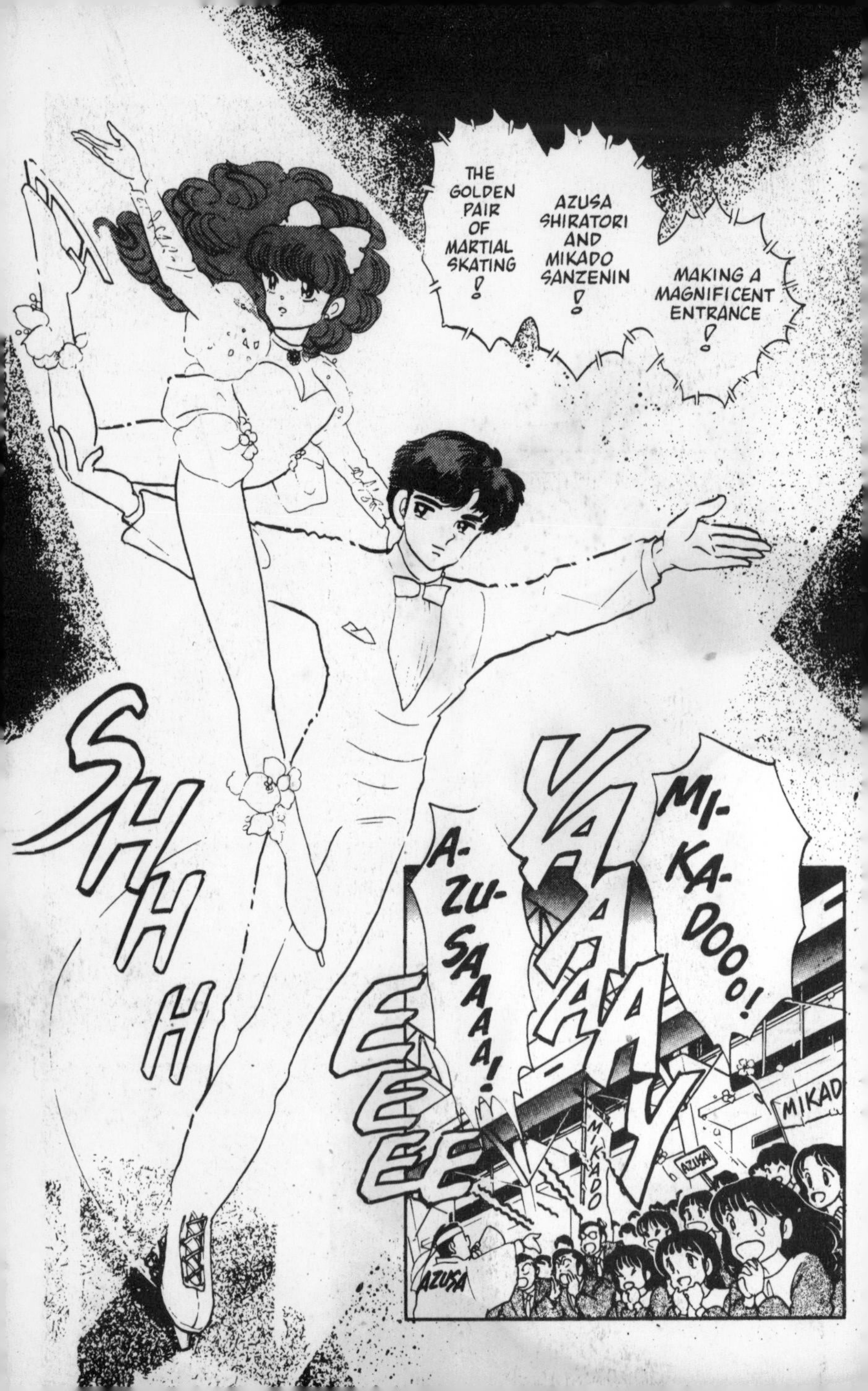

THE GOLDEN PAIR OF MARTIAL SKATING!
AZUSA SHIRATORI AND MIKADO SANZENIN!
MAKING A MAGNIFICENT ENTRANCE!
SHHHH
A-ZU-SAAAAA!
YAAAAY
EEEE
MI-KA-DOOOO!
MIKADO
AZUSA
MIKAD
AZUSA

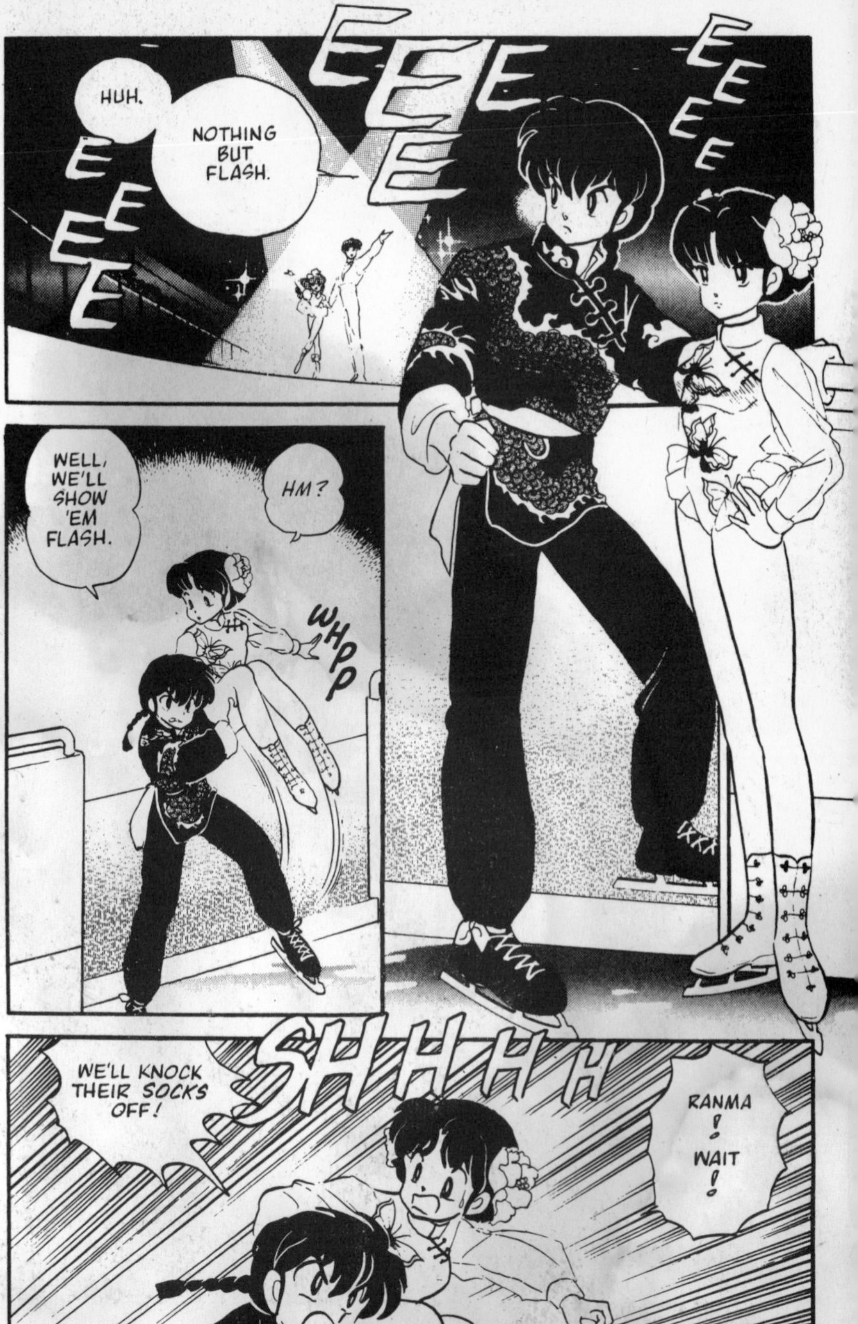
EEEE
HUH.
NOTHING BUT FLASH.
EEEEE
EEEE
WELL, WE'LL SHOW 'EM FLASH.
HM?
WHPP
WE'LL KNOCK THEIR SOCKS OFF!
SHHHHH
RANMA! WAIT!

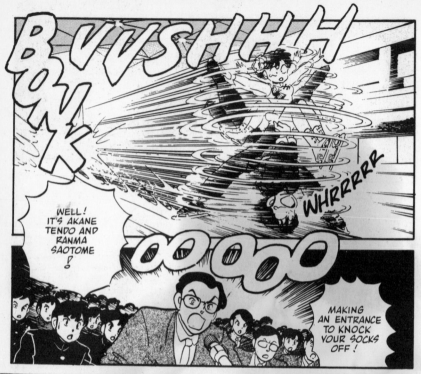

BVVSHHHH
BONK
WHRRRRR

WELL! IT'S AKANE TENDO AND RANMA SAOTOME!

OO OOO

MAKING AN ENTRANCE TO KNOCK YOUR SOCKS OFF!

TEE HEE HEE HEE HEE HEE!

HEE HEE HEE HEE HEE HEE HEE HEE HEE HEE!

AH, SHADDUP!

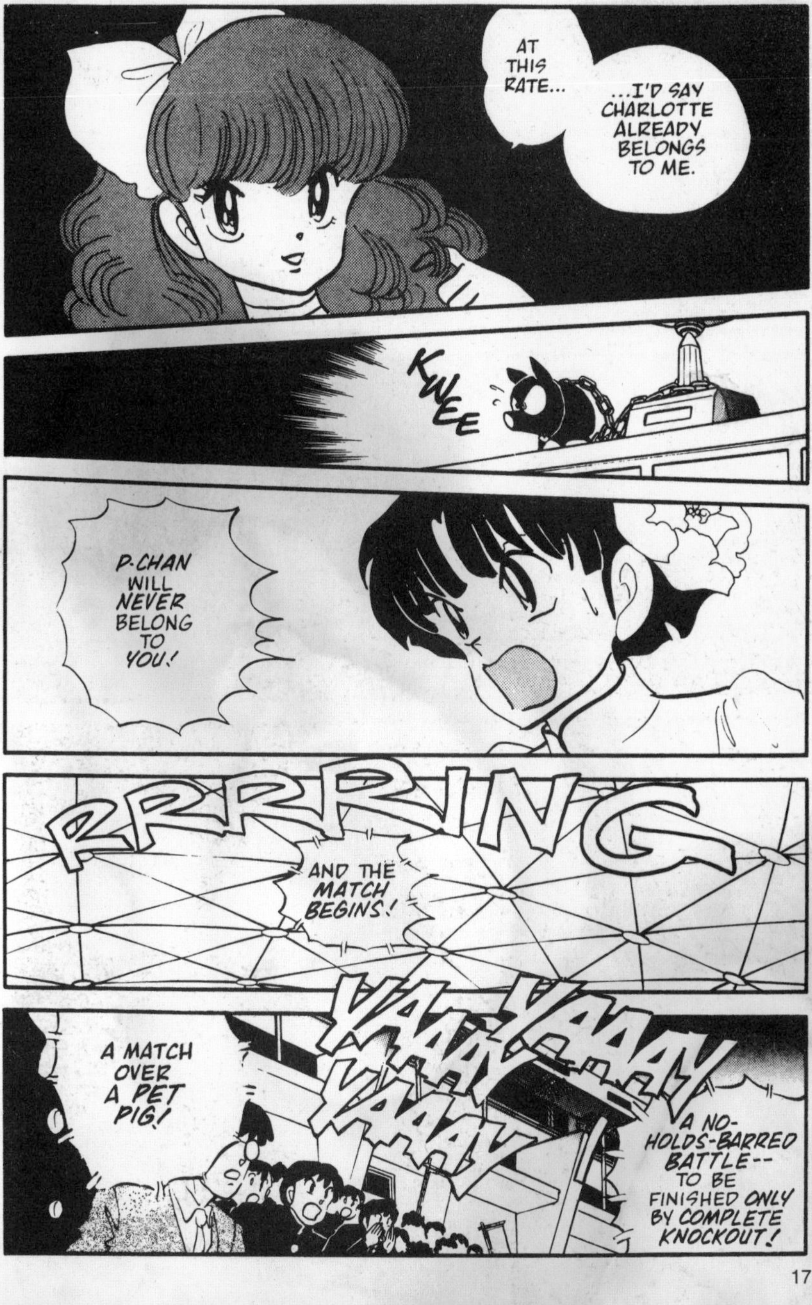
AT THIS RATE...
...I'D SAY CHARLOTTE ALREADY BELONGS TO ME.
KWEE
P-CHAN WILL NEVER BELONG TO YOU!
RRRRING
AND THE MATCH BEGINS!
A MATCH OVER A PET PIG!
YAAAY YAAAY YAAAY
A NO-HOLDS-BARRED BATTLE-- TO BE FINISHED ONLY BY COMPLETE KNOCKOUT!

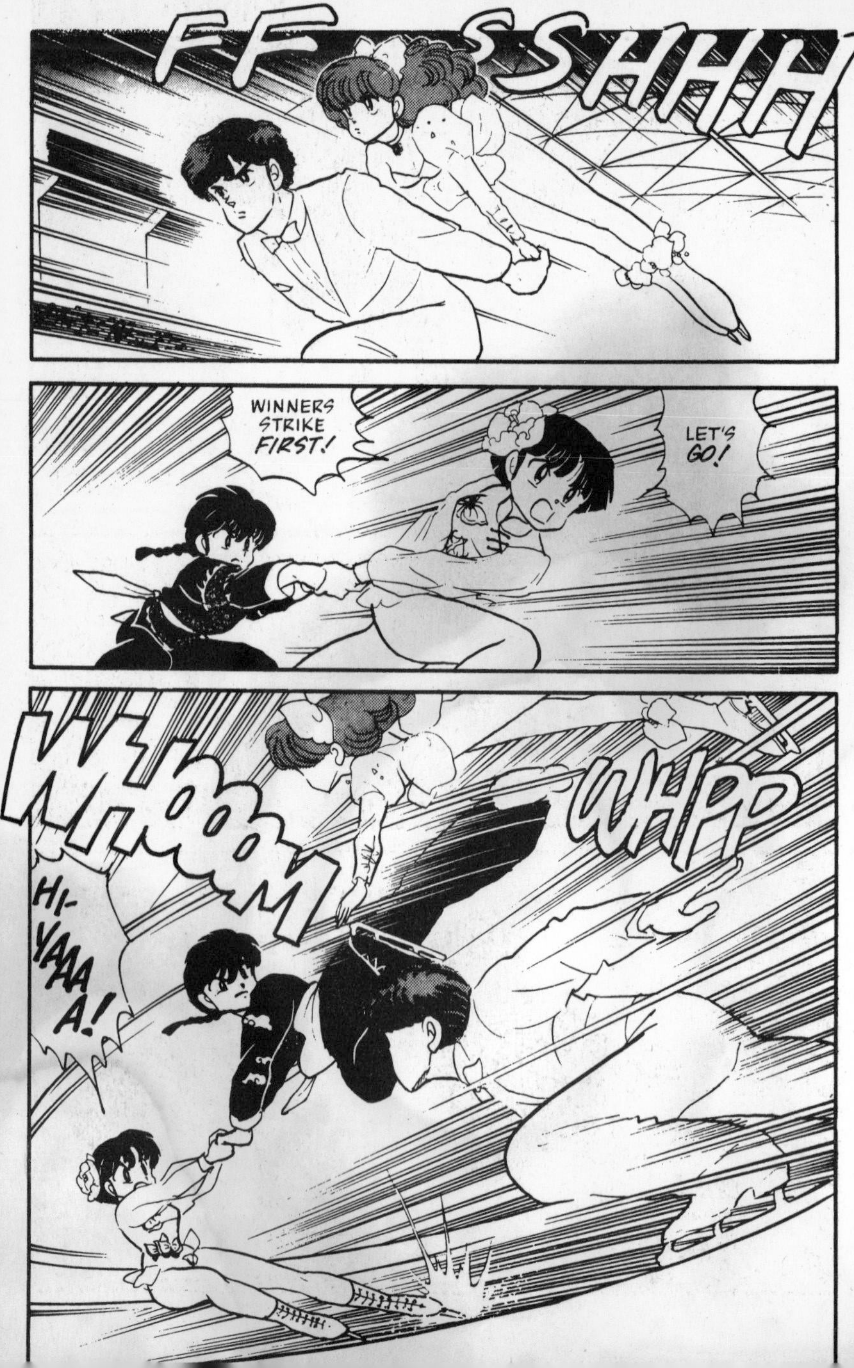
FF SSHHH
WINNERS STRIKE FIRST!
LET'S GO!
WHOOOM
WHPP
HI-YAAAAA!

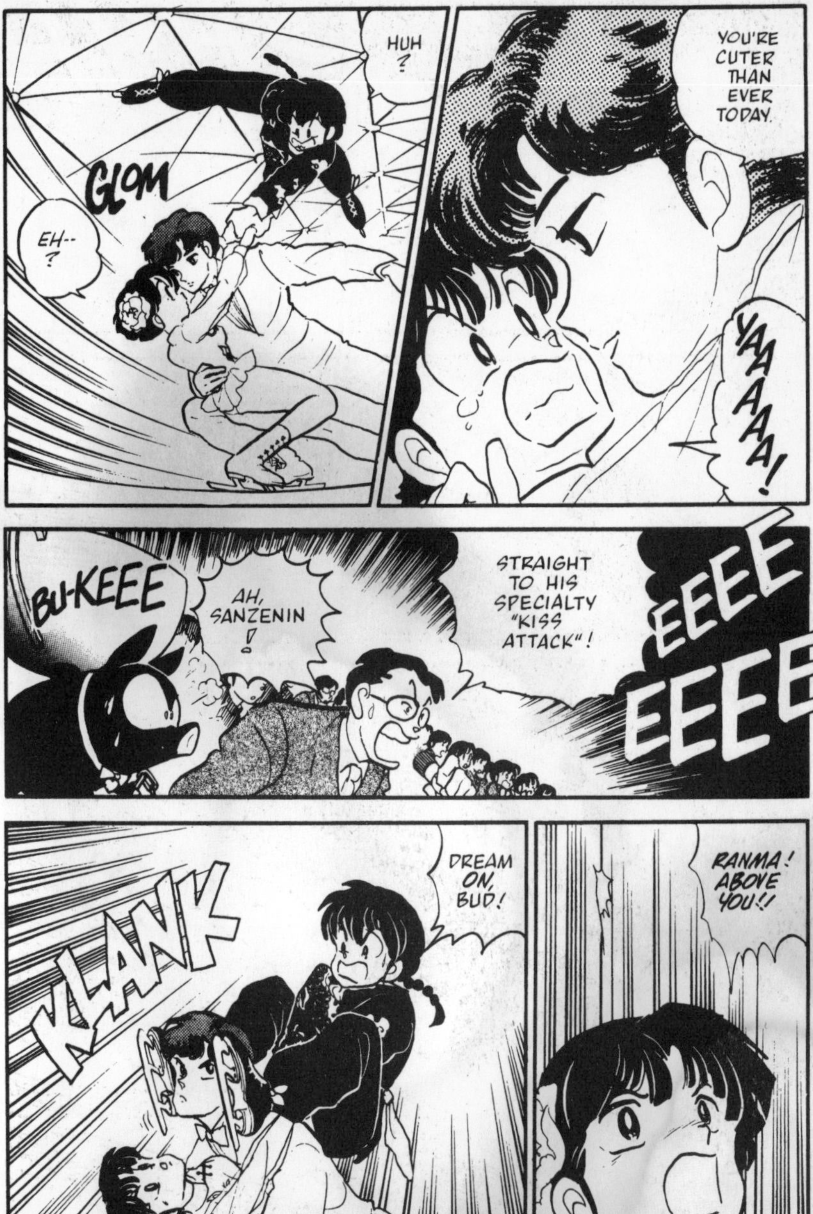
HUH ?
GLOM
EH-- ?
YOU'RE CUTER THAN EVER TODAY.
YAAAAAA!
BU-KEEE
AH, SANZENIN !
STRAIGHT TO HIS SPECIALTY "KISS ATTACK"!
EEEE EEEE
KLANK
DREAM ON, BUD!
RANMA! ABOVE YOU!!

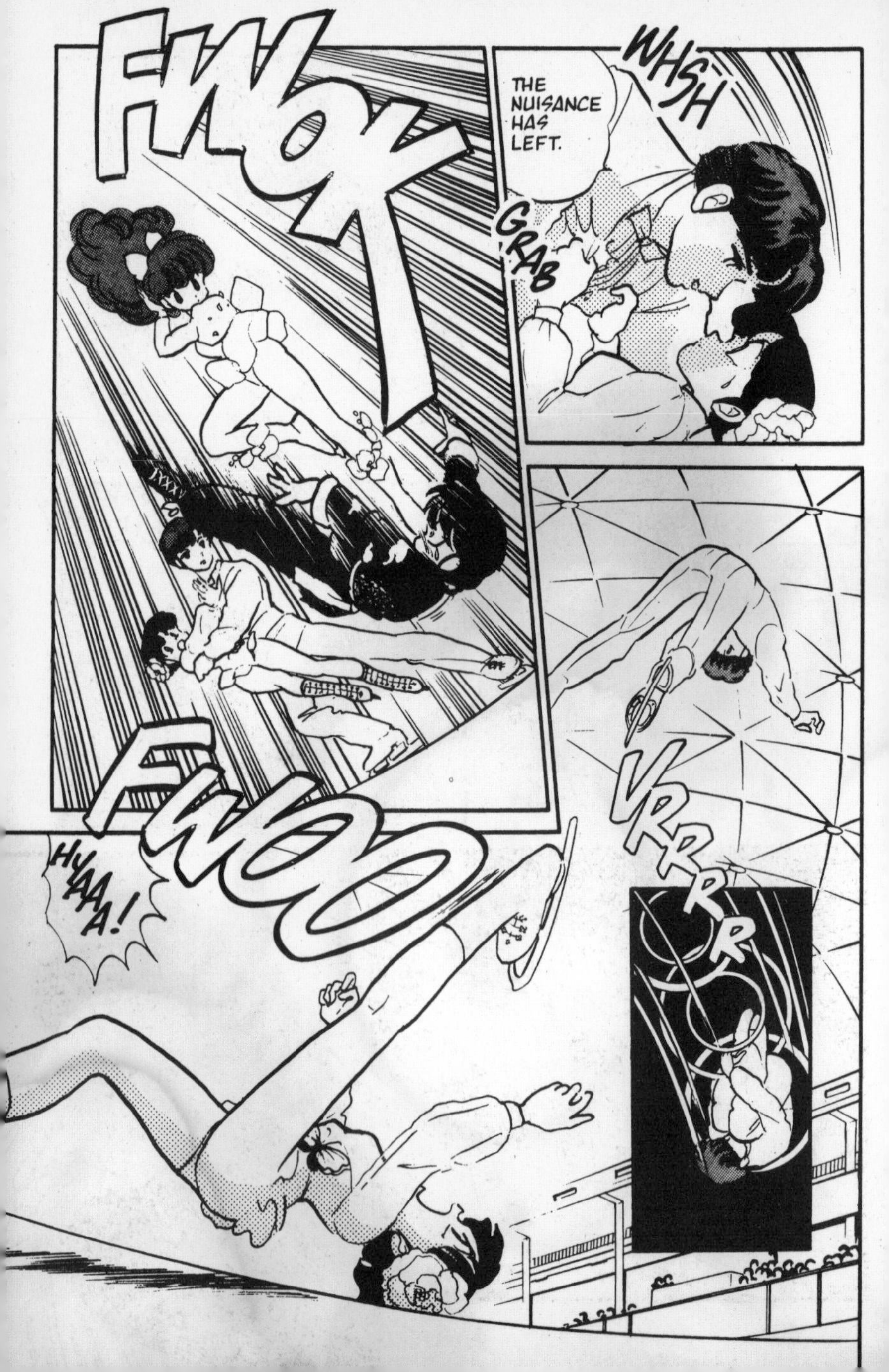

FWOY
FWOO
THE NUISANCE HAS LEFT.
WHSH
GRAB
HYAAAA!
VRRRRR

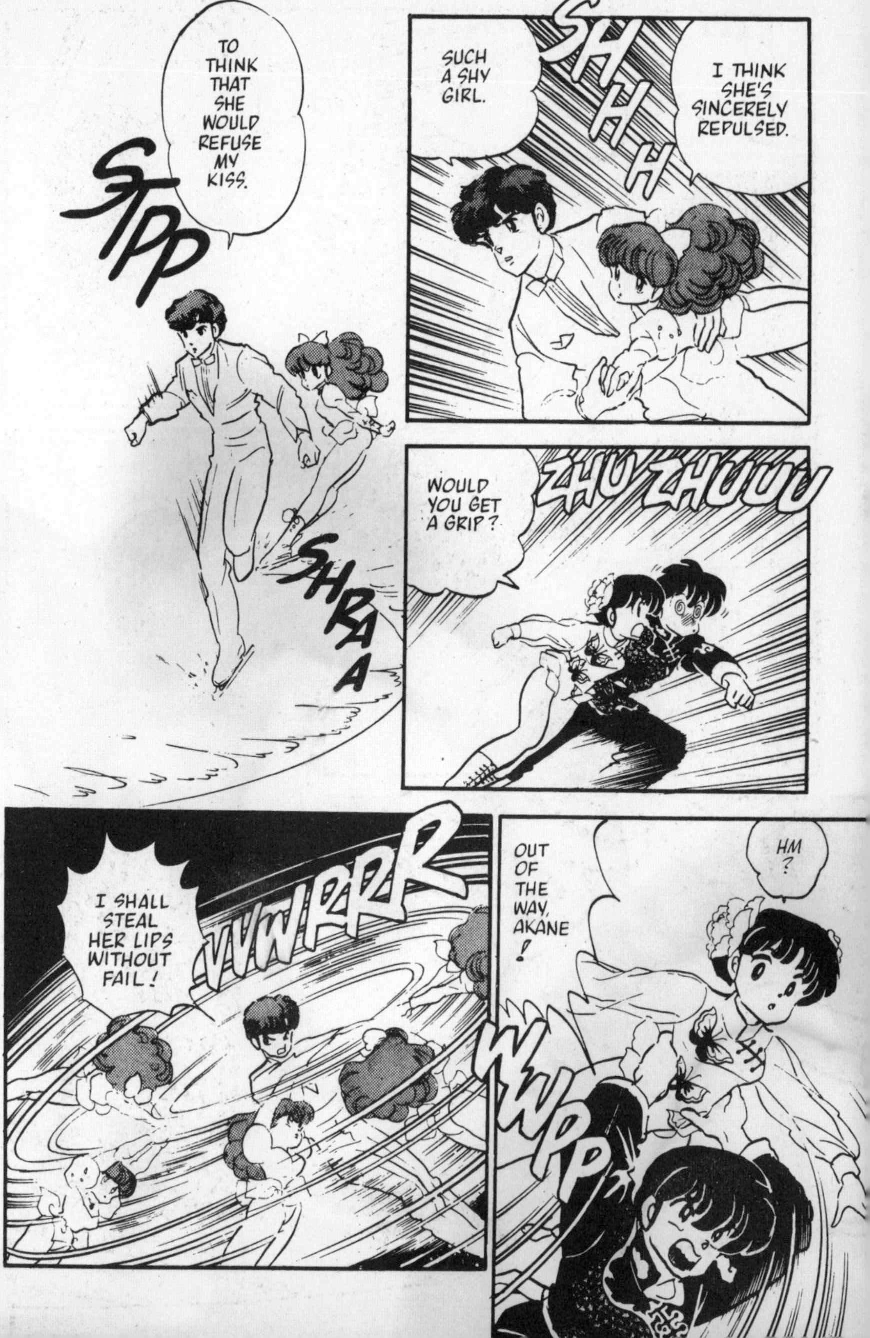
TO THINK THAT SHE WOULD REFUSE MY KISS.
STPP
SHRAA
SUCH A SHY GIRL.
SHHH
I THINK SHE'S SINCERELY REPULSED.
WOULD YOU GET A GRIP?
ZHU ZHUUU
I SHALL STEAL HER LIPS WITHOUT FAIL!
VVWRRR
OUT OF THE WAY, AKANE!
HM?
WWPP

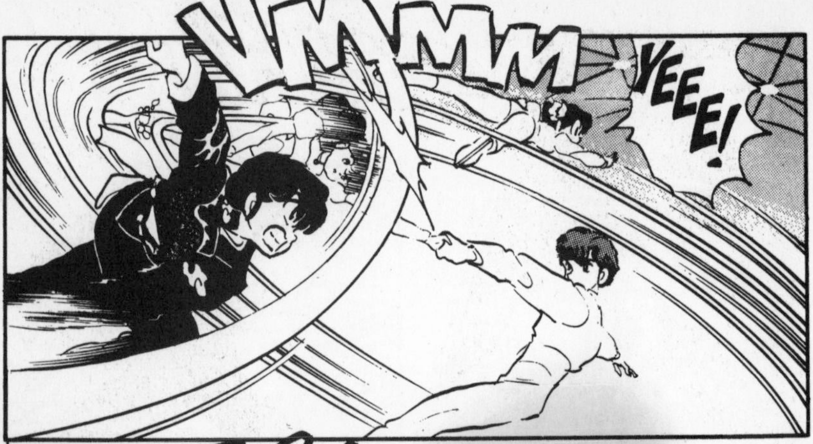
VMMMM
YEEEE!
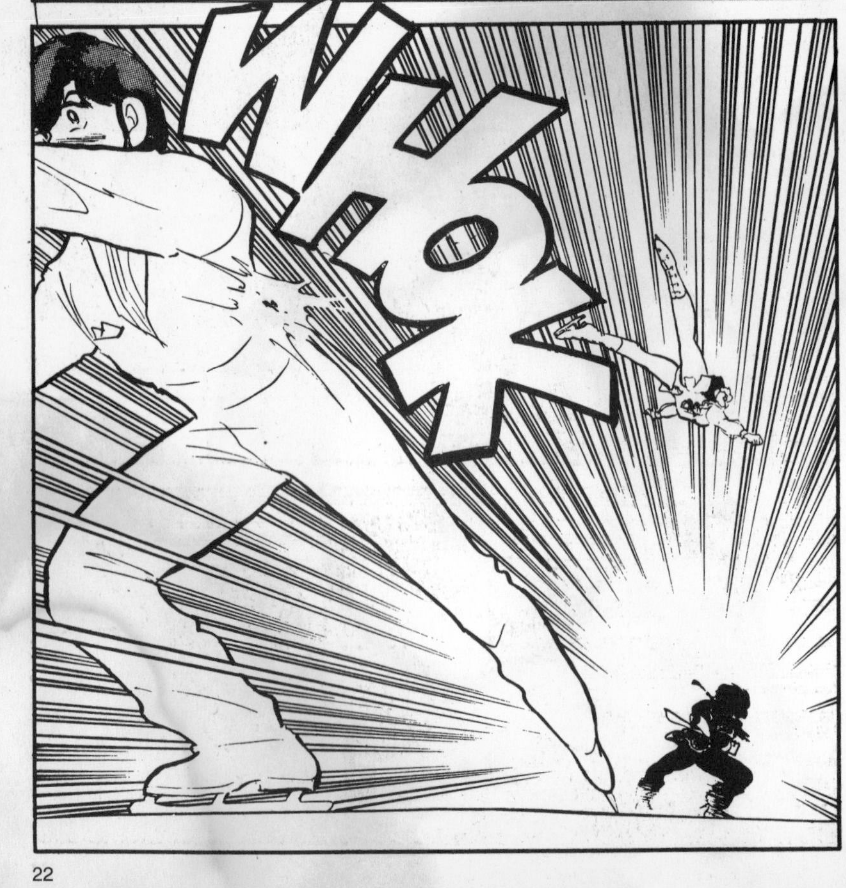
WHOK

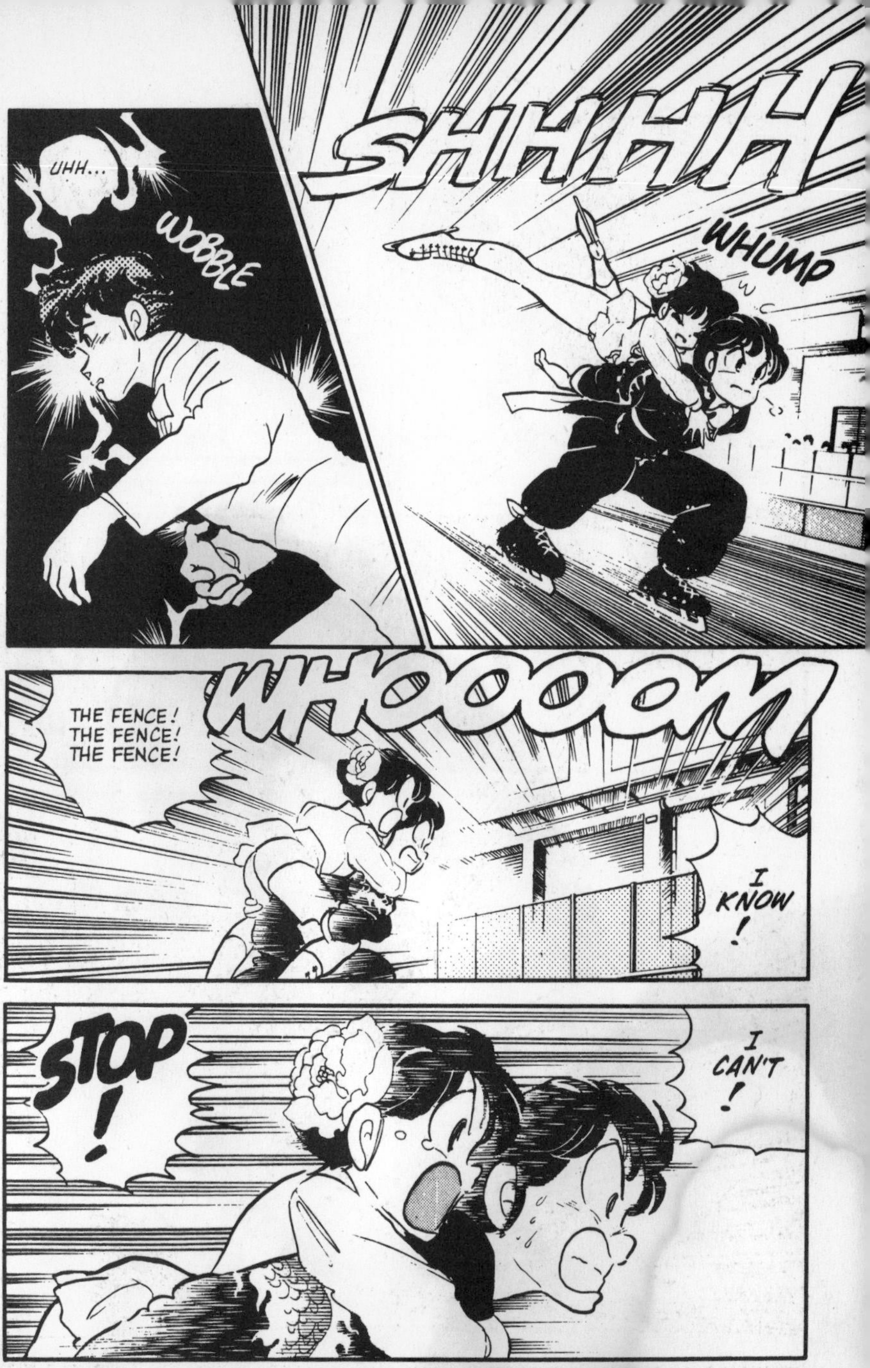
UHH...
WOBBLE
SHHHHH
WHUMP
WHOOOOM
THE FENCE! THE FENCE! THE FENCE!
I KNOW!
STOP!
I CAN'T!

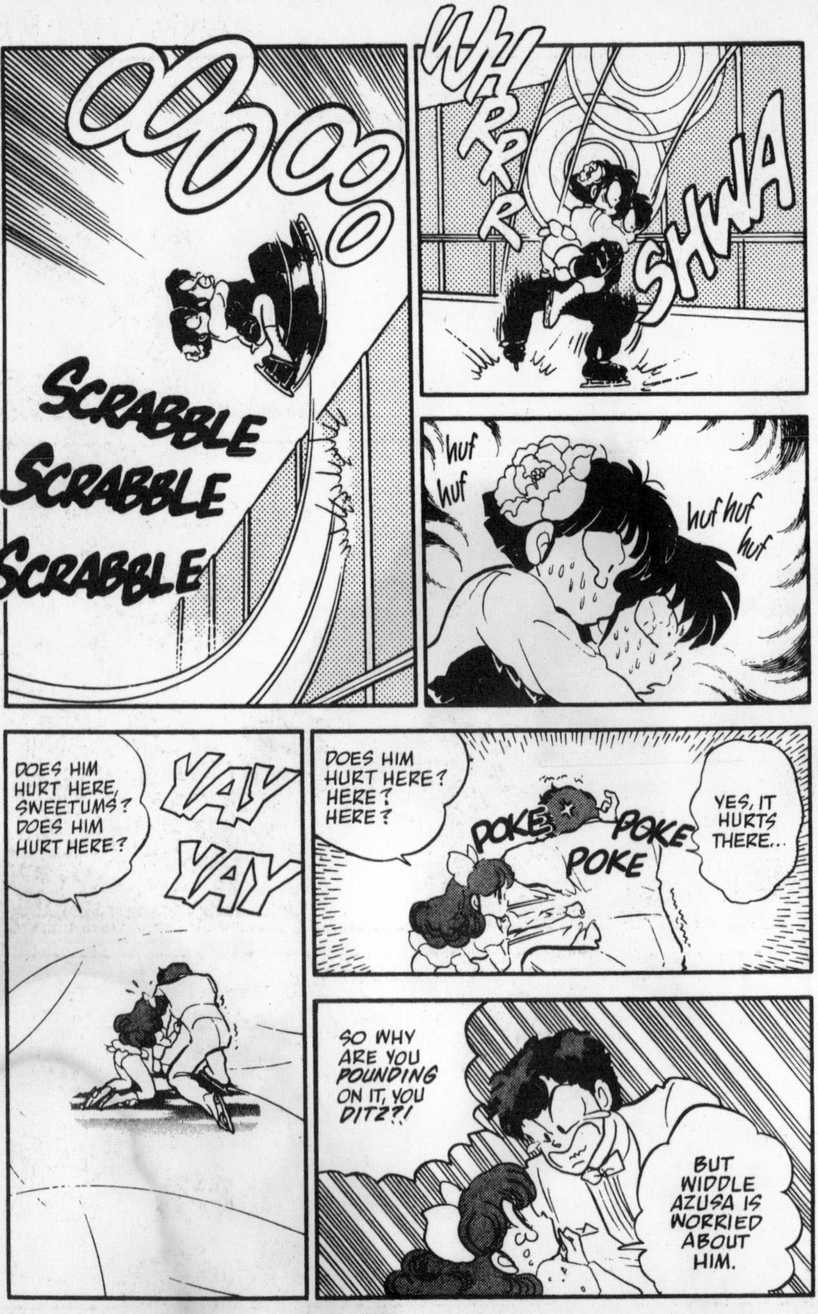
OOOOOOO
SCRABBLE SCRABBLE SCRABBLE
WHIRRR
SHWA
huf huf
huf huf huf
DOES HIM HURT HERE, SWEETUMS? DOES HIM HURT HERE?
YAY YAY
DOES HIM HURT HERE? HERE? HERE?
POKE POKE POKE
YES, IT HURTS THERE...
SO WHY ARE YOU *POUNDING* ON IT, YOU *DITZ?!*
BUT WIDDLE AZUSA IS WORRIED ABOUT HIM.

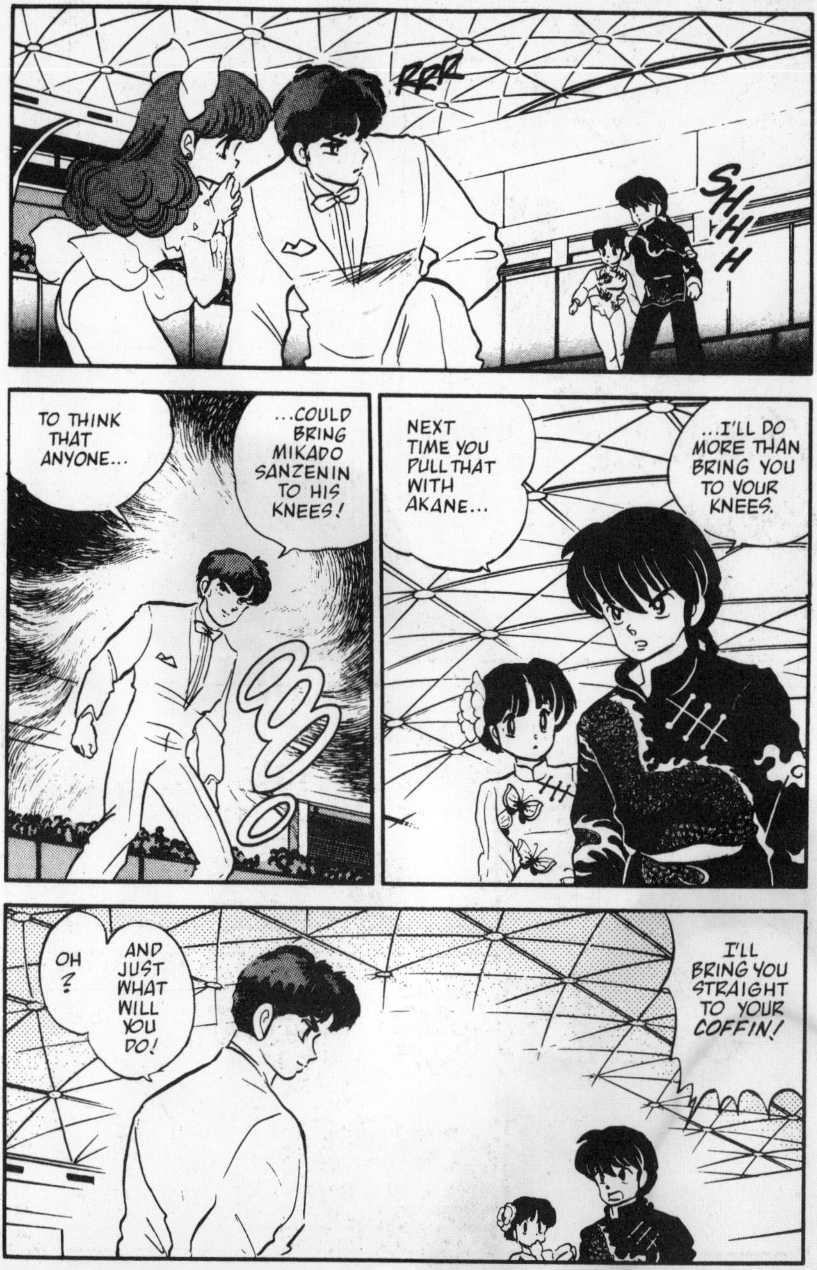
RRR
SHHHH
TO THINK THAT ANYONE...
...COULD BRING MIKADO SANZENIN TO HIS KNEES!
NEXT TIME YOU PULL THAT WITH AKANE...
...I'LL DO MORE THAN BRING YOU TO YOUR KNEES.
OH?
AND JUST WHAT WILL YOU DO!
I'LL BRING YOU STRAIGHT TO YOUR COFFIN!

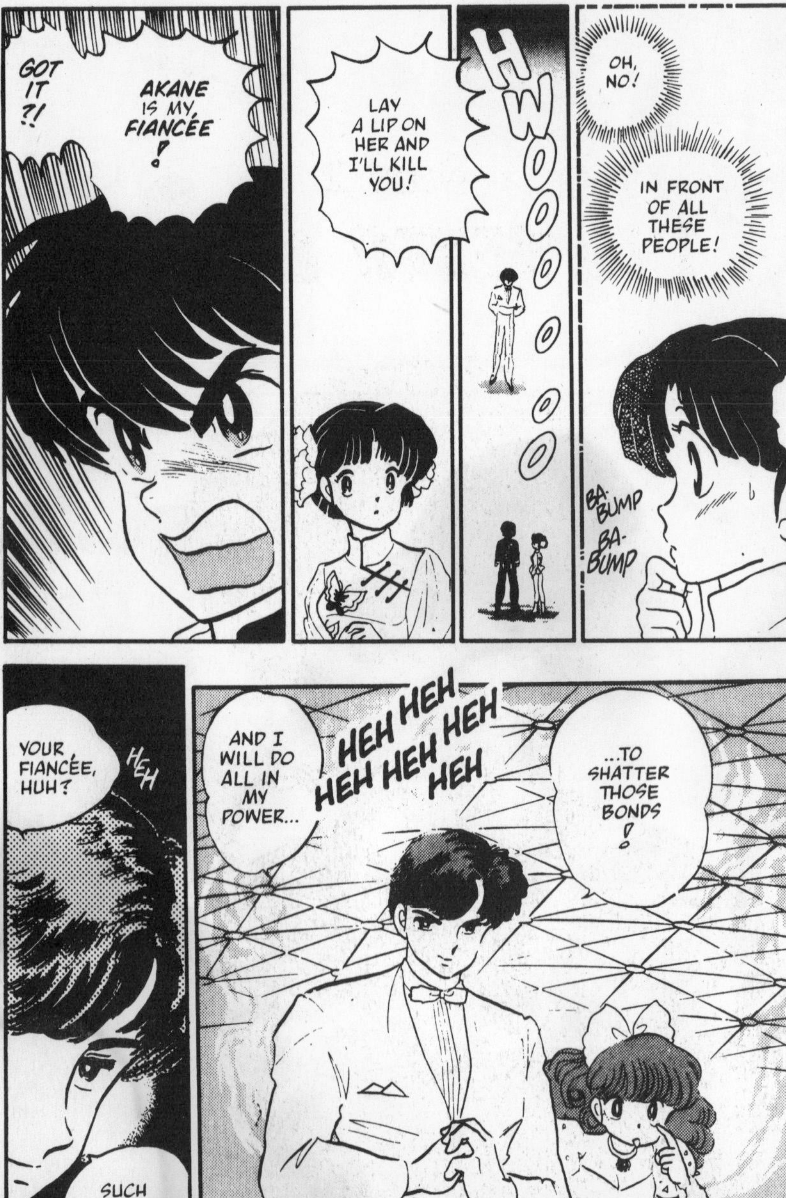
GOT IT ?!
AKANE IS MY FIANCÉE !
LAY A LIP ON HER AND I'LL KILL YOU!
HWOOOOOOOOO
OH, NO!
IN FRONT OF ALL THESE PEOPLE!
BA-BUMP
BA-BUMP
YOUR FIANCÉE, HUH?
HEH
SUCH BONDS ARE FRAGILE.
AND I WILL DO ALL IN MY POWER...
HEH HEH HEH HEH HEH HEH
...TO SHATTER THOSE BONDS!

Part 2
I'LL NEVER LET GO

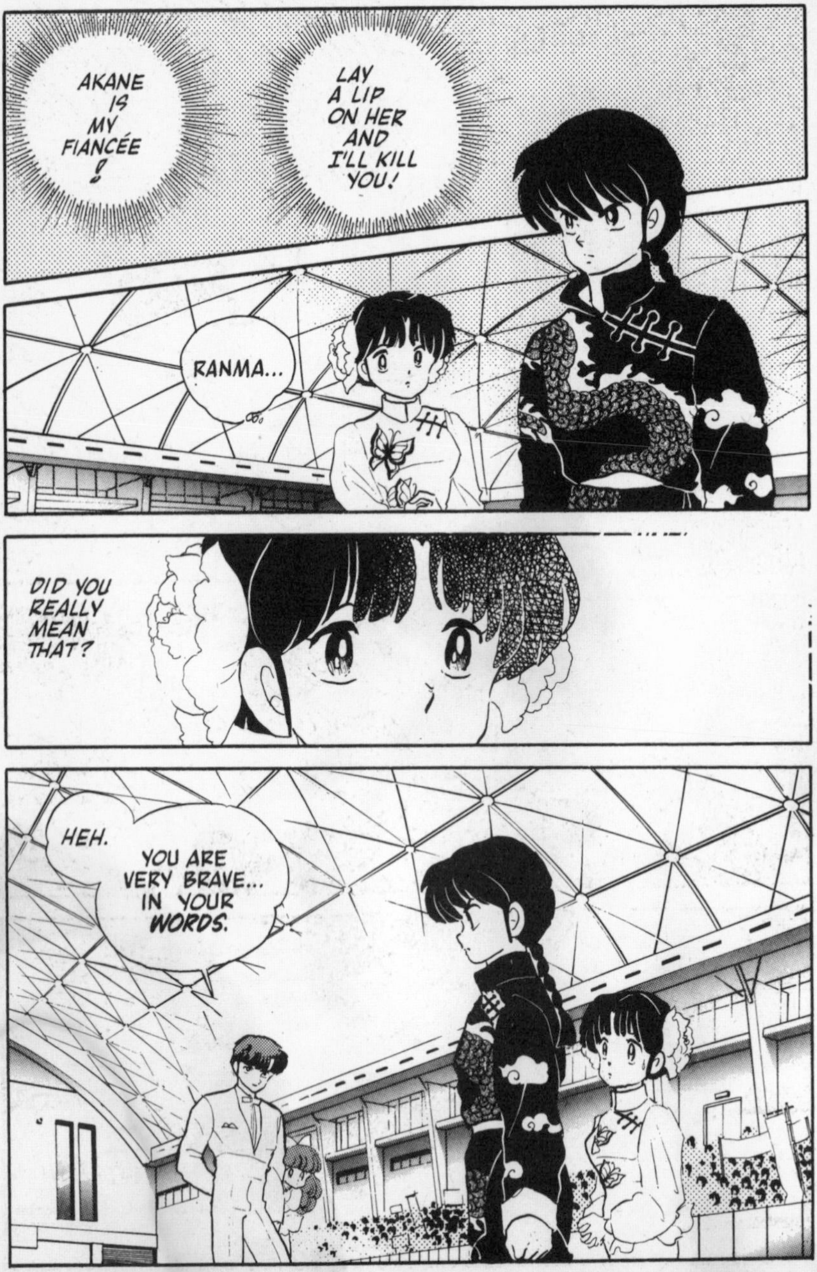
AKANE IS MY FIANCÉE!
LAY A LIP ON HER AND I'LL KILL YOU!
RANMA...
DID YOU REALLY MEAN THAT?
HEH.
YOU ARE VERY BRAVE... IN YOUR WORDS.

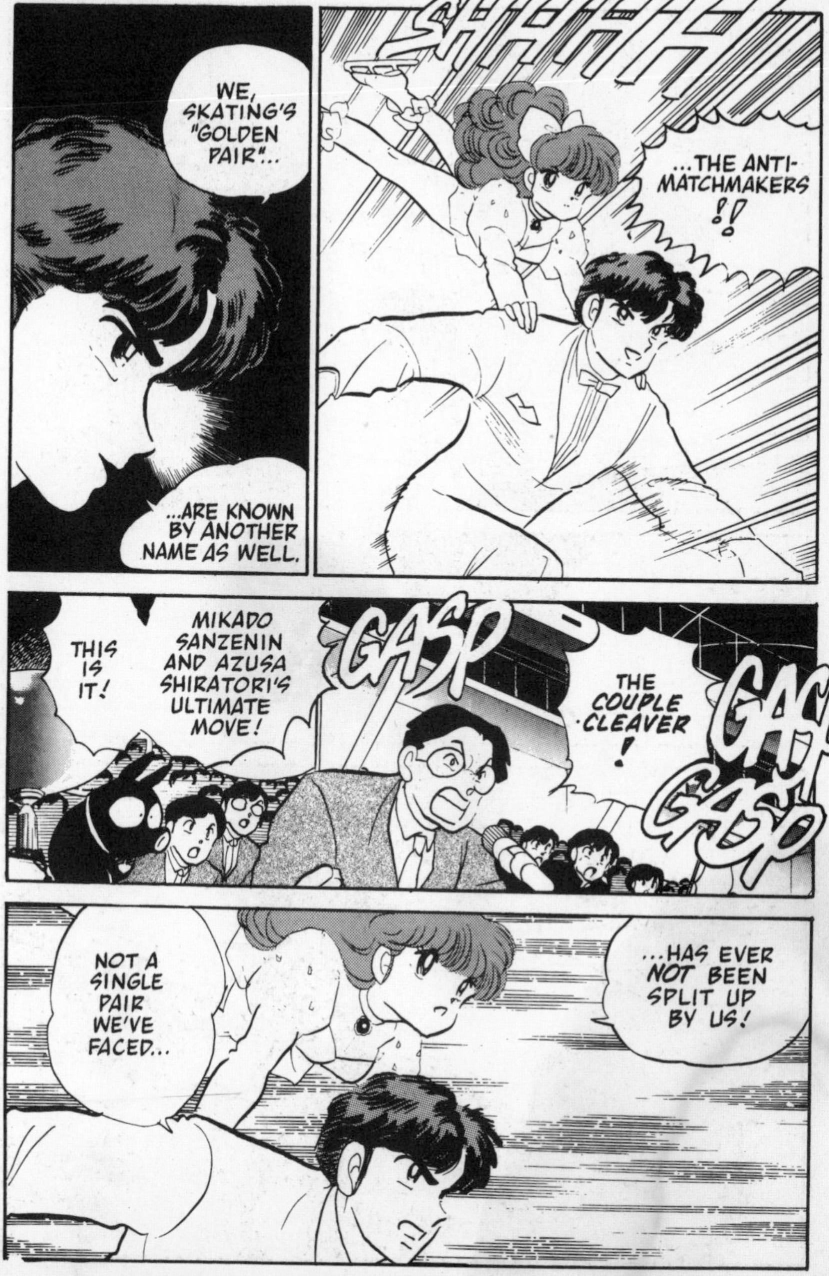
WE, SKATING'S "GOLDEN PAIR"...
...ARE KNOWN BY ANOTHER NAME AS WELL.
SHHHHHH
...THE ANTI-MATCHMAKERS !!
THIS IS IT!
MIKADO SANZENIN AND AZUSA SHIRATORI'S ULTIMATE MOVE!
GASP
THE COUPLE CLEAVER!
GASP GASP
NOT A SINGLE PAIR WE'VE FACED...
...HAS EVER NOT BEEN SPLIT UP BY US!

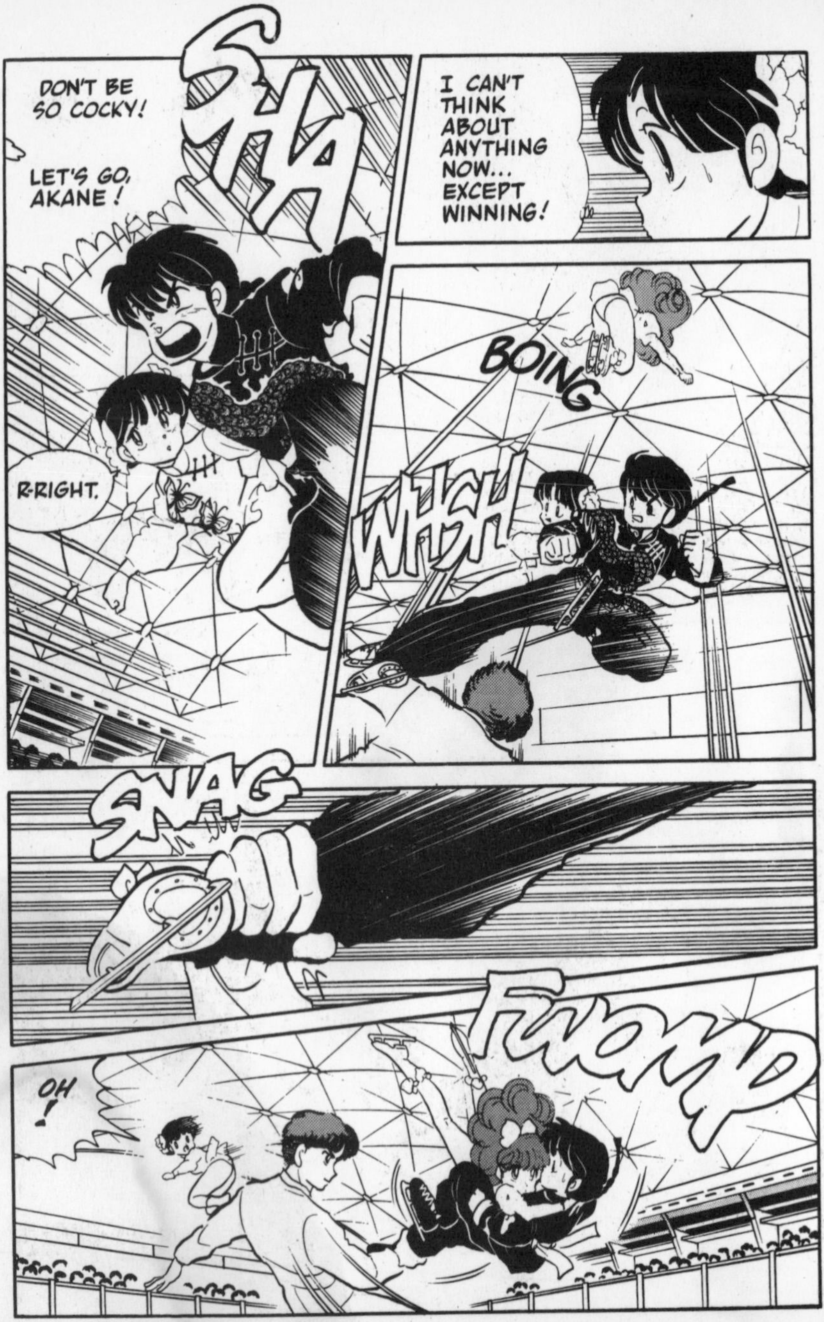
DON'T BE SO COCKY!
LET'S GO, AKANE!
SHA
R-RIGHT.
I CAN'T THINK ABOUT ANYTHING NOW... EXCEPT WINNING!
BOING
WHSH
SNAG
OH!
FWOMP

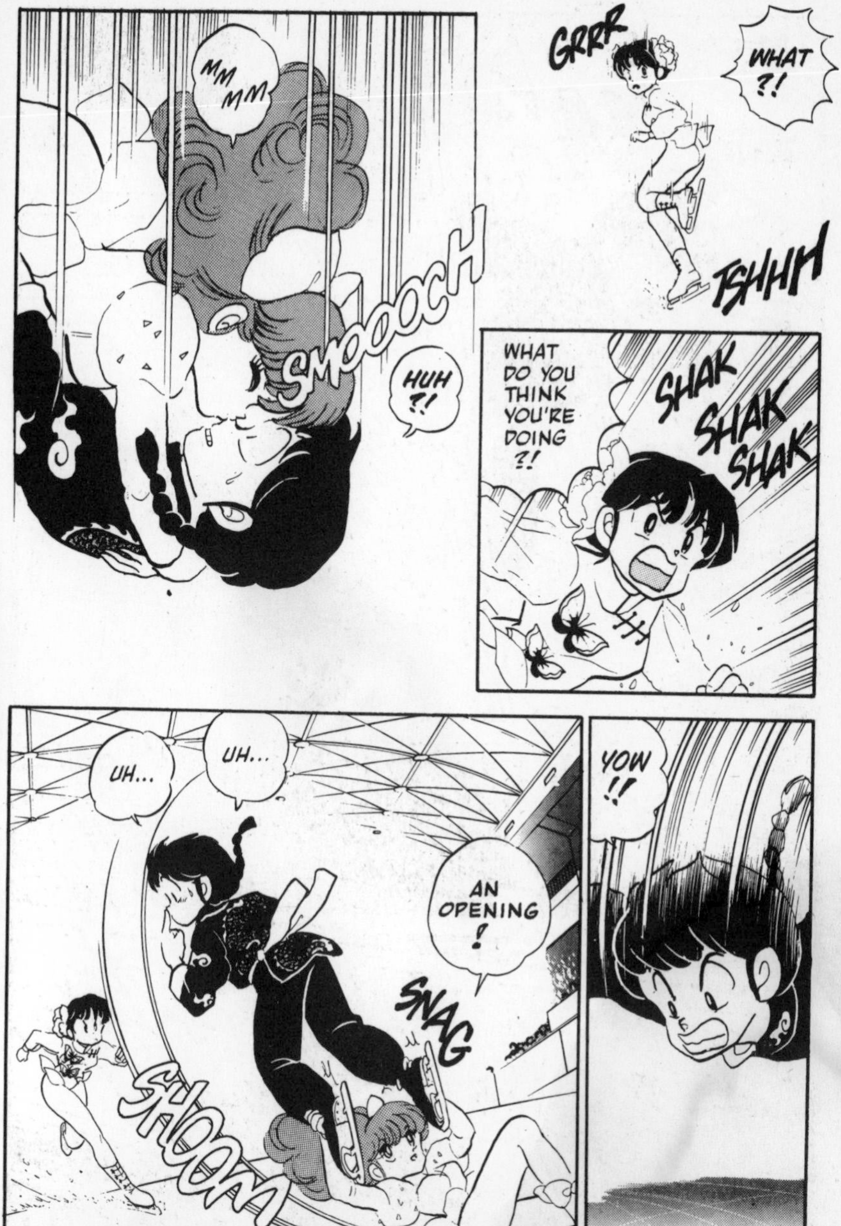
MM MM
SMOOOCH
HUH ?!
GRRR
WHAT ?!
TSHHH
WHAT DO YOU THINK YOU'RE DOING ?!
SHAK SHAK SHAK
UH...
UH...
AN OPENING !
SNAG
SHOOM
YOW !!

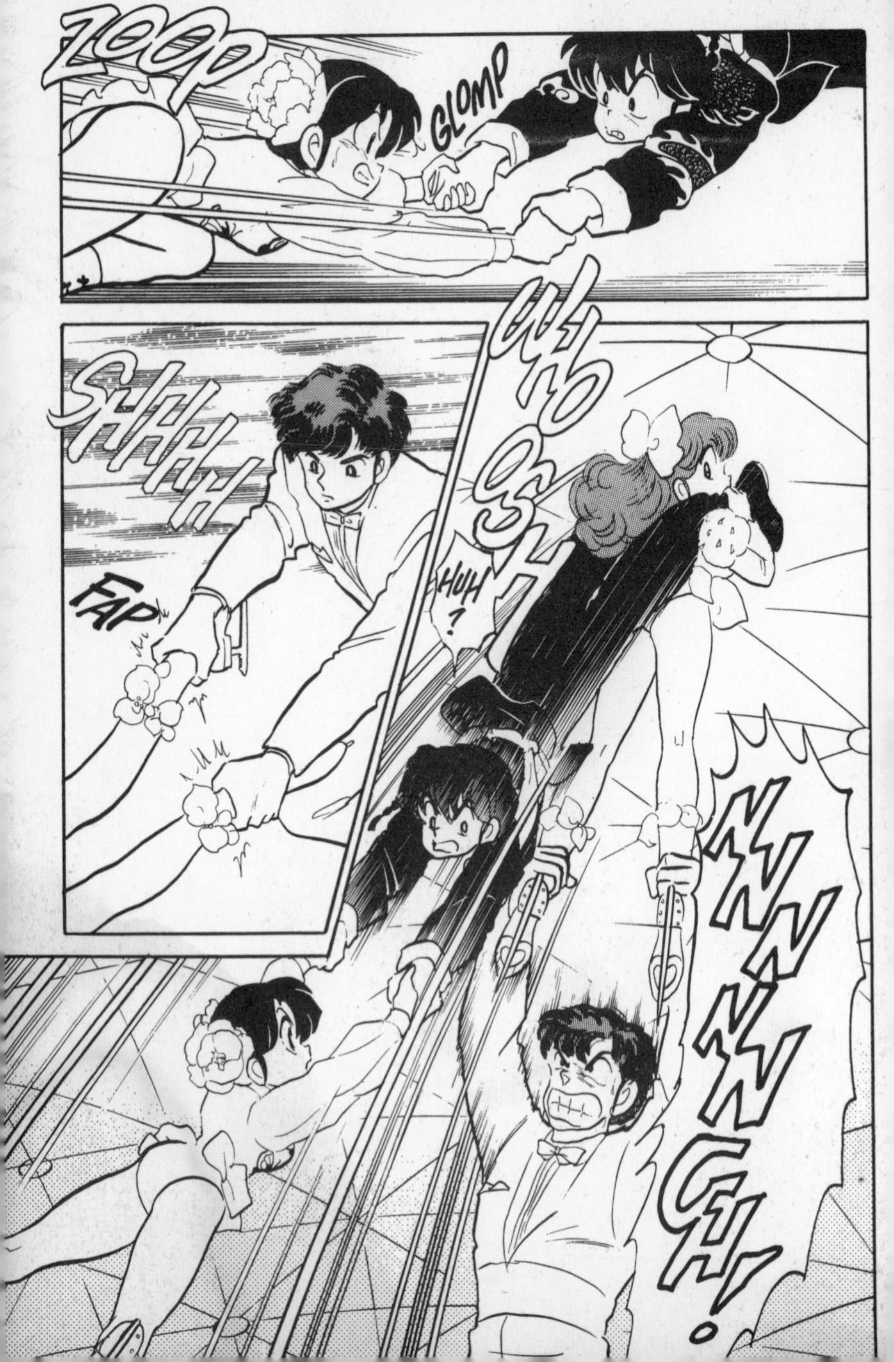
ZOOP
GLOMP
SHHHH
FAP
WHOOSH
HUH ?
NNNNNGH!

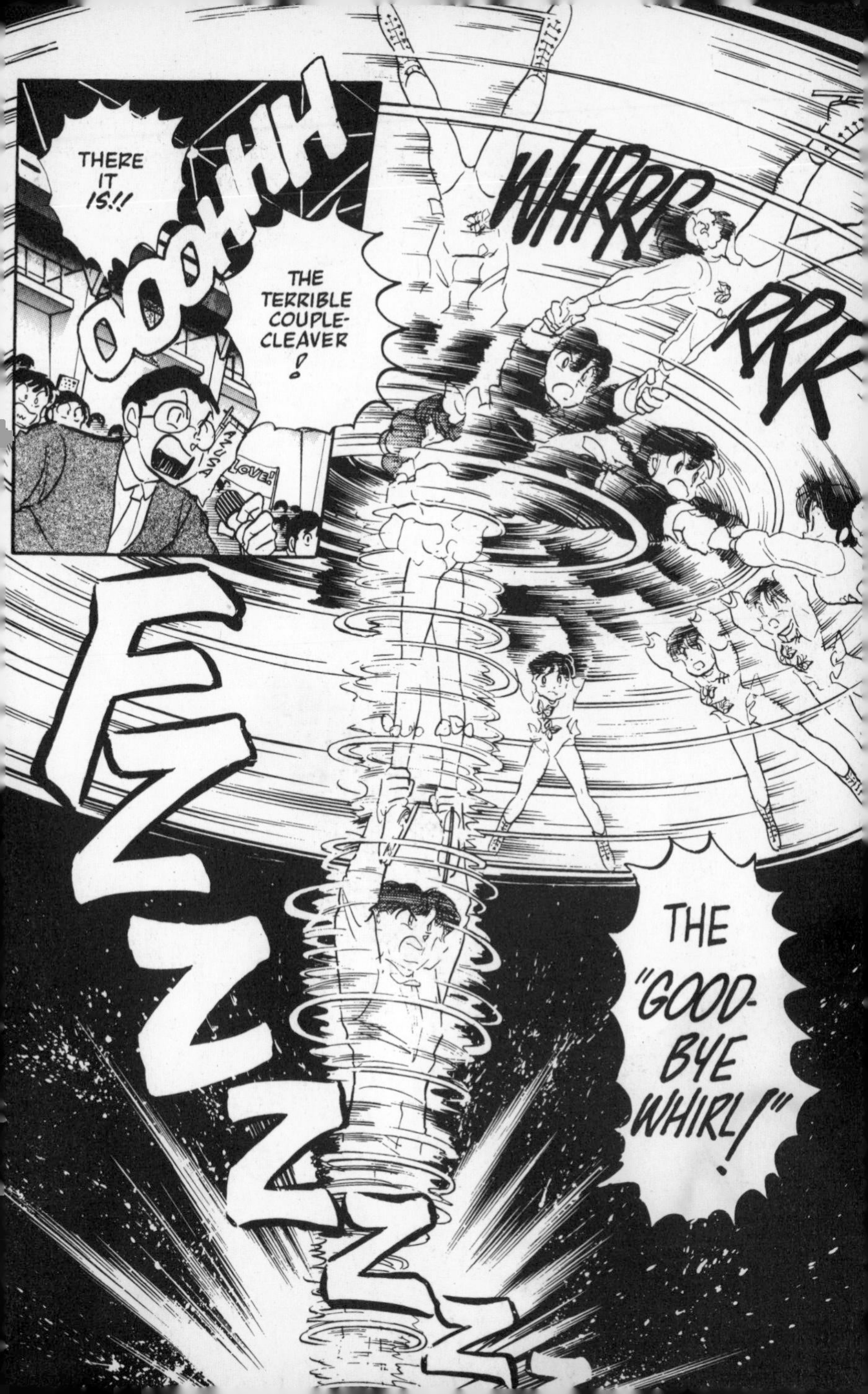
THERE IT IS!!
OOOHHH
THE TERRIBLE COUPLE-CLEAVER!
LOVE!
WHIRRRRRK
THE "GOOD-BYE WHIRL!"
ZZZZ

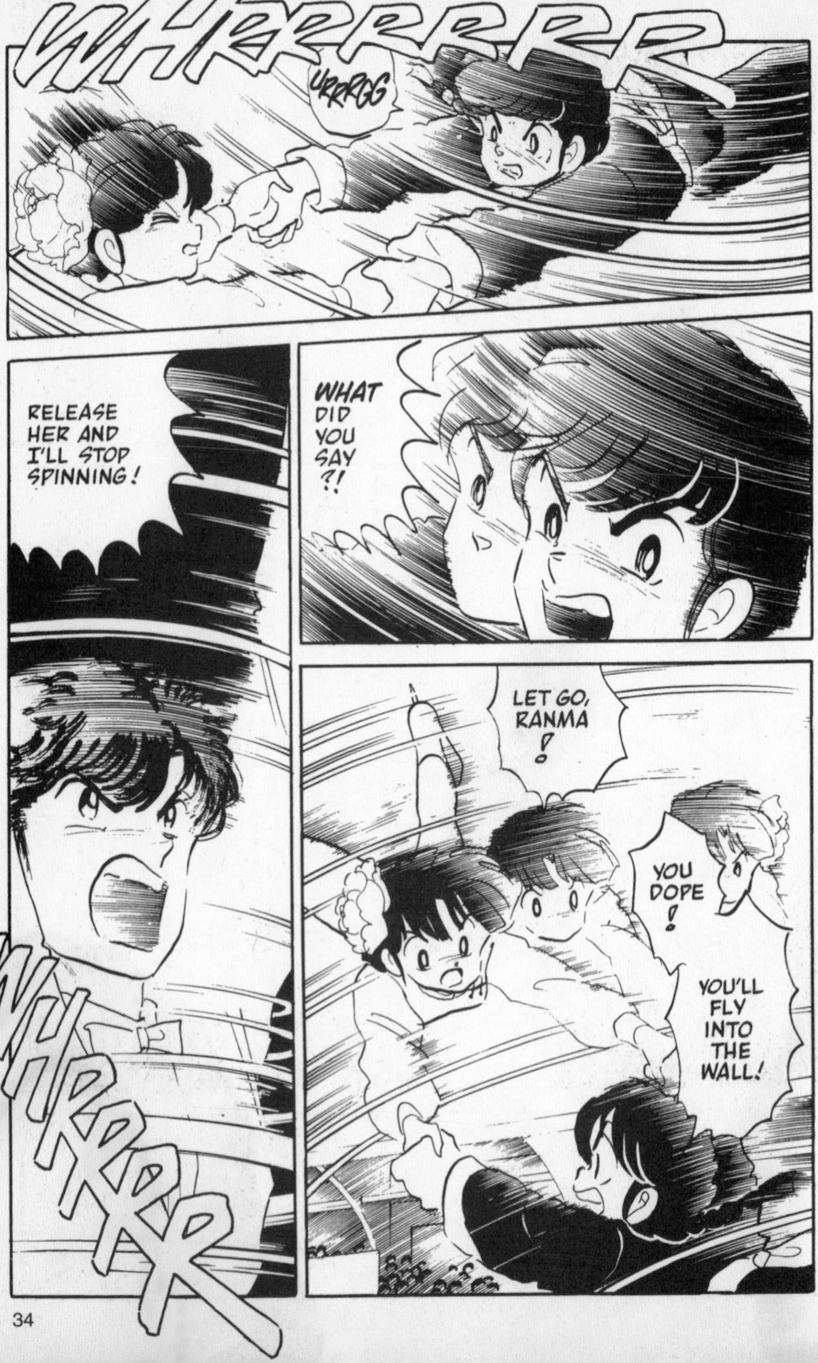
WHIRRRRRR
URRRGG
RELEASE HER AND I'LL STOP SPINNING!
WHAT DID YOU SAY ?!
WHIRRRRR
LET GO, RANMA!
YOU DOPE!
YOU'LL FLY INTO THE WALL!

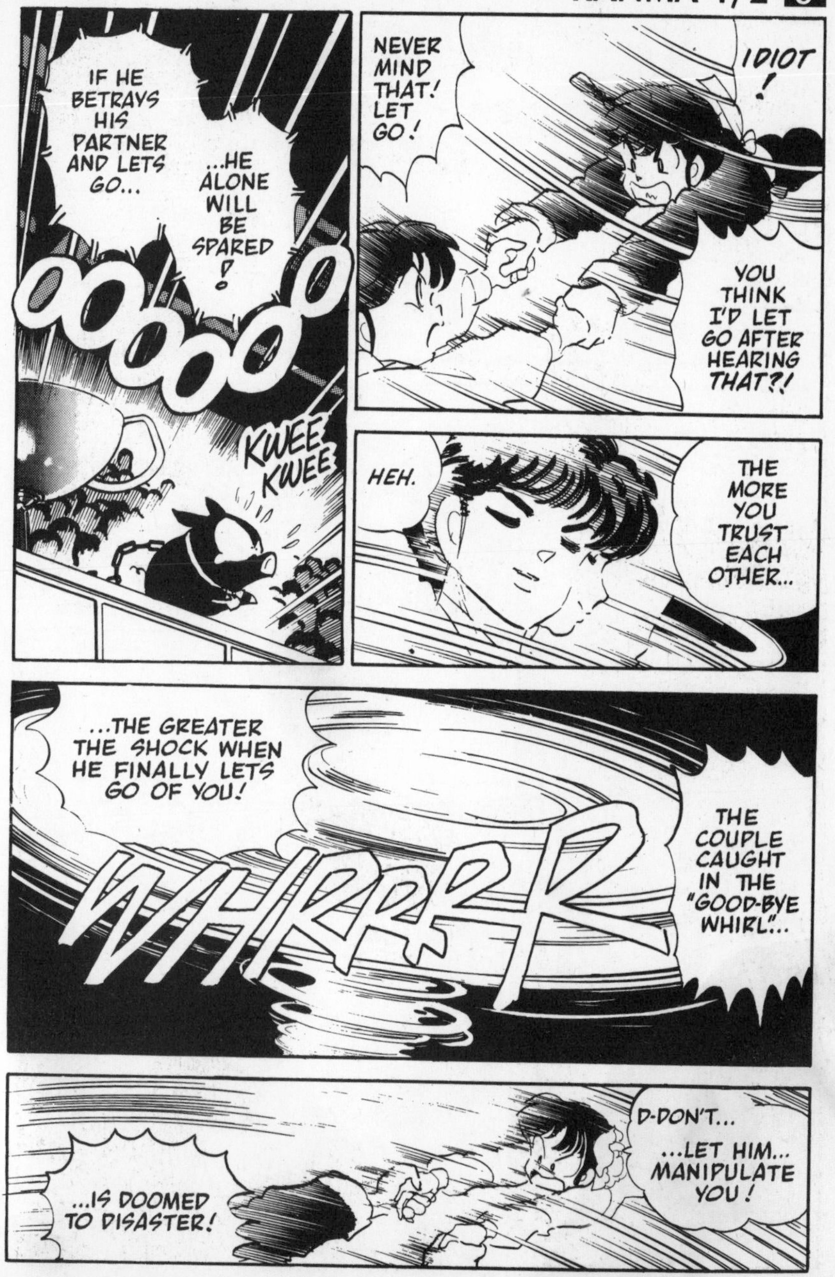
IF HE BETRAYS HIS PARTNER AND LETS GO...
...HE ALONE WILL BE SPARED!
OOOOO
KWEE KWEE
NEVER MIND THAT! LET GO!
IDIOT!
YOU THINK I'D LET GO AFTER HEARING THAT?!
HEH.
THE MORE YOU TRUST EACH OTHER...
...THE GREATER THE SHOCK WHEN HE FINALLY LETS GO OF YOU!
WHIRRRR
THE COUPLE CAUGHT IN THE "GOOD-BYE WHIRL"...
...IS DOOMED TO DISASTER!
D-DON'T...
...LET HIM... MANIPULATE YOU!

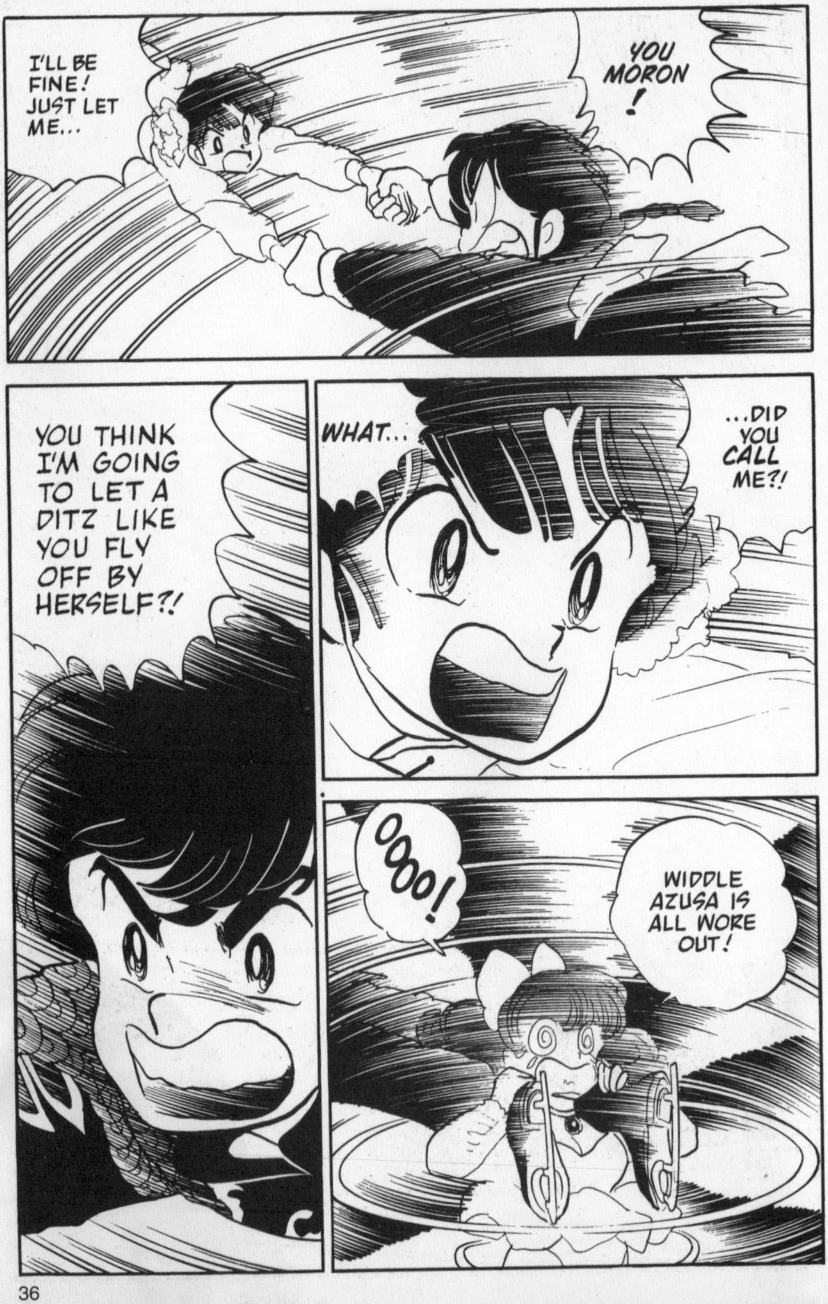
I'LL BE FINE! JUST LET ME...
YOU MORON!
YOU THINK I'M GOING TO LET A DITZ LIKE YOU FLY OFF BY HERSELF?!
WHAT...
...DID YOU CALL ME?!
OOOO!
WIDDLE AZUSA IS ALL WORE OUT!

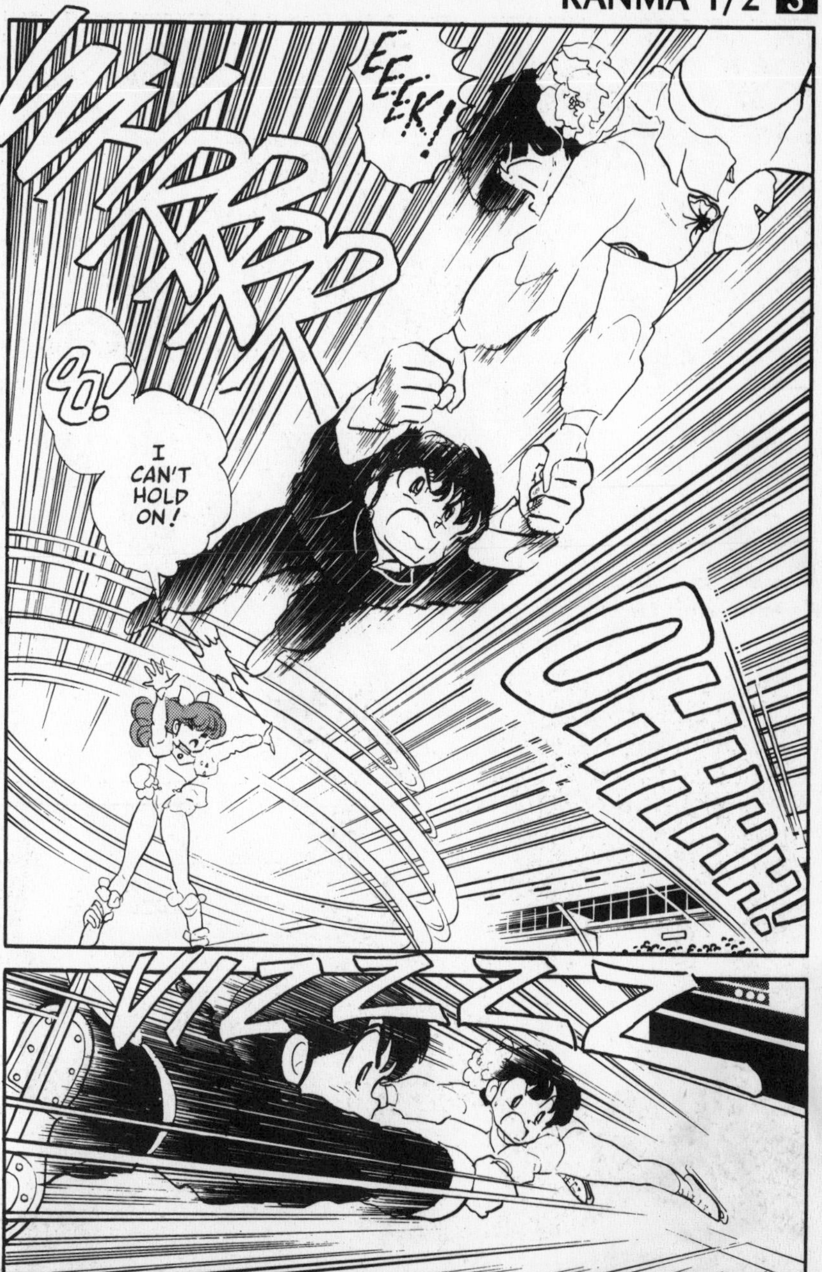
WHRRRRRD
EEEEK!
OO!
I CAN'T HOLD ON!
OHHHHH!
VIZZZZ

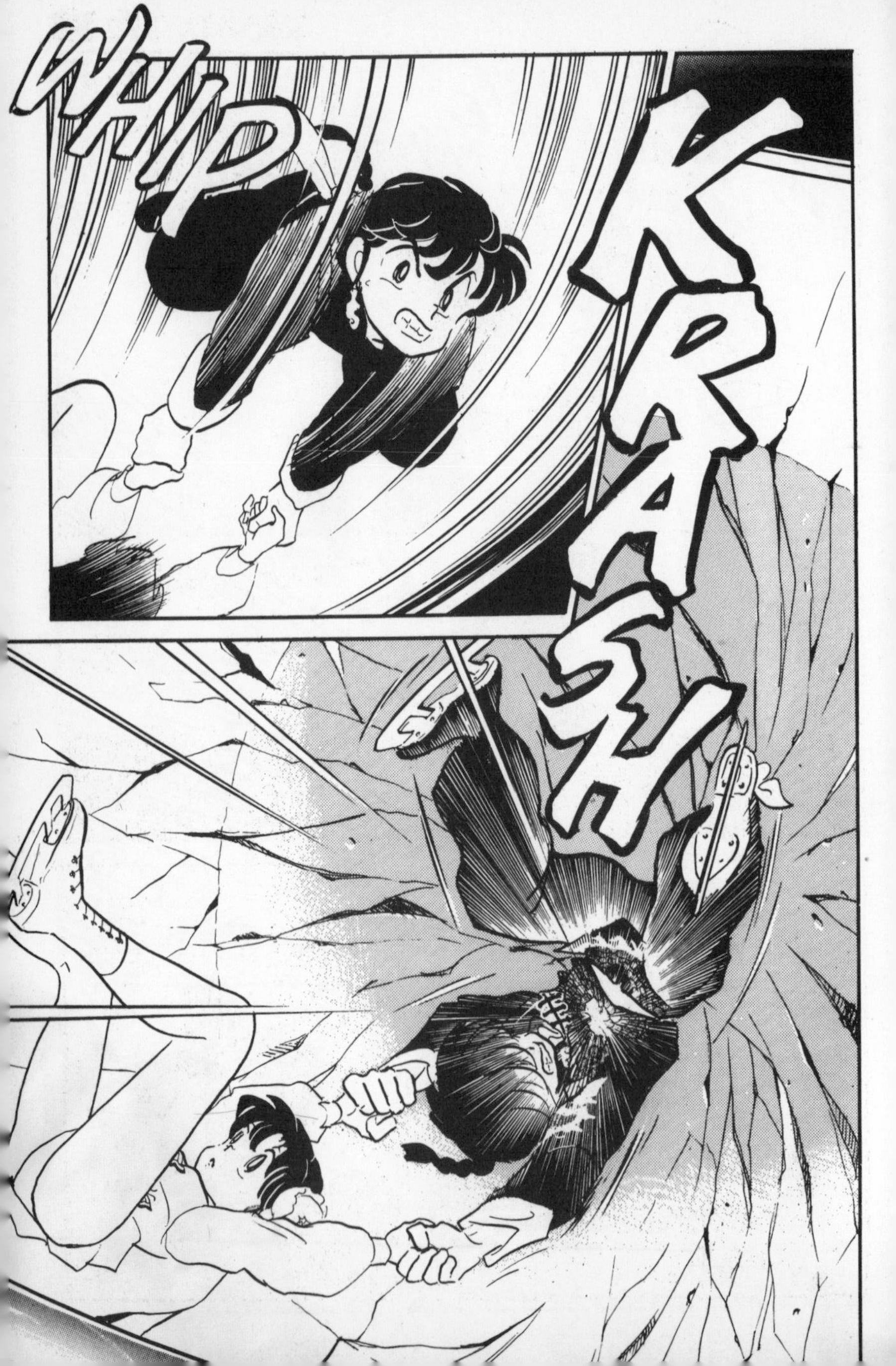
WHIP
KRASH

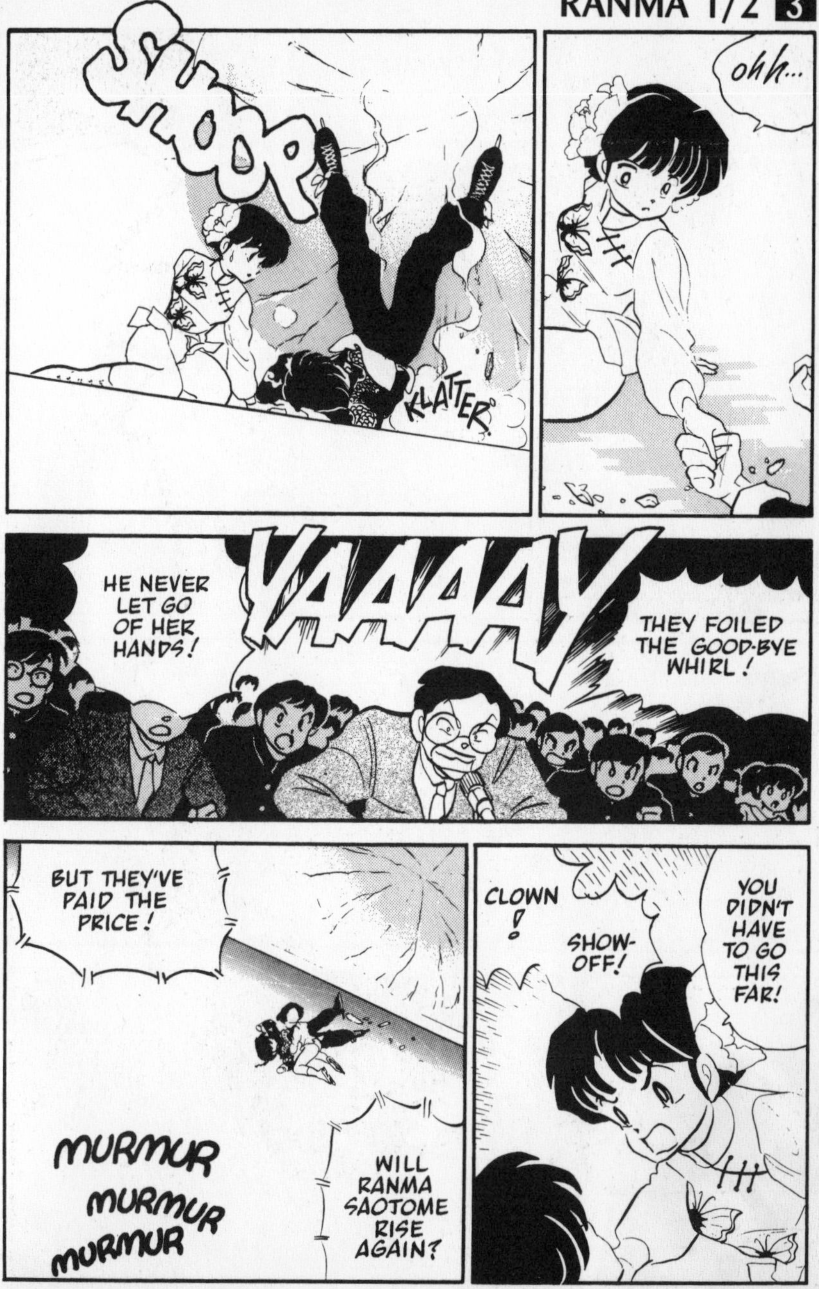
SHOOP
KLATTER!
ohh...
HE NEVER LET GO OF HER HANDS!
YAAAAY
THEY FOILED THE GOOD-BYE WHIRL!
BUT THEY'VE PAID THE PRICE!
MURMUR MURMUR MURMUR
WILL RANMA SAOTOME RISE AGAIN?
CLOWN!
SHOW-OFF!
YOU DIDN'T HAVE TO GO THIS FAR!

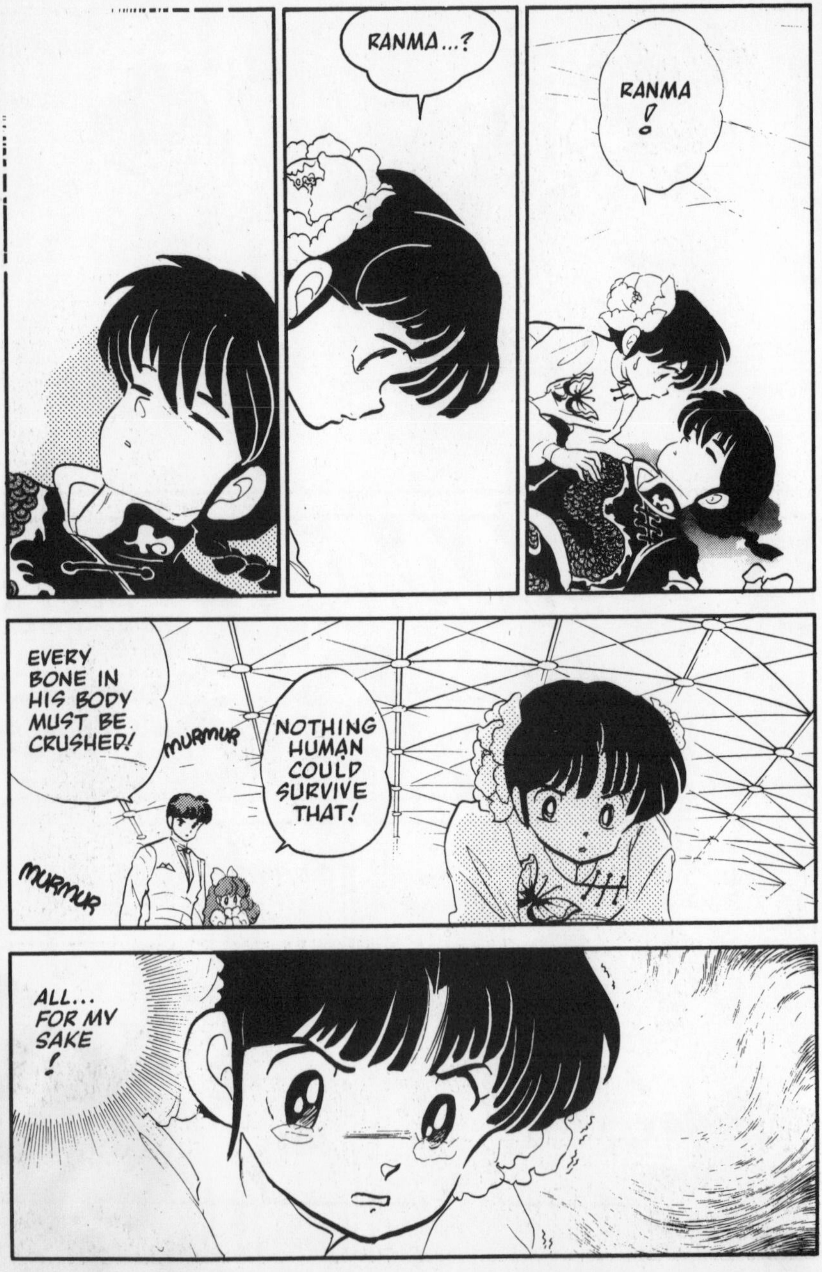
RANMA...?
RANMA!
EVERY BONE IN HIS BODY MUST BE CRUSHED!
MURMUR
NOTHING HUMAN COULD SURVIVE THAT!
MURMUR
ALL... FOR MY SAKE!

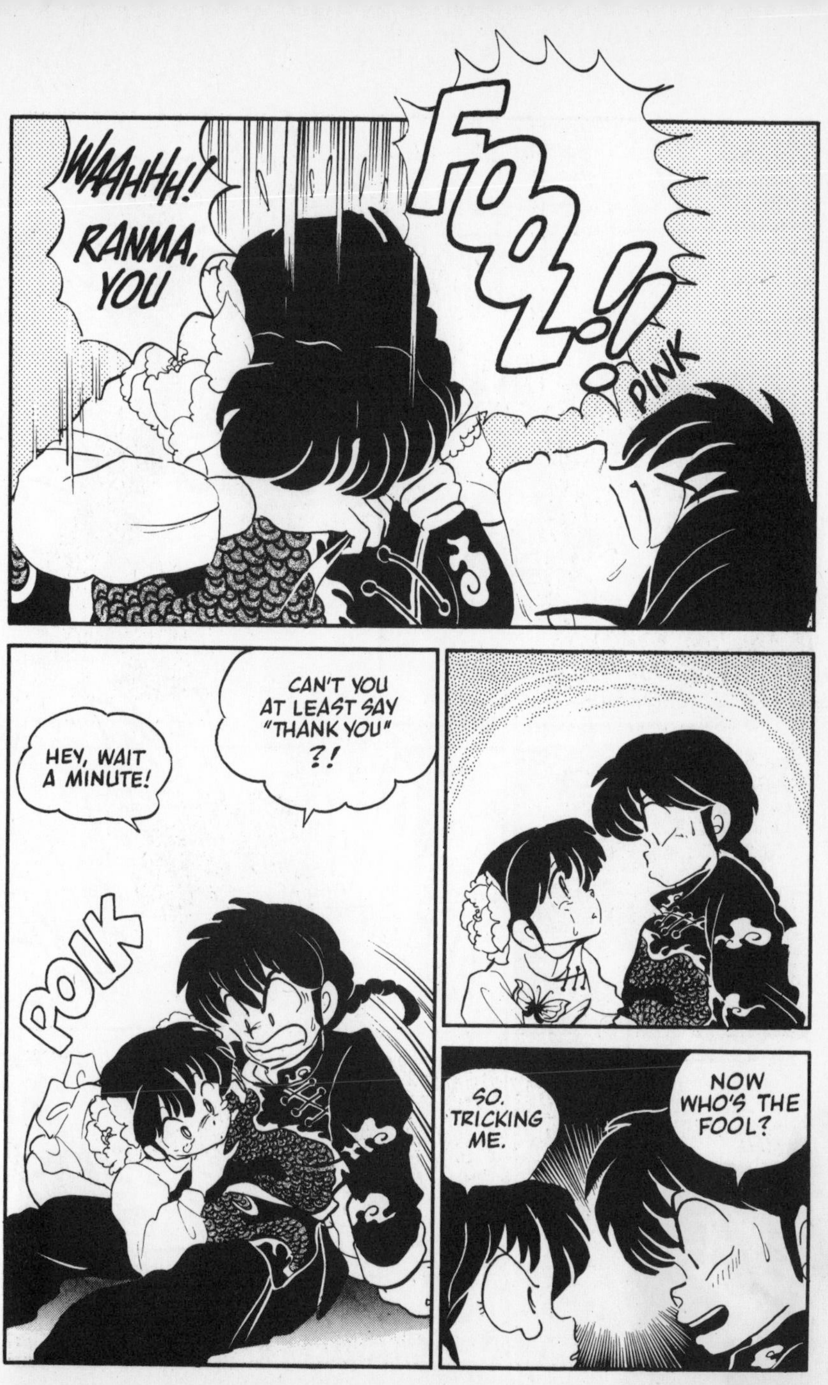
WAAHHH! RANMA, YOU
FOOL!!
PINK
HEY, WAIT A MINUTE!
CAN'T YOU AT LEAST SAY "THANK YOU" ?!
POIK
SO. TRICKING ME.
NOW WHO'S THE FOOL?

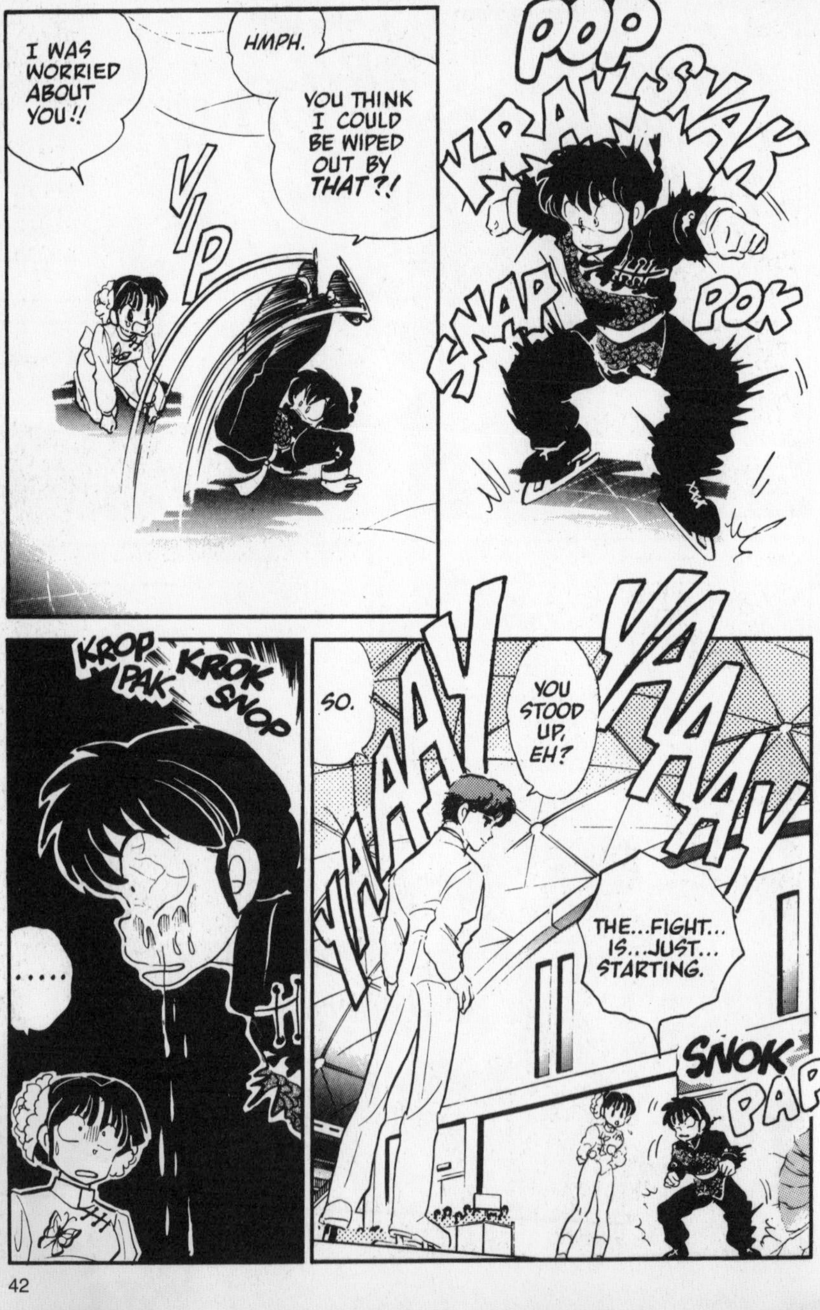
I WAS WORRIED ABOUT YOU!!
HMPH.
YOU THINK I COULD BE WIPED OUT BY THAT?!
VIP
POP
KRAK
SNAK
SNAP
POK
KROP
PAK
KROK
SNOP
......
YAAAY
YAAAY
SO.
YOU STOOD UP, EH?
THE...FIGHT... IS...JUST... STARTING.
SNOK
PAP

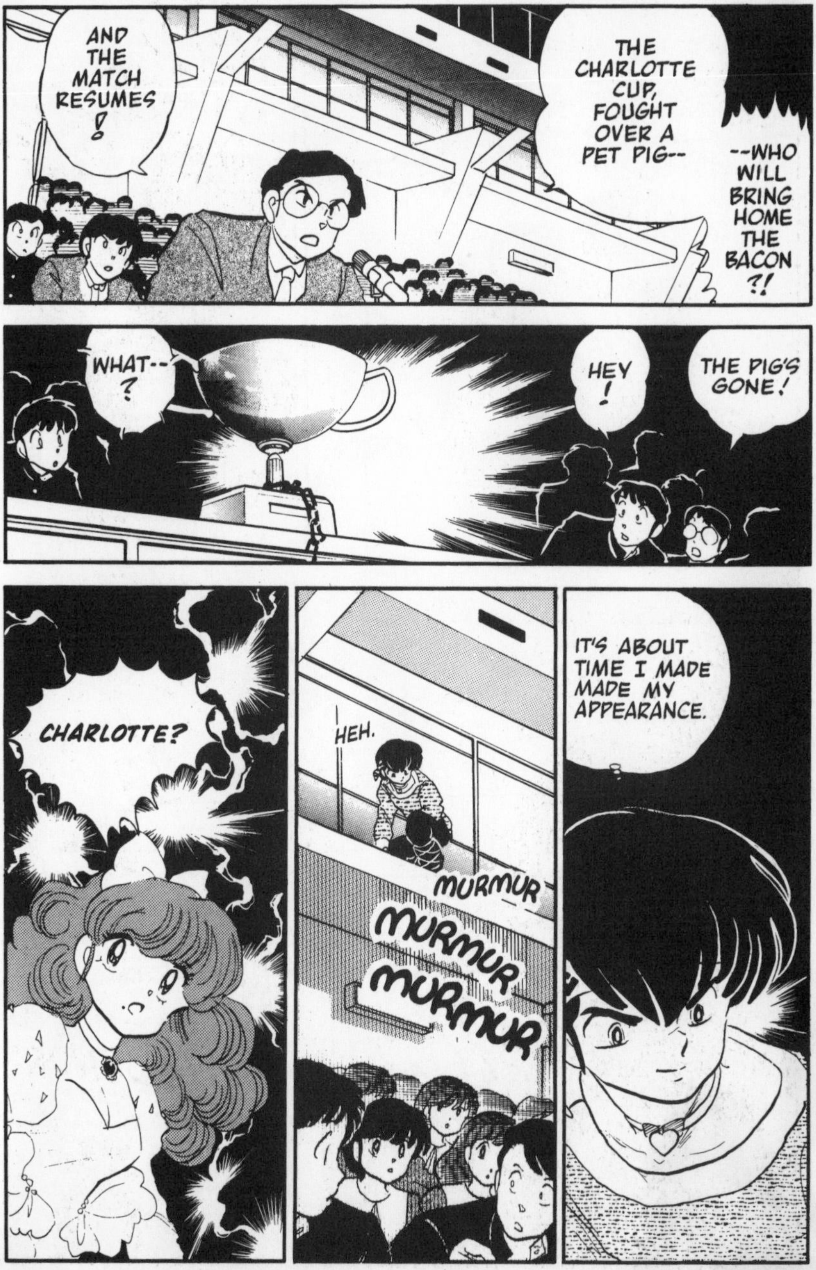
AND THE MATCH RESUMES!
THE CHARLOTTE CUP, FOUGHT OVER A PET PIG--
--WHO WILL BRING HOME THE BACON?!
WHAT--?
HEY!
THE PIG'S GONE!
CHARLOTTE?
HEH.
MURMUR
MURMUR
MURMUR
MURMUR
IT'S ABOUT TIME I MADE MADE MY APPEARANCE.

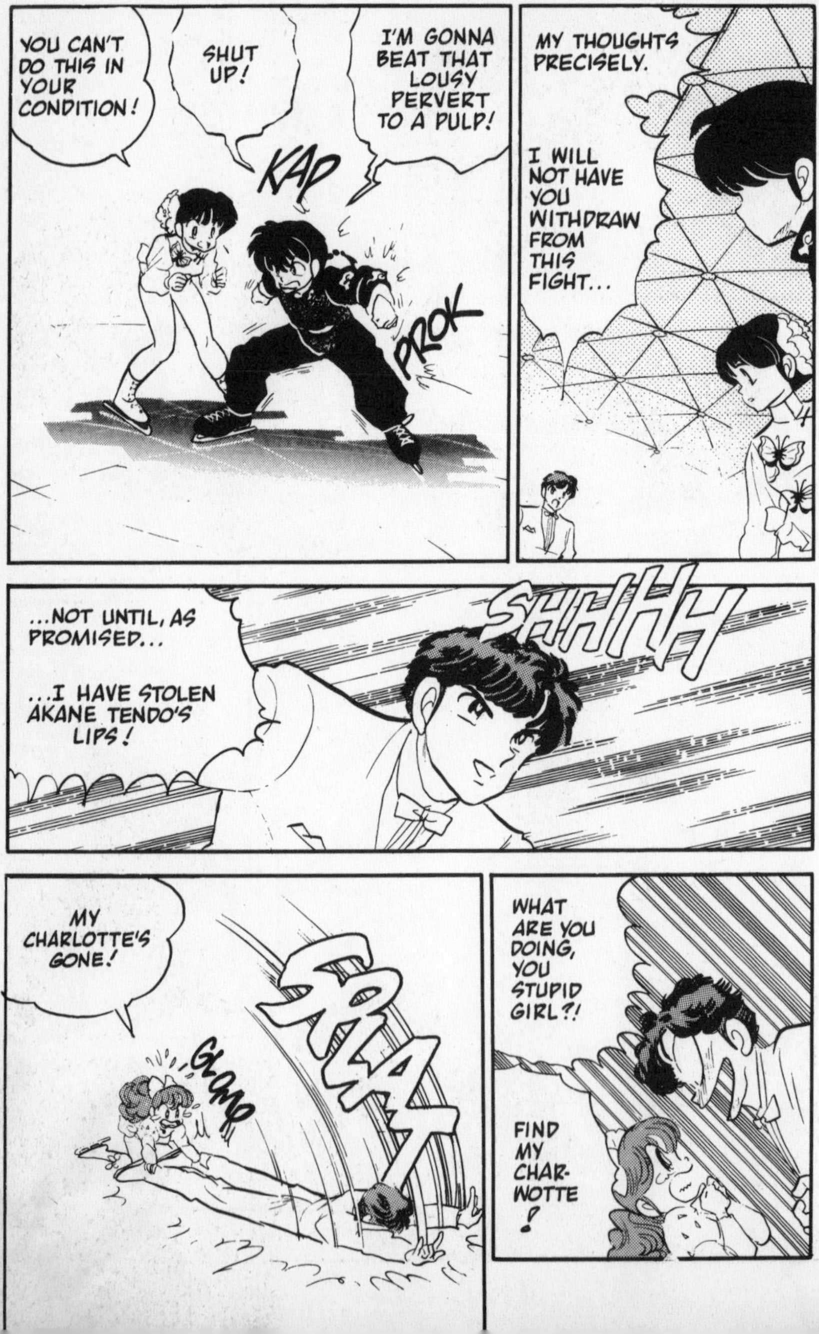
YOU CAN'T DO THIS IN YOUR CONDITION!
SHUT UP!
I'M GONNA BEAT THAT LOUSY PERVERT TO A PULP!
KAP
PROK
MY THOUGHTS PRECISELY.
I WILL NOT HAVE YOU WITHDRAW FROM THIS FIGHT...
...NOT UNTIL, AS PROMISED...
...I HAVE STOLEN AKANE TENDO'S LIPS!
SHHHH
MY CHARLOTTE'S GONE!
SPLAT
GLOMP
WHAT ARE YOU DOING, YOU STUPID GIRL?!
FIND MY CHAR-WOTTE!

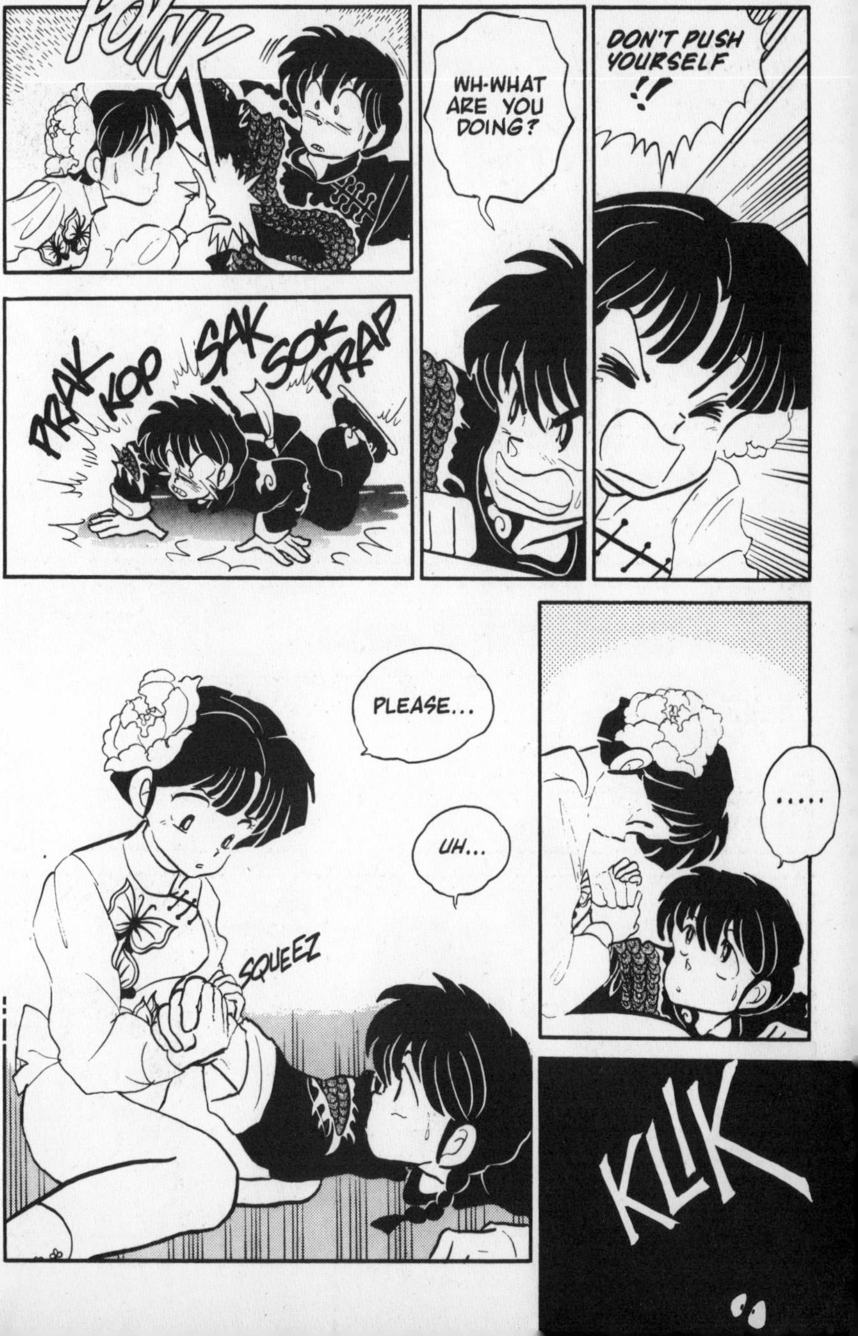
POINK
PRAK KOP SAK SOK PRAP
WH-WHAT ARE YOU DOING?
DON'T PUSH YOURSELF !!
PLEASE...
UH...
SQUEEZ
.....
KLIK

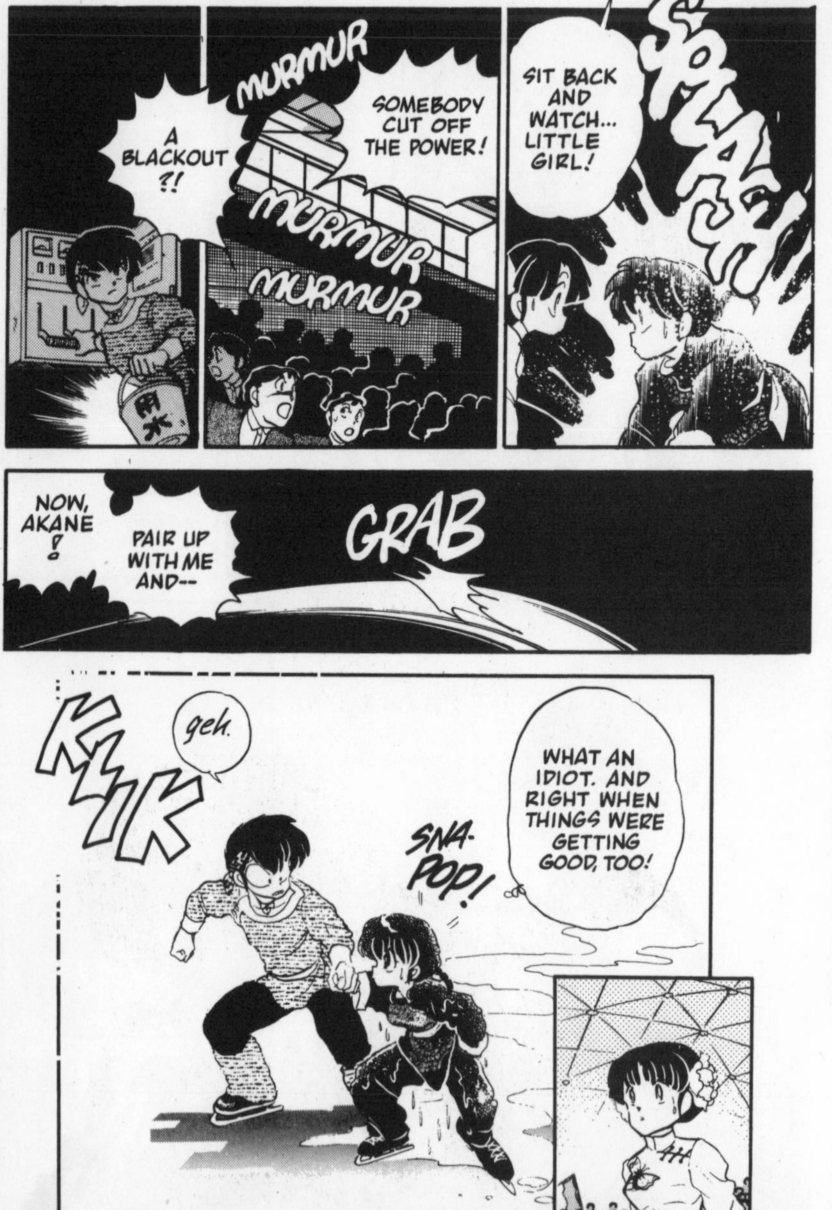
A BLACKOUT ?!
MURMUR
SOMEBODY CUT OFF THE POWER!
MURMUR
MURMUR
SIT BACK AND WATCH... LITTLE GIRL!
SPLASH!!
NOW, AKANE!
PAIR UP WITH ME AND--
GRAB
KLIK
geh.
SNA-POP!
WHAT AN IDIOT. AND RIGHT WHEN THINGS WERE GETTING GOOD, TOO!

Part 3
BURNING THE BRIDGES

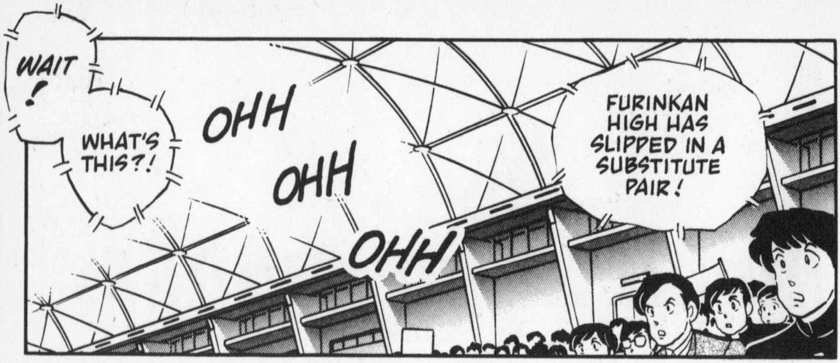
WAIT!
WHAT'S THIS?!
OHH
OHH
OHH
FURINKAN HIGH HAS SLIPPED IN A SUBSTITUTE PAIR!

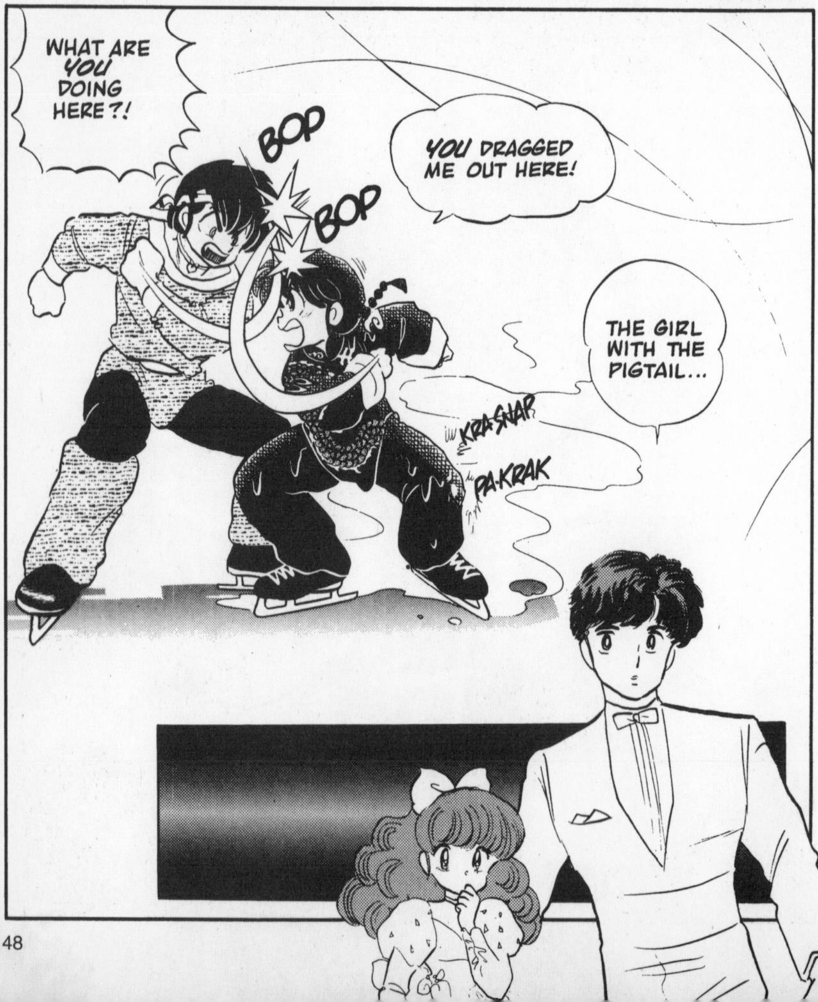
WHAT ARE YOU DOING HERE?!
BOP
BOP
YOU DRAGGED ME OUT HERE!
THE GIRL WITH THE PIGTAIL...
KRA-SNAP
PA-KRAK

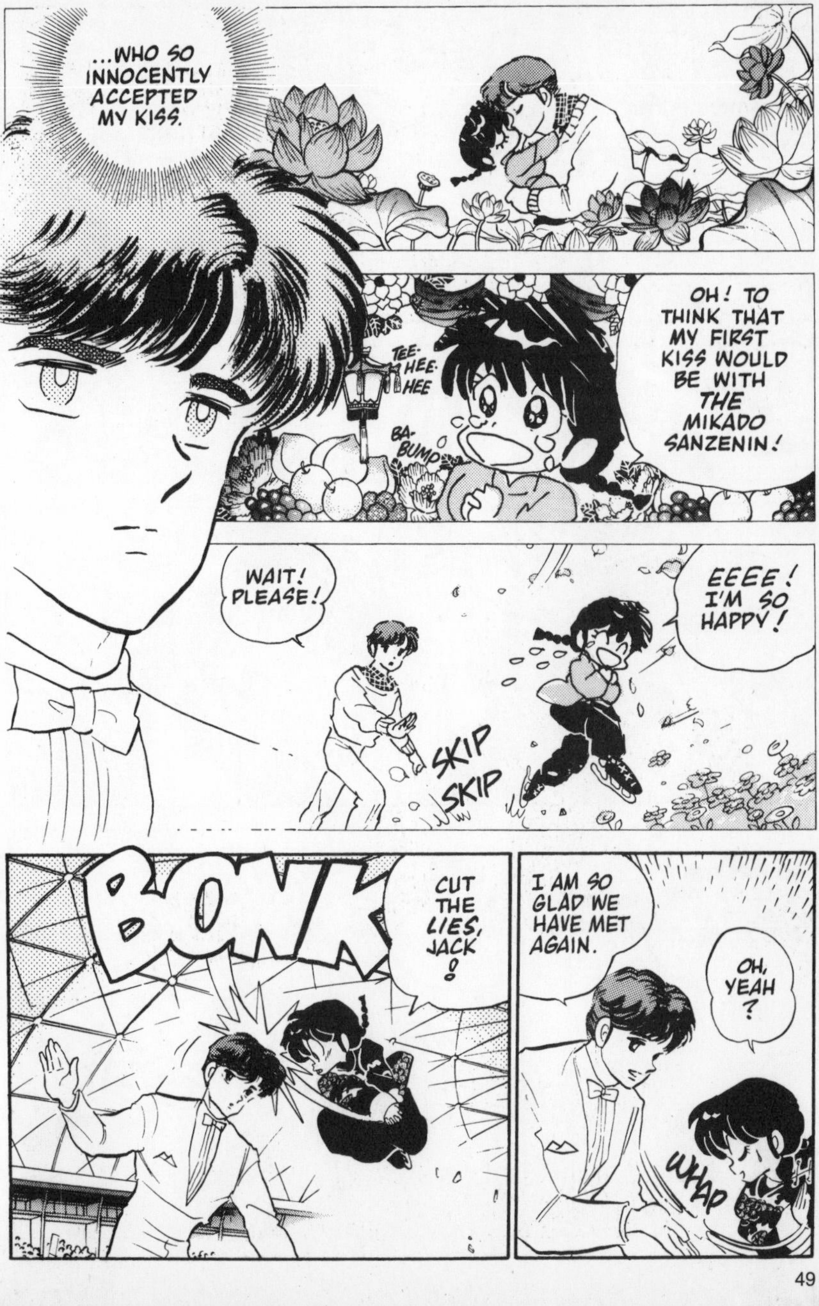
...WHO SO INNOCENTLY ACCEPTED MY KISS.
TEE-HEE-HEE
BA-BUMP
OH! TO THINK THAT MY FIRST KISS WOULD BE WITH THE MIKADO SANZENIN!
WAIT! PLEASE!
EEEE! I'M SO HAPPY!
SKIP SKIP
BONK
CUT THE LIES, JACK!
I AM SO GLAD WE HAVE MET AGAIN.
OH, YEAH?
WHAP

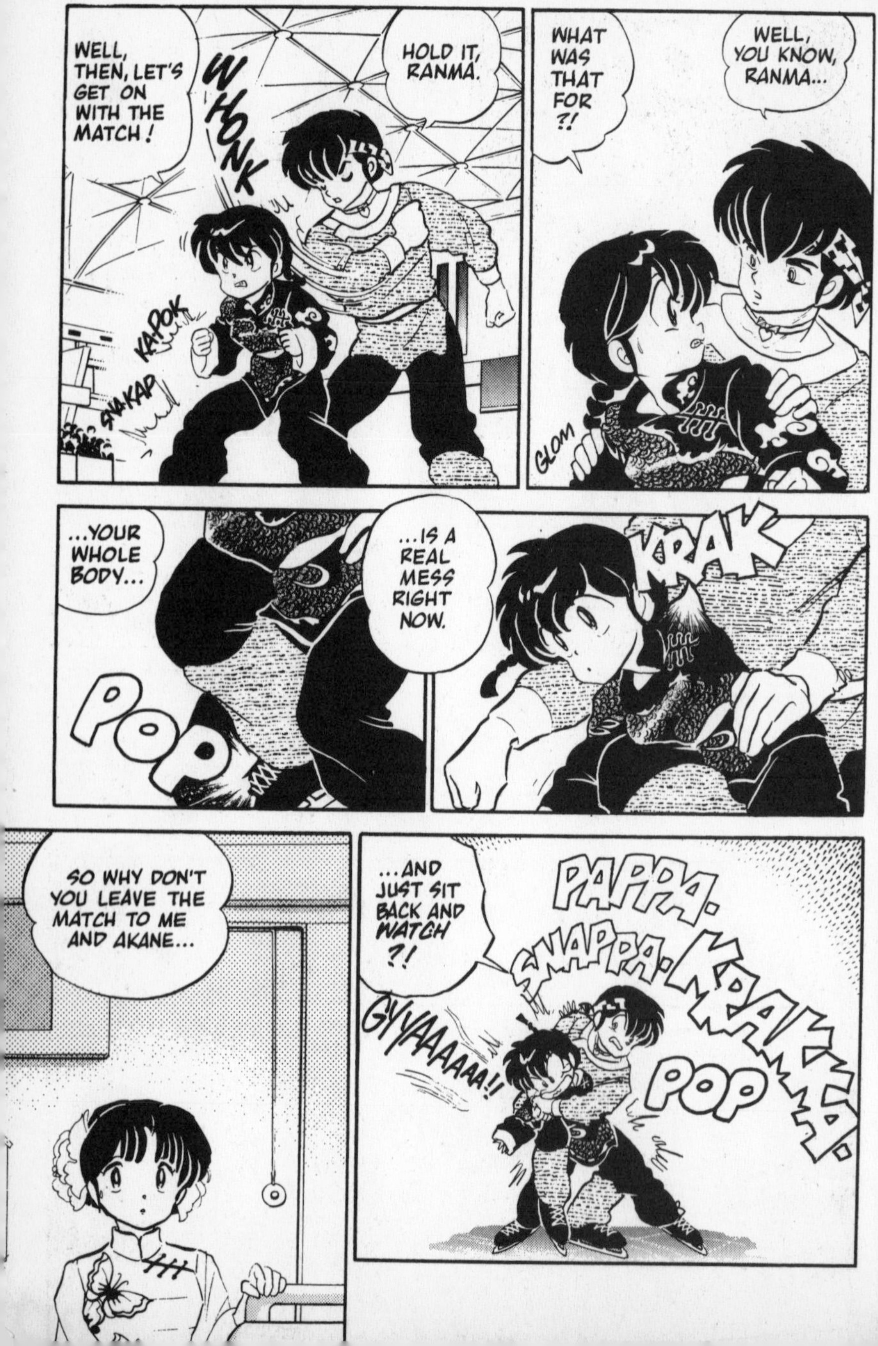
WELL, THEN, LET'S GET ON WITH THE MATCH!
WHONK
HOLD IT, RANMA.
KA-POK
SNA-KAP
WHAT WAS THAT FOR ?!
WELL, YOU KNOW, RANMA...
GLOM
...YOUR WHOLE BODY...
...IS A REAL MESS RIGHT NOW.
POP
KRAK
SO WHY DON'T YOU LEAVE THE MATCH TO ME AND AKANE...
...AND JUST SIT BACK AND WATCH ?!
PAPPA-SNAPPA-KRAKKA-KA-
GYYAAAAAAA!!
POP

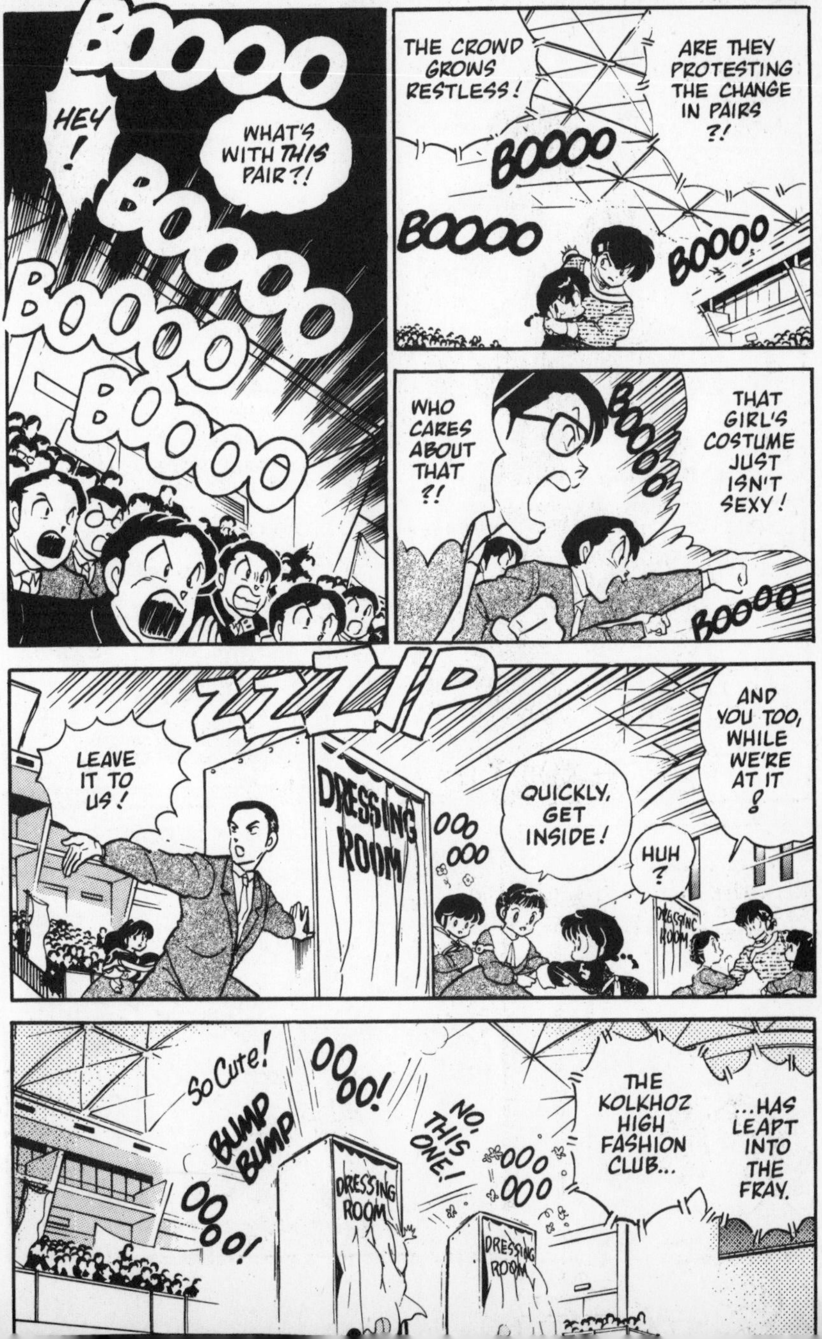
BOOOO
HEY!
WHAT'S WITH THIS PAIR?!
BOOOO
BOOOO
BOOOO
THE CROWD GROWS RESTLESS!
BOOOO
ARE THEY PROTESTING THE CHANGE IN PAIRS?!
BOOOO
BOOOO
WHO CARES ABOUT THAT?!
BOOOO
THAT GIRL'S COSTUME JUST ISN'T SEXY!
BOOOO
ZZZIP
LEAVE IT TO US!
DRESSING ROOM
OOO OOO
QUICKLY, GET INSIDE!
HUH?
AND YOU TOO, WHILE WE'RE AT IT!
So Cute!
BUMP BUMP
OOOO!
OOOO!
DRESSING ROOM
NO, THIS ONE!
OOO OOO
DRESSING ROOM
THE KOLKHOZ HIGH FASHION CLUB...
...HAS LEAPT INTO THE FRAY.

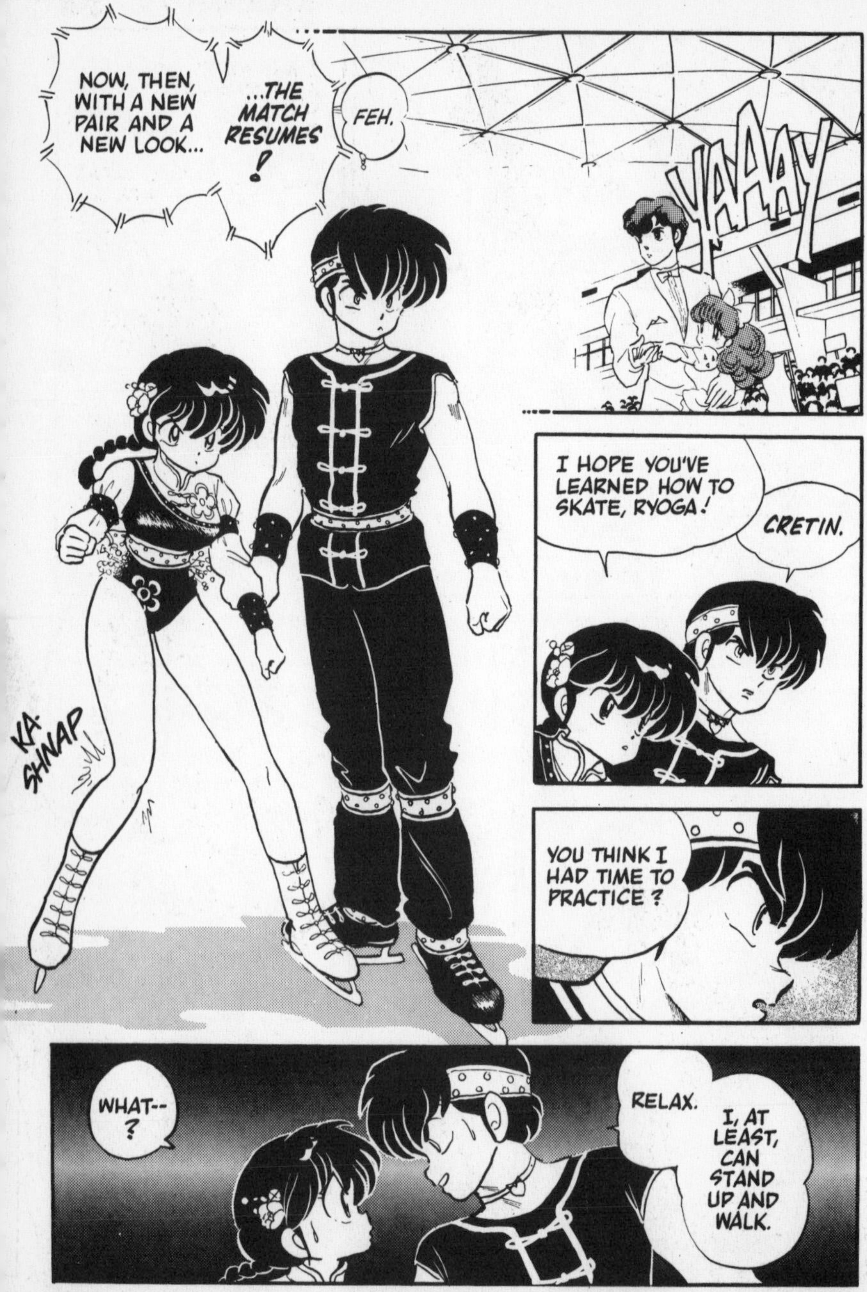
NOW, THEN, WITH A NEW PAIR AND A NEW LOOK...
...THE MATCH RESUMES!
FEH.
YAAAY
KA-SHNAP
I HOPE YOU'VE LEARNED HOW TO SKATE, RYOGA!
CRETIN.
YOU THINK I HAD TIME TO PRACTICE?
WHAT--?
RELAX.
I, AT LEAST, CAN STAND UP AND WALK.

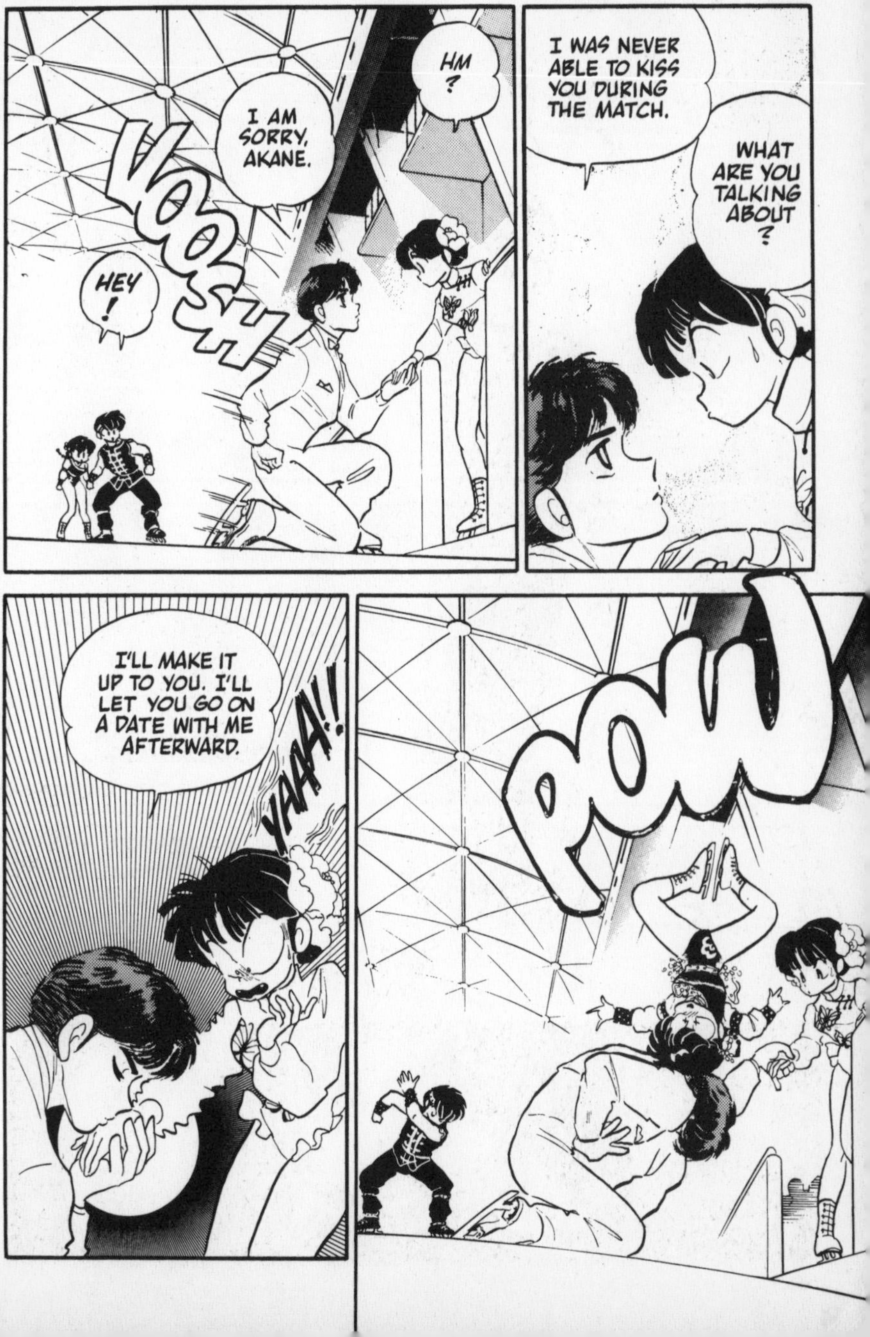
HM ?
I AM SORRY, AKANE.
VOOSH
HEY !
I WAS NEVER ABLE TO KISS YOU DURING THE MATCH.
WHAT ARE YOU TALKING ABOUT ?
I'LL MAKE IT UP TO YOU. I'LL LET YOU GO ON A DATE WITH ME AFTERWARD.
YAAA!!
POW

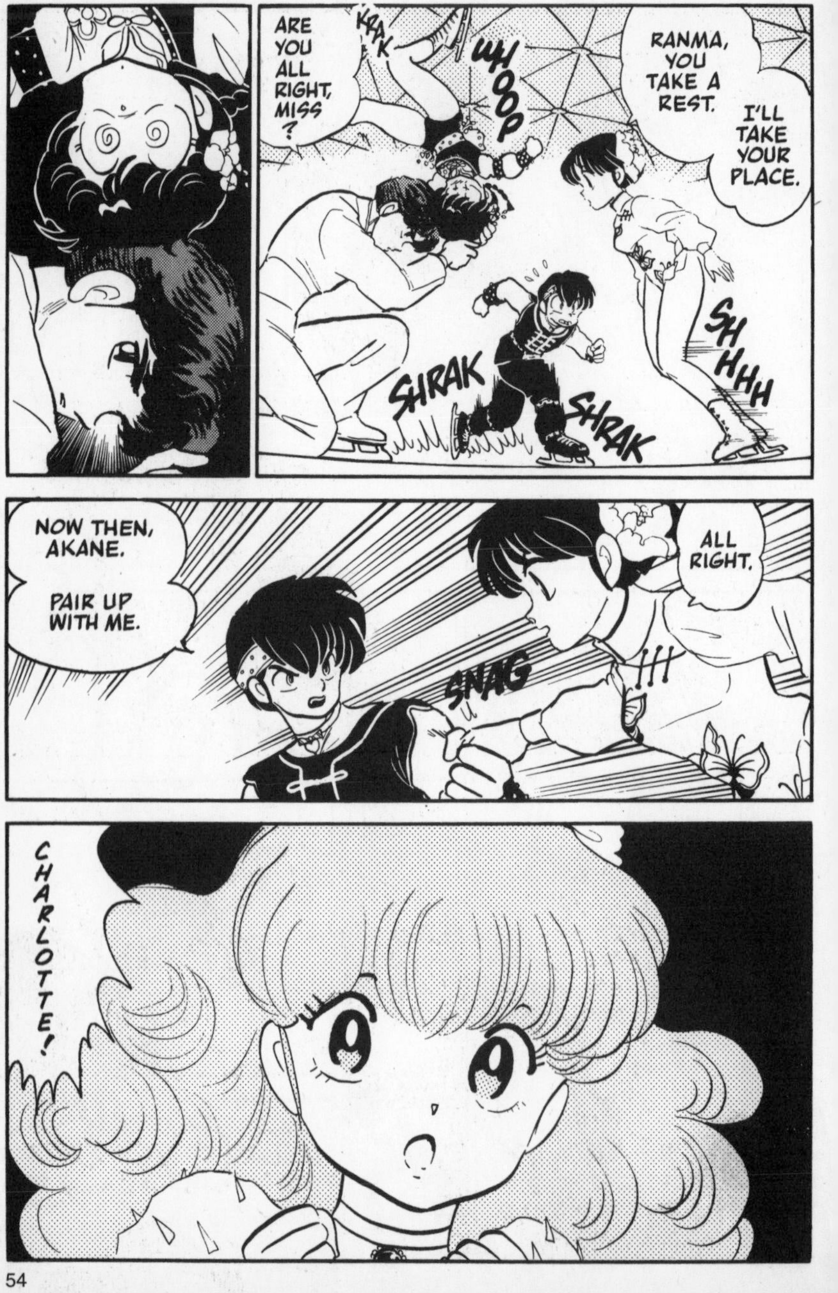
ARE YOU ALL RIGHT, MISS?
KRAK
WHOOOP
RANMA, YOU TAKE A REST.
I'LL TAKE YOUR PLACE.
SHRAK
SHRAK
SHHHH
NOW THEN, AKANE.
PAIR UP WITH ME.
SNAG
ALL RIGHT.
!!!
CHARLOTTE!

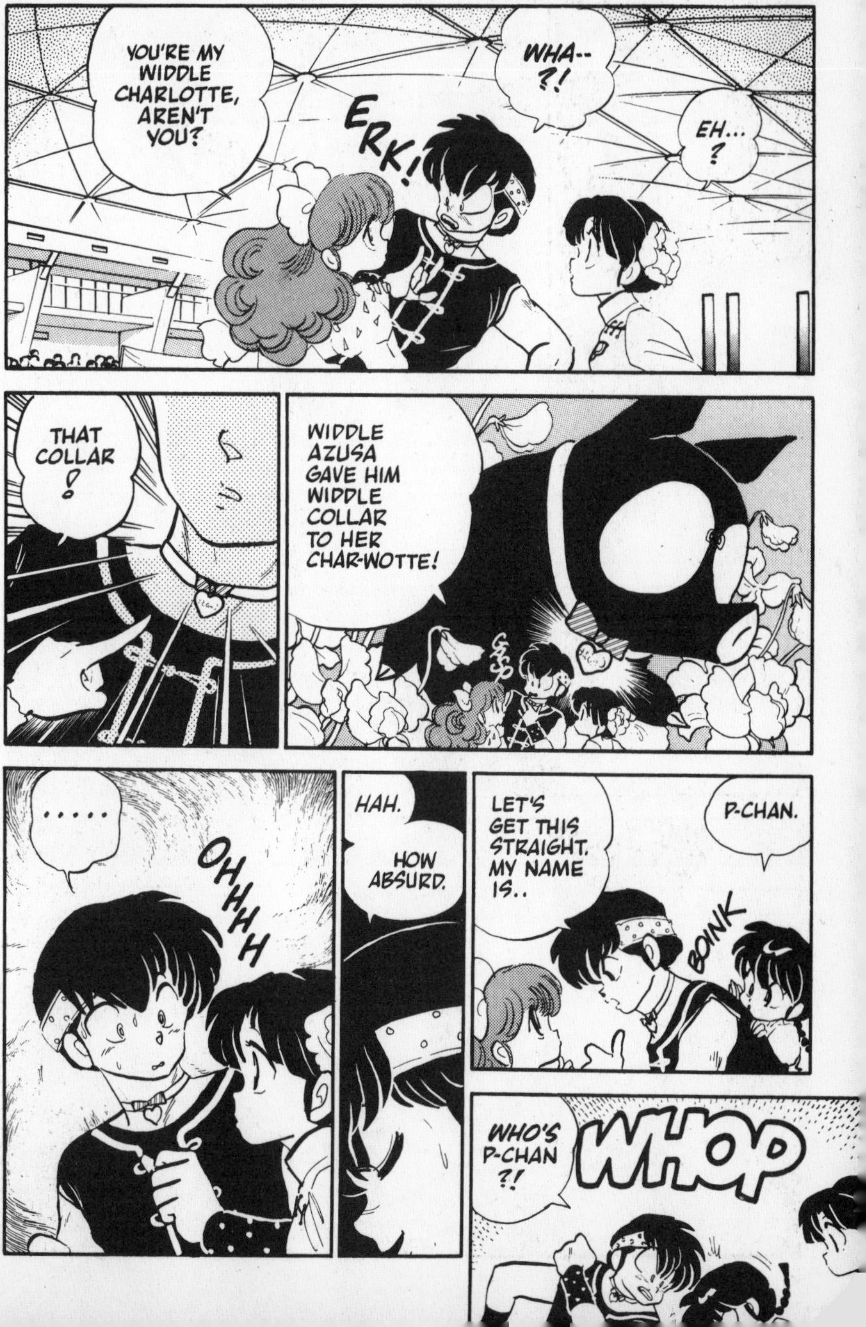
YOU'RE MY WIDDLE CHARLOTTE, AREN'T YOU?
ERK!
WHA-- ?!
EH... ?
THAT COLLAR!
WIDDLE AZUSA GAVE HIM WIDDLE COLLAR TO HER CHAR-WOTTE!
.....
OHHHH
HAH.
HOW ABSURD.
LET'S GET THIS STRAIGHT. MY NAME IS..
P-CHAN.
BOINK
WHO'S P-CHAN ?!
WHOP

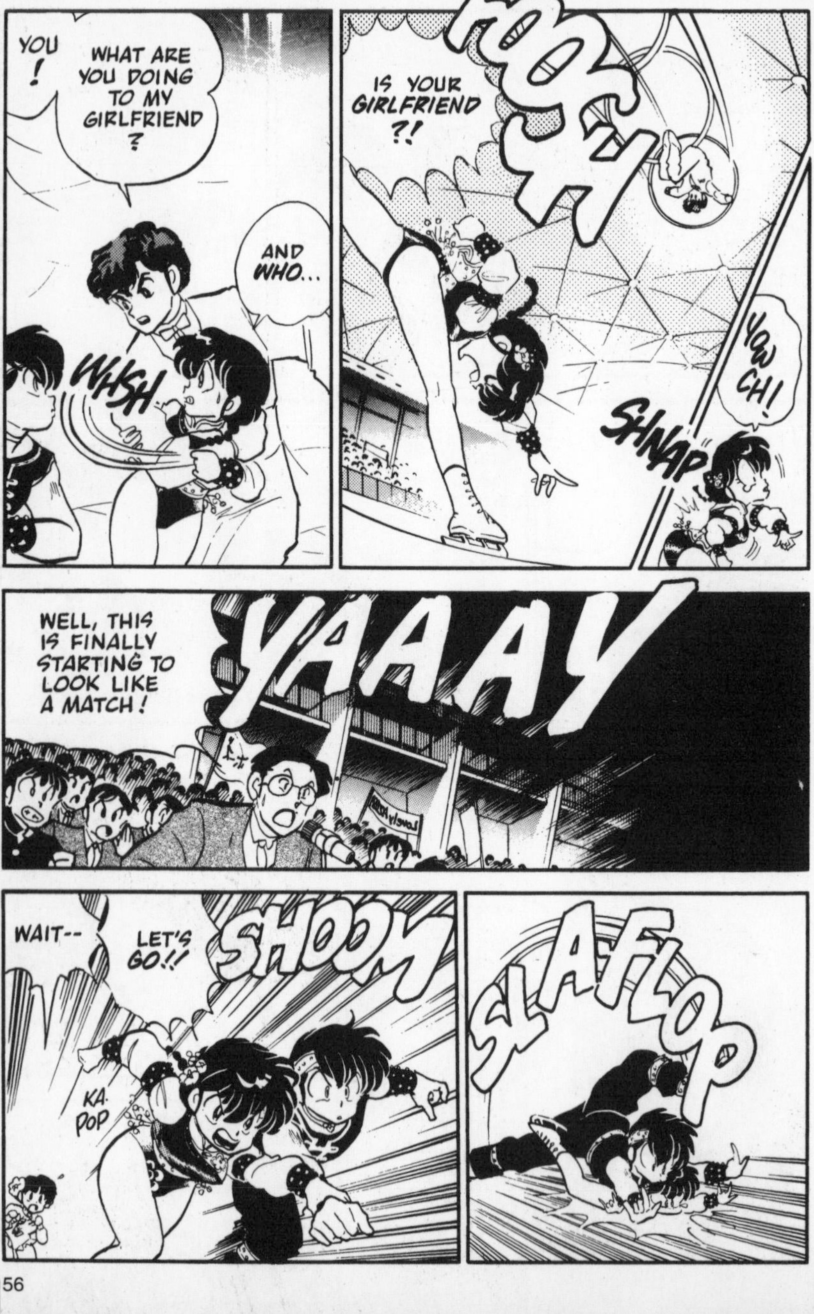
YOU!
WHAT ARE YOU DOING TO MY GIRLFRIEND?
AND WHO...
WHSH
FOOSH
IS YOUR GIRLFRIEND?!
YOWCH!
SHNAP
WELL, THIS IS FINALLY STARTING TO LOOK LIKE A MATCH!
YAAAY
WAIT--
LET'S GO!!
SHOOM
KA.POP
SLAFLOP

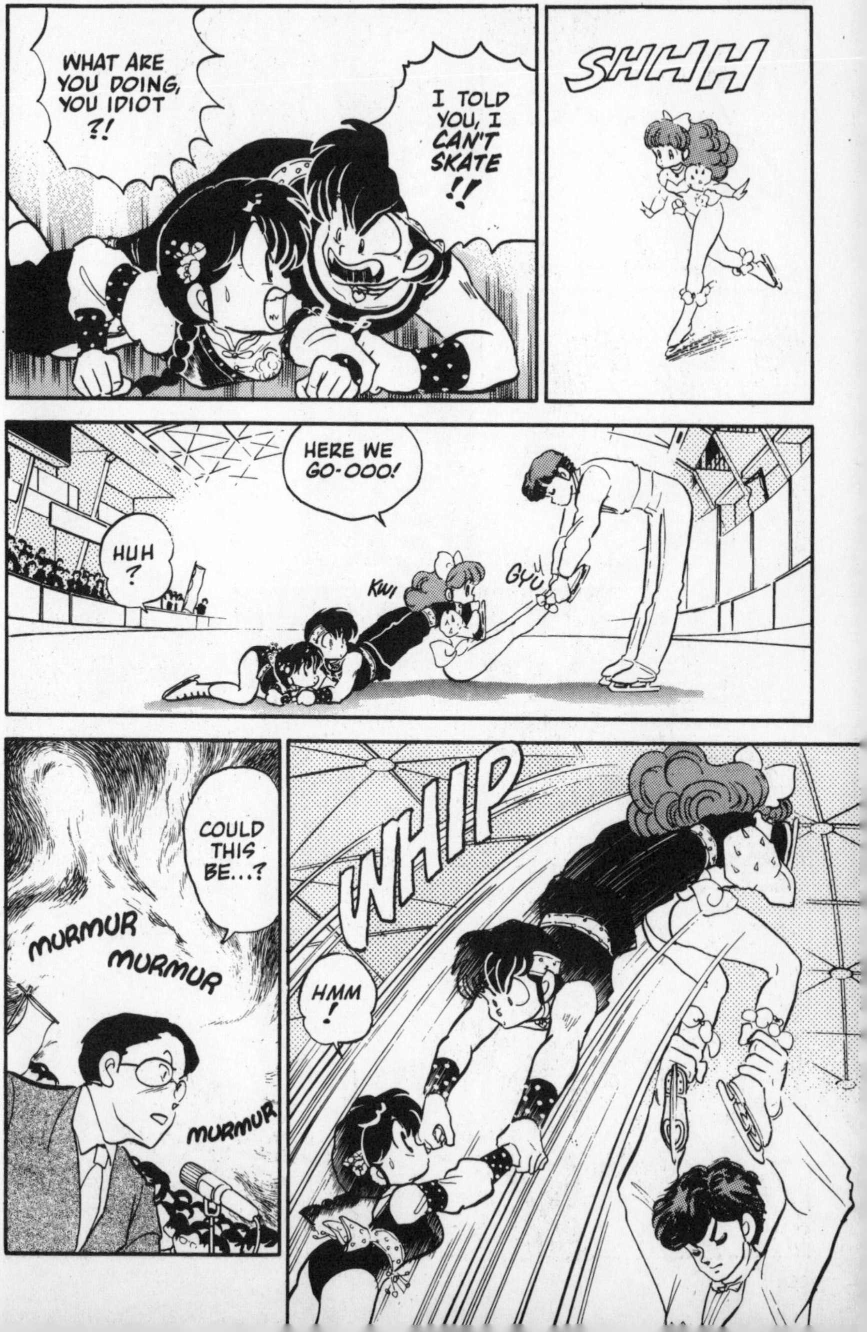
WHAT ARE YOU DOING, YOU IDIOT ?!
I TOLD YOU, I CAN'T SKATE !!
SHHH
HERE WE GO-OOO!
HUH ?
KWI
GYU
COULD THIS BE...?
MURMUR
MURMUR
MURMUR
WHIP
HMM !

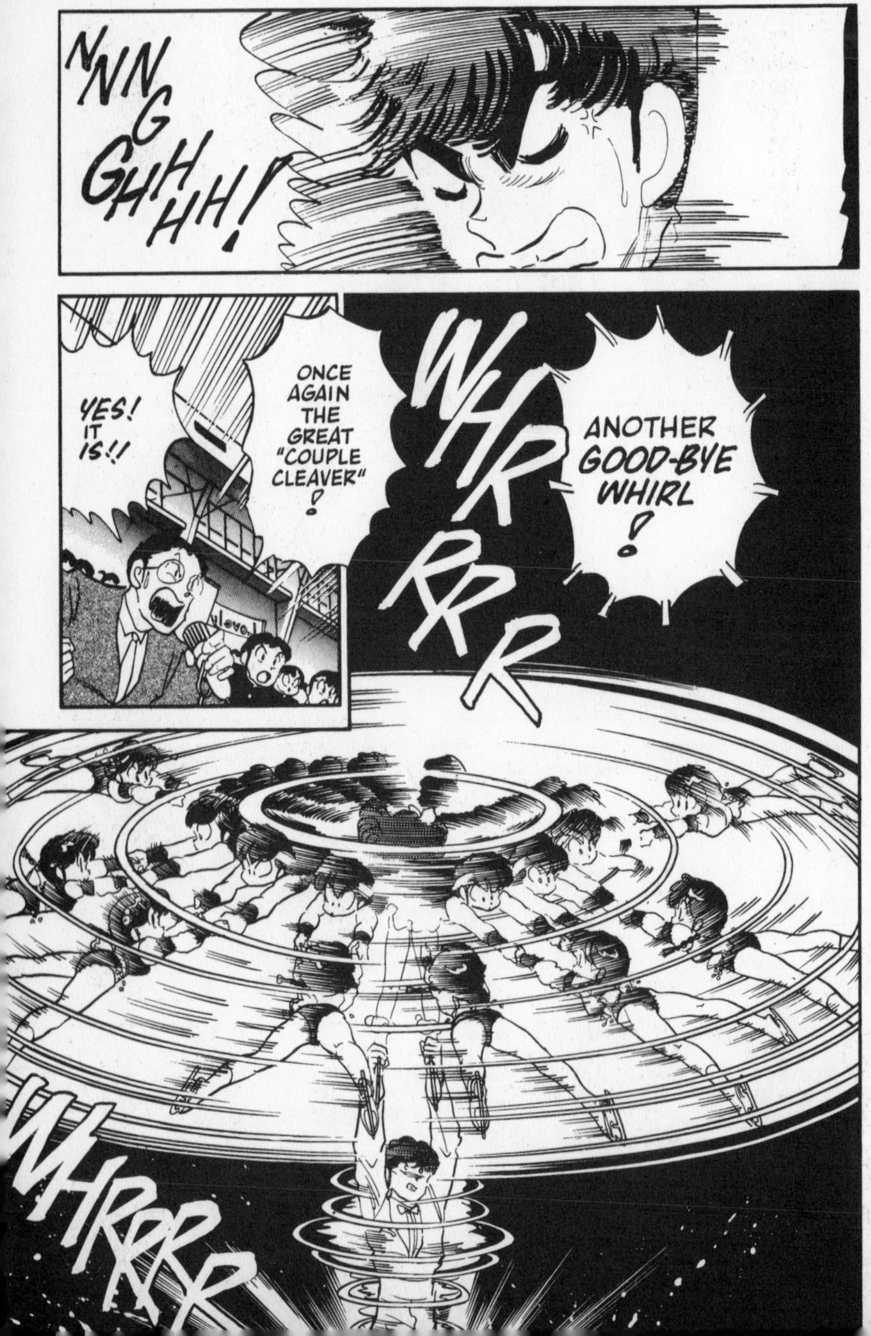
NNNG GHHHH!
YES! IT IS!!
ONCE AGAIN THE GREAT "COUPLE CLEAVER"!
WHRRRR
ANOTHER GOOD-BYE WHIRL!
WHRRRR

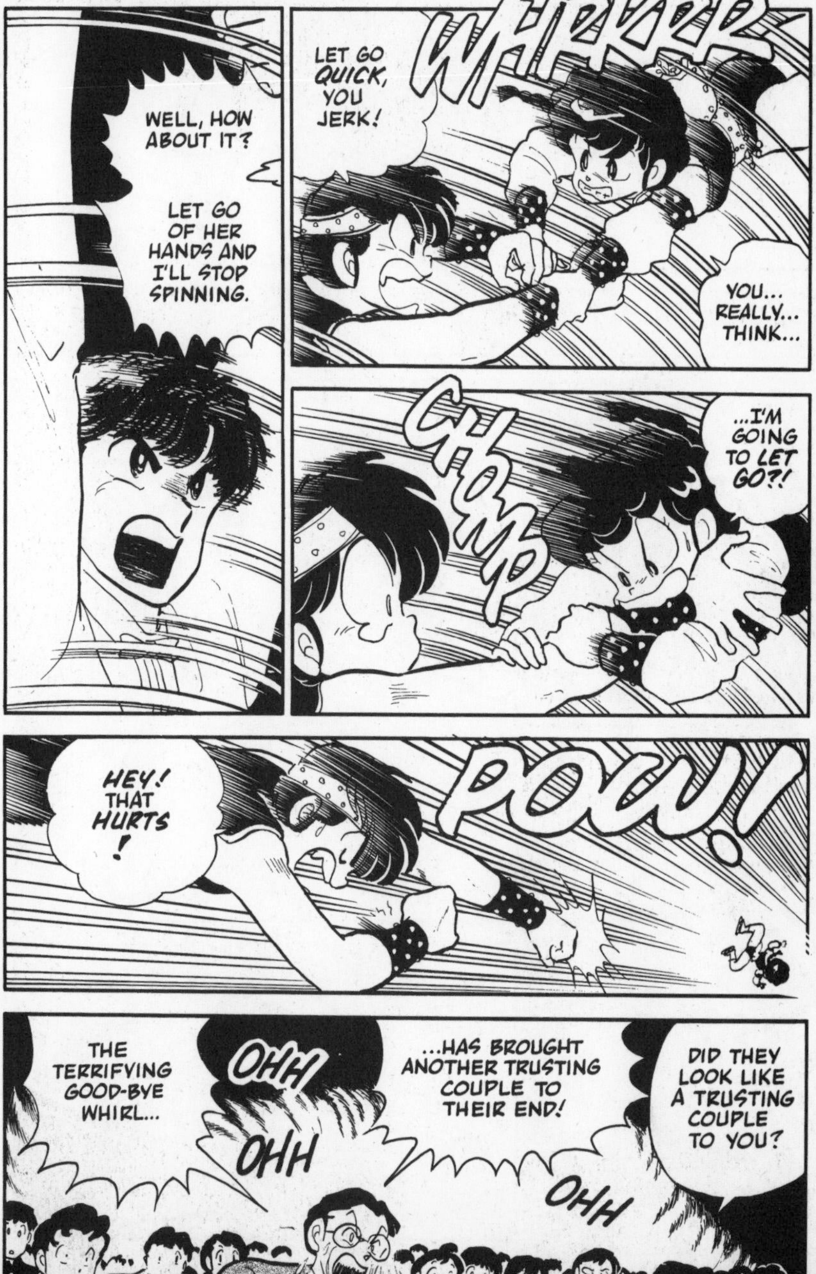

WELL, HOW ABOUT IT?
LET GO OF HER HANDS AND I'LL STOP SPINNING.
LET GO QUICK, YOU JERK!
WHIRRRR
YOU... REALLY... THINK...
CHOMP
...I'M GOING TO LET GO?!
HEY! THAT HURTS!
POW!
THE TERRIFYING GOOD-BYE WHIRL...
OHH
OHH
...HAS BROUGHT ANOTHER TRUSTING COUPLE TO THEIR END!
OHH
DID THEY LOOK LIKE A TRUSTING COUPLE TO YOU?

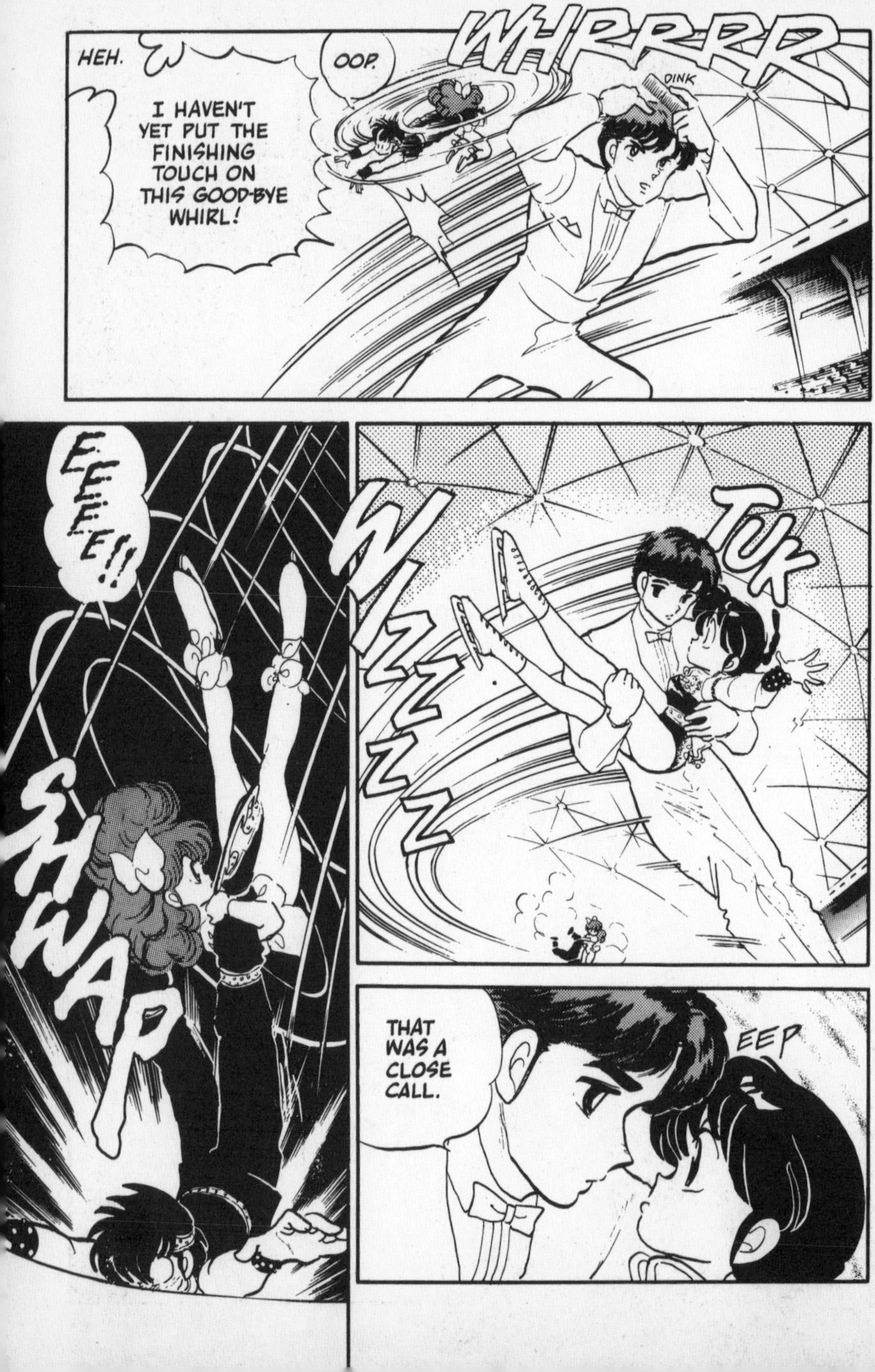
HEH.
I HAVEN'T YET PUT THE FINISHING TOUCH ON THIS GOOD-BYE WHIRL!
OOP.
WHRRRR
DINK
EEEE!!
SHWAP
TUK
THAT WAS A CLOSE CALL.
EEP

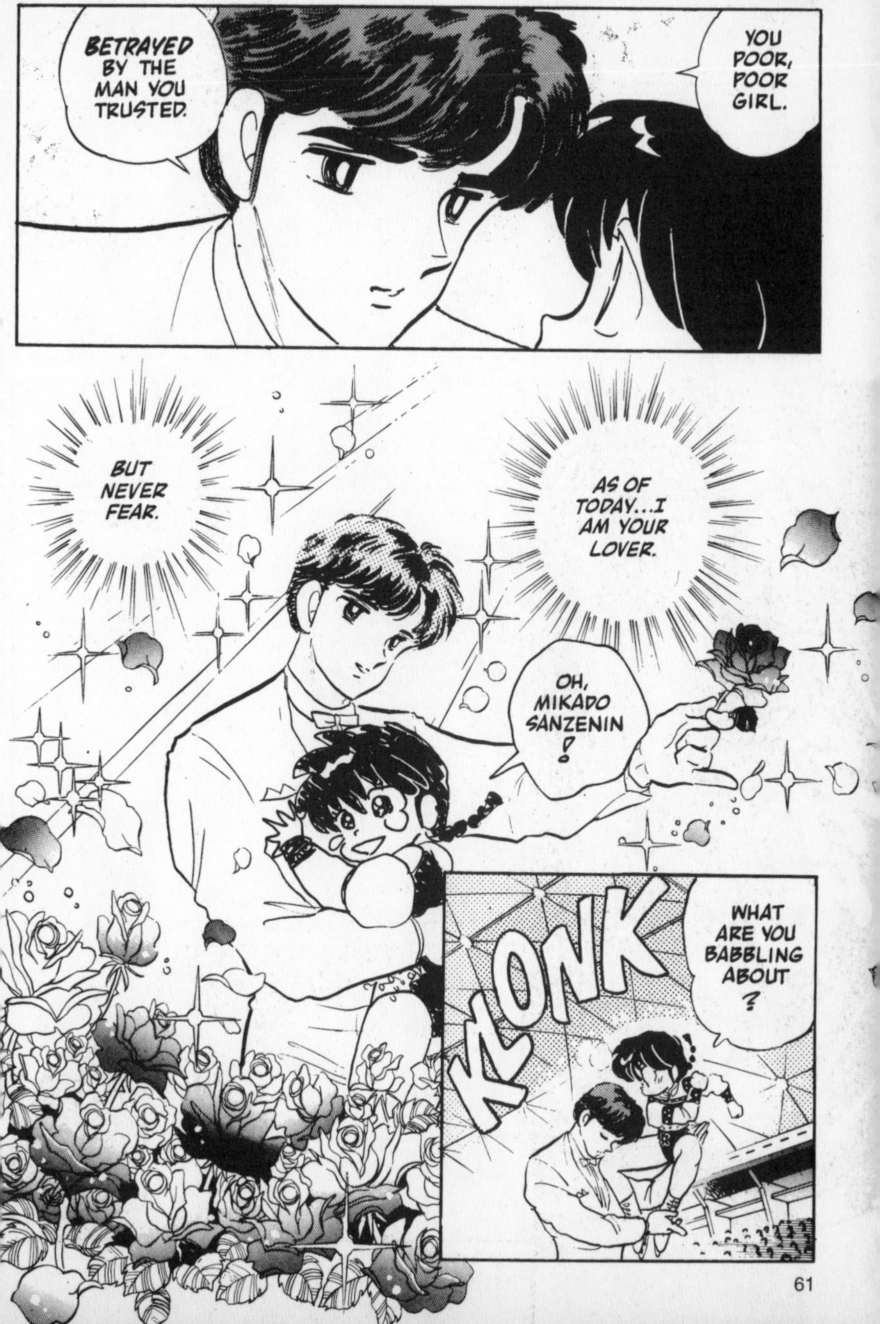
BETRAYED BY THE MAN YOU TRUSTED.
YOU POOR, POOR GIRL.
BUT NEVER FEAR.
AS OF TODAY...I AM YOUR LOVER.
OH, MIKADO SANZENIN!
KLONK
WHAT ARE YOU BABBLING ABOUT?

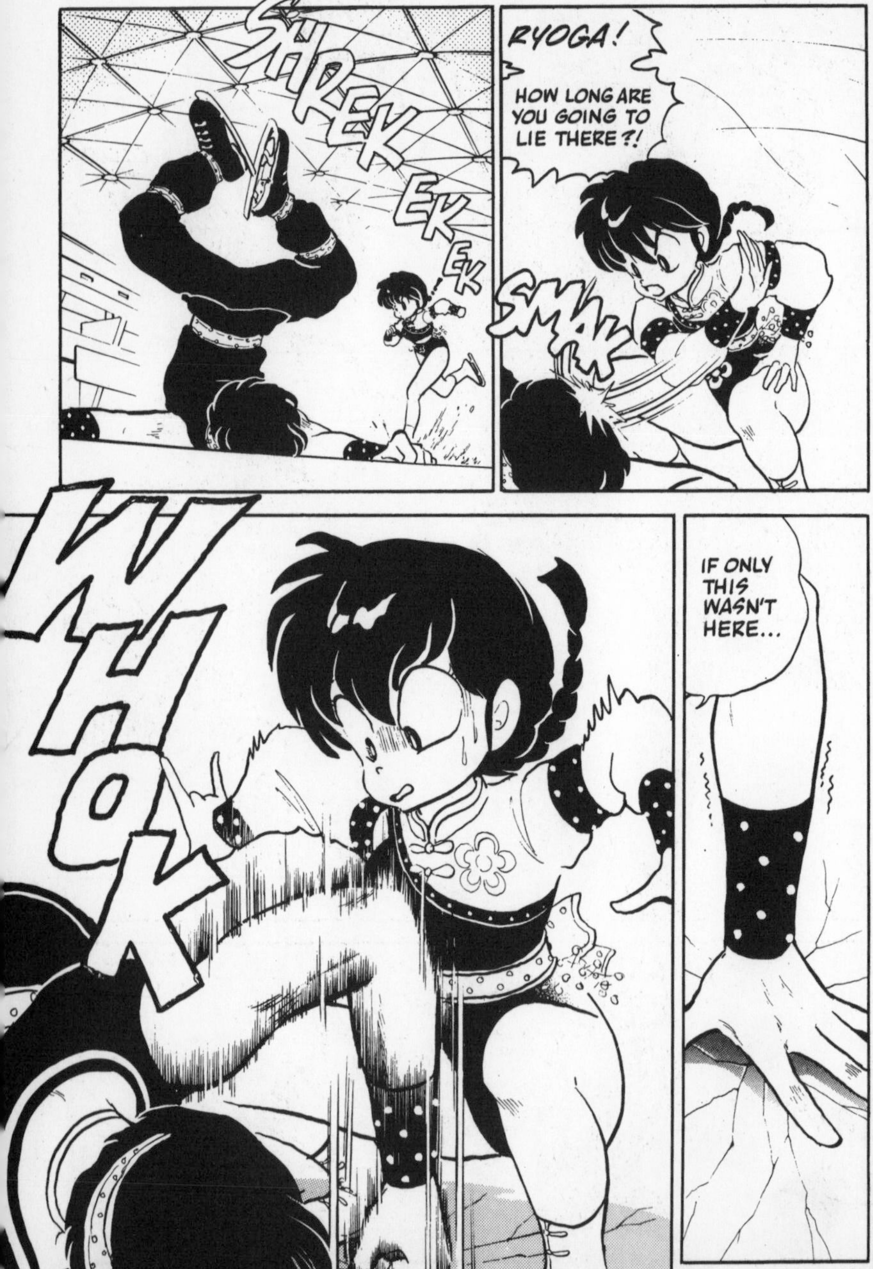
RYOGA!
HOW LONG ARE YOU GOING TO LIE THERE?!
SMAK
SHREK
EK
EK
IF ONLY THIS WASN'T HERE...
WHOK

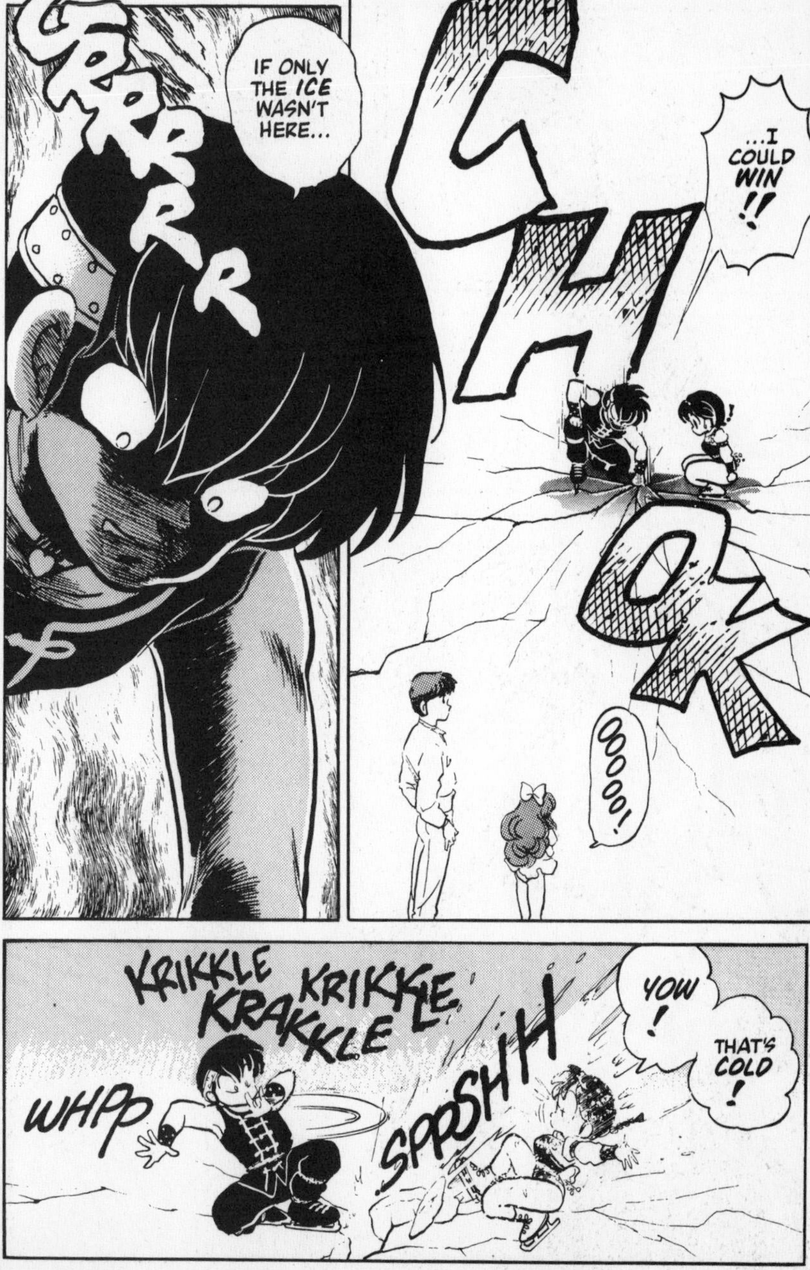
GRRRRR
IF ONLY THE ICE WASN'T HERE...
CHOK
...I COULD WIN!!
OOOOOO!
KRIKKLE
KRIKKLE
KRAKKLE
WHPP
SPPSHH
YOW!
THAT'S COLD!

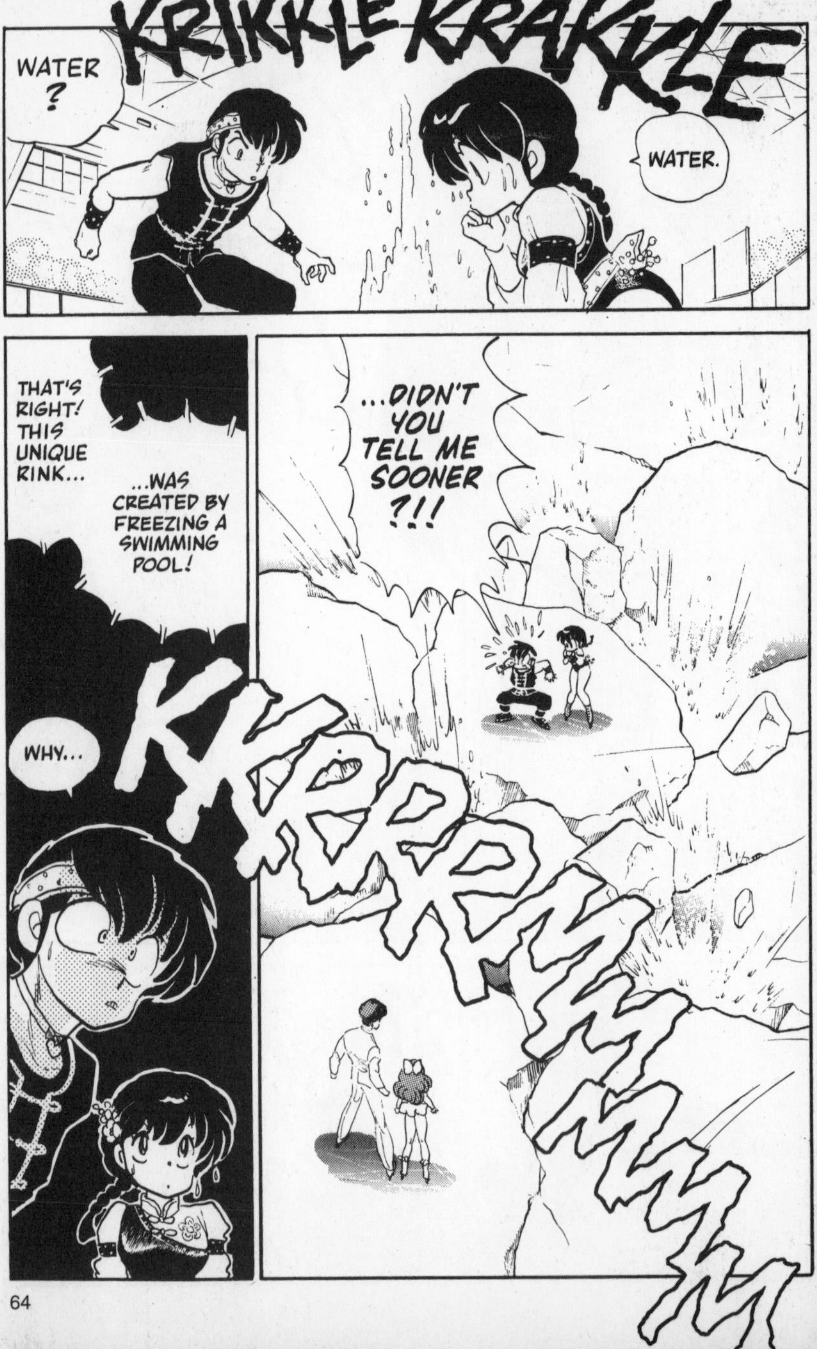
KRIKKLE KRAKKLE
WATER ?
WATER.
THAT'S RIGHT! THIS UNIQUE RINK...
...WAS CREATED BY FREEZING A SWIMMING POOL!
WHY...
...DIDN'T YOU TELL ME SOONER ?!!

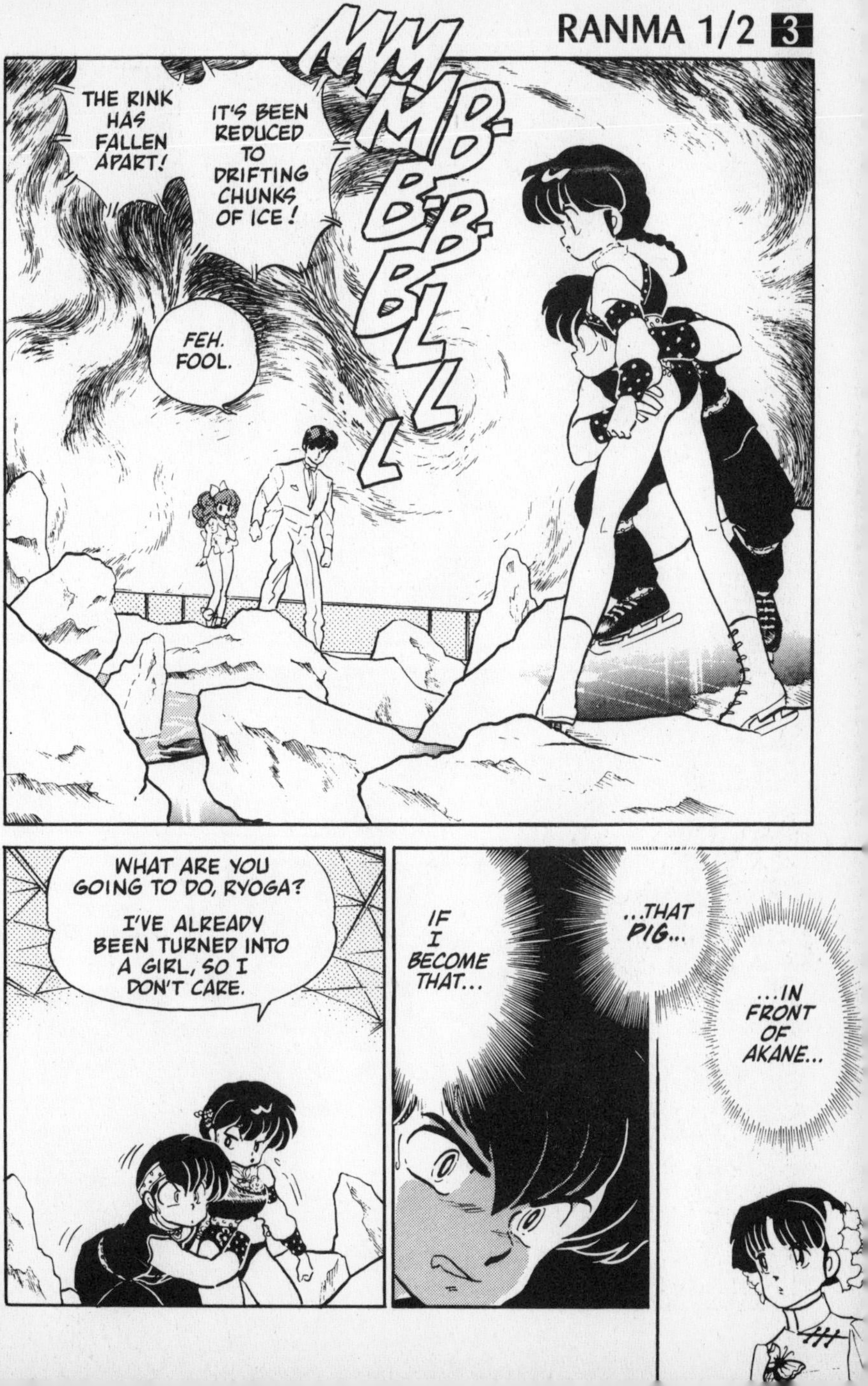
MMMB-B-B-BLLL
THE RINK HAS FALLEN APART!
IT'S BEEN REDUCED TO DRIFTING CHUNKS OF ICE!
FEH. FOOL.
WHAT ARE YOU GOING TO DO, RYOGA?
I'VE ALREADY BEEN TURNED INTO A GIRL, SO I DON'T CARE.
IF I BECOME THAT...
...THAT PIG...
...IN FRONT OF AKANE...

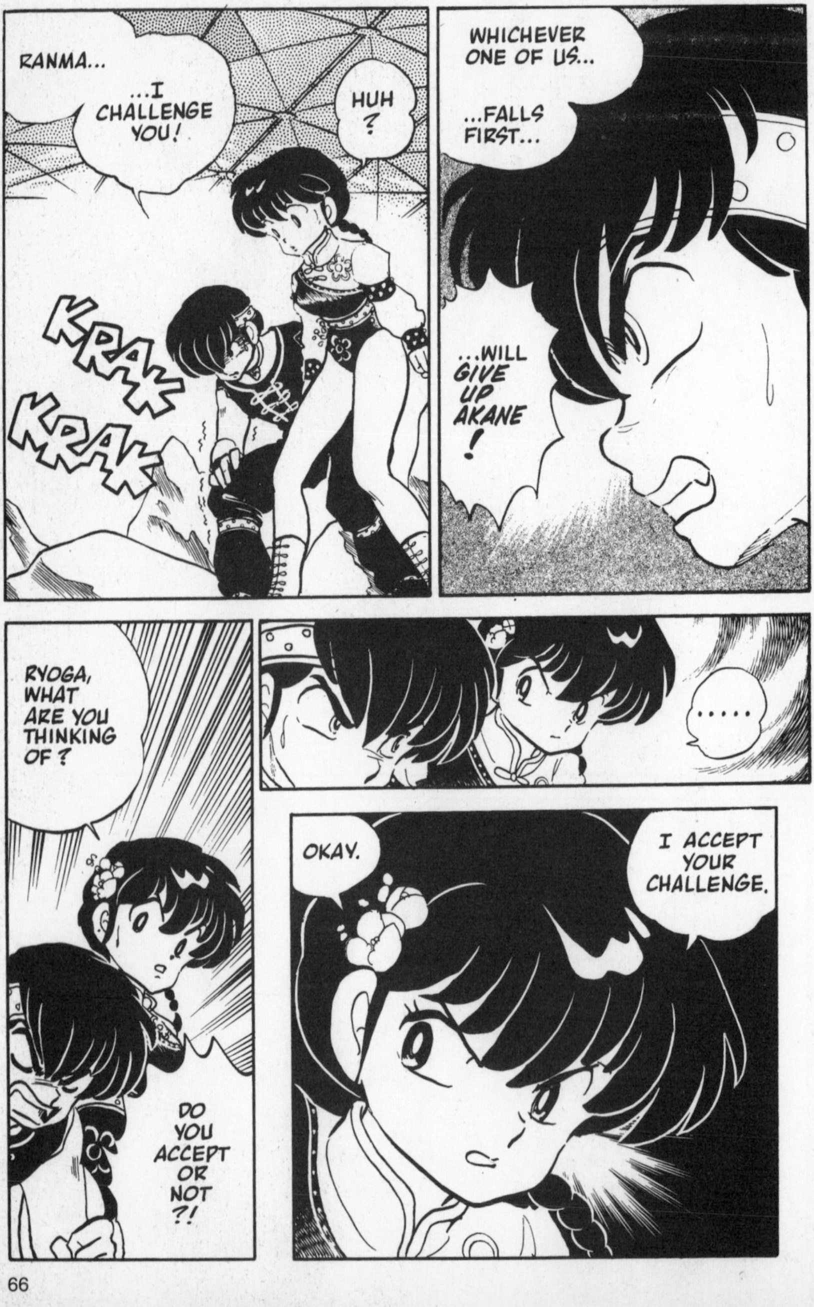
RANMA...
...I CHALLENGE YOU!
HUH?
KRAK
KRAK
WHICHEVER ONE OF US...
...FALLS FIRST...
...WILL GIVE UP AKANE!
RYOGA, WHAT ARE YOU THINKING OF?
.....
DO YOU ACCEPT OR NOT?!
OKAY.
I ACCEPT YOUR CHALLENGE.

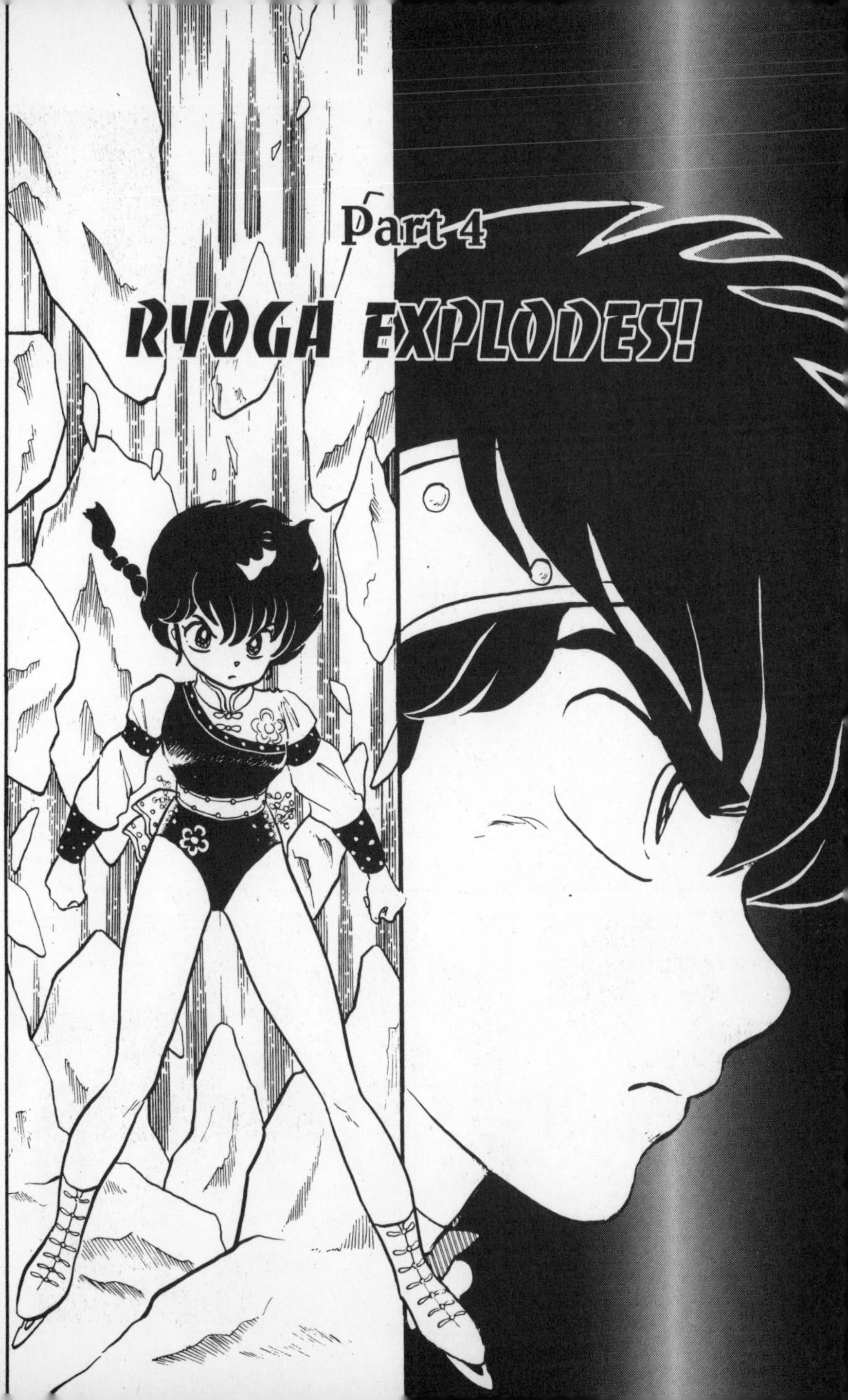
Part 4
RYOGA EXPLODES!

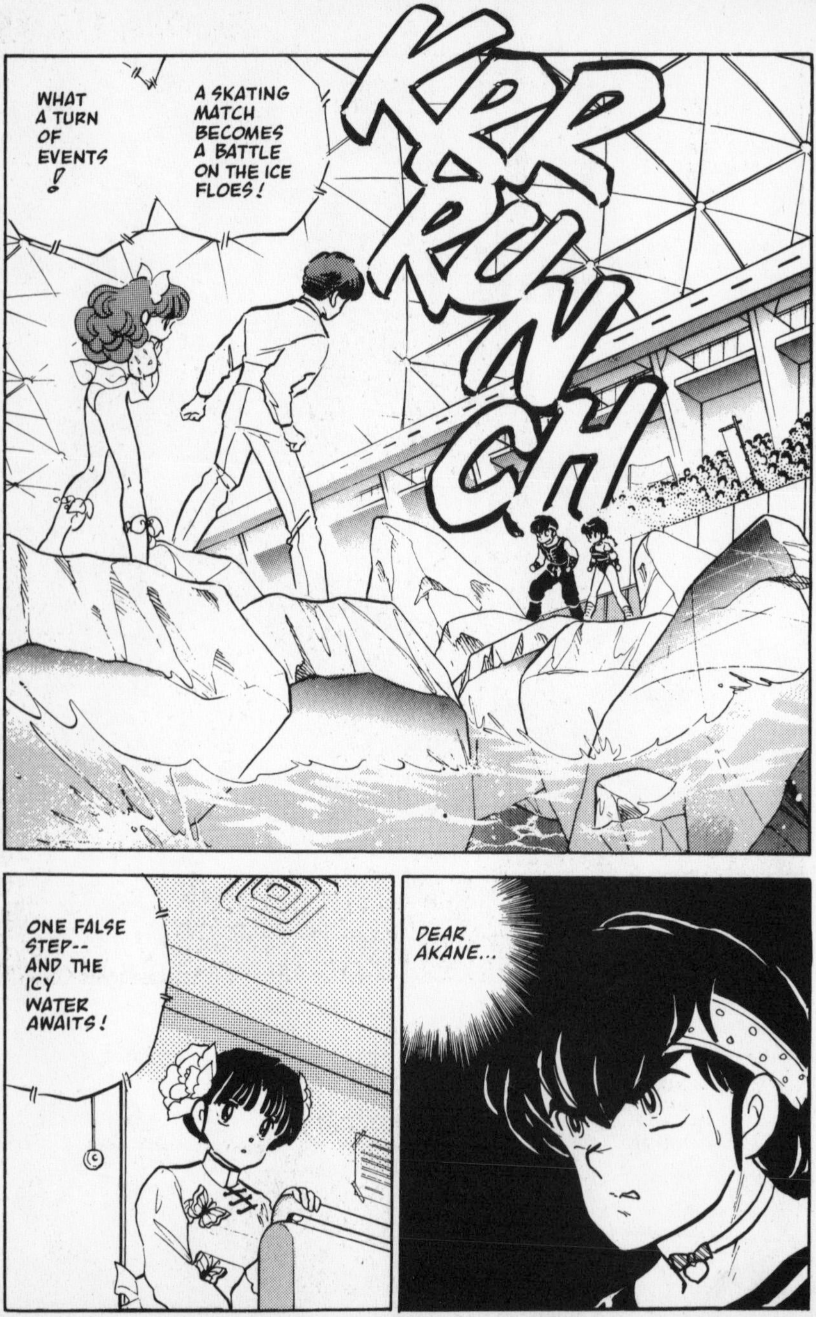
WHAT A TURN OF EVENTS!
A SKATING MATCH BECOMES A BATTLE ON THE ICE FLOES!
KRRRUNCH
ONE FALSE STEP-- AND THE ICY WATER AWAITS!
DEAR AKANE...

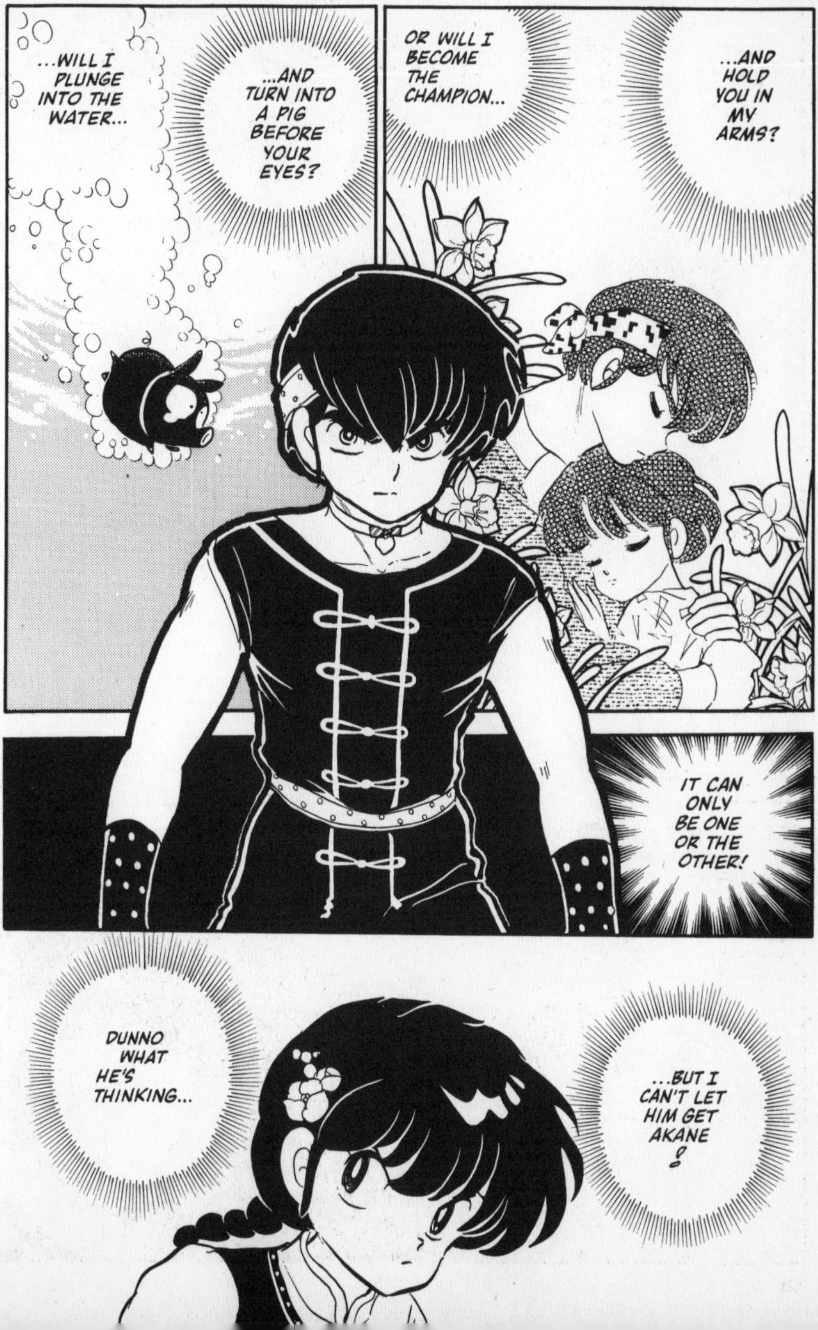
...WILL I PLUNGE INTO THE WATER...
...AND TURN INTO A PIG BEFORE YOUR EYES?
OR WILL I BECOME THE CHAMPION...
...AND HOLD YOU IN MY ARMS?
IT CAN ONLY BE ONE OR THE OTHER!
DUNNO WHAT HE'S THINKING...
...BUT I CAN'T LET HIM GET AKANE!

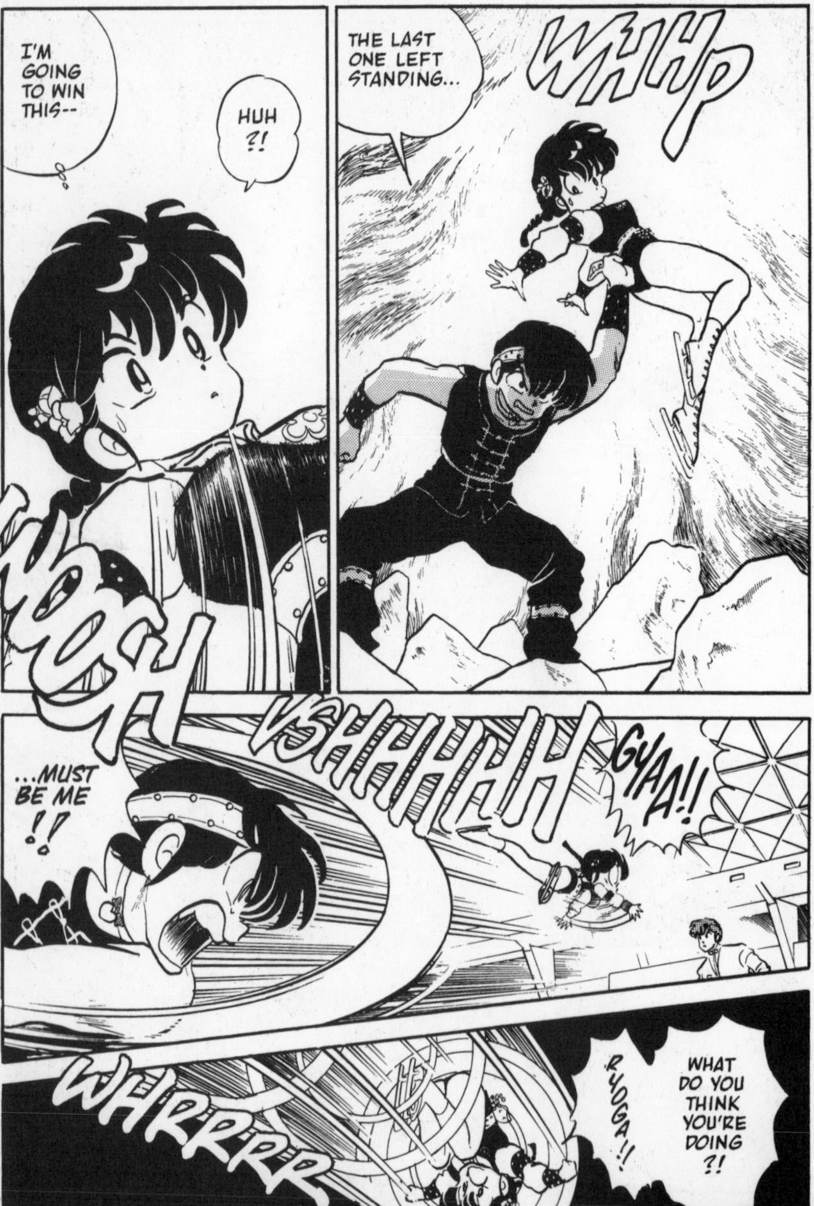
THE LAST ONE LEFT STANDING...
WHHP
I'M GOING TO WIN THIS--
HUH ?!
WOOSH
VSHHHHHH
GYAA!!
...MUST BE ME !!
WHAT DO YOU THINK YOU'RE DOING ?!
RYOGA!!
WHRRRRR

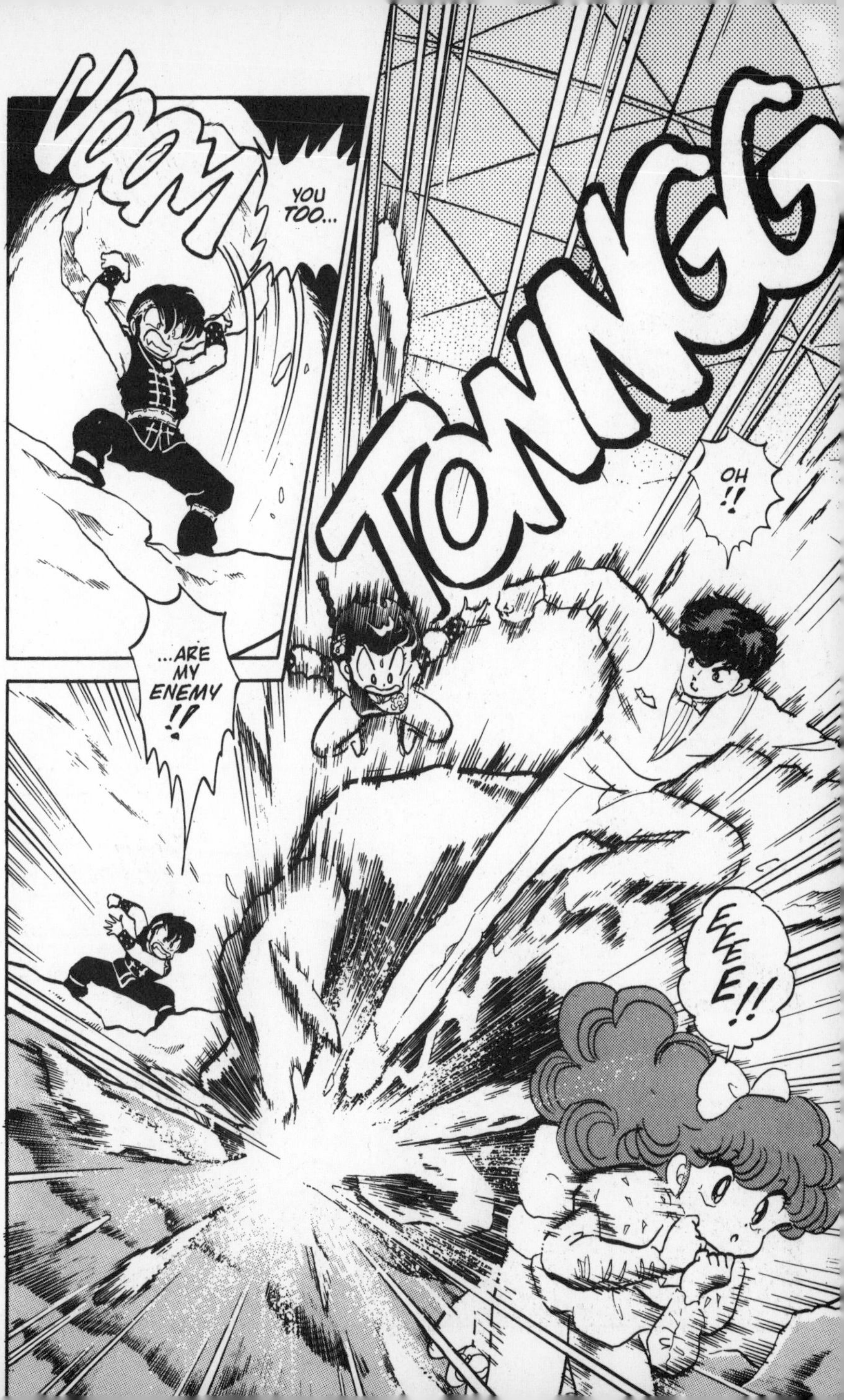
VOOM
YOU TOO...
...ARE MY ENEMY!!
TOWNGG
OH!!
EEEEE!!

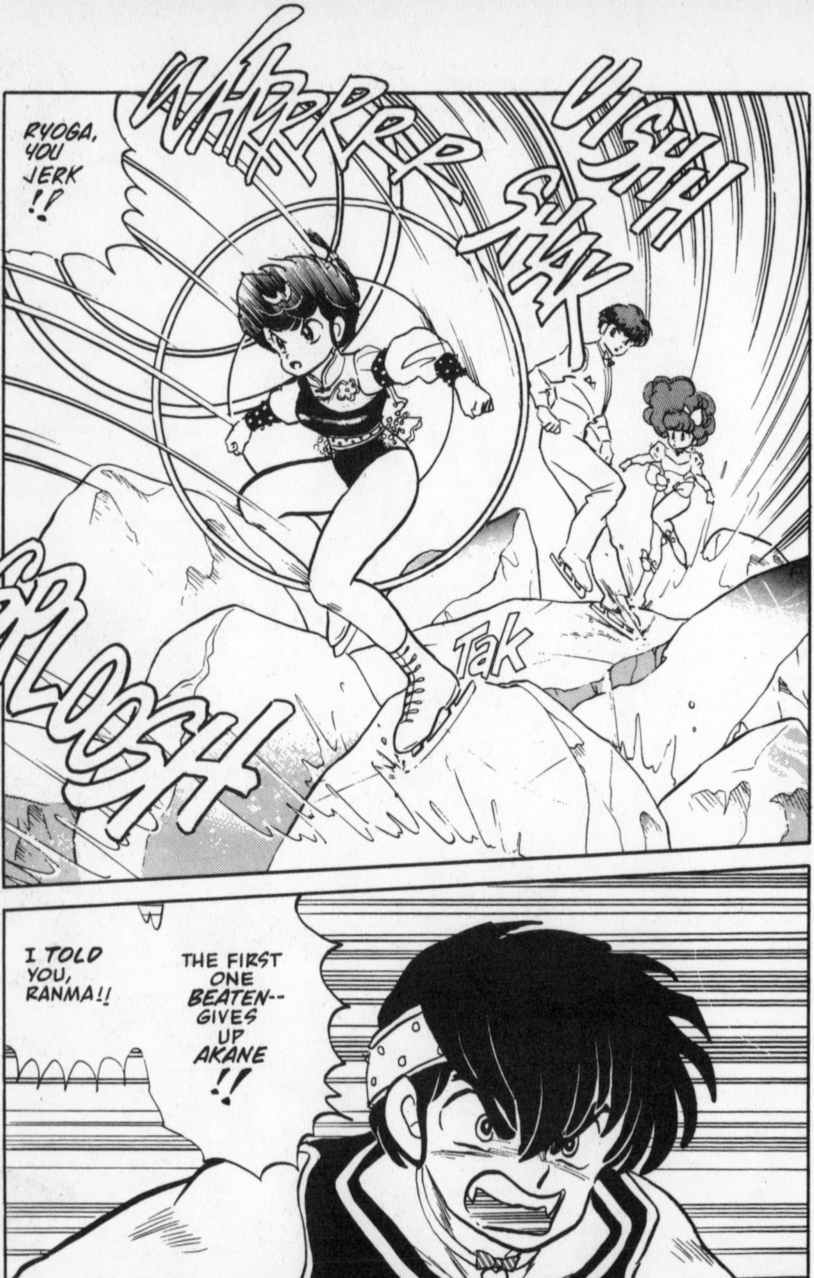
WHIRRRR
UISHH
SHAK
RYOGA, YOU JERK!!
SPLOOSH
TAK
I TOLD YOU, RANMA!!
THE FIRST ONE BEATEN--GIVES UP AKANE!!

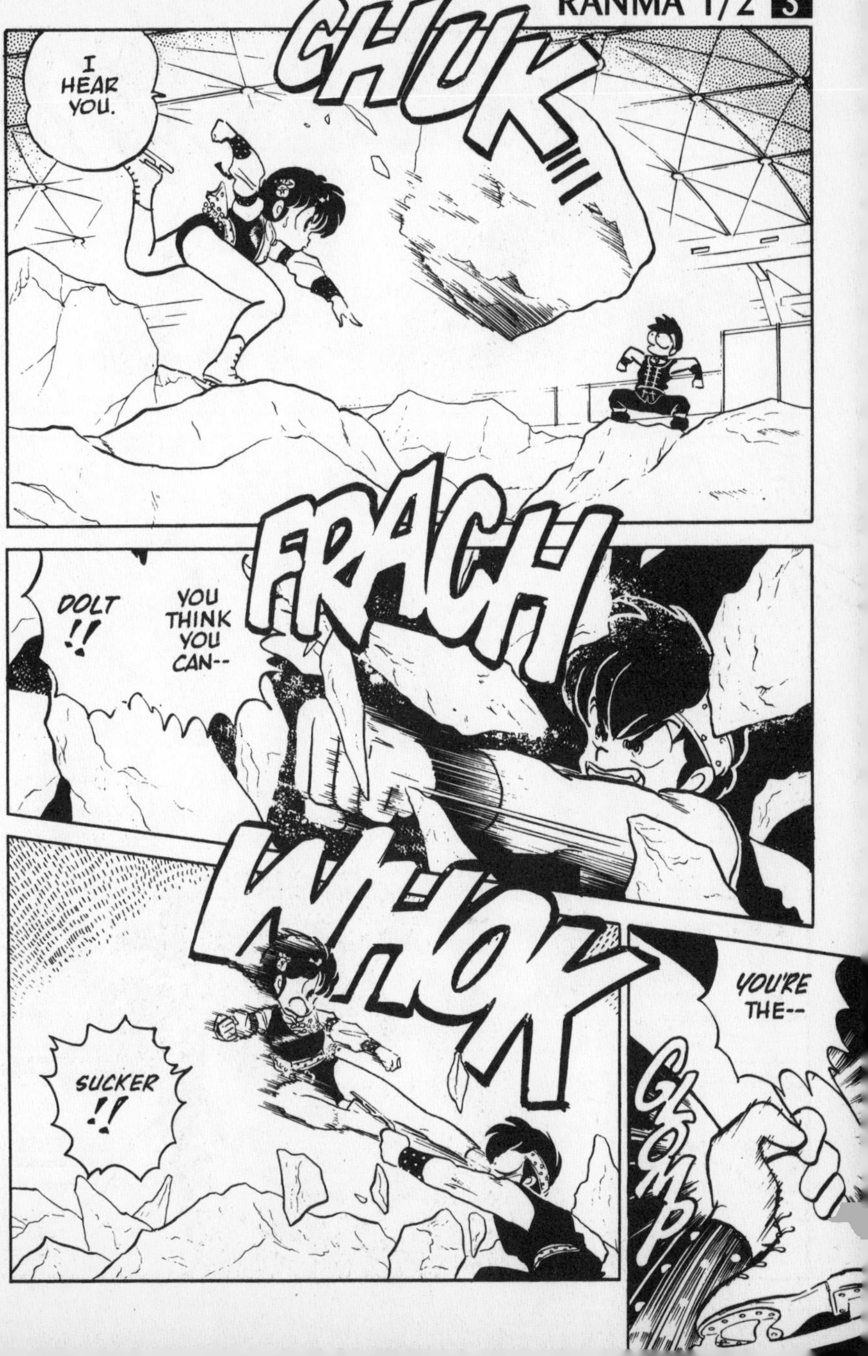
CHUK
I HEAR YOU.
FRACH
DOLT !!
YOU THINK YOU CAN--
WHOK
SUCKER !!
YOU'RE THE--
GLOMP

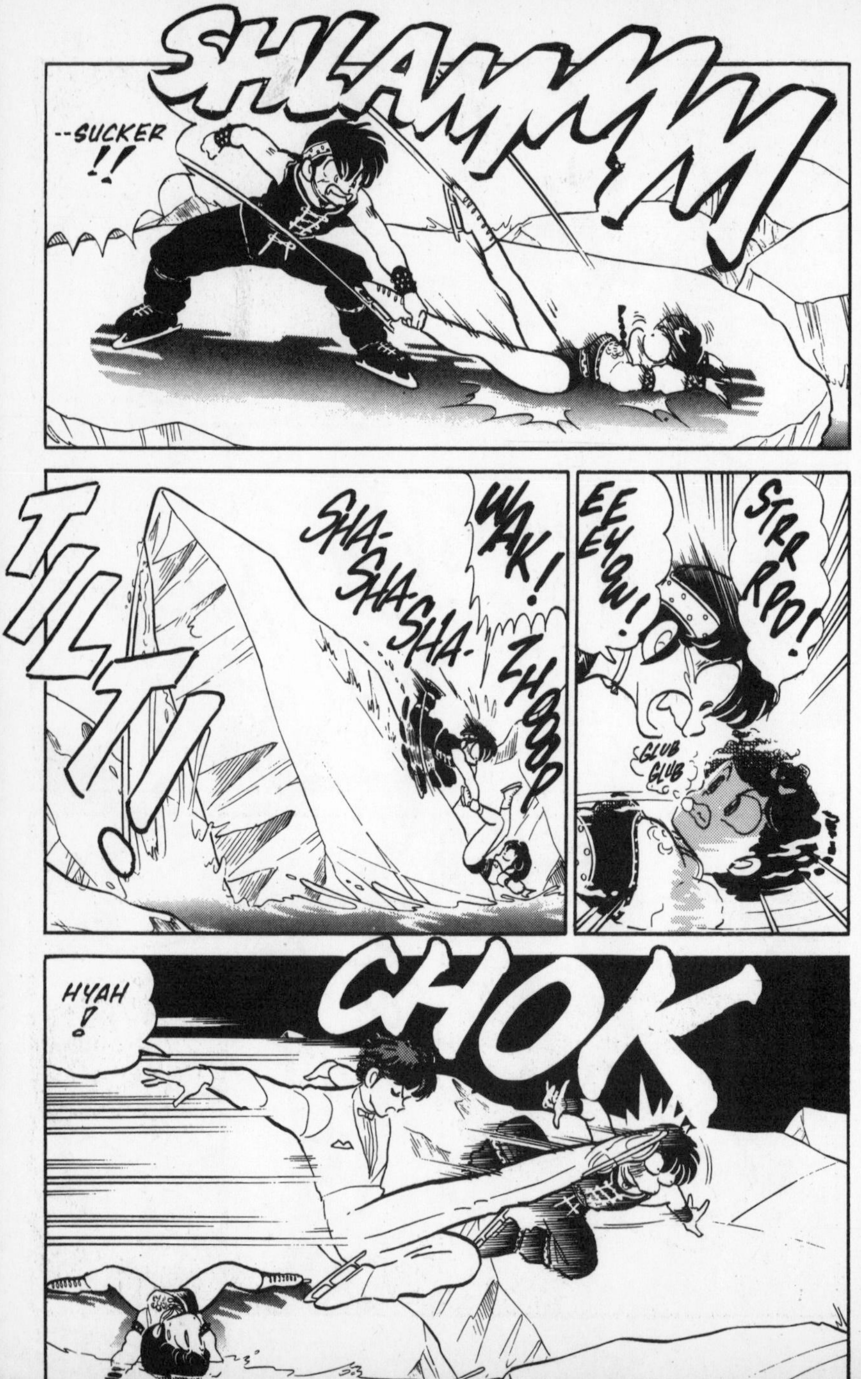
SHLAMMM
--SUCKER !!
TILT!
SHA-SHA-SHA-
WAK!
ZHOOOO
EEYOW!
STRRRPO!
GLUB GLUB
HYAH!
CHOK

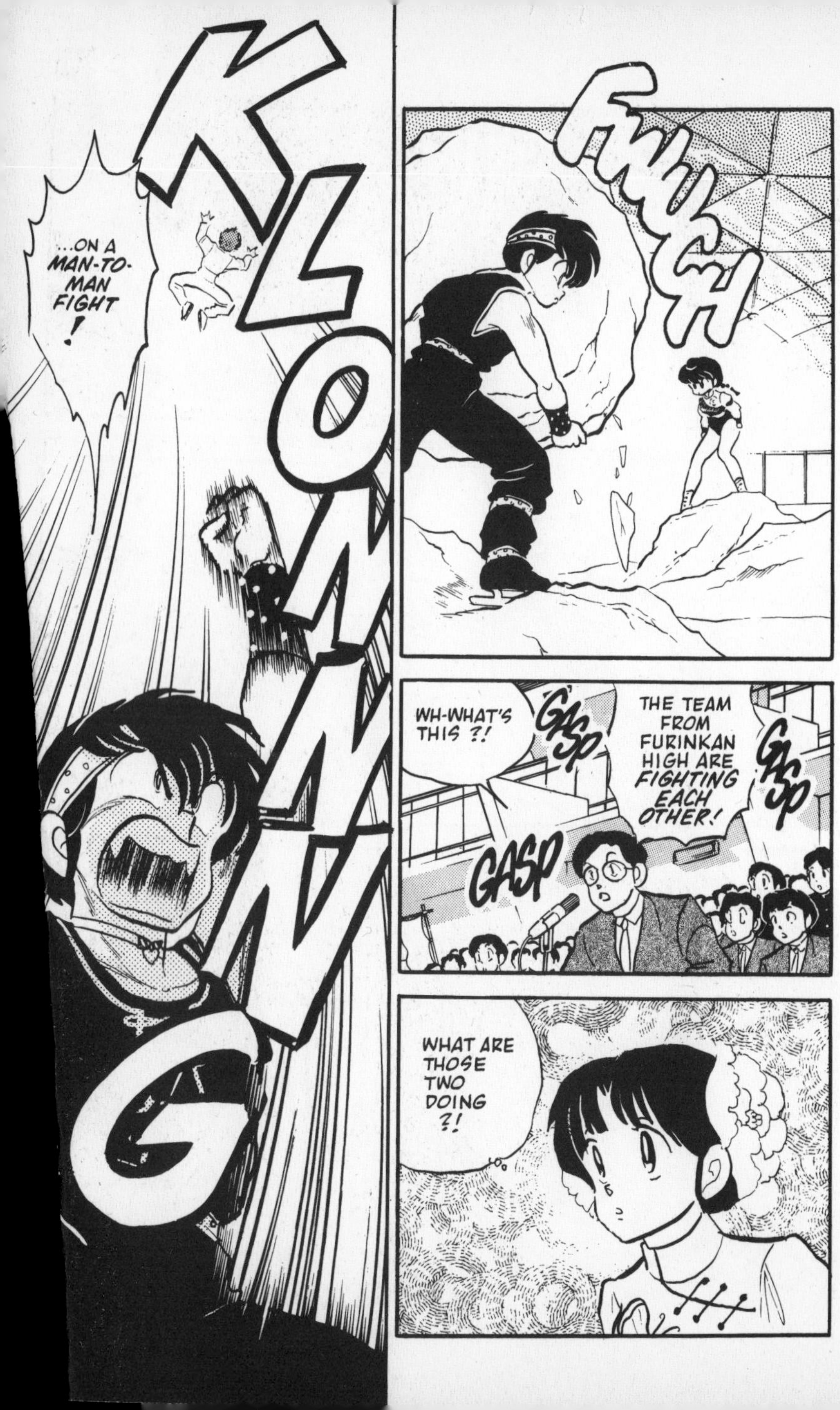
GASP
THE TEAM FROM FURINKAN HIGH ARE FIGHTING EACH OTHER!
GASP
WH-WHAT'S THIS ?!
GASP
WHAT ARE THOSE TWO DOING ?!
...ON A MAN-TO-MAN FIGHT!

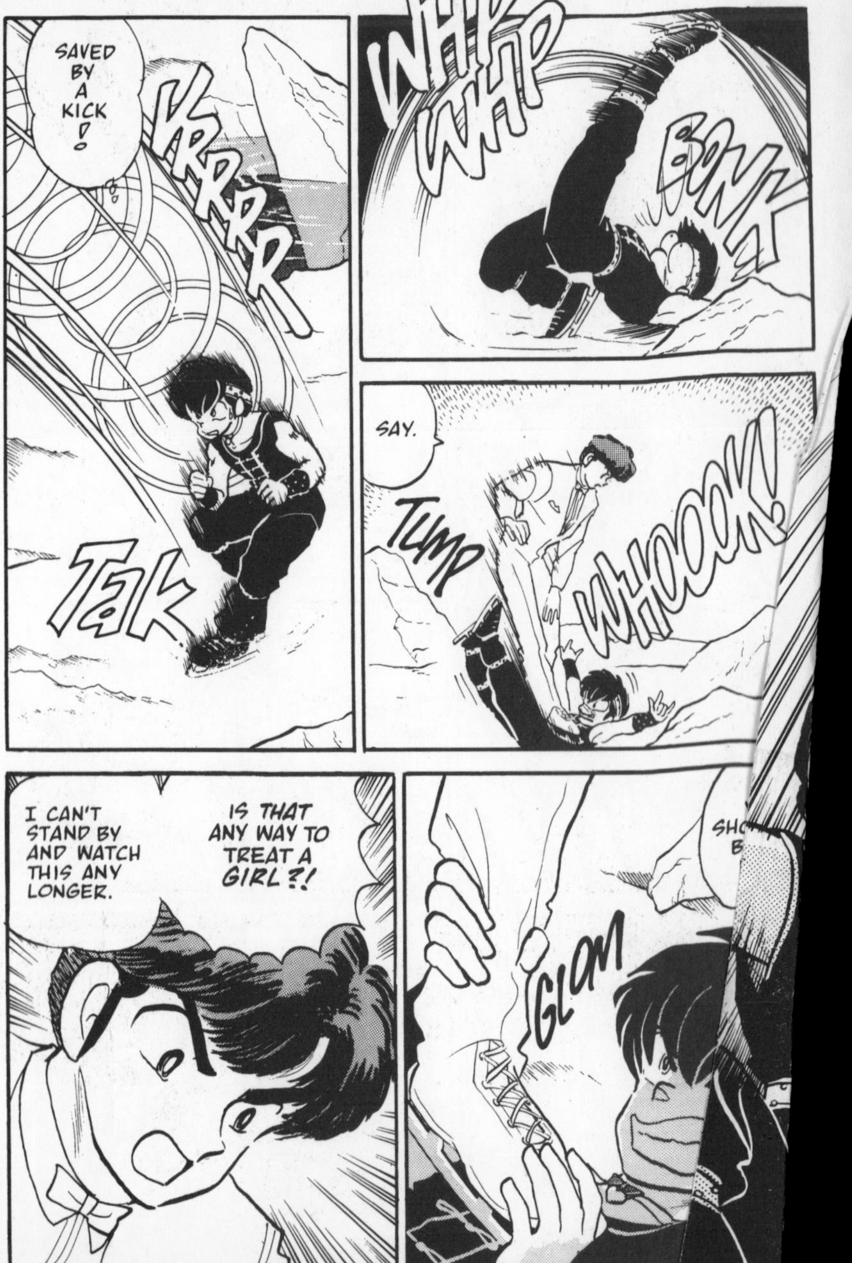
SAVED BY A KICK!
KRRRR
TAK
WHIP WHIP
BONK
SAY.
TUMP
WHOOOK!
I CAN'T STAND BY AND WATCH THIS ANY LONGER.
IS THAT ANY WAY TO TREAT A GIRL?!
GLOM

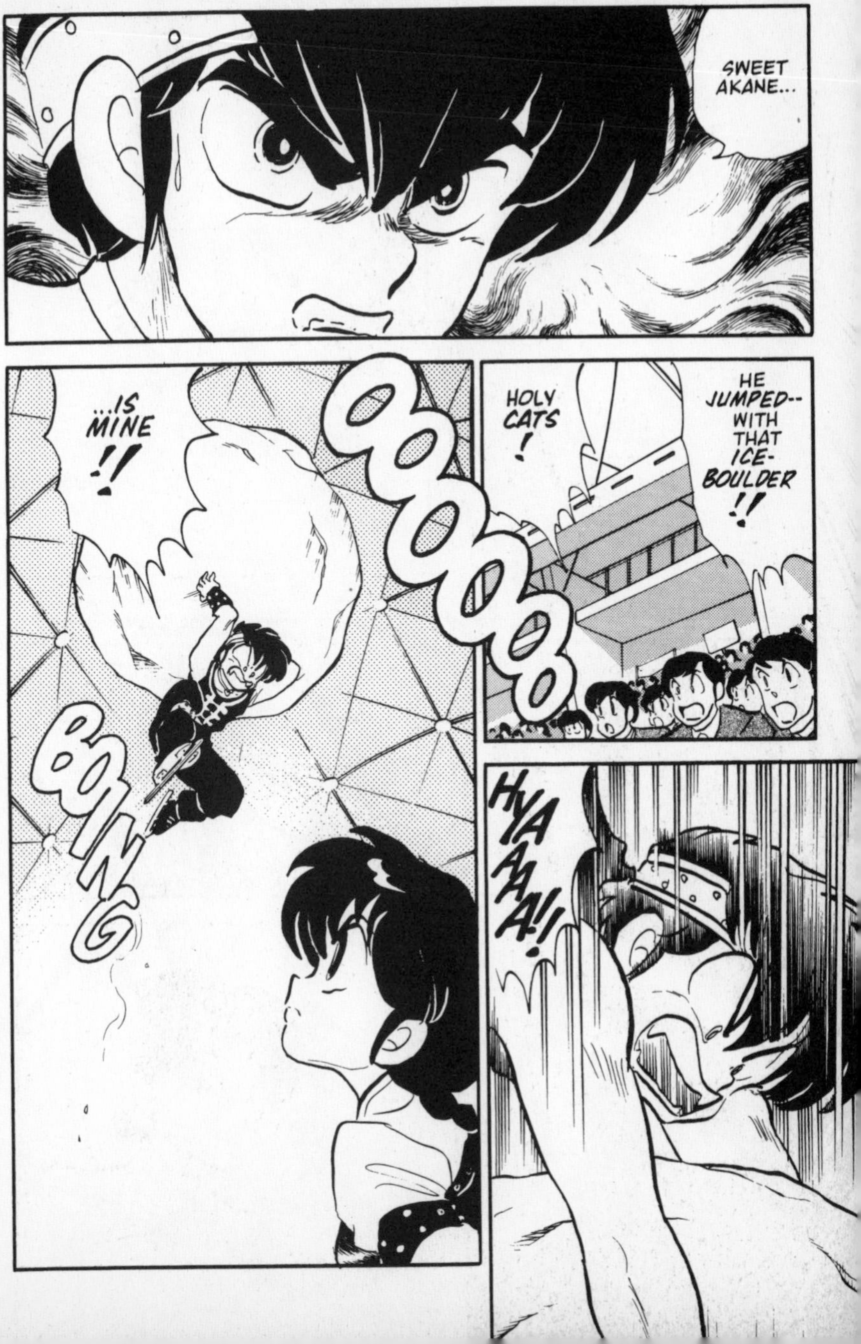
SWEET AKANE...
...IS MINE !!
OOOOOO
BOING
HOLY CATS!
HE JUMPED--WITH THAT ICE-BOULDER!!
HYAAAA!!

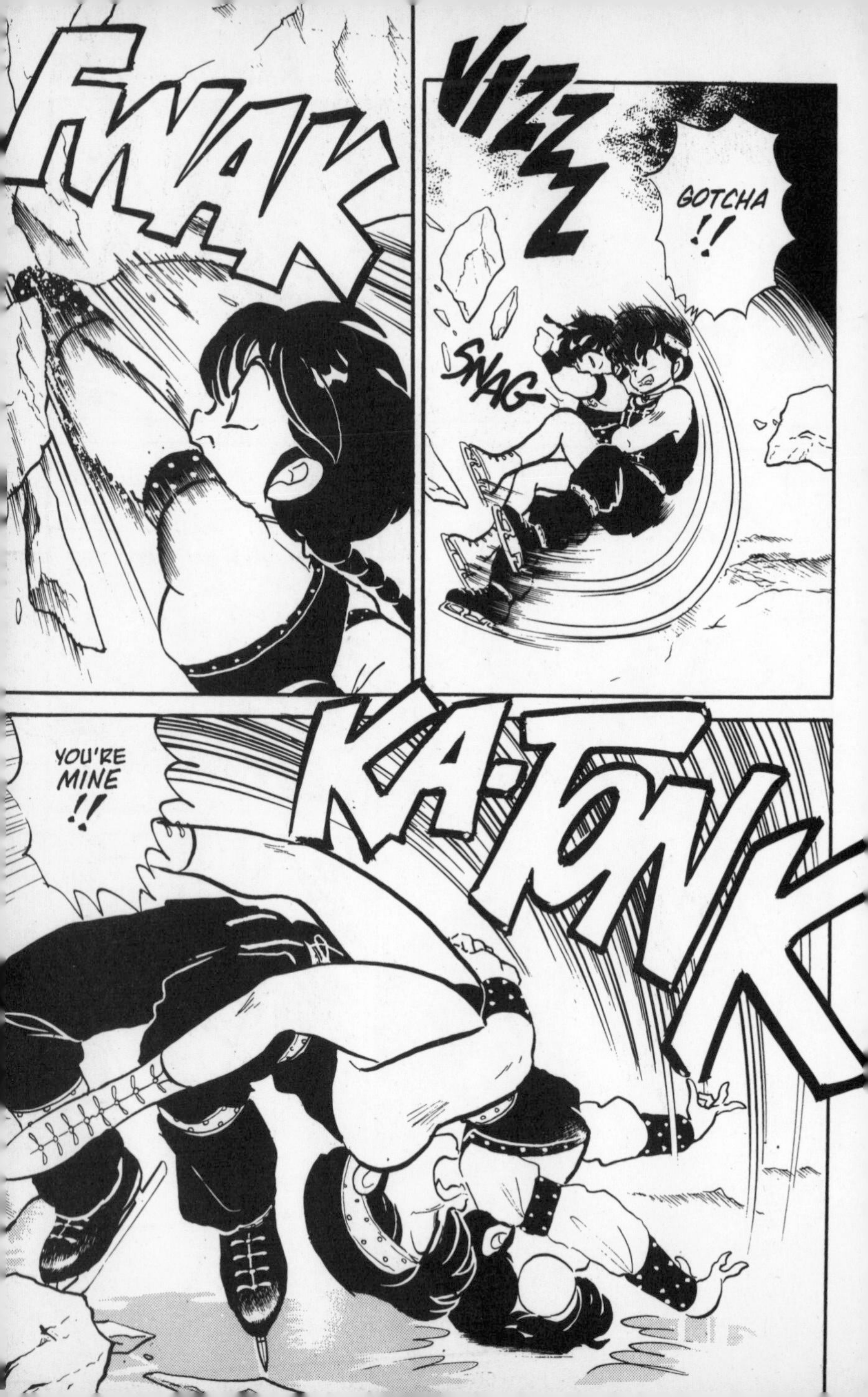

FWAK
VIZZZ
GOTCHA !!
SNAG
YOU'RE MINE !!
KA-TONK

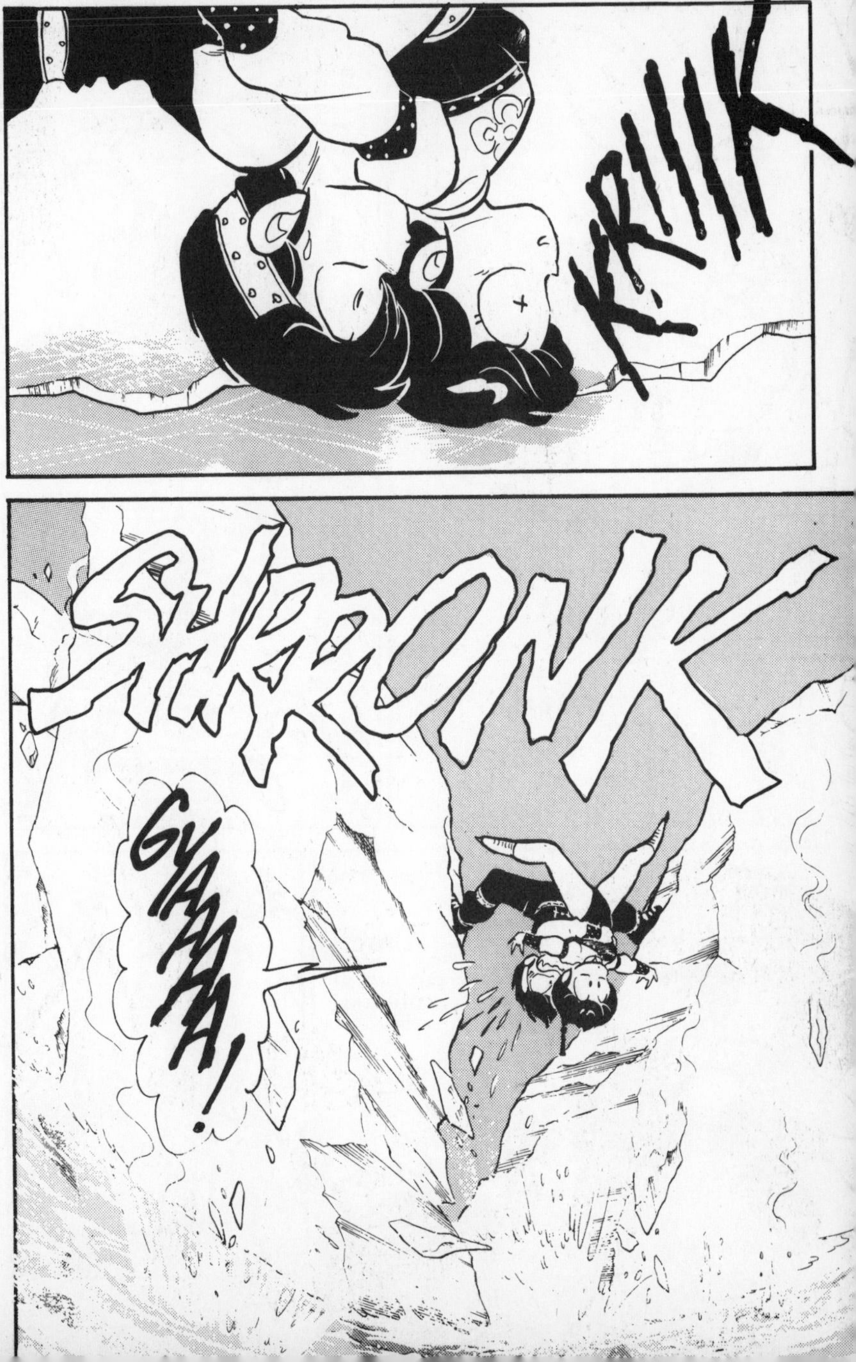
KRIIIK
SHRONK
GYAAAA!

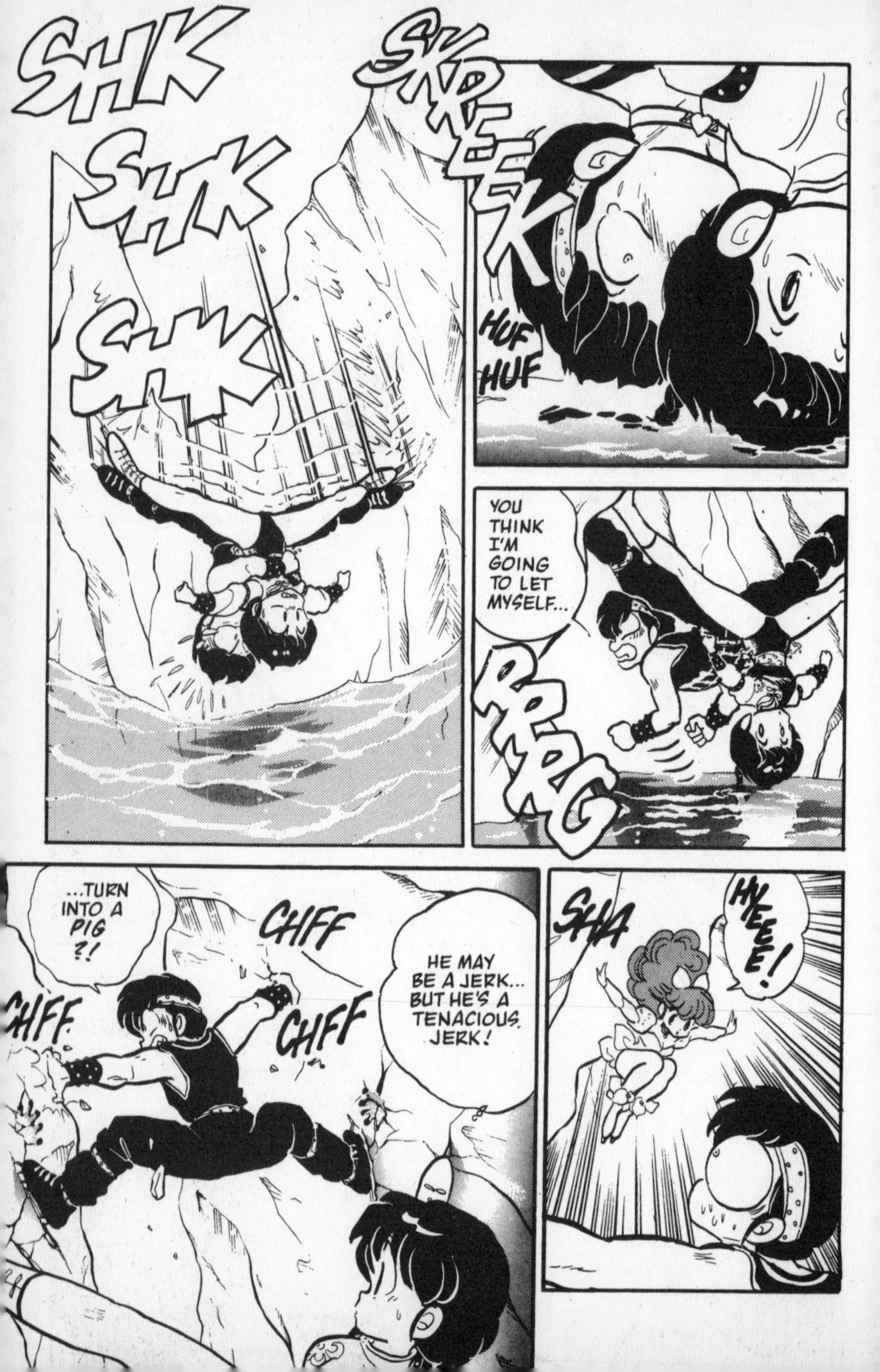
SHK
SHK
SHK
SKREEEK
HUF HUF
YOU THINK I'M GOING TO LET MYSELF...
RRRAG
...TURN INTO A PIG ?!
CHFF
CHFF
CHFF
HE MAY BE A JERK... BUT HE'S A TENACIOUS JERK!
SHA
HYEEEE!

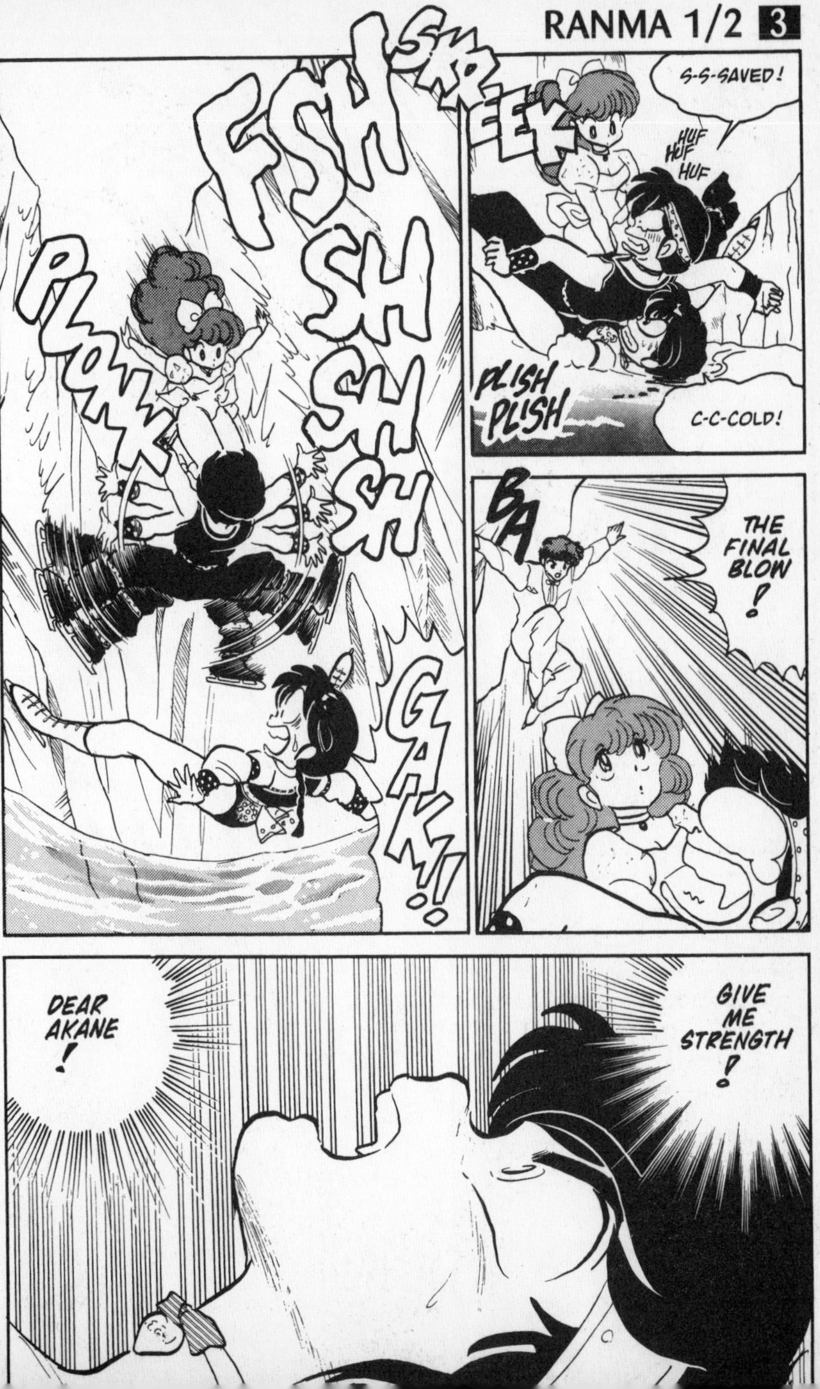
FSH
SKREEK
PLONK
SH SH SH SH
GAK!!
S-S-SAVED!
HUF HUF HUF
PLISH PLISH
C-C-COLD!
BA
THE FINAL BLOW!
DEAR AKANE!
GIVE ME STRENGTH!

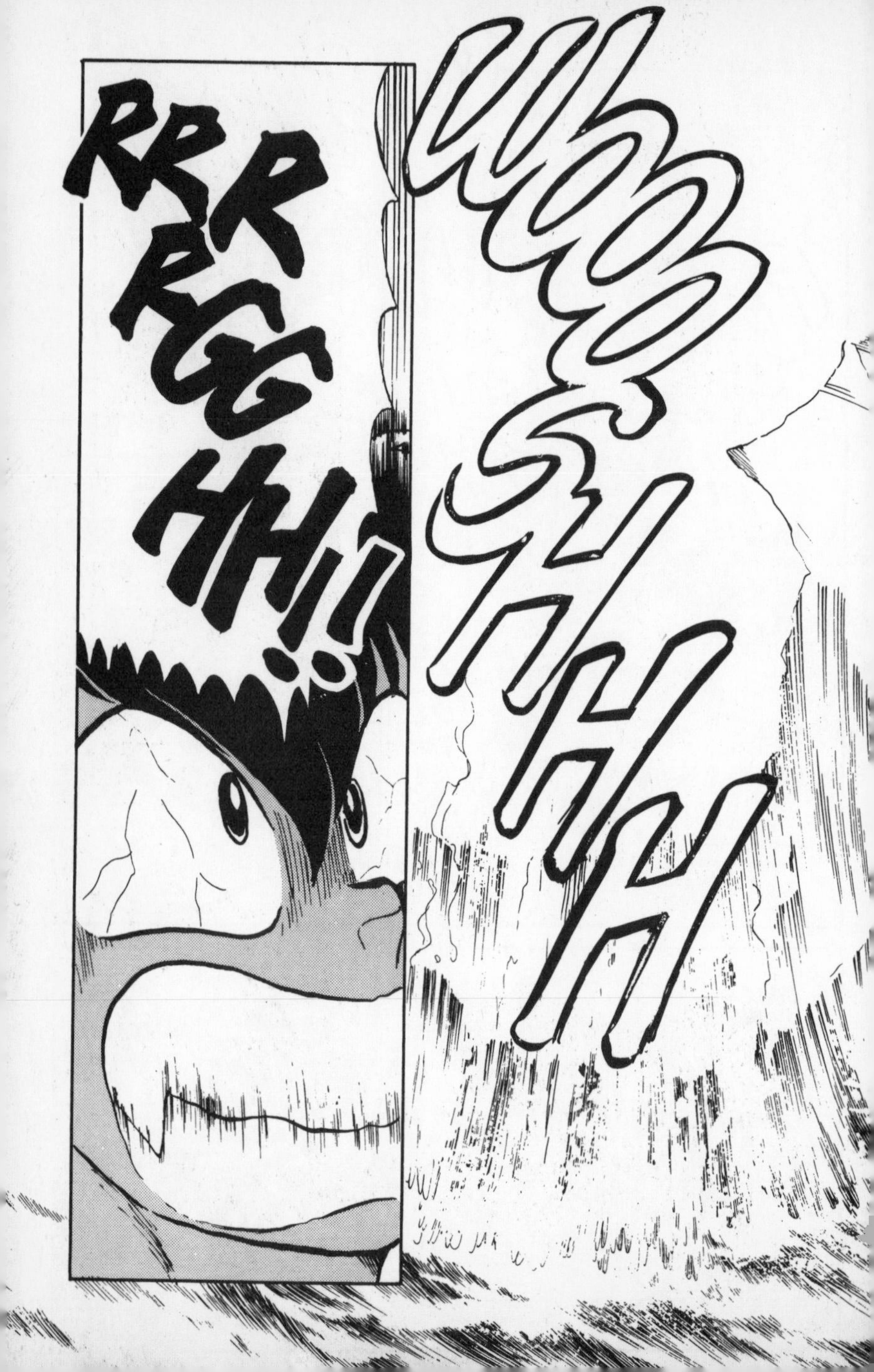
RRRRGGHH!!
WHOOOSHHHH

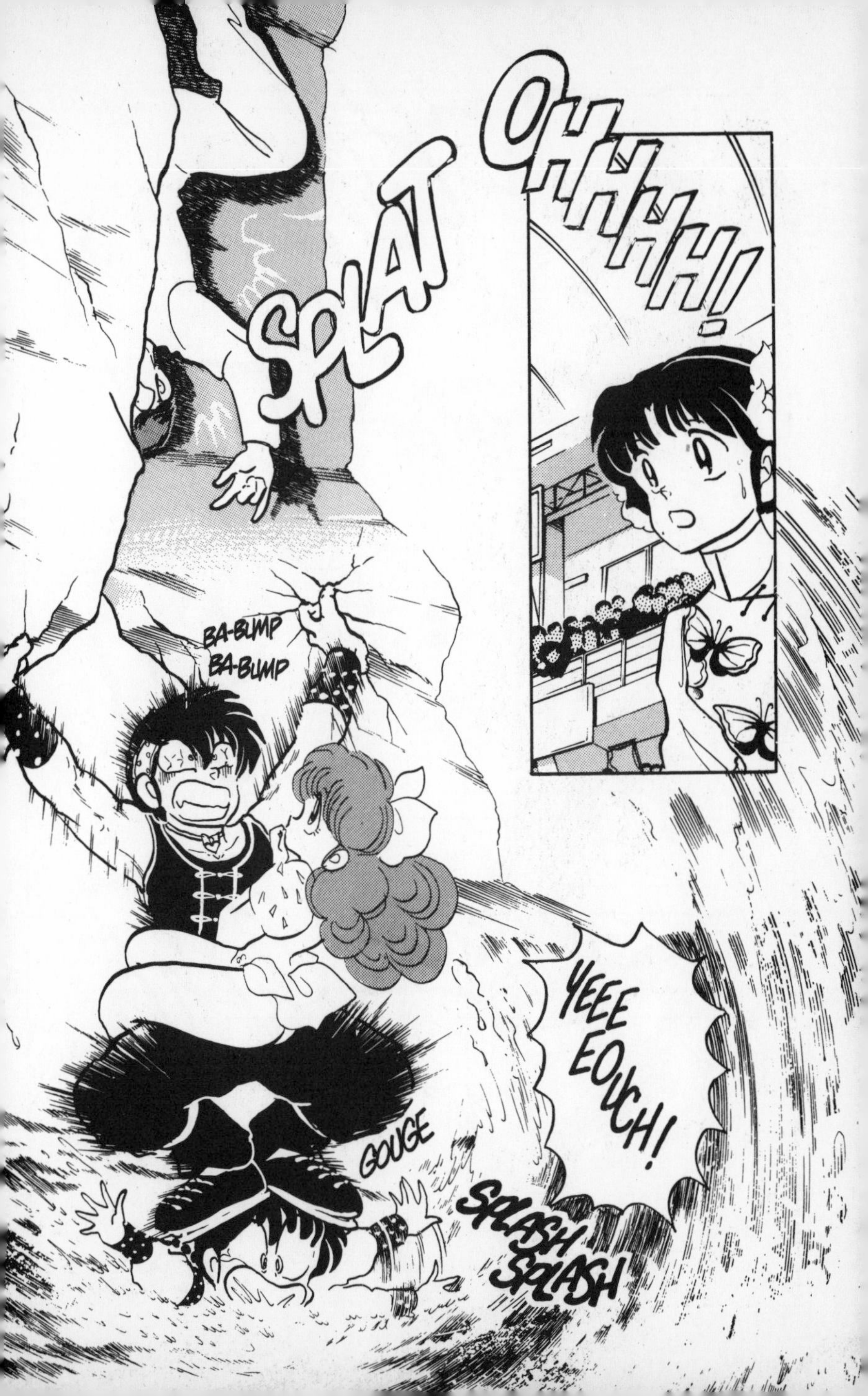
SPLAT
OHHHHH!
BA-BUMP
BA-BUMP
YEEE EOUCH!
GOUGE
SPLASH
SPLASH

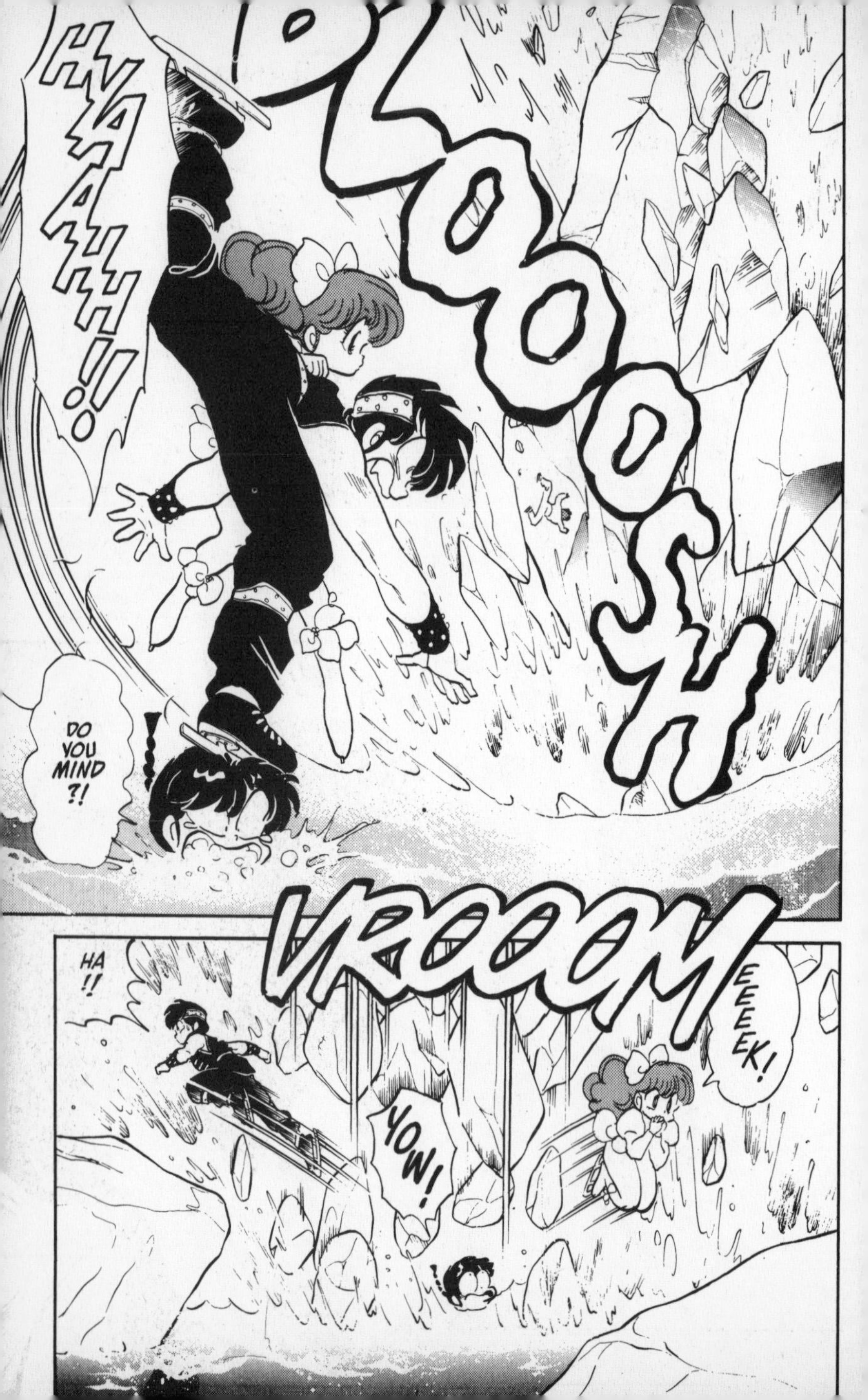
HYAAAAH!!!
PLOOOOOSH
DO YOU MIND ?!
VROOOM
HA !!
EEEEK!
YOW!

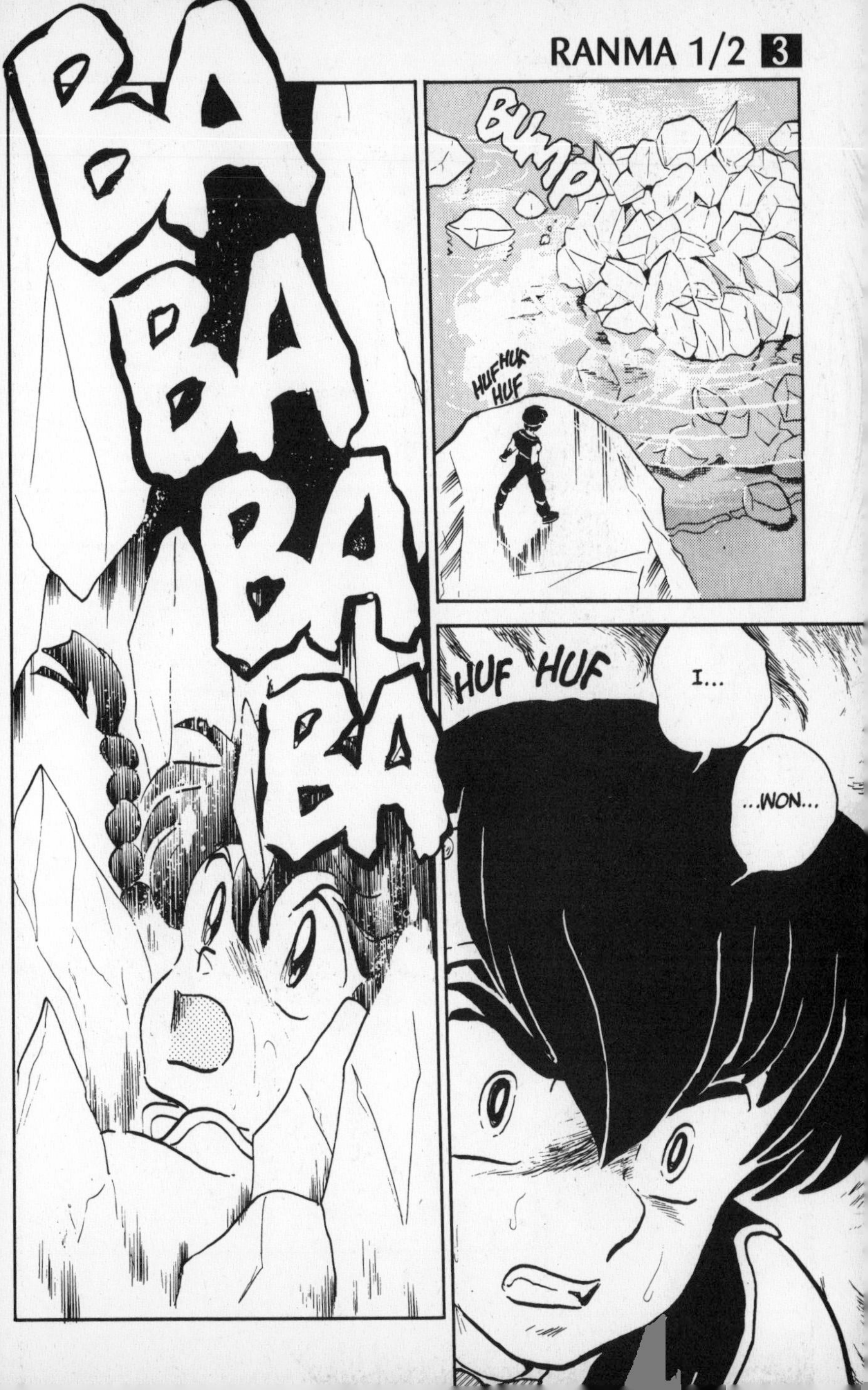
BA
BA
BA
BA
BUMP
HUF HUF
HUF
HUF HUF
I...
...WON...

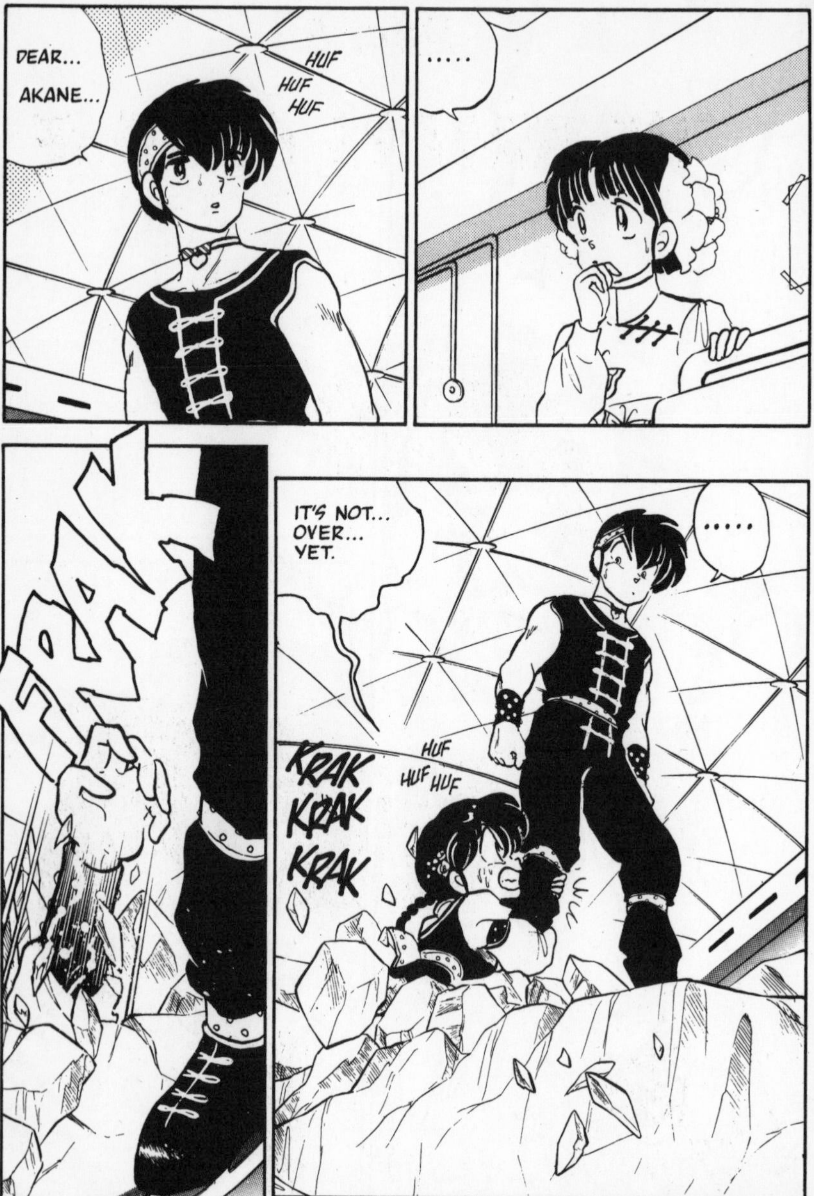
DEAR...
AKANE...
HUF
HUF
HUF
.....
IT'S NOT... OVER... YET.
.....
KRAK
KRAK
KRAK
HUF
HUF HUF

Part 5

THE WATERS OF LOVE

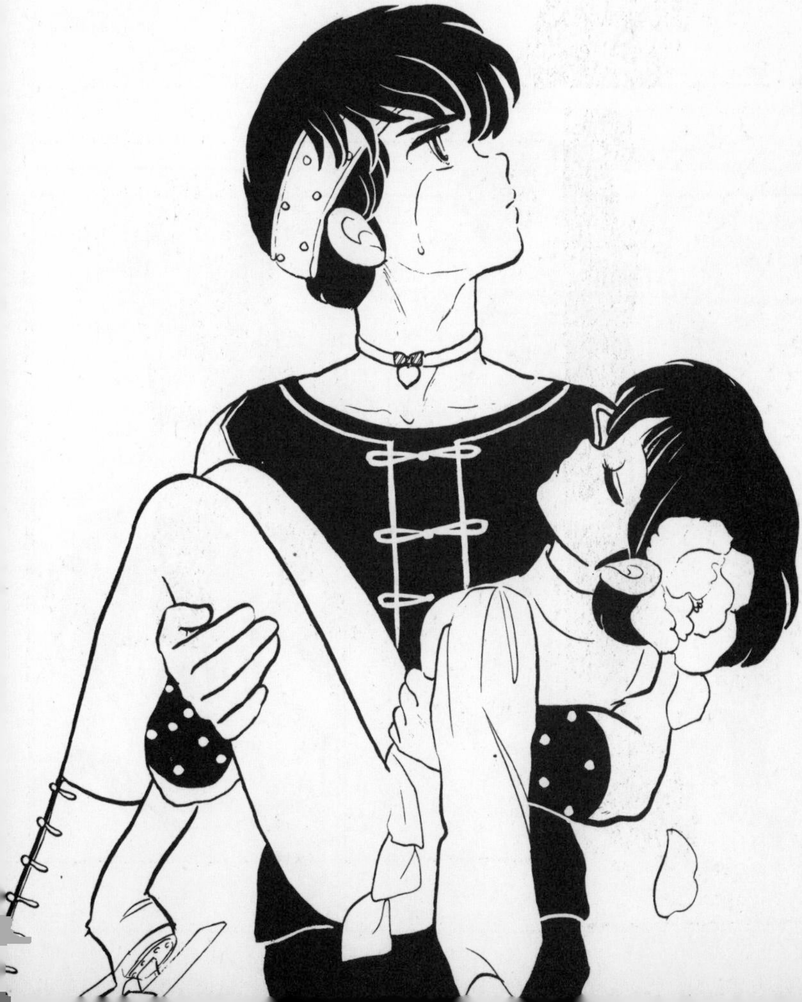

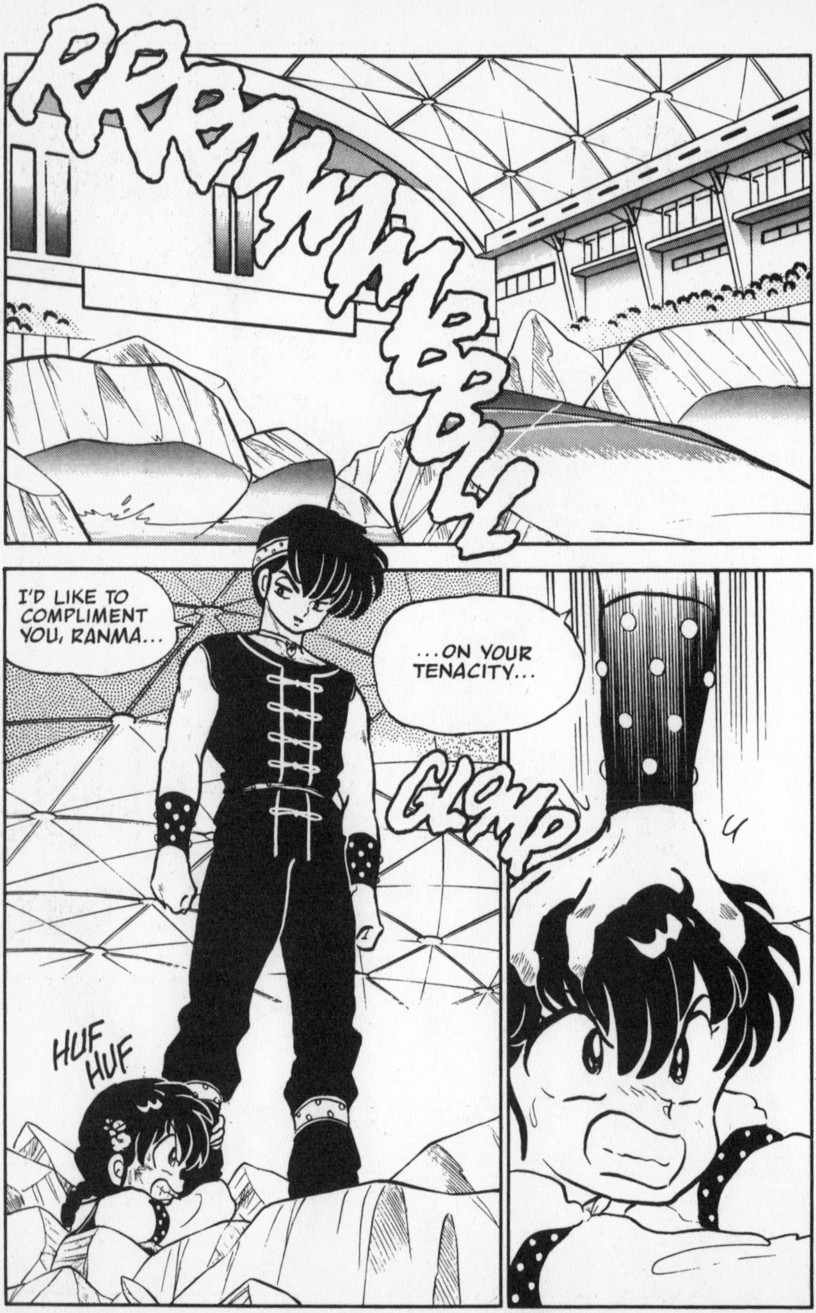
RRRAMMBBLL
I'D LIKE TO COMPLIMENT YOU, RANMA...
...ON YOUR TENACITY...
HUF HUF
GLOMP

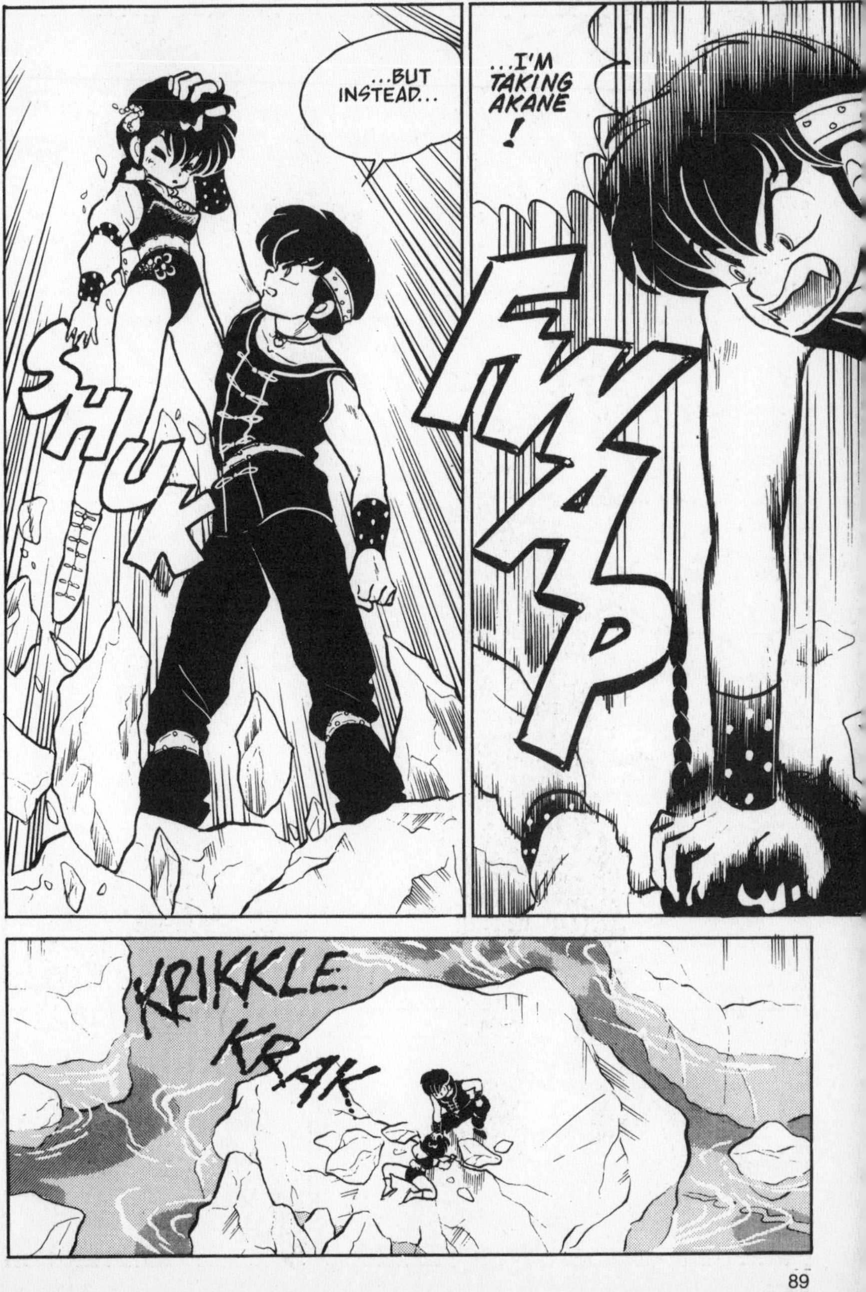
...BUT INSTEAD...
SHUK
...I'M TAKING AKANE!
FWAP
KRIKKLE
KRAK

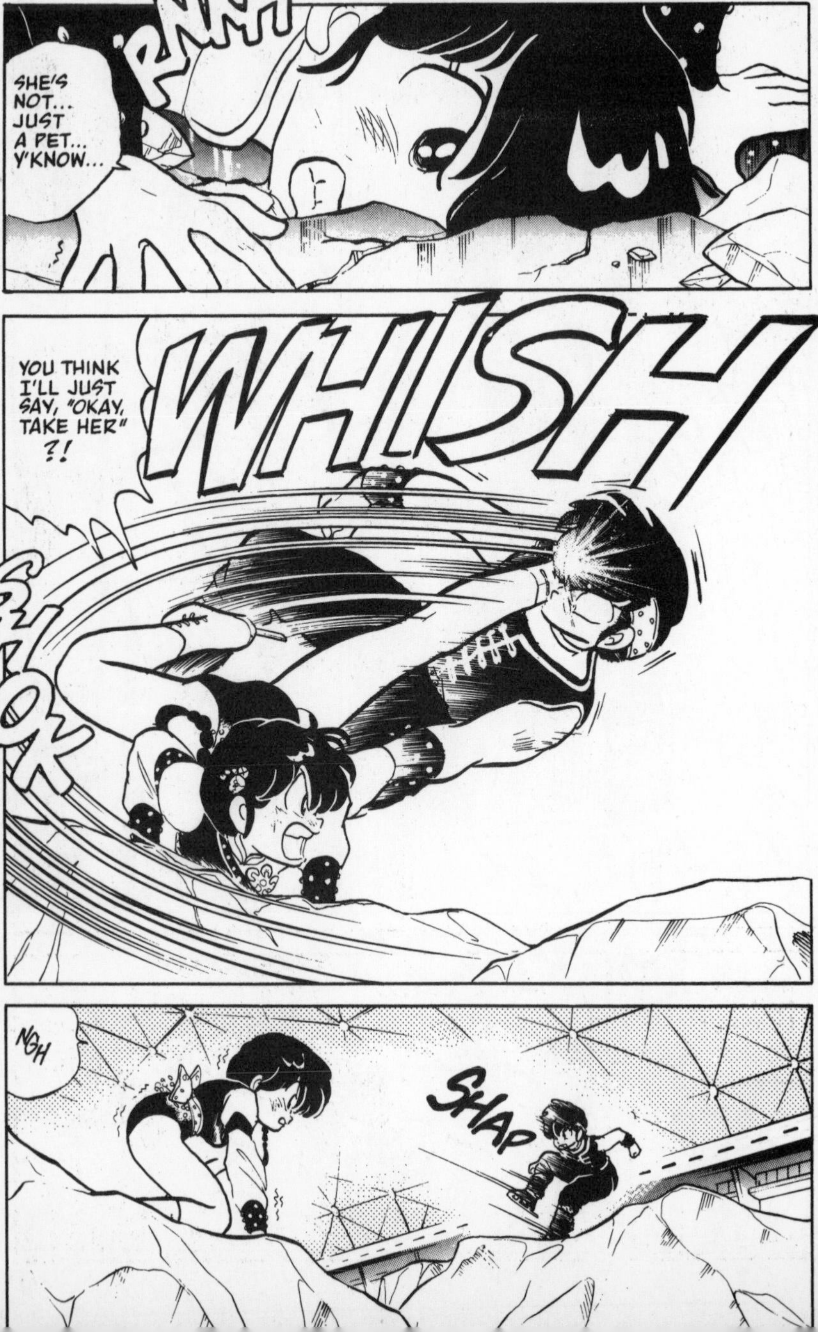
RNKH
SHE'S NOT... JUST A PET... Y'KNOW...
YOU THINK I'LL JUST SAY, "OKAY, TAKE HER" ?!
WHISH
SHOK
NGH
SHAP

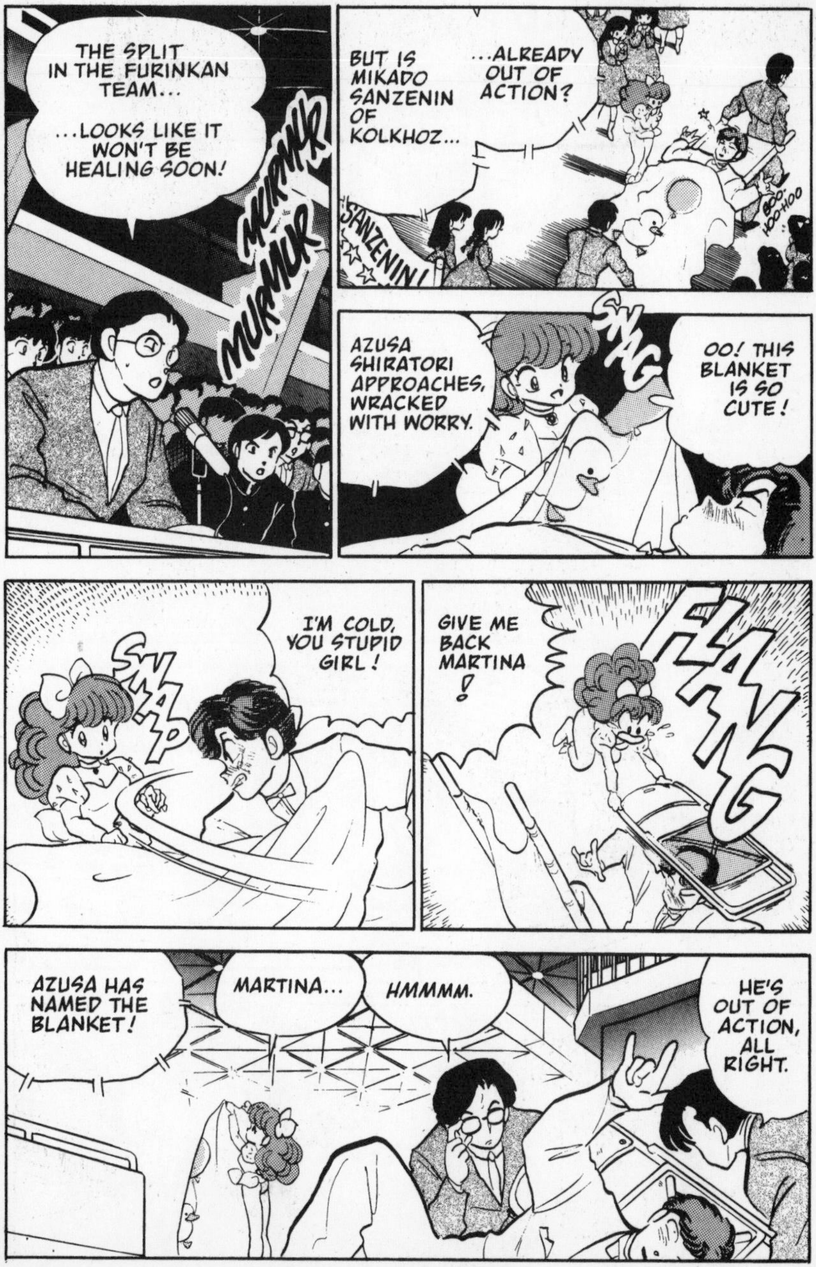
THE SPLIT IN THE FURINKAN TEAM...
...LOOKS LIKE IT WON'T BE HEALING SOON!
MURMUR MURMUR
BUT IS MIKADO SANZENIN OF KOLKHOZ...
...ALREADY OUT OF ACTION?
SANZENIN!
BOO-HOO-HOO
AZUSA SHIRATORI APPROACHES, WRACKED WITH WORRY.
SNAG
OO! THIS BLANKET IS SO CUTE!
SNAP
I'M COLD, YOU STUPID GIRL!
GIVE ME BACK MARTINA!
FLANG
AZUSA HAS NAMED THE BLANKET!
MARTINA...
HMMMM.
HE'S OUT OF ACTION, ALL RIGHT.

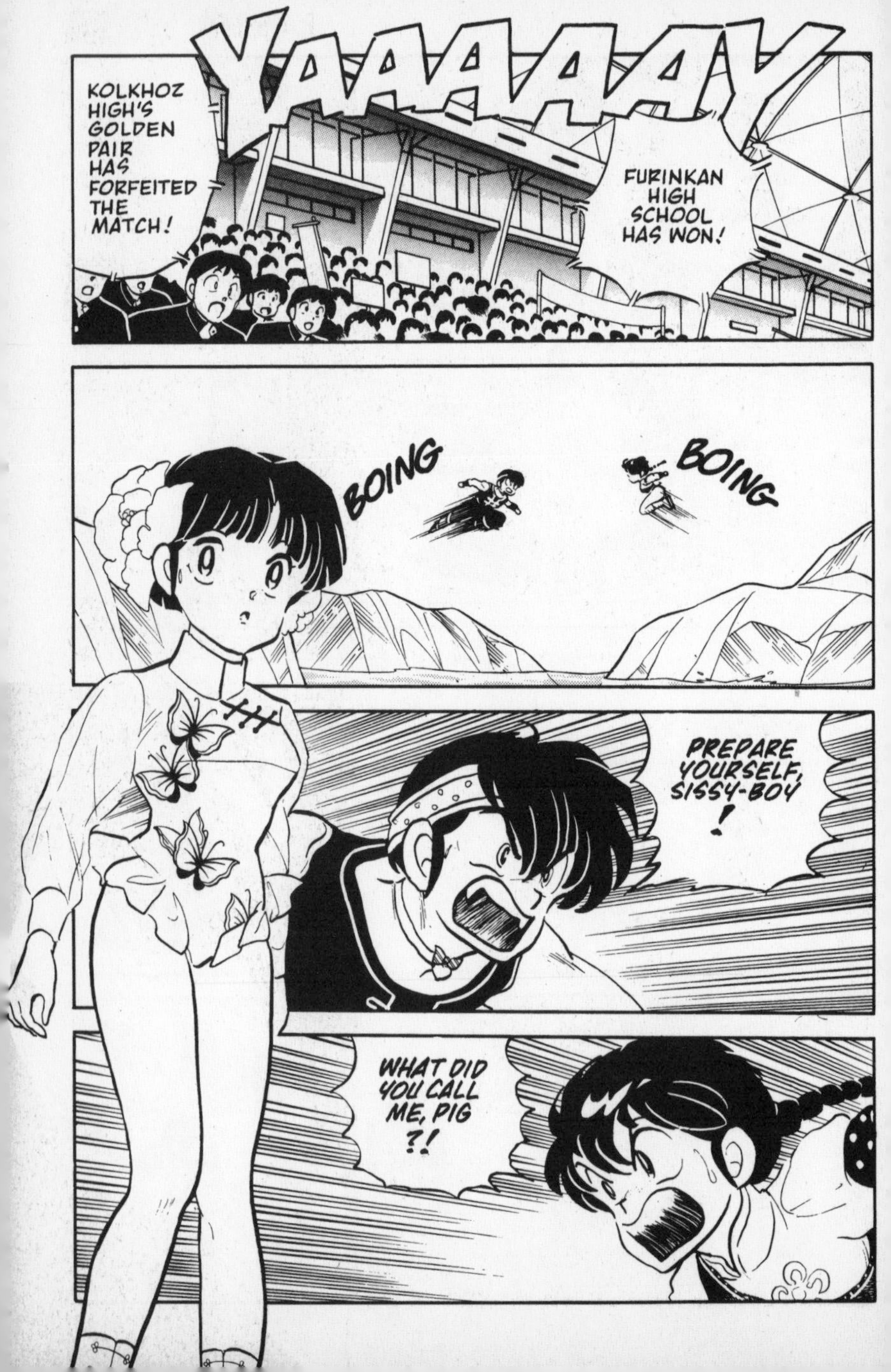
YAAAAAY
KOLKHOZ HIGH'S GOLDEN PAIR HAS FORFEITED THE MATCH!
FURINKAN HIGH SCHOOL HAS WON!
BOING
BOING
PREPARE YOURSELF, SISSY-BOY!
WHAT DID YOU CALL ME, PIG?!

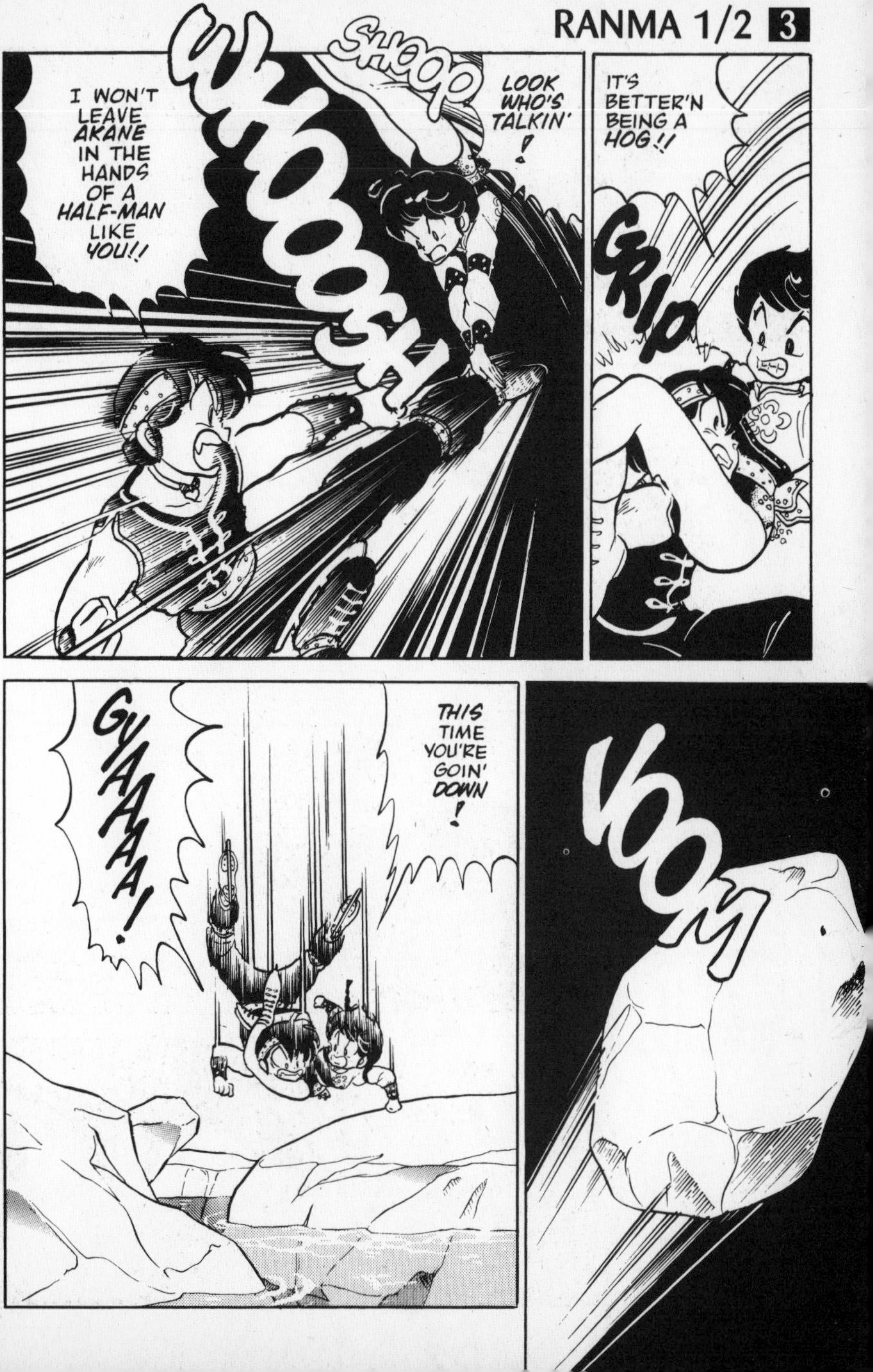
SHOOP
WHOOOSH
I WON'T LEAVE AKANE IN THE HANDS OF A HALF-MAN LIKE YOU!!
LOOK WHO'S TALKIN'!
IT'S BETTER'N BEING A HOG!!
GRIP
GYAAAAAA!
THIS TIME YOU'RE GOIN' DOWN!
VOOM

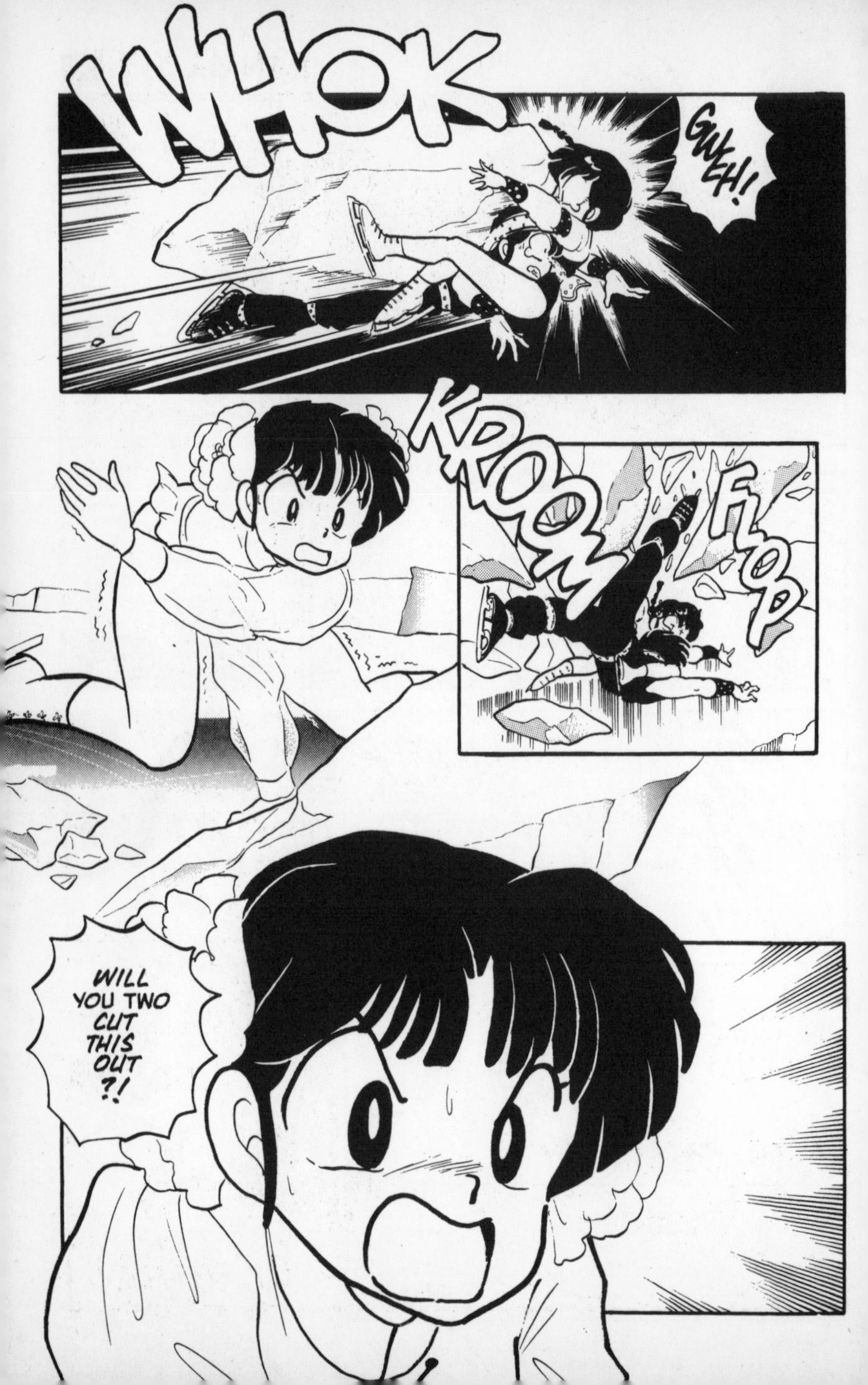
WHOK
GULCH!
KROOM
FLOP
WILL YOU TWO CUT THIS OUT ?!

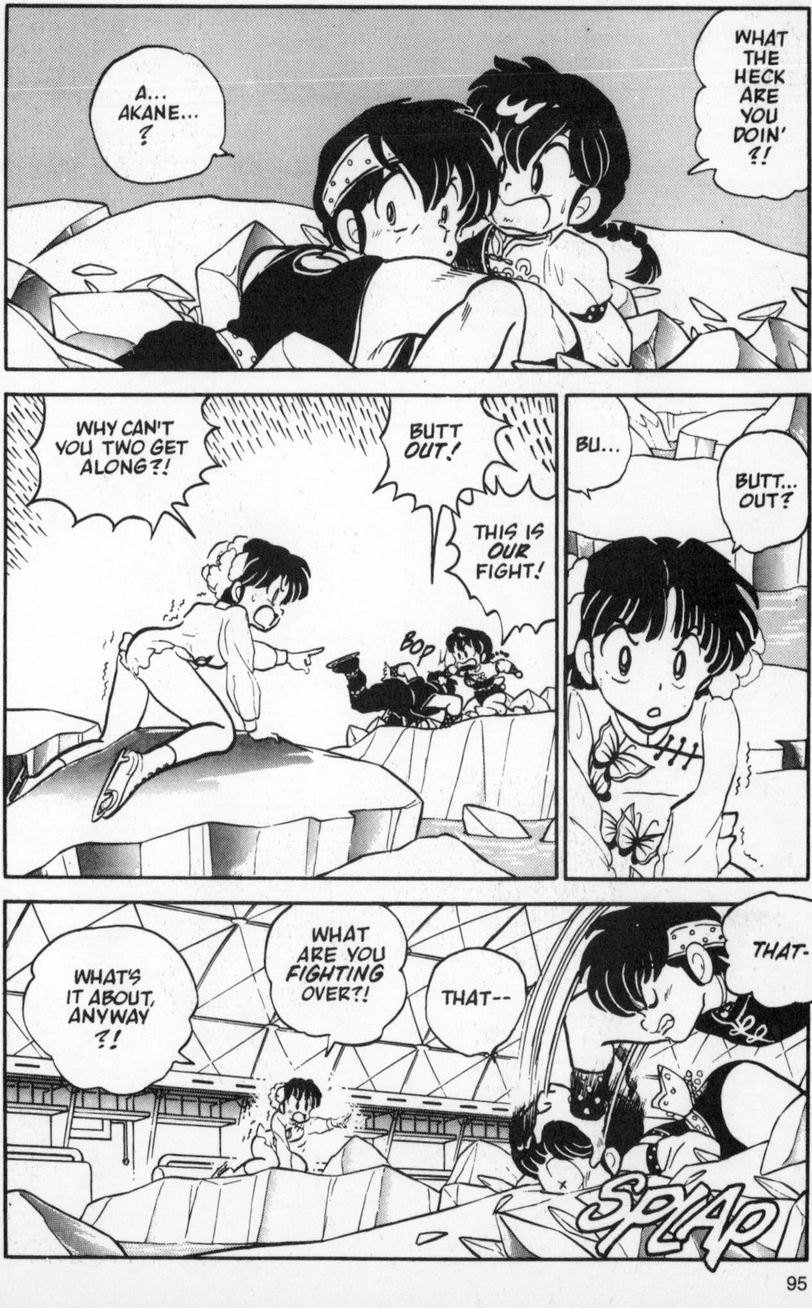
A... AKANE... ?
WHAT THE HECK ARE YOU DOIN' ?!
WHY CAN'T YOU TWO GET ALONG?!
BUTT OUT!
THIS IS OUR FIGHT!
BOP
BU...
BUTT... OUT?
WHAT'S IT ABOUT, ANYWAY ?!
WHAT ARE YOU FIGHTING OVER?!
THAT--
THAT--
SPLAP

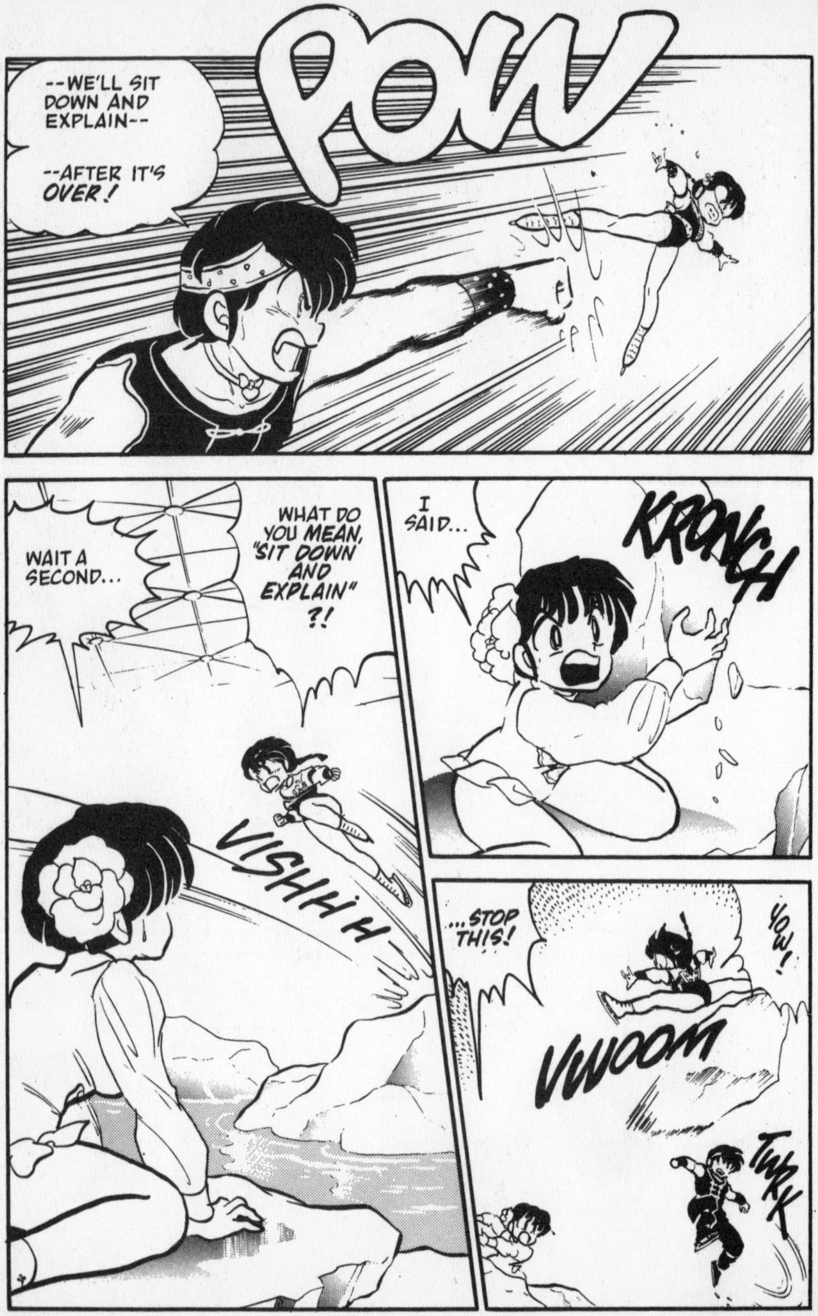
POW
--WE'LL SIT DOWN AND EXPLAIN--
--AFTER IT'S OVER!
WAIT A SECOND...
WHAT DO YOU MEAN, "SIT DOWN AND EXPLAIN" ?!
VISHHHH
I SAID...
KRONCH
...STOP THIS!
YOW!
VWOOM
THUNK

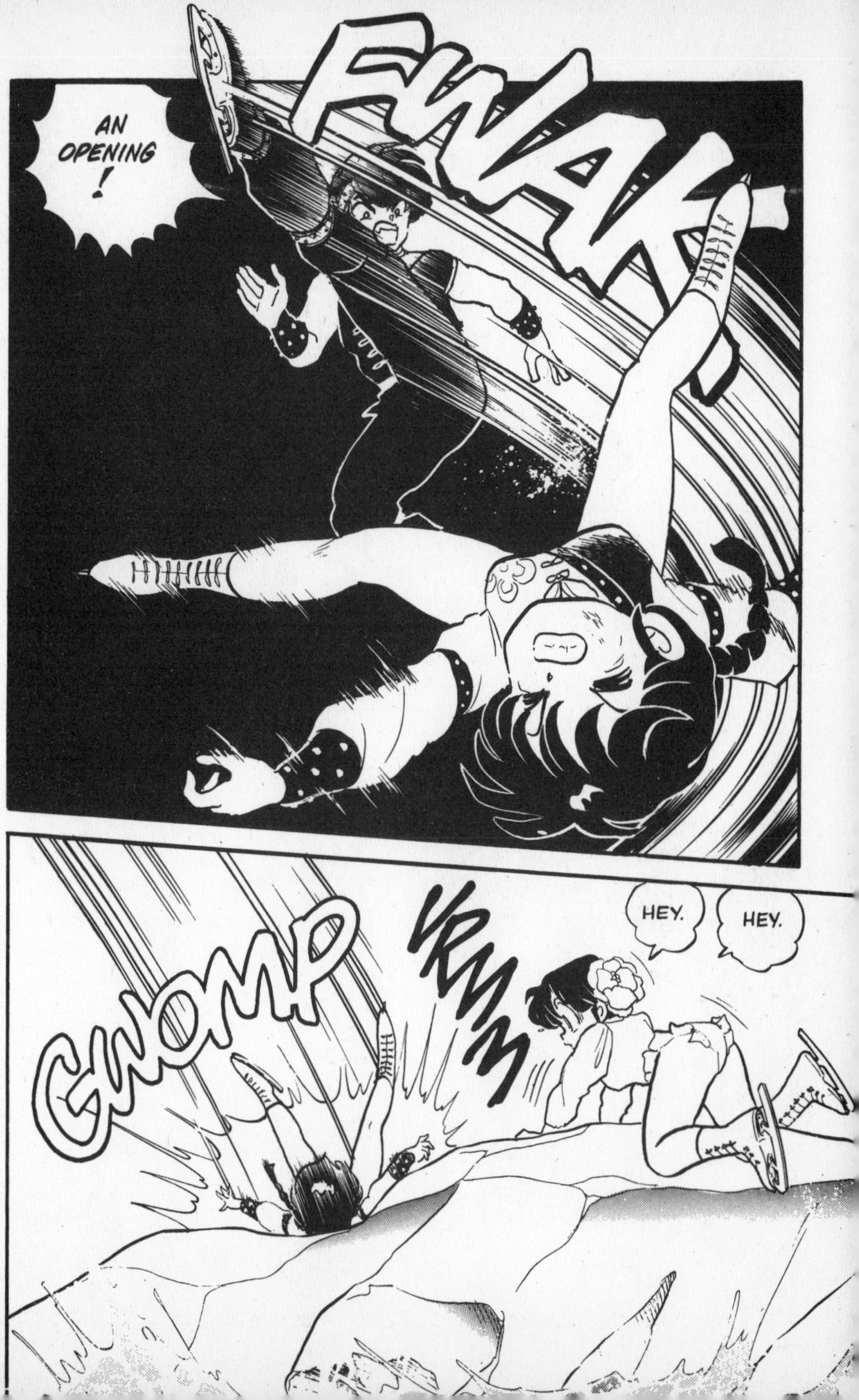
FWAK
AN OPENING!
HEY.
HEY.
VRMMM
GWOMP

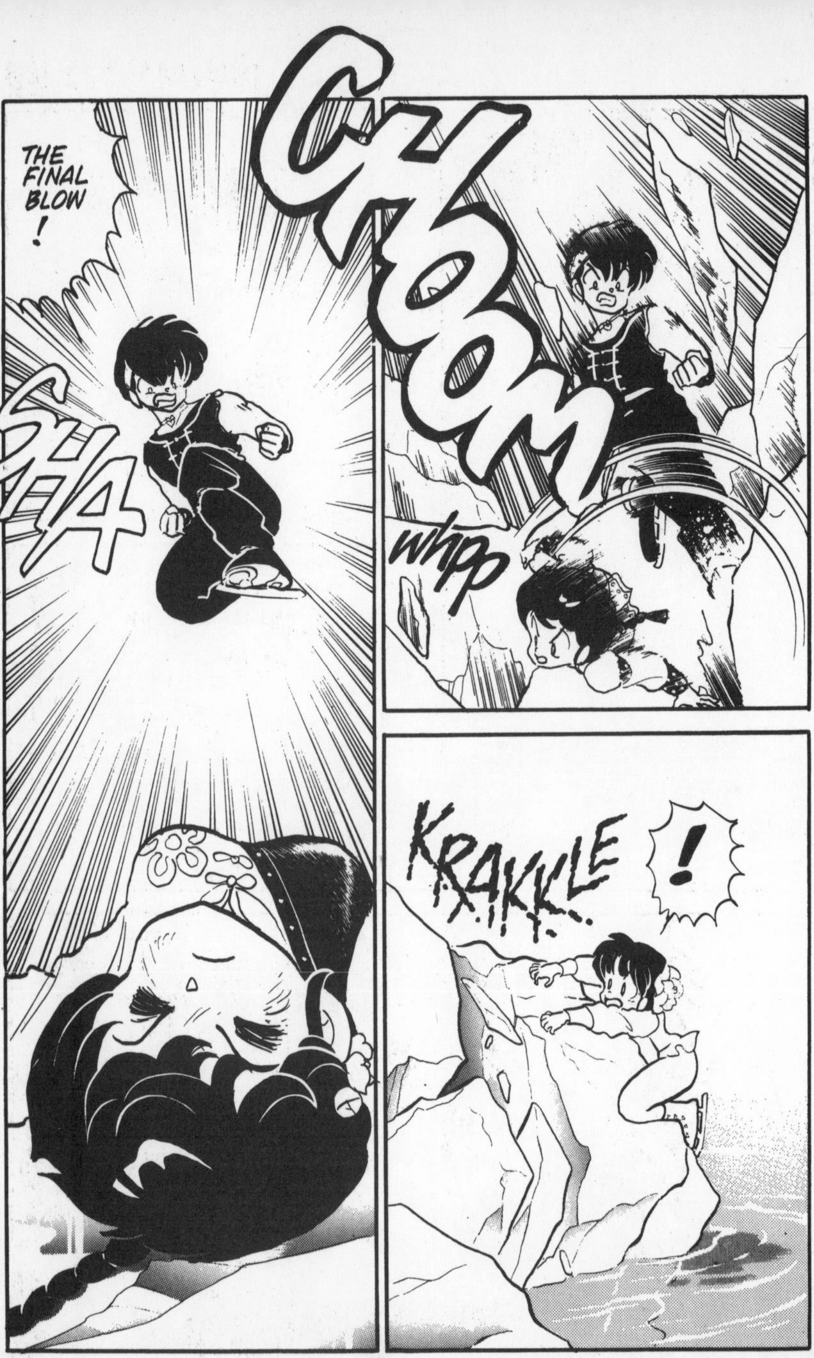
CRUNCH
THE FINAL BLOW!
CHOOM
SHA
whpp
KRAKKLE
!

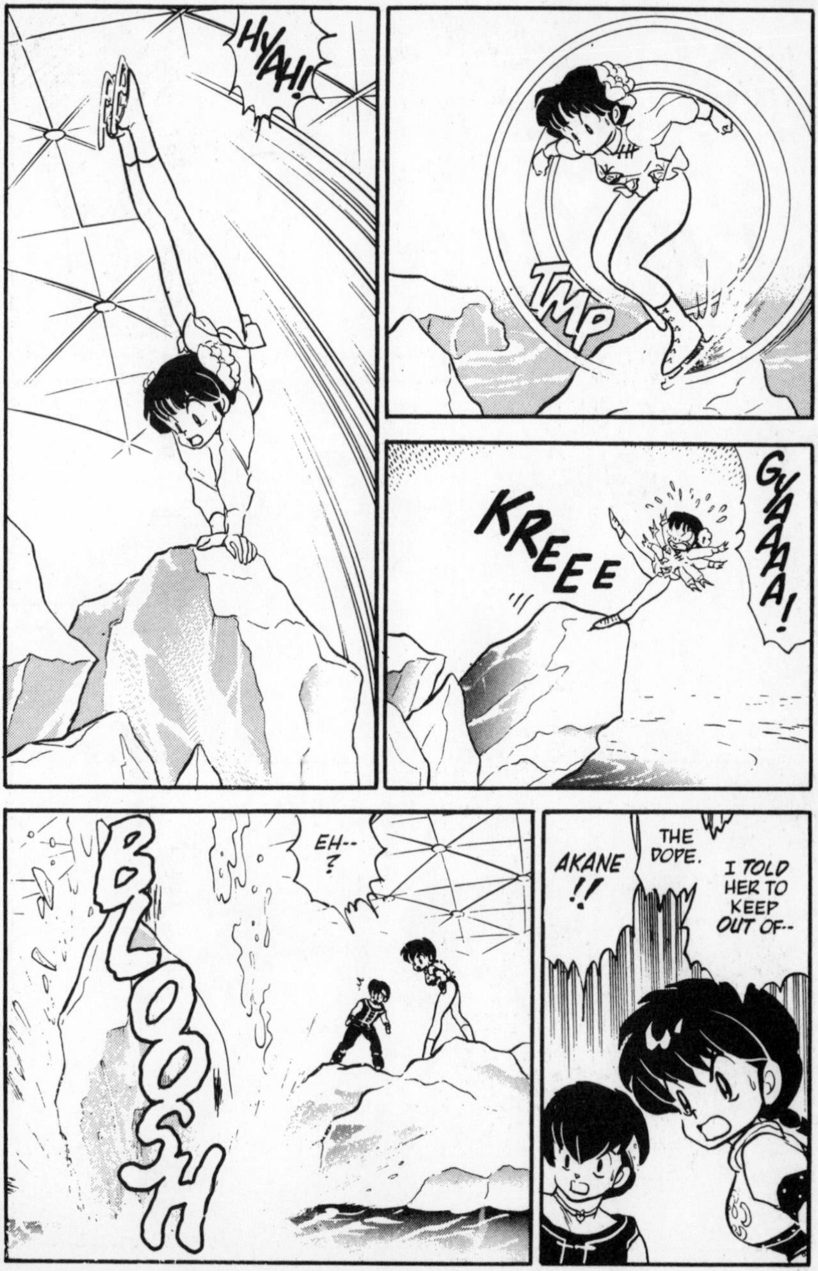
HYAAH!
TMP
KREEEE
GYAAAA!
BLOOOSH
EH--?
AKANE!!
THE DOPE.
I TOLD HER TO KEEP OUT OF--

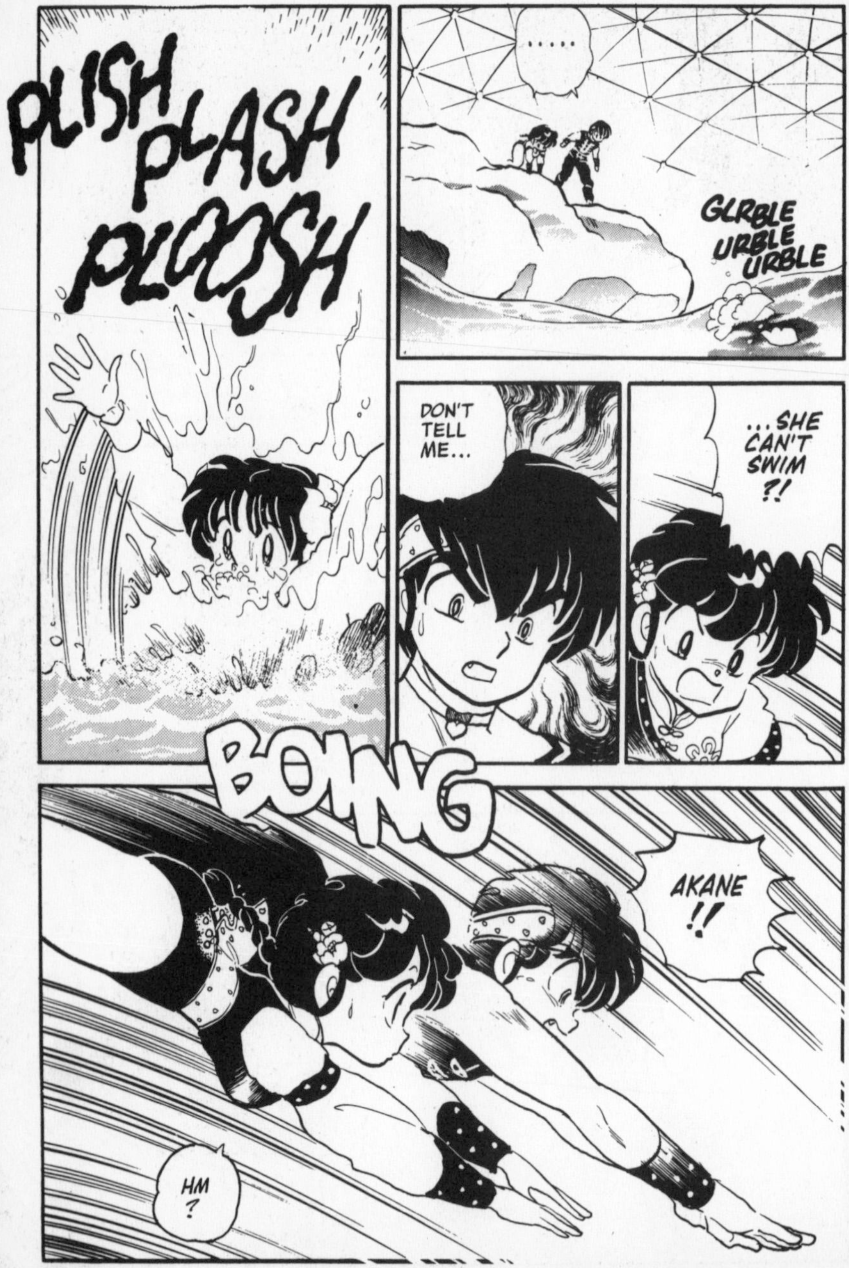
PLISH PLASH PLOOSH
.....
GLRBLE URBLE URBLE
DON'T TELL ME...
...SHE CAN'T SWIM ?!
BOING
AKANE !!
HM ?

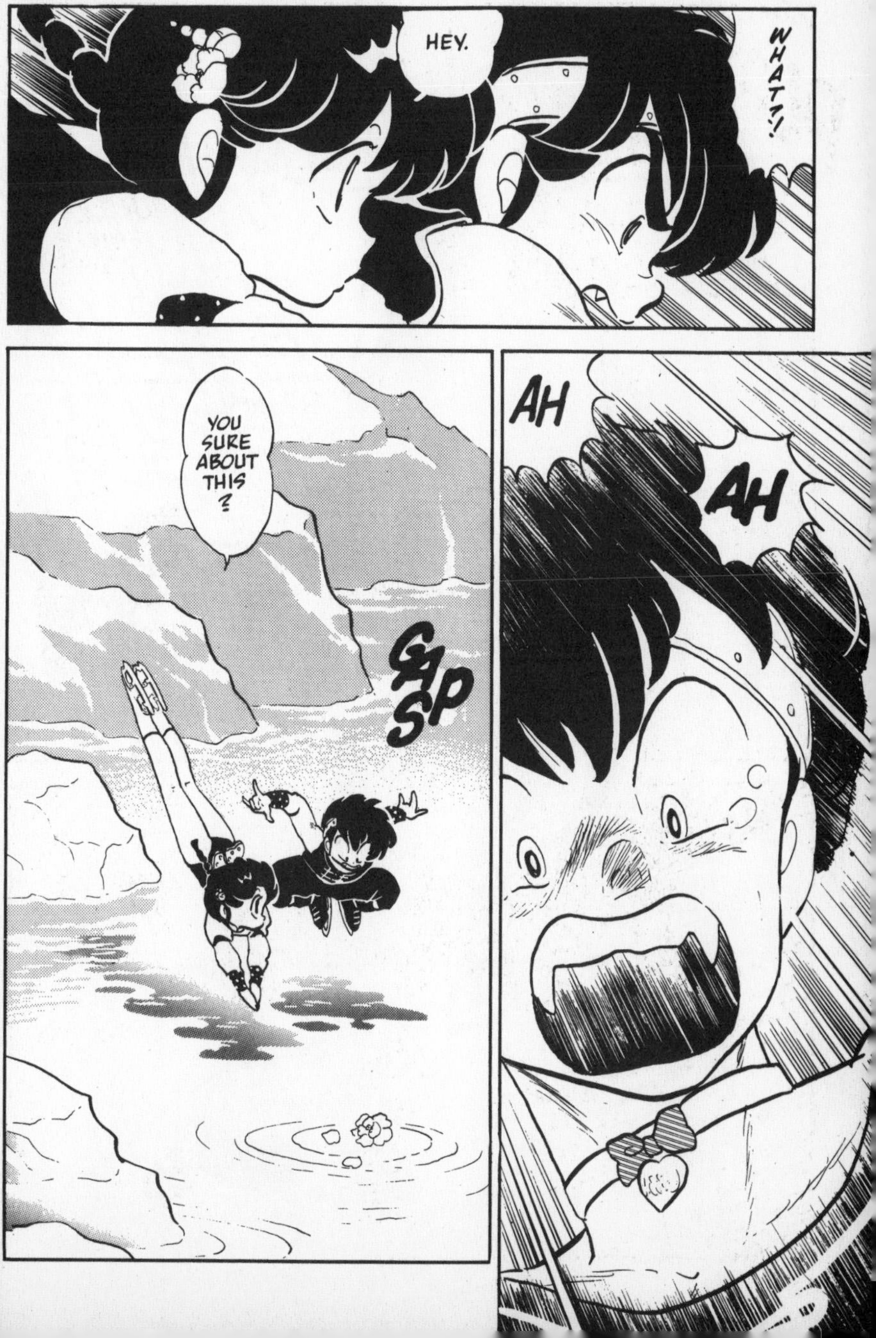
HEY.
WHAT?!
YOU SURE ABOUT THIS?
GASP
AH
AH

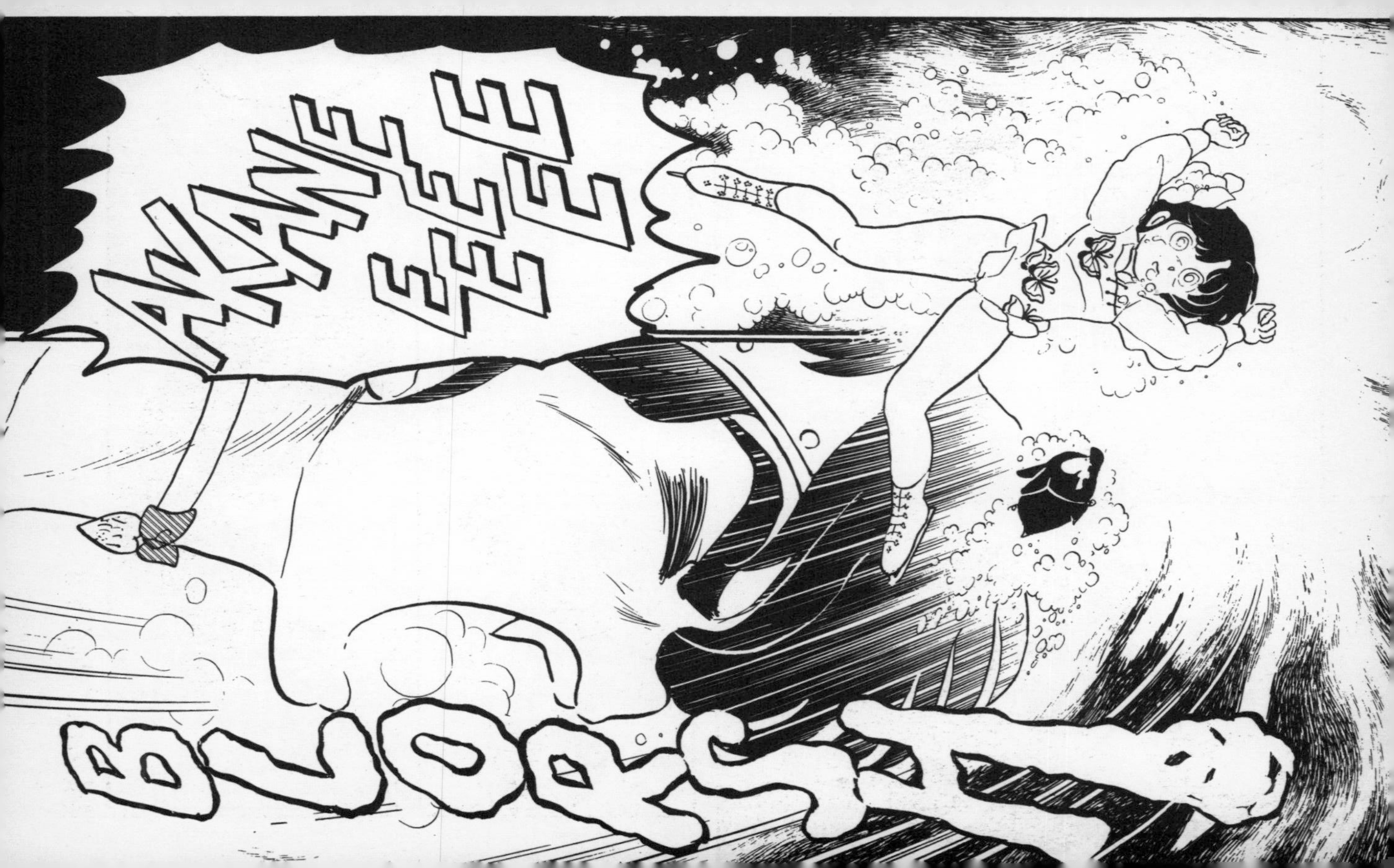
AKANEEEEEE
BLOPSH

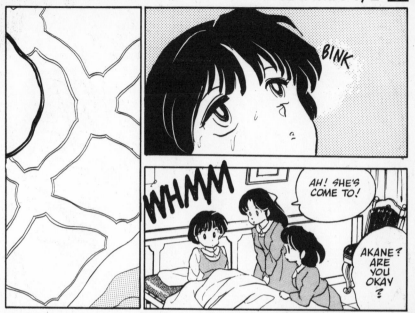

BINK

WHMM

AH! SHE'S COME TO!

AKANE? ARE YOU OKAY?

AHCHOO

.....

GULP.

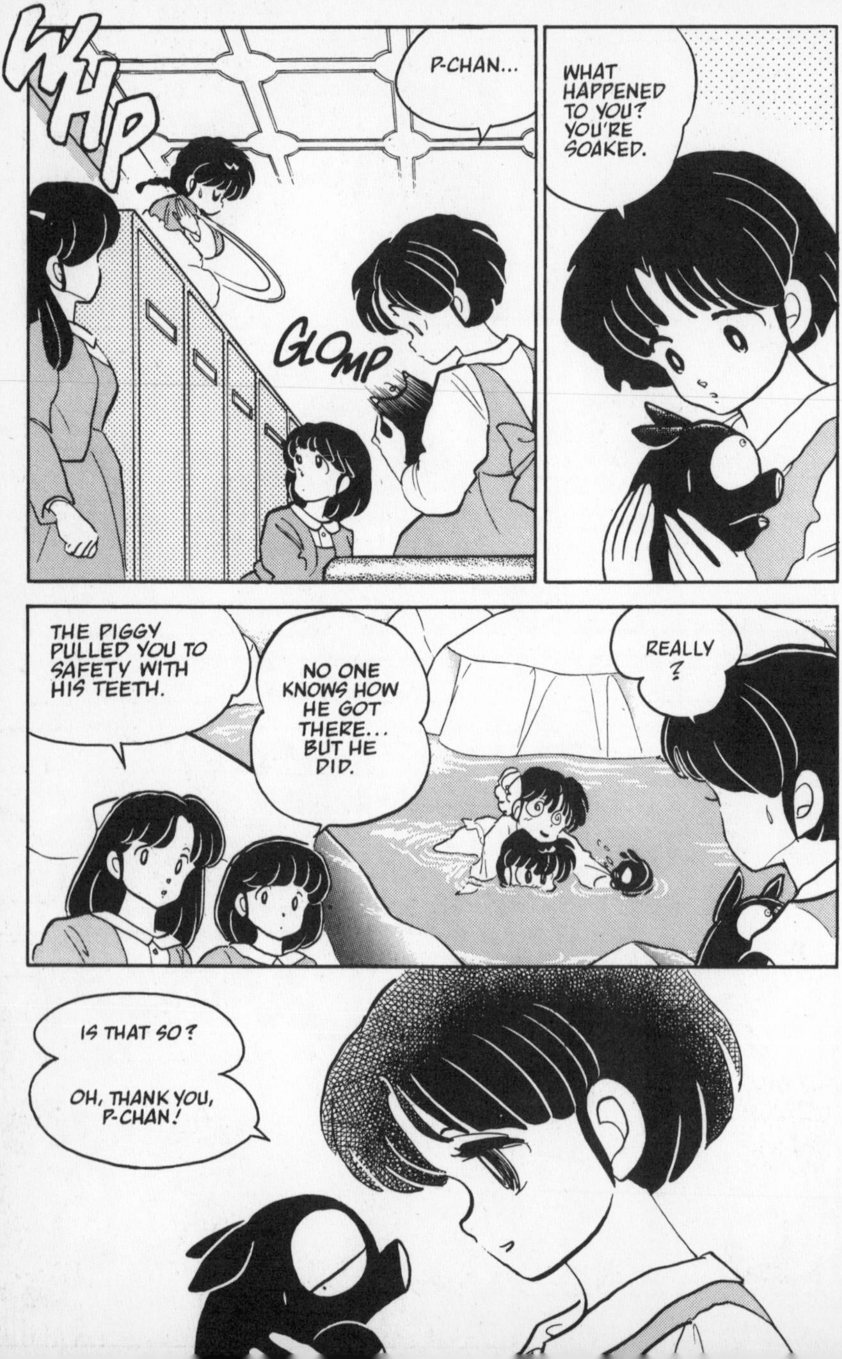
WHP
GLOMP
P-CHAN...
WHAT HAPPENED TO YOU? YOU'RE SOAKED.
THE PIGGY PULLED YOU TO SAFETY WITH HIS TEETH.
NO ONE KNOWS HOW HE GOT THERE... BUT HE DID.
REALLY?
IS THAT SO?
OH, THANK YOU, P-CHAN!

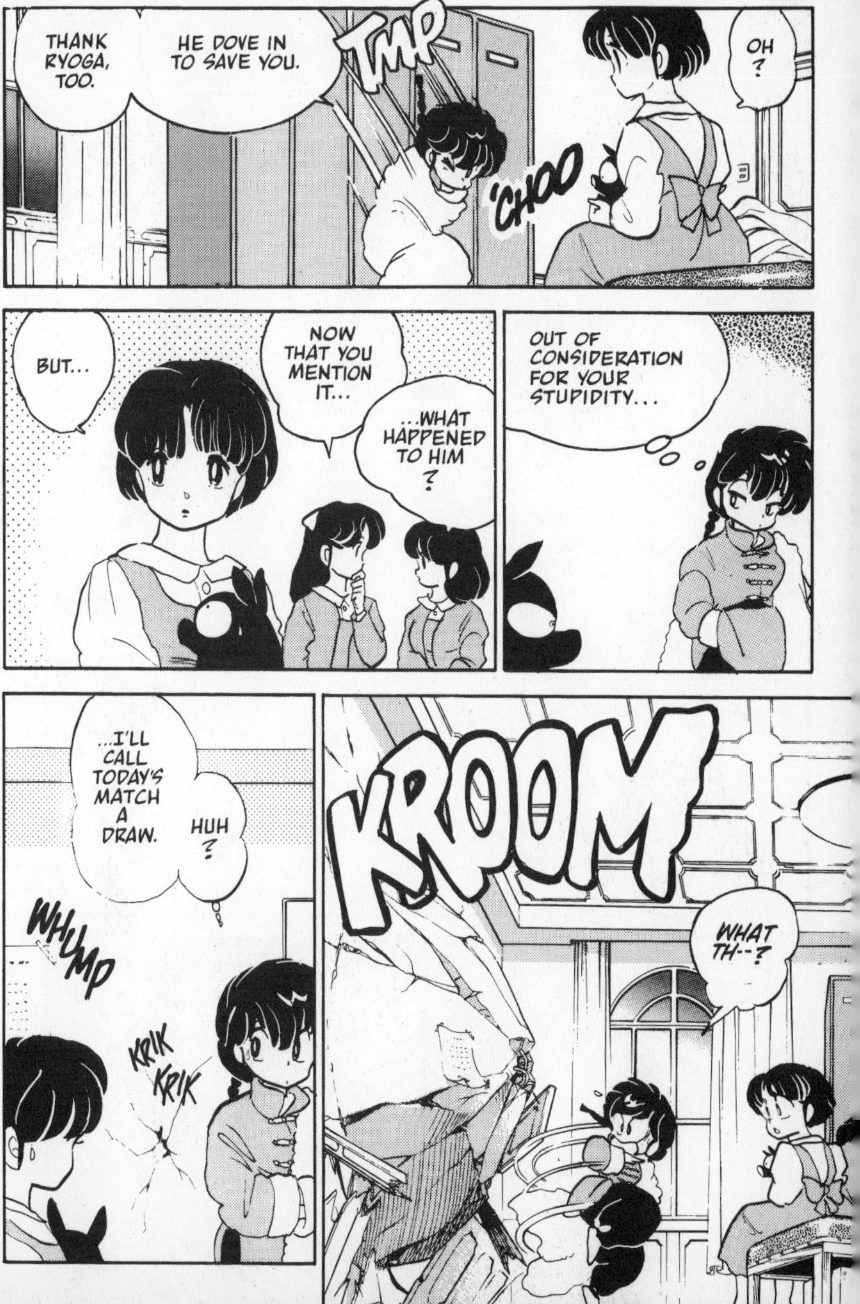
THANK RYOGA, TOO.
HE DOVE IN TO SAVE YOU.
TMP
OH?
'CHOO
BUT...
NOW THAT YOU MENTION IT...
...WHAT HAPPENED TO HIM?
OUT OF CONSIDERATION FOR YOUR STUPIDITY...
...I'LL CALL TODAY'S MATCH A DRAW.
HUH?
WHUMP
KRIK
KRIK
KROOM
WHAT TH--?

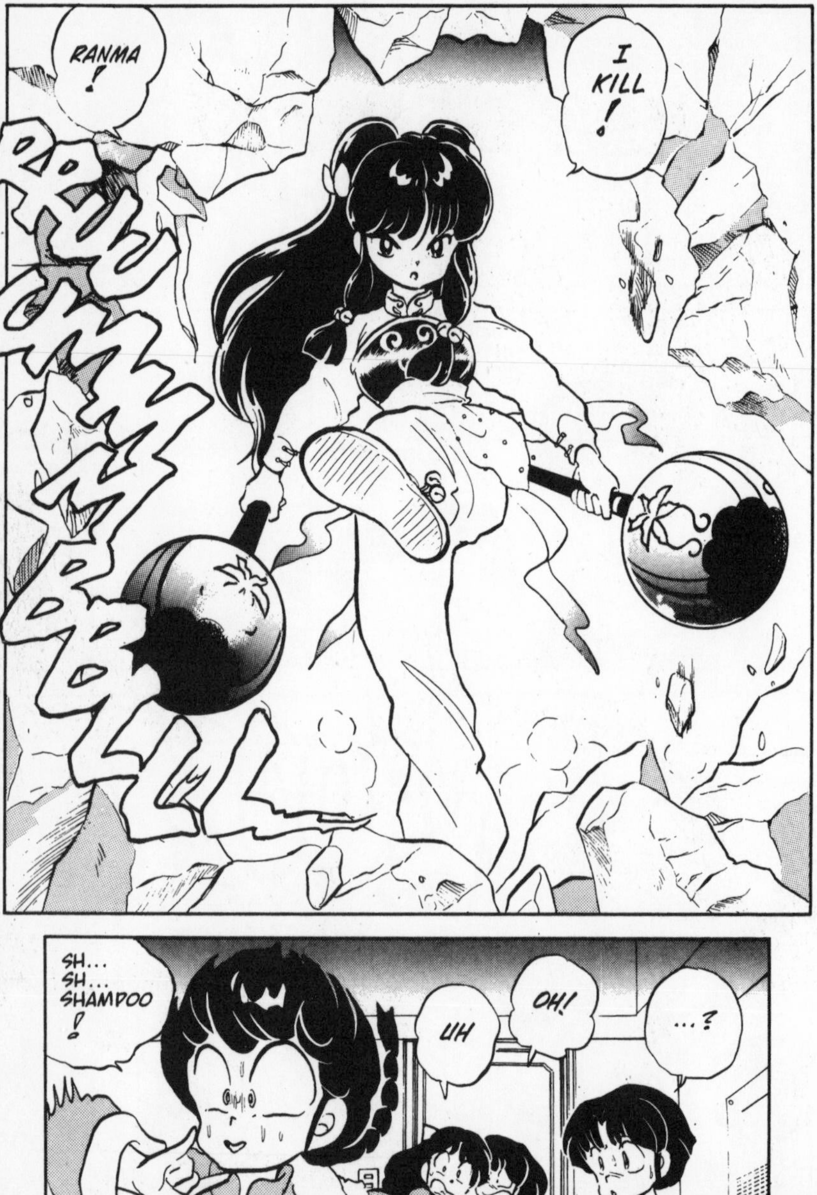
RANMA!
RUMMMBBLL
I KILL!
SH... SH... SHAMPOO!
UH
OH!
...?

Part 6

KISS OF DEATH

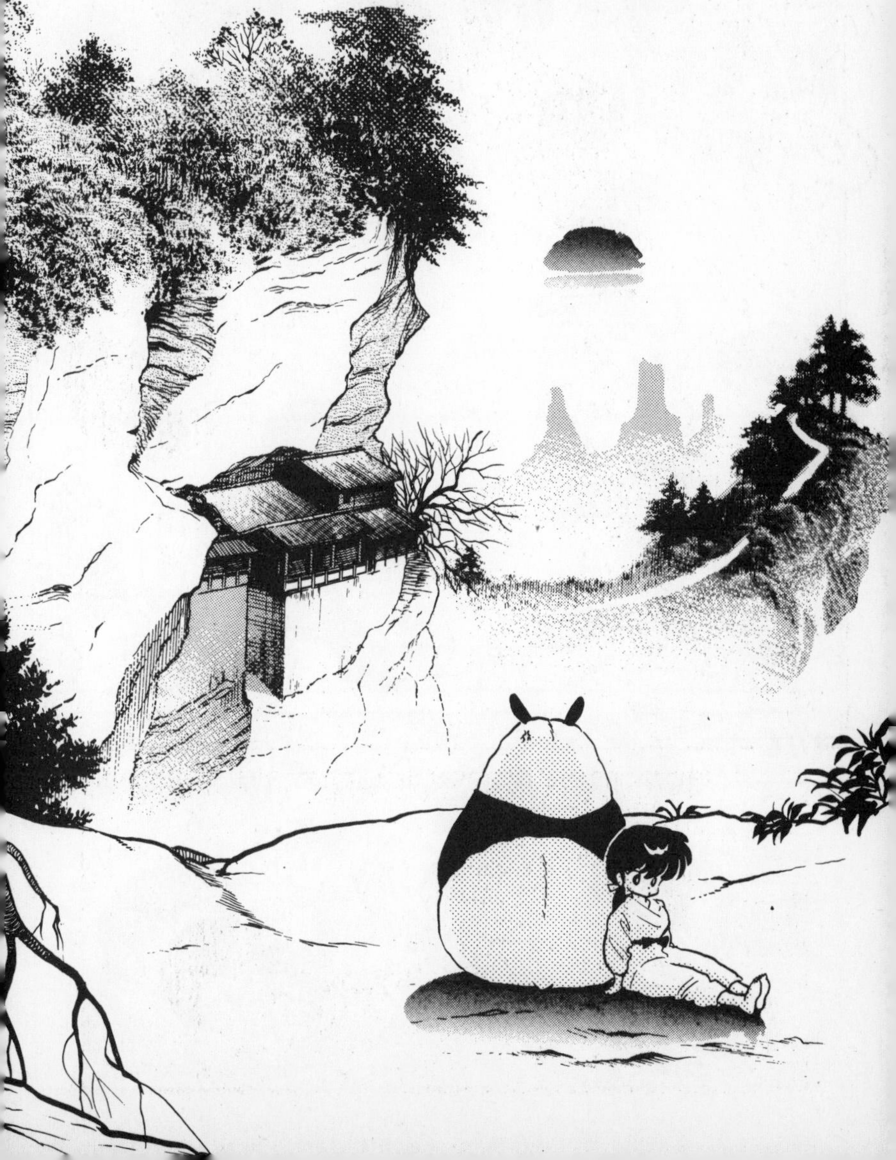

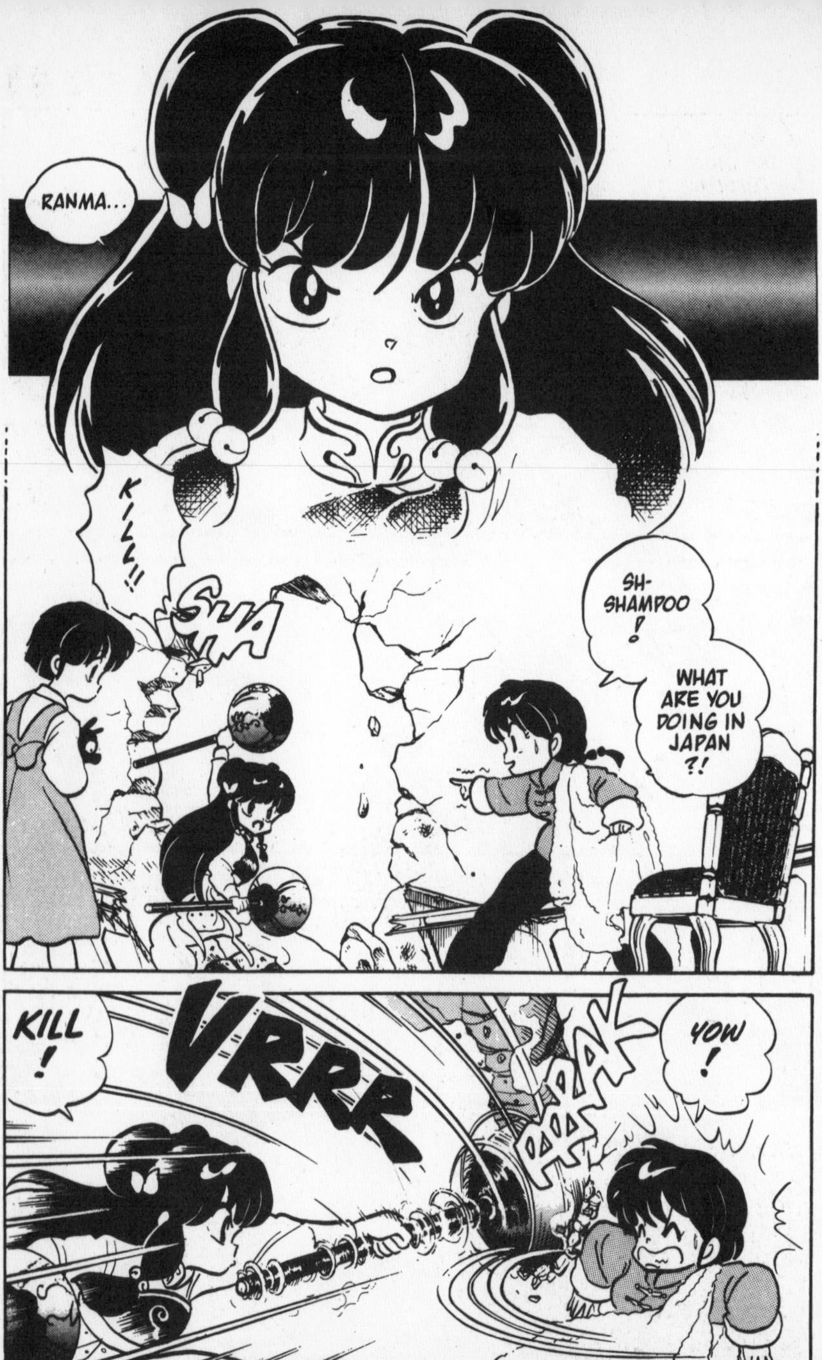
RANMA...
KILL!!
SHA
SH-SHAMPOO!
WHAT ARE YOU DOING IN JAPAN?!
KILL!
VRRR
YOW!

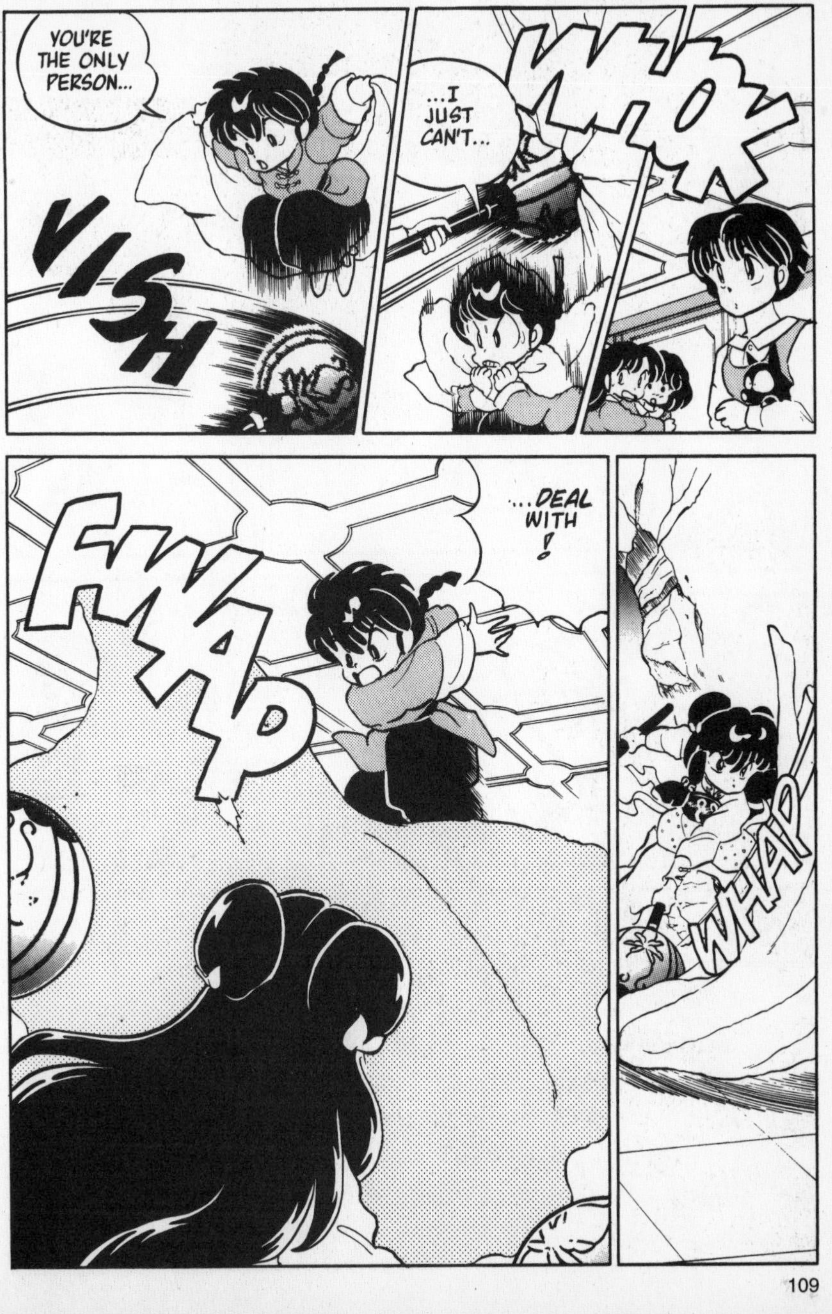
YOU'RE THE ONLY PERSON...
VISH
...I JUST CAN'T...
WHOK
...DEAL WITH!
FWAP
WHAP

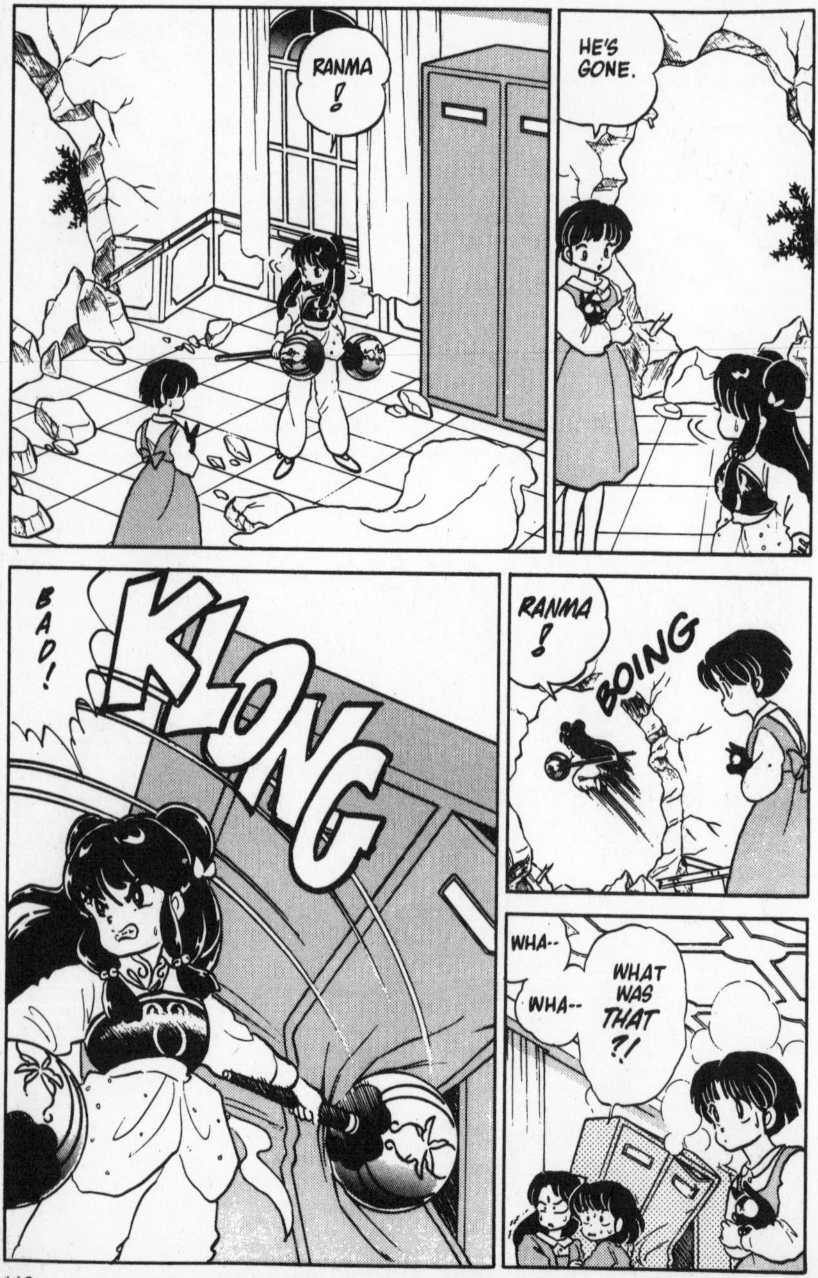
RANMA!
HE'S GONE.
BAD!
KLONG
RANMA!
BOING
WHA--
WHA--
WHAT WAS THAT?!

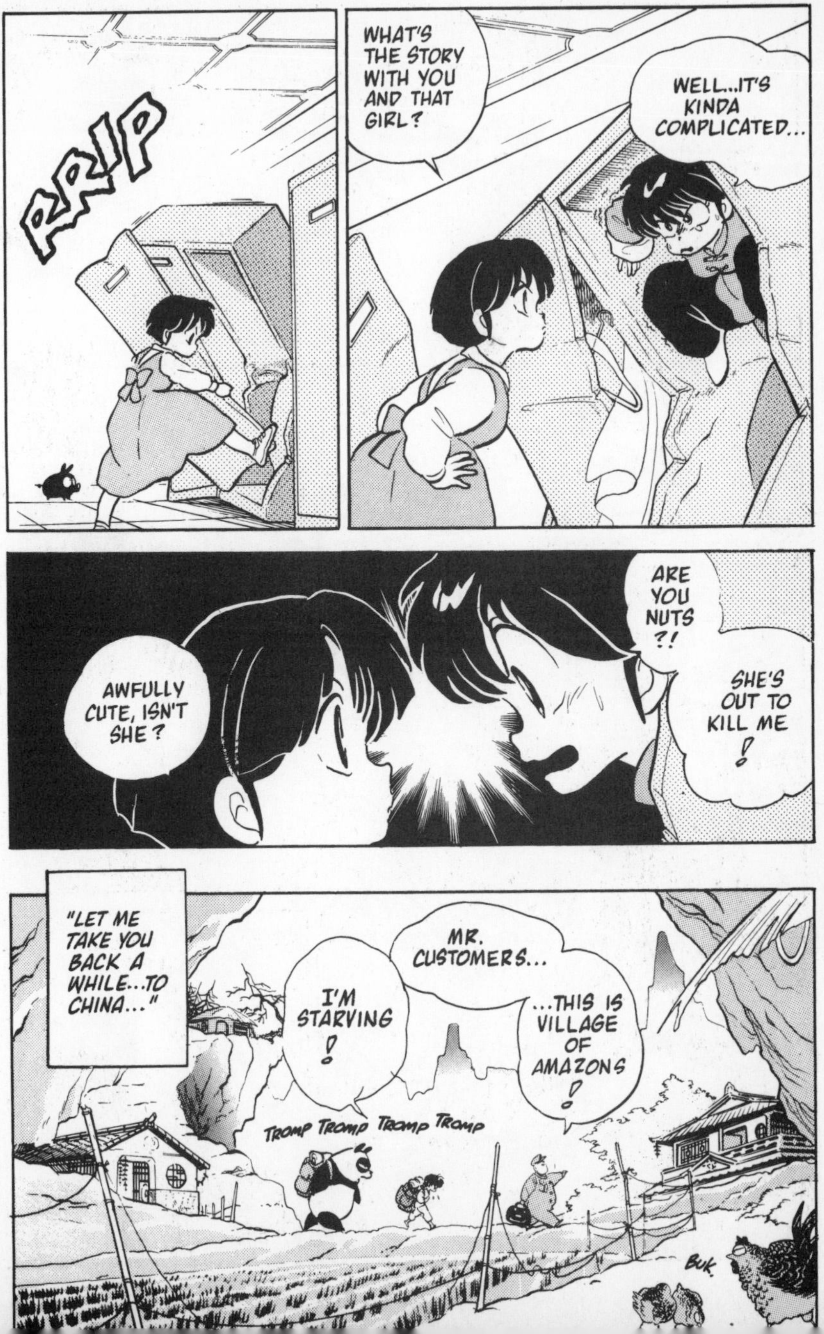
RRIP
WHAT'S THE STORY WITH YOU AND THAT GIRL?
WELL...IT'S KINDA COMPLICATED...
AWFULLY CUTE, ISN'T SHE?
ARE YOU NUTS?!
SHE'S OUT TO KILL ME!
"LET ME TAKE YOU BACK A WHILE...TO CHINA..."
MR. CUSTOMERS...
I'M STARVING!
...THIS IS VILLAGE OF AMAZONS!
TROMP TROMP TROMP TROMP
BUK.

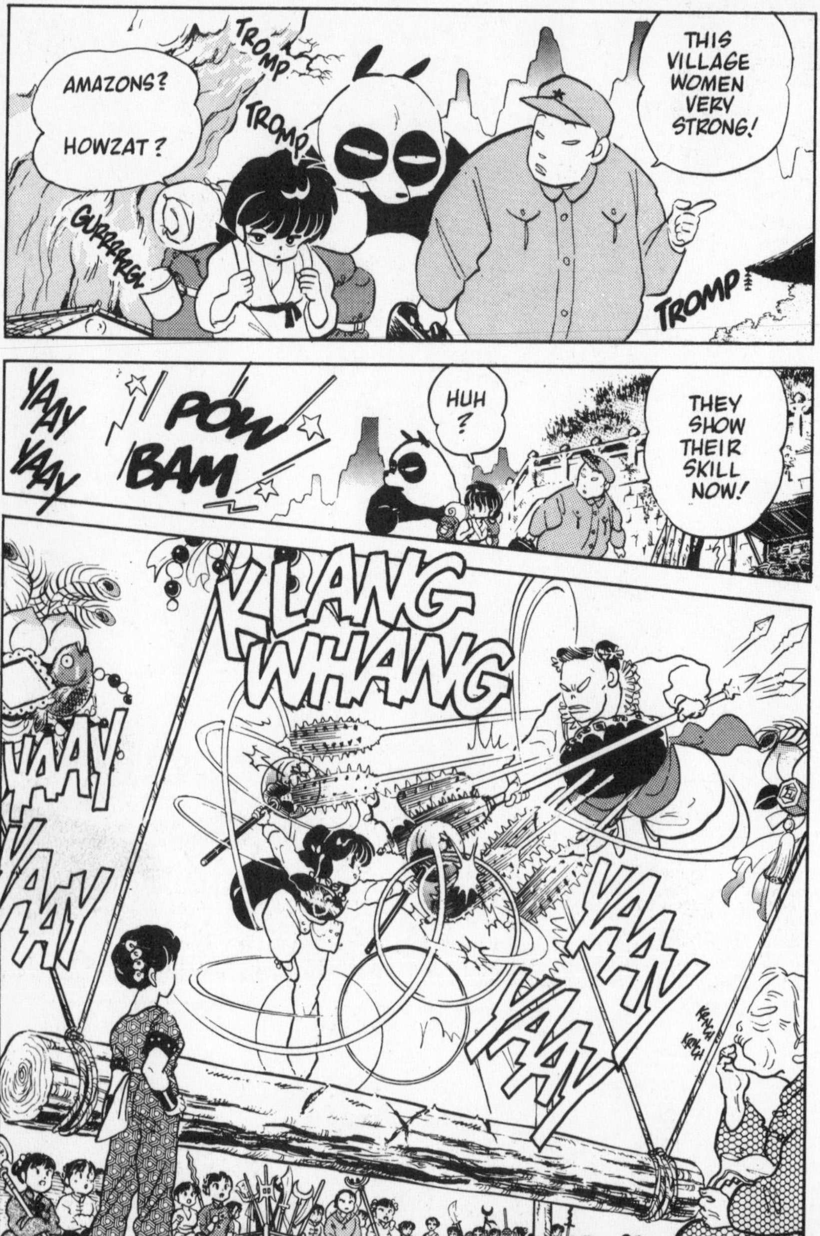
AMAZONS?
HOWZAT?
TROMP
TROMP
GURRRRRGL
THIS VILLAGE WOMEN VERY STRONG!
TROMP
YAAAY YAAAY
POW
BAM
HUH?
THEY SHOW THEIR SKILL NOW!
KLANG
WHANG
YAAAY
YAAAY
YAAAY
YAAAY
KRNCH KRNCH

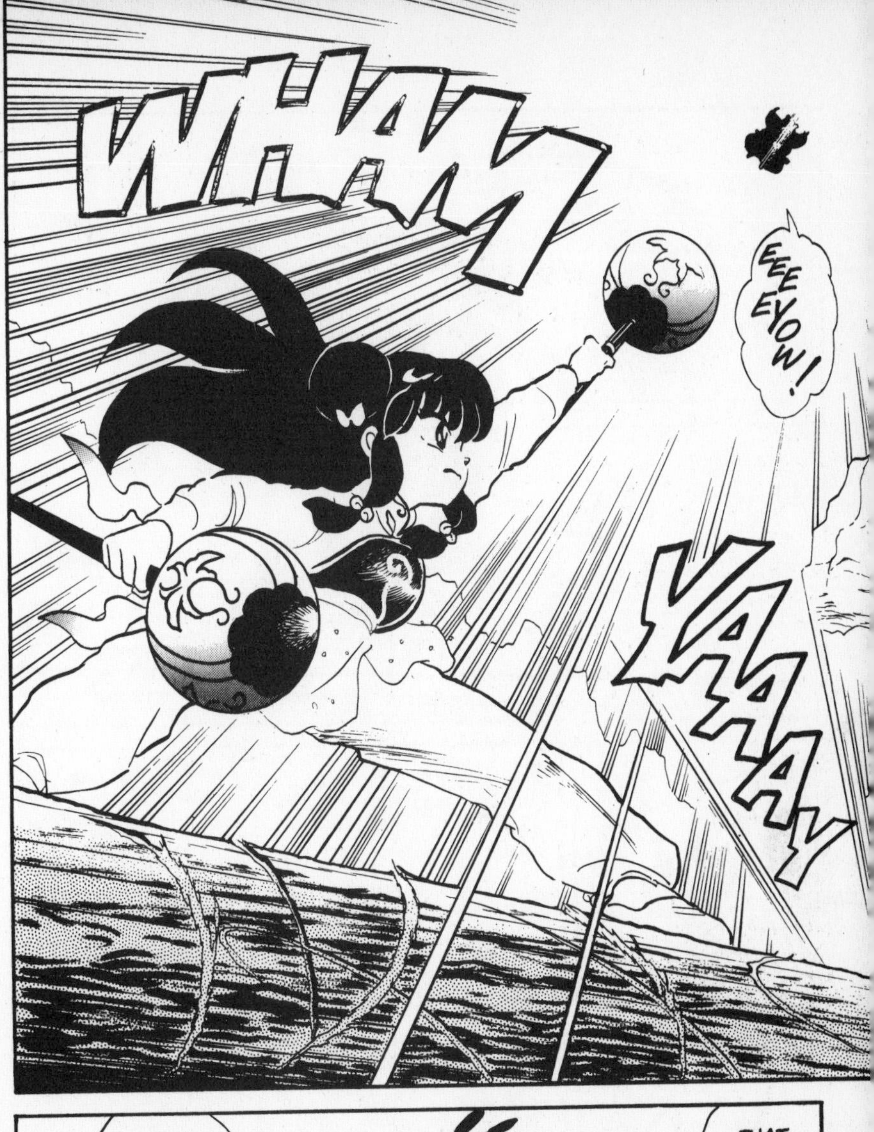
WHAM
EEE EYOW!
YAAAW

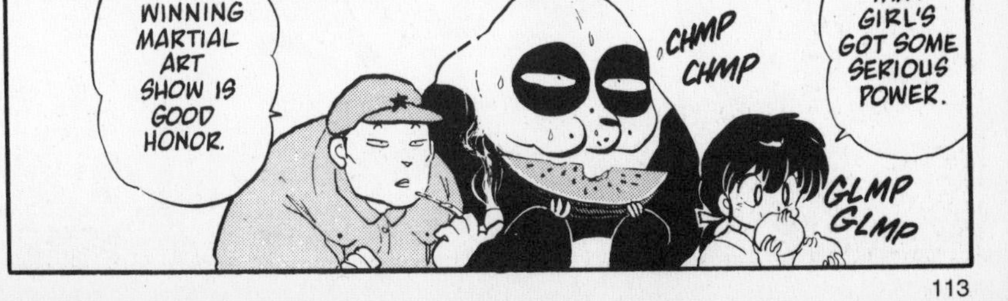
WINNING MARTIAL ART SHOW IS GOOD HONOR.
CHMP CHMP
THAT GIRL'S GOT SOME SERIOUS POWER.
GLMP GLMP

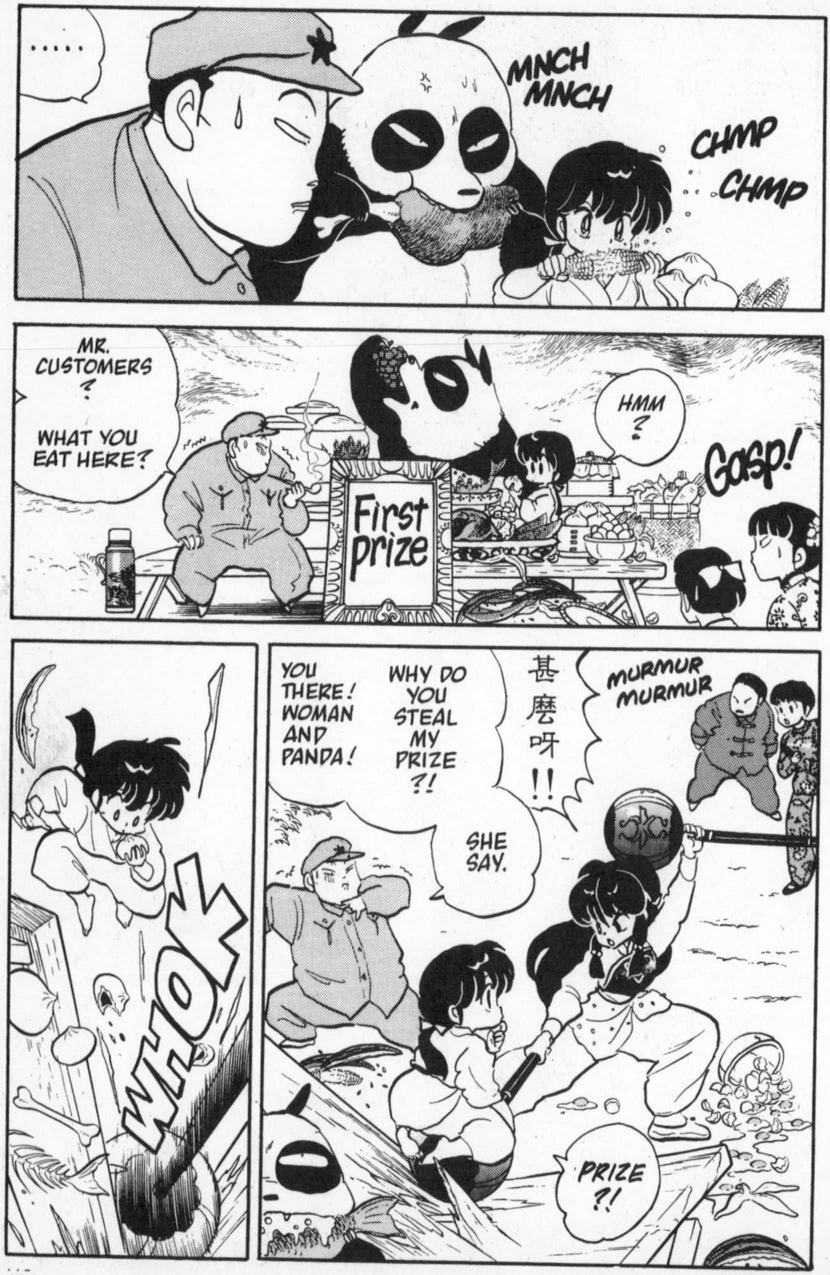
.....
MNCH MNCH
CHMP CHMP
MR. CUSTOMERS? WHAT YOU EAT HERE?
First prize
HMM?
Gasp!
WHOK
YOU THERE! WOMAN AND PANDA!
WHY DO YOU STEAL MY PRIZE?!
甚麼呀!!
SHE SAY.
MURMUR MURMUR
PRIZE?!

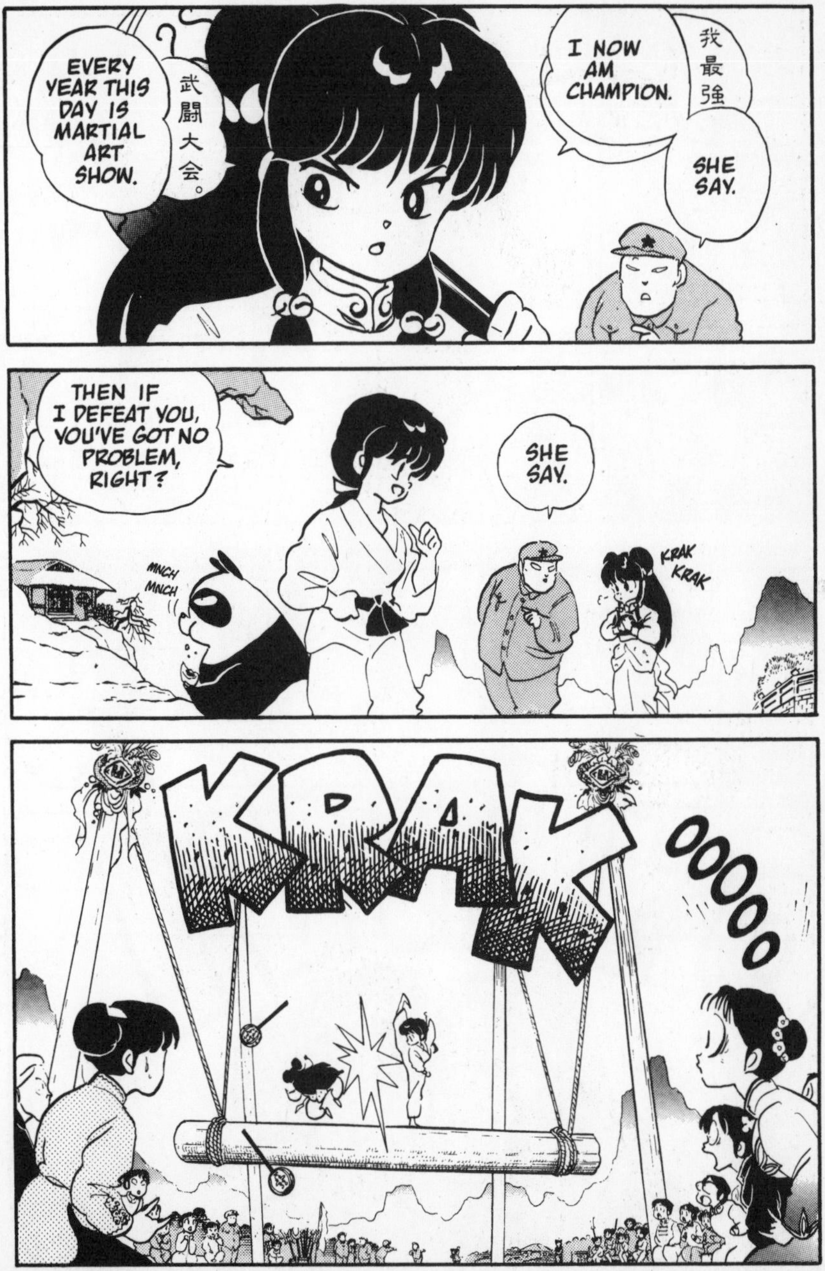
武闘大会。
EVERY YEAR THIS DAY IS MARTIAL ART SHOW.
我最強
I NOW AM CHAMPION.
SHE SAY.
THEN IF I DEFEAT YOU, YOU'VE GOT NO PROBLEM, RIGHT?
SHE SAY.
MNCH MNCH
KRAK KRAK
KRAK
OOOOO

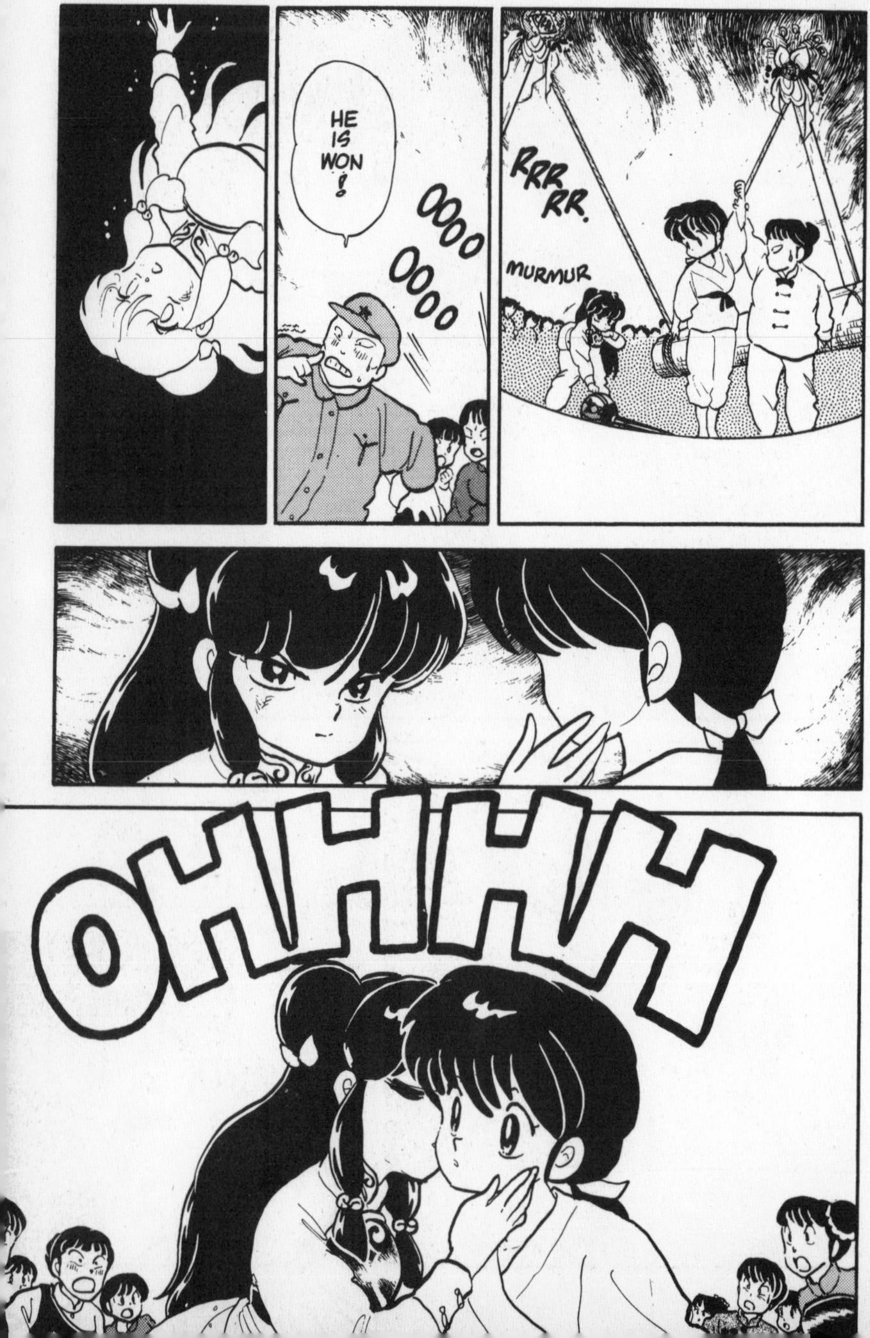
HE IS WON!
OOOO OOOO
RRRRR.
MURMUR
OHHHH

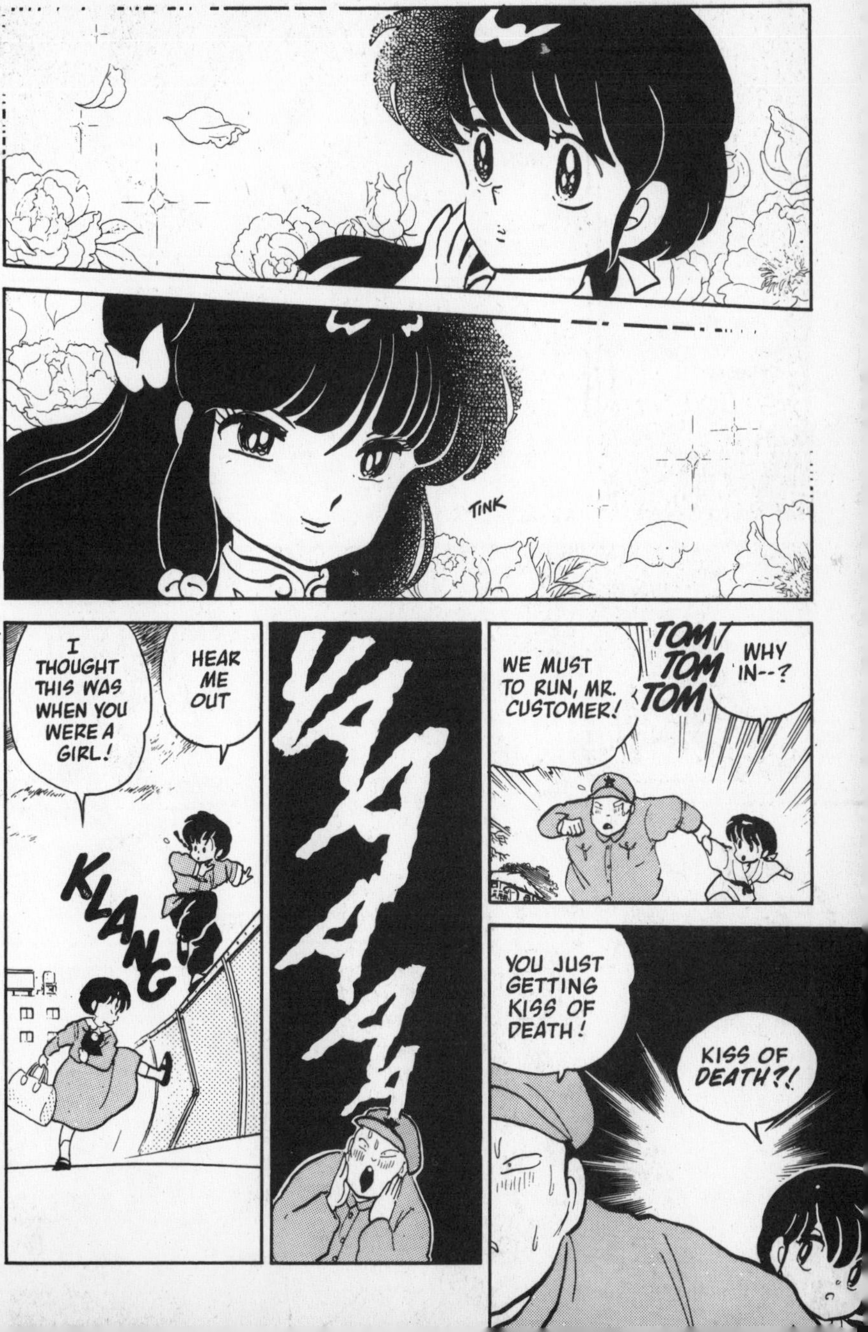
TINK
I THOUGHT THIS WAS WHEN YOU WERE A GIRL!
HEAR ME OUT
KLANG
YAAAAA
WE MUST TO RUN, MR. CUSTOMER!
TOM TOM TOM TOM
WHY IN--?
YOU JUST GETTING KISS OF DEATH!
KISS OF DEATH?!

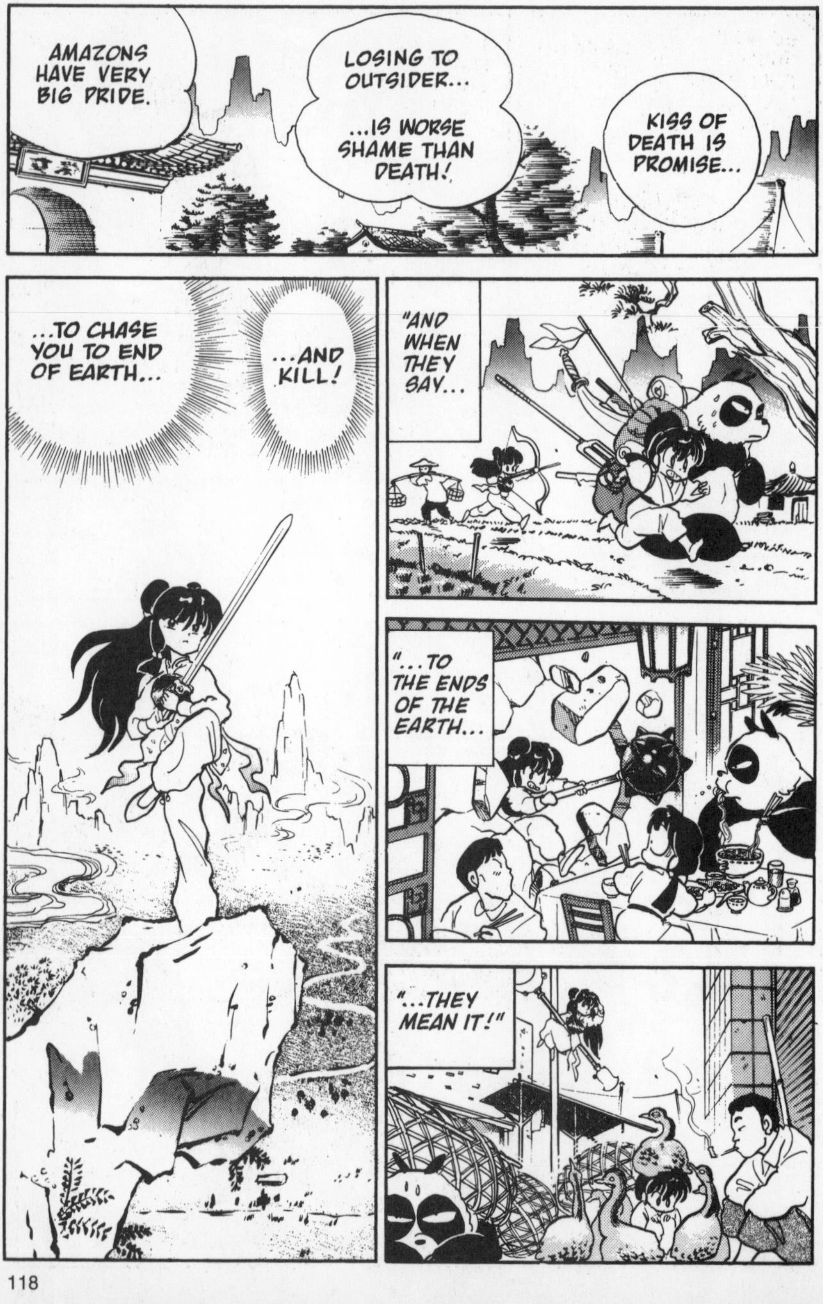
AMAZONS HAVE VERY BIG PRIDE.
LOSING TO OUTSIDER...
...IS WORSE SHAME THAN DEATH!
KISS OF DEATH IS PROMISE...
...TO CHASE YOU TO END OF EARTH...
...AND KILL!
"AND WHEN THEY SAY...
"...TO THE ENDS OF THE EARTH...
"...THEY MEAN IT!"

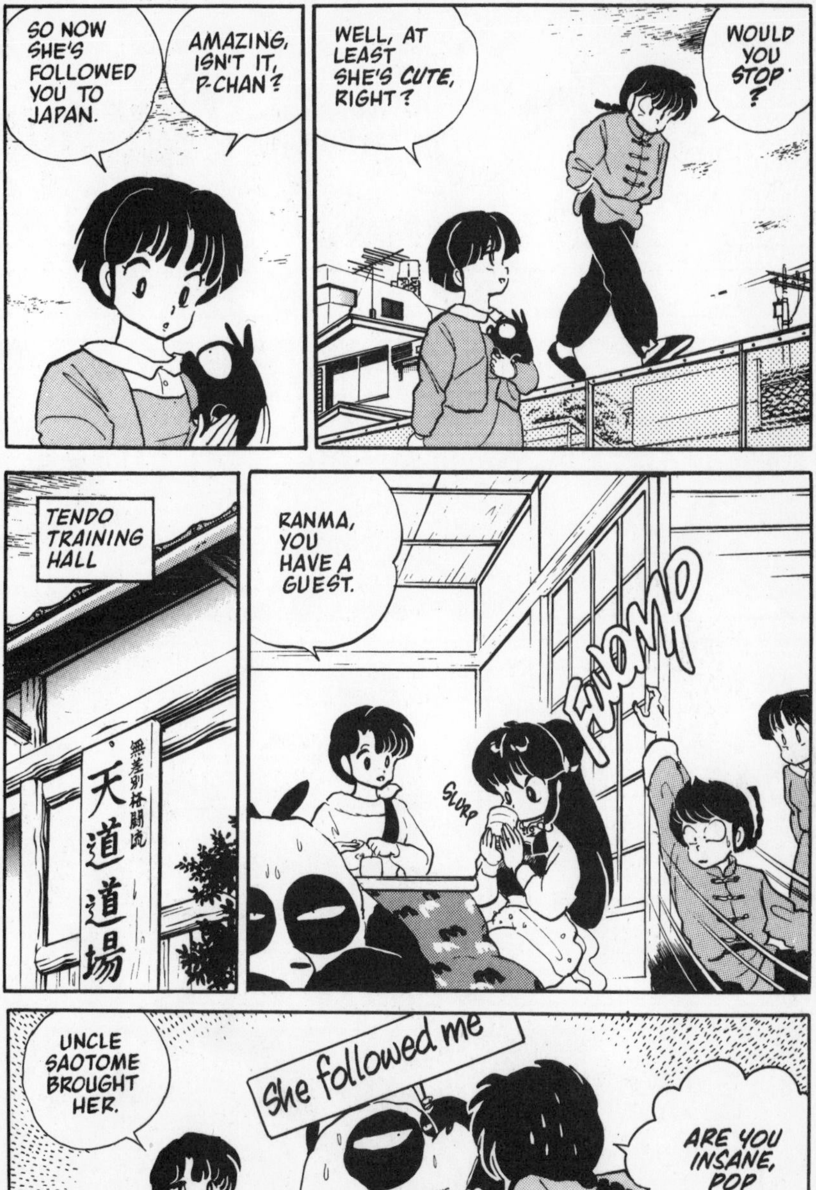
SO NOW SHE'S FOLLOWED YOU TO JAPAN.
AMAZING, ISN'T IT, P-CHAN?
WELL, AT LEAST SHE'S *CUTE*, RIGHT?
WOULD YOU STOP?
TENDO TRAINING HALL
無差別格闘流
天道道場
RANMA, YOU HAVE A GUEST.
FWOMP
SLURP
UNCLE SAOTOME BROUGHT HER.
She followed me
ARE YOU INSANE, POP?!

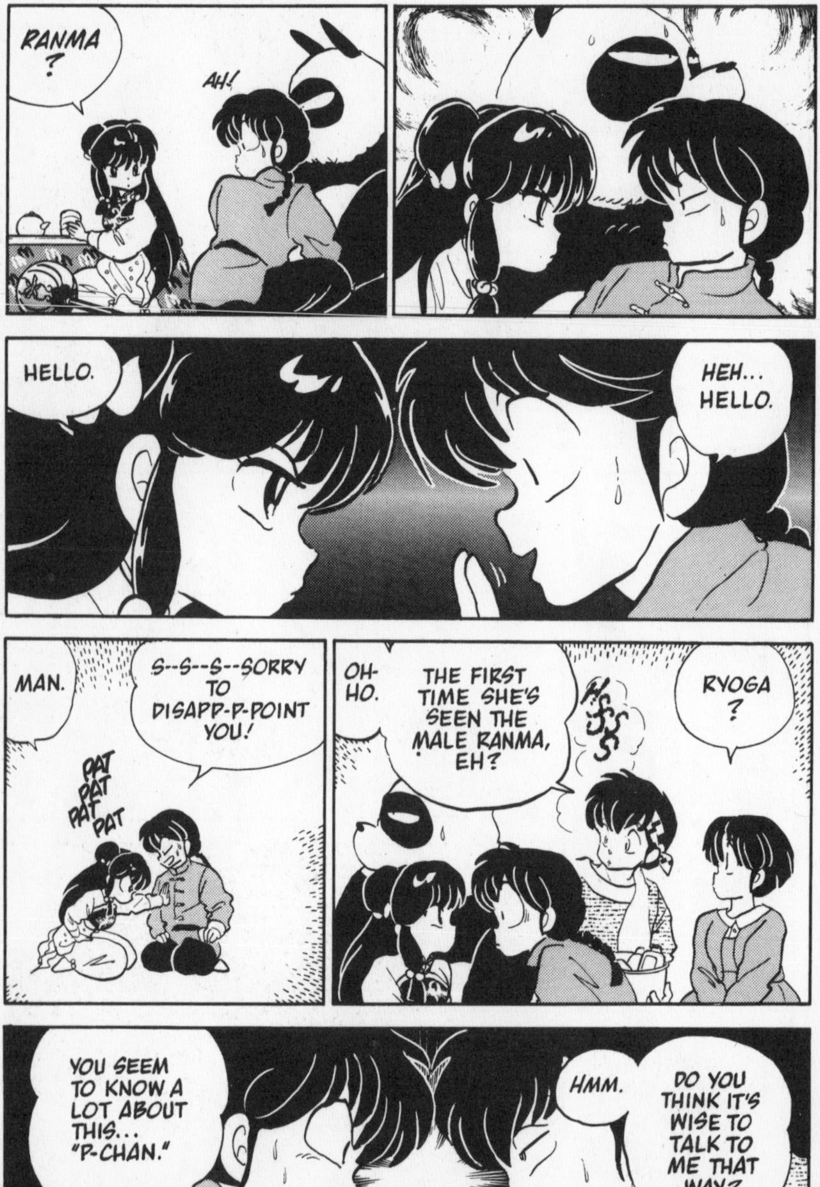
RANMA ?
AH!
HELLO.
HEH... HELLO.
MAN.
S--S--S--SORRY TO DISAPP-P-POINT YOU!
PAT PAT PAT PAT
OH-HO.
THE FIRST TIME SHE'S SEEN THE MALE RANMA, EH?
RYOGA ?
YOU SEEM TO KNOW A LOT ABOUT THIS... "P-CHAN."
HMM.
DO YOU THINK IT'S WISE TO TALK TO ME THAT WAY?

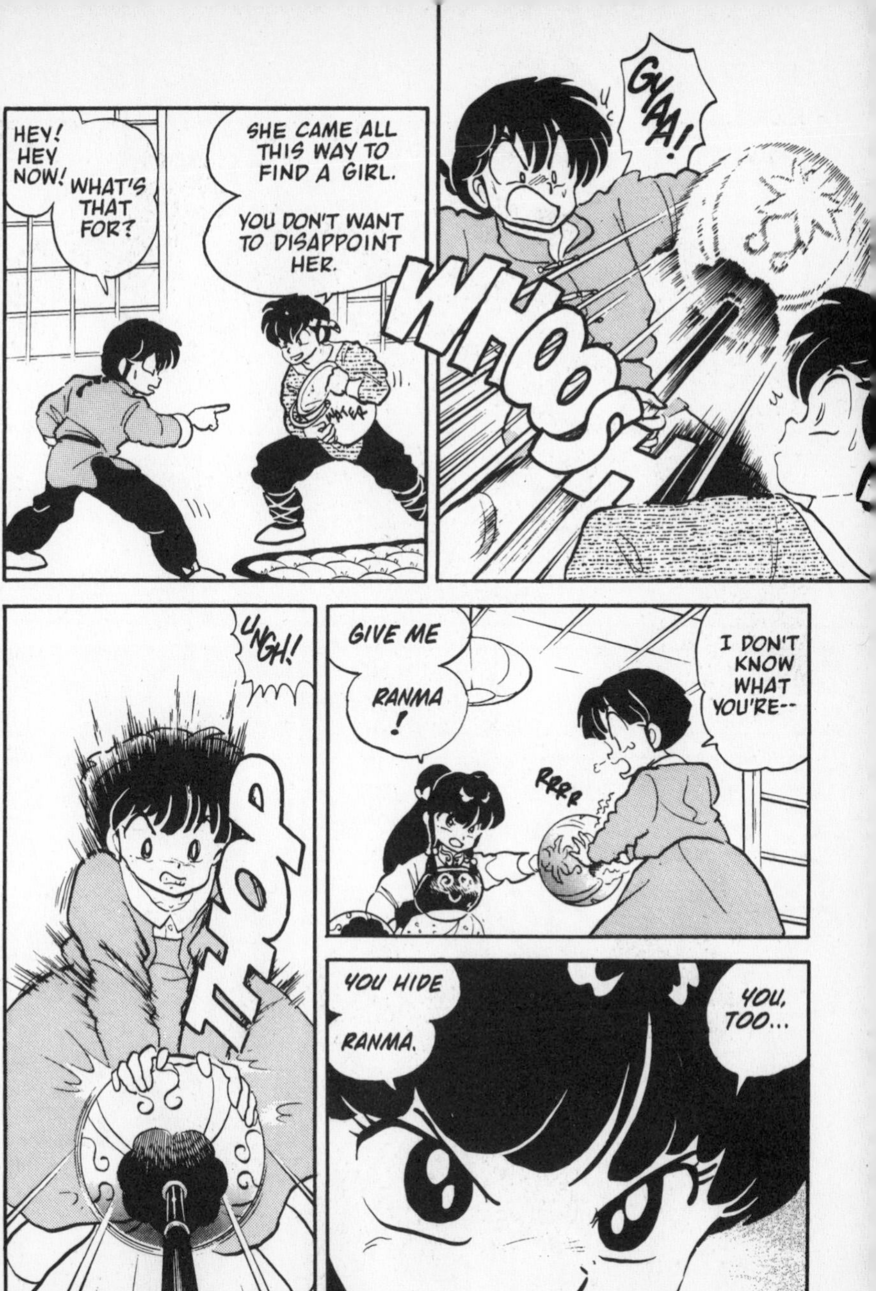
HEY! HEY NOW!
WHAT'S THAT FOR?
SHE CAME ALL THIS WAY TO FIND A GIRL.
YOU DON'T WANT TO DISAPPOINT HER.
GYAAA!
WHOOSH!
UNGH!
THOP
GIVE ME RANMA!
I DON'T KNOW WHAT YOU'RE--
RRRR
YOU HIDE RANMA.
YOU, TOO...

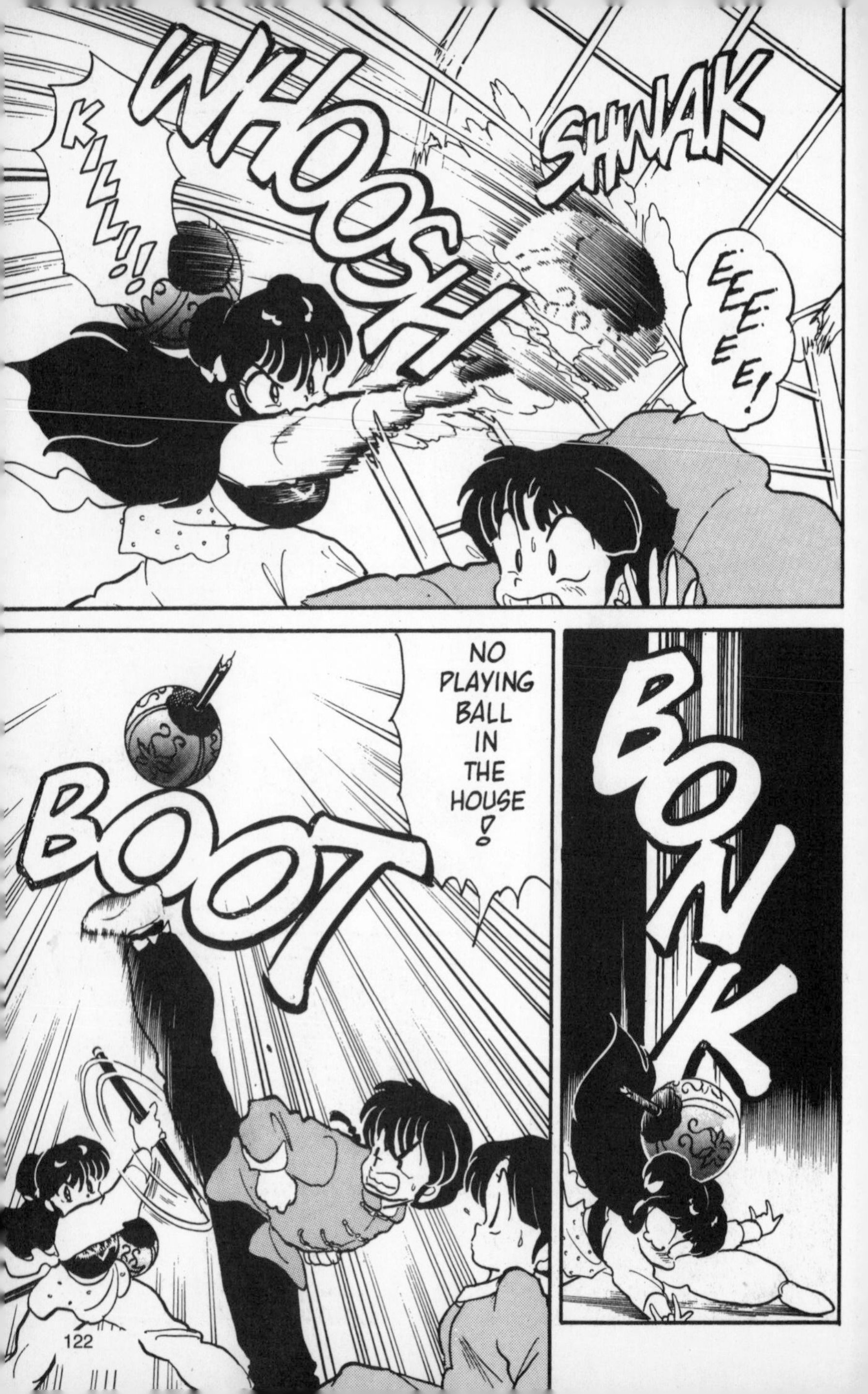
KILL!!
WHOOSH
SHWAK
EEEEEE!
BOOT
NO PLAYING BALL IN THE HOUSE!
BONK

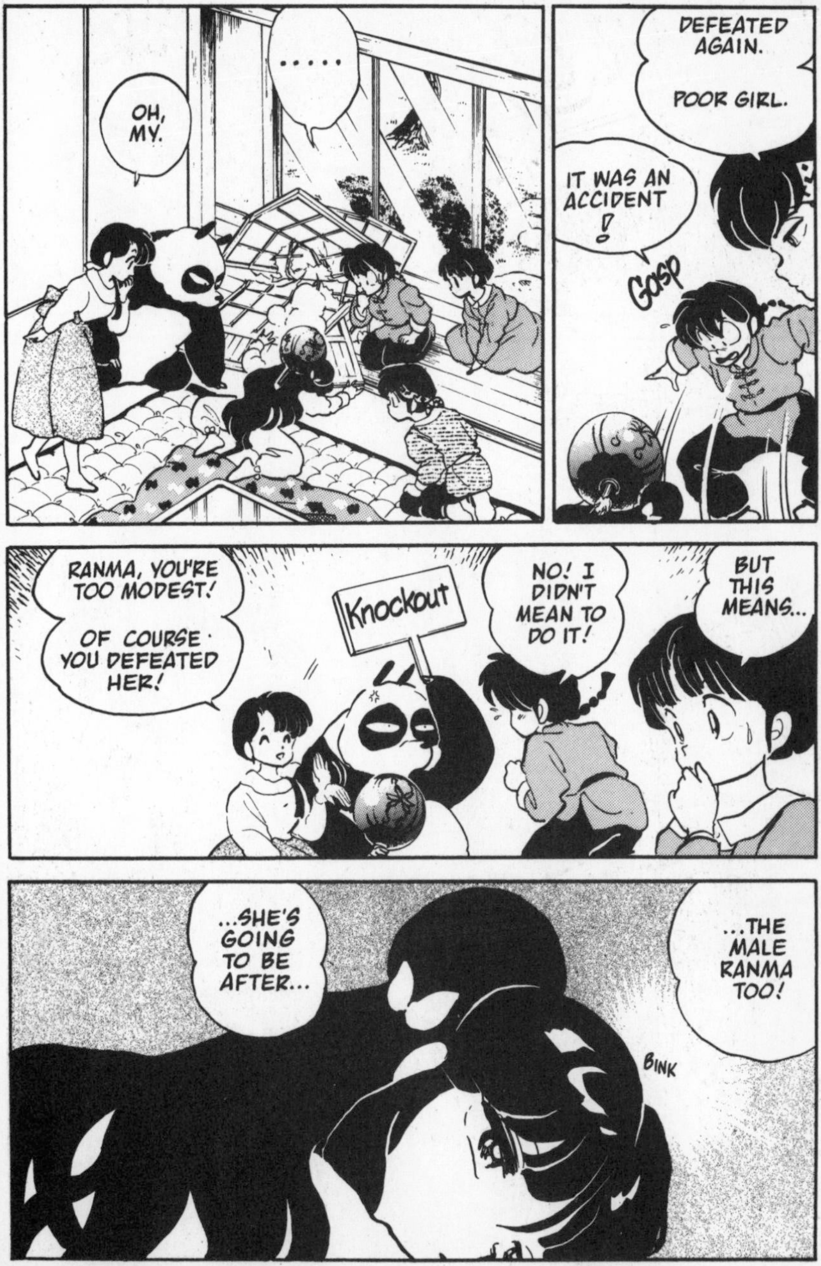
OH, MY.
.....
DEFEATED AGAIN.
POOR GIRL.
IT WAS AN ACCIDENT!
Gasp
RANMA, YOU'RE TOO MODEST!
OF COURSE YOU DEFEATED HER!
Knockout
NO! I DIDN'T MEAN TO DO IT!
BUT THIS MEANS...
...SHE'S GOING TO BE AFTER...
...THE MALE RANMA TOO!
BINK

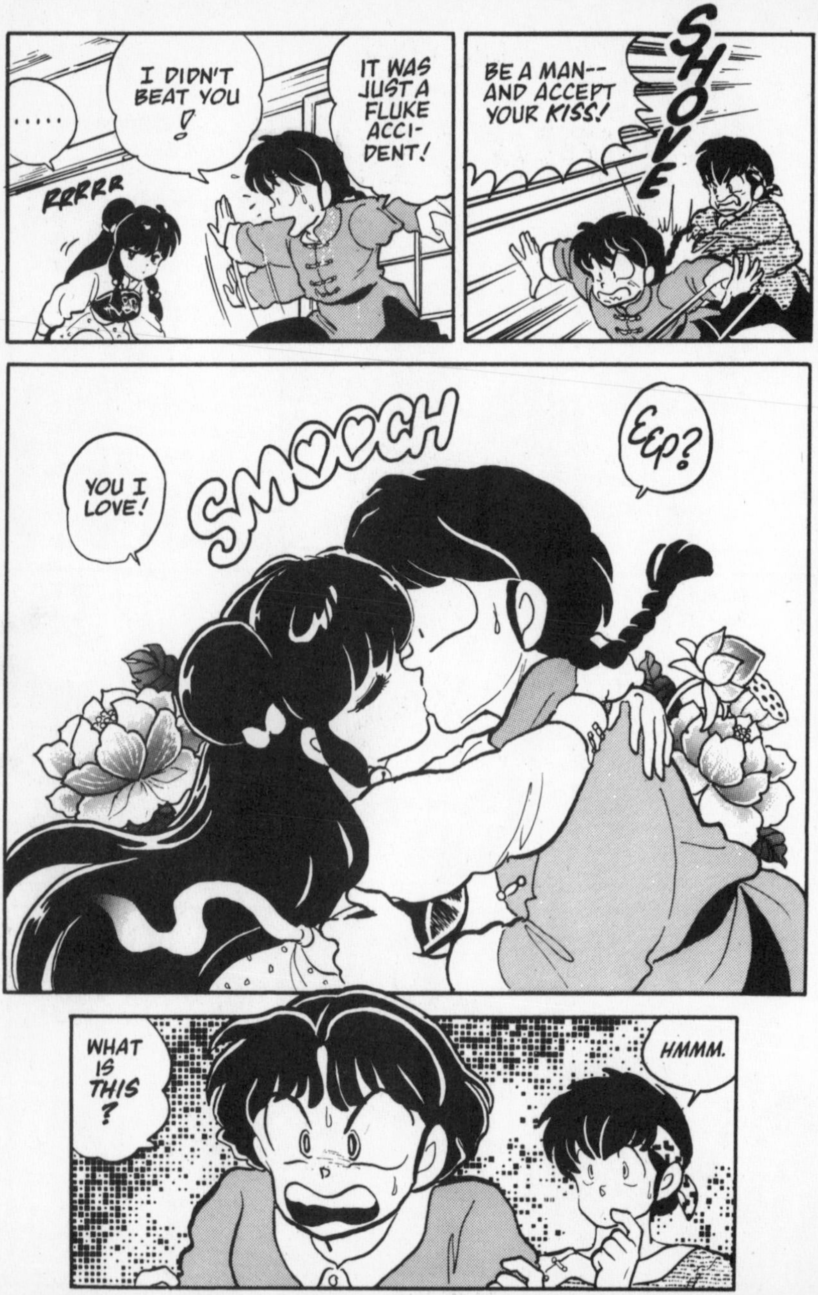
.....
I DIDN'T BEAT YOU!
IT WAS JUST A FLUKE ACCI-DENT!
RRRRR
BE A MAN-- AND ACCEPT YOUR KISS!
SHOVE
YOU I LOVE!
SMOOCH
EEP?
WHAT IS THIS?
HMMM.

Part 7
YOU I LOVE

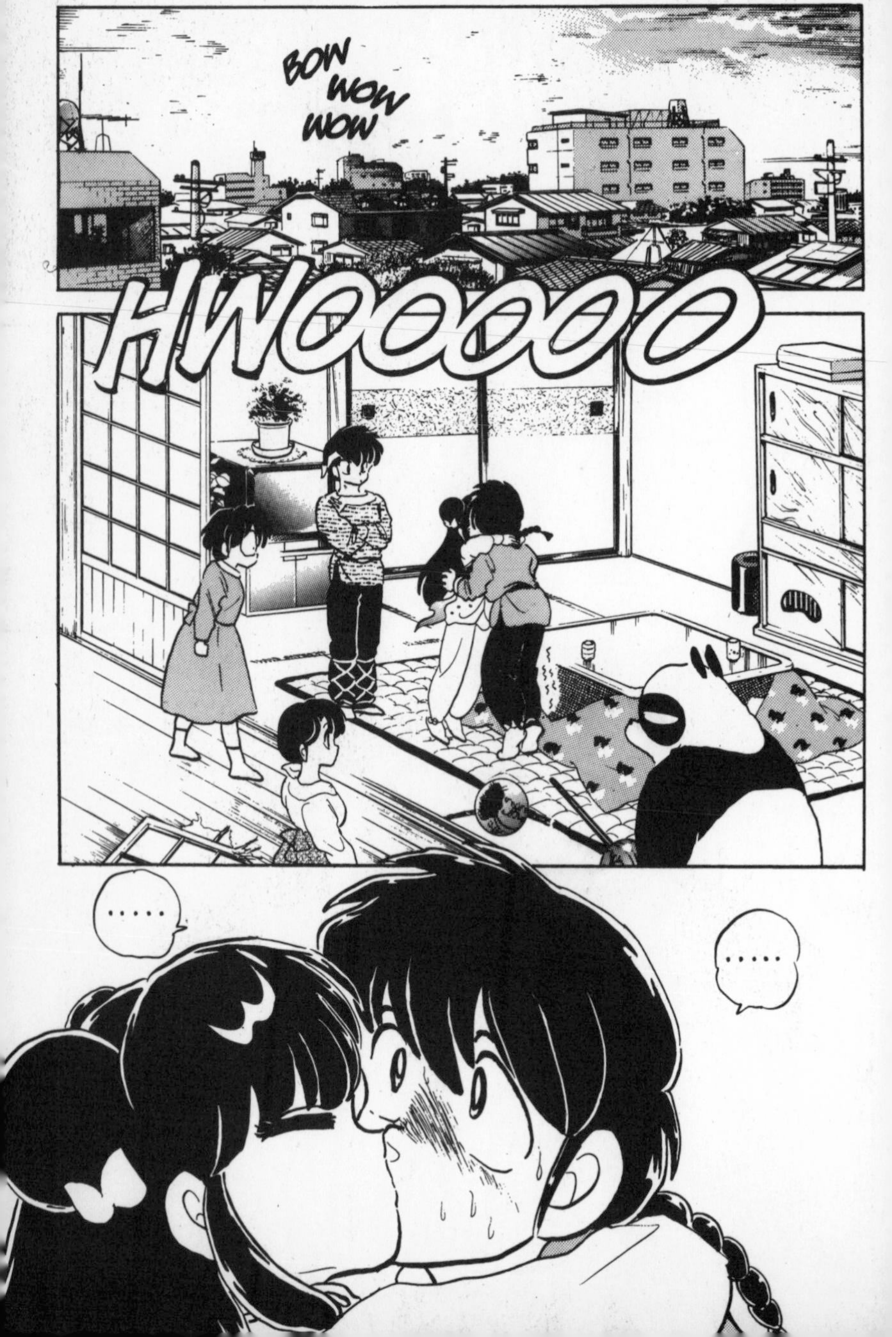
BOW WOW WOW
HWOOOOO
......
......

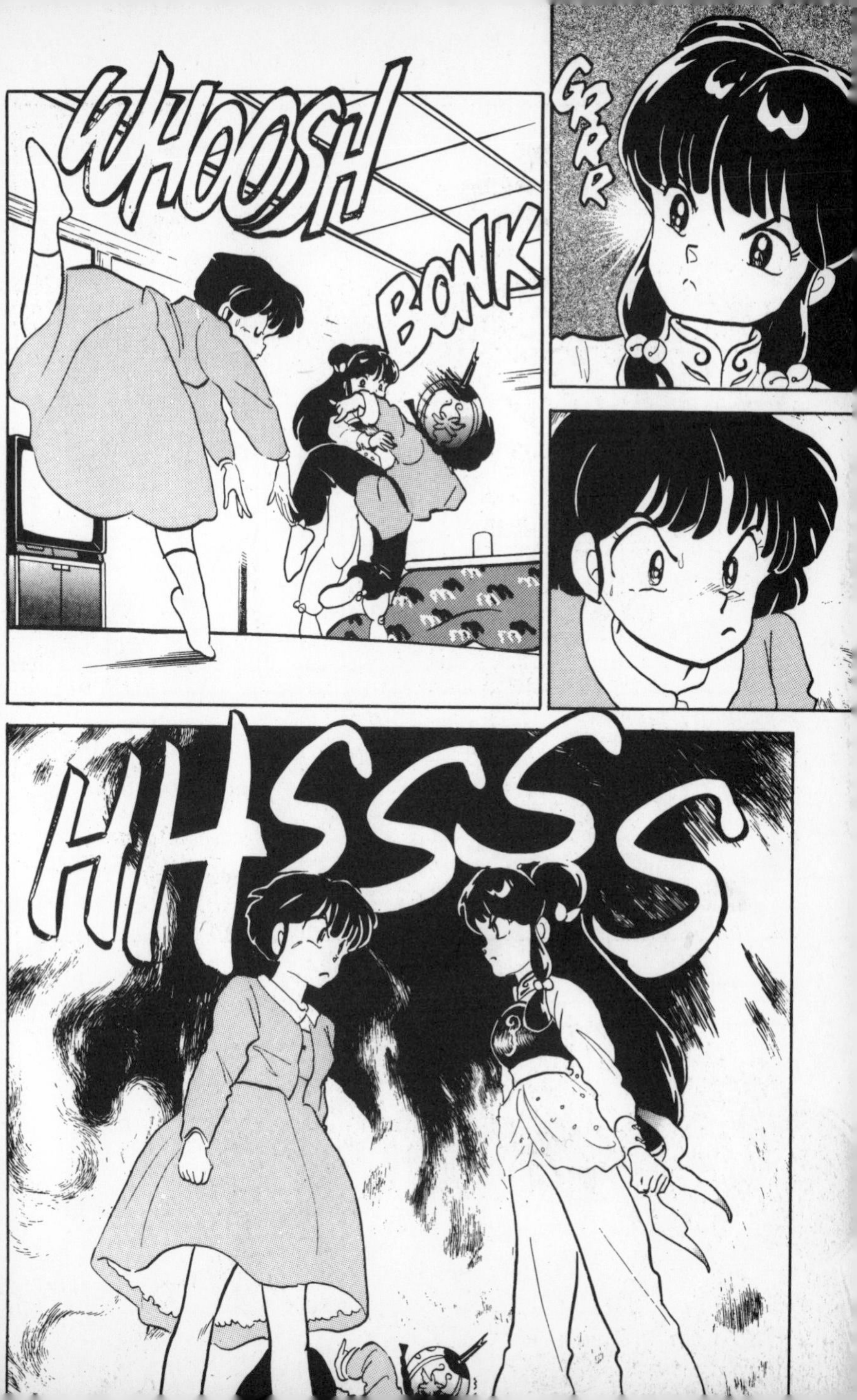
WHOOSH
BONK
GRRR
HSSSS

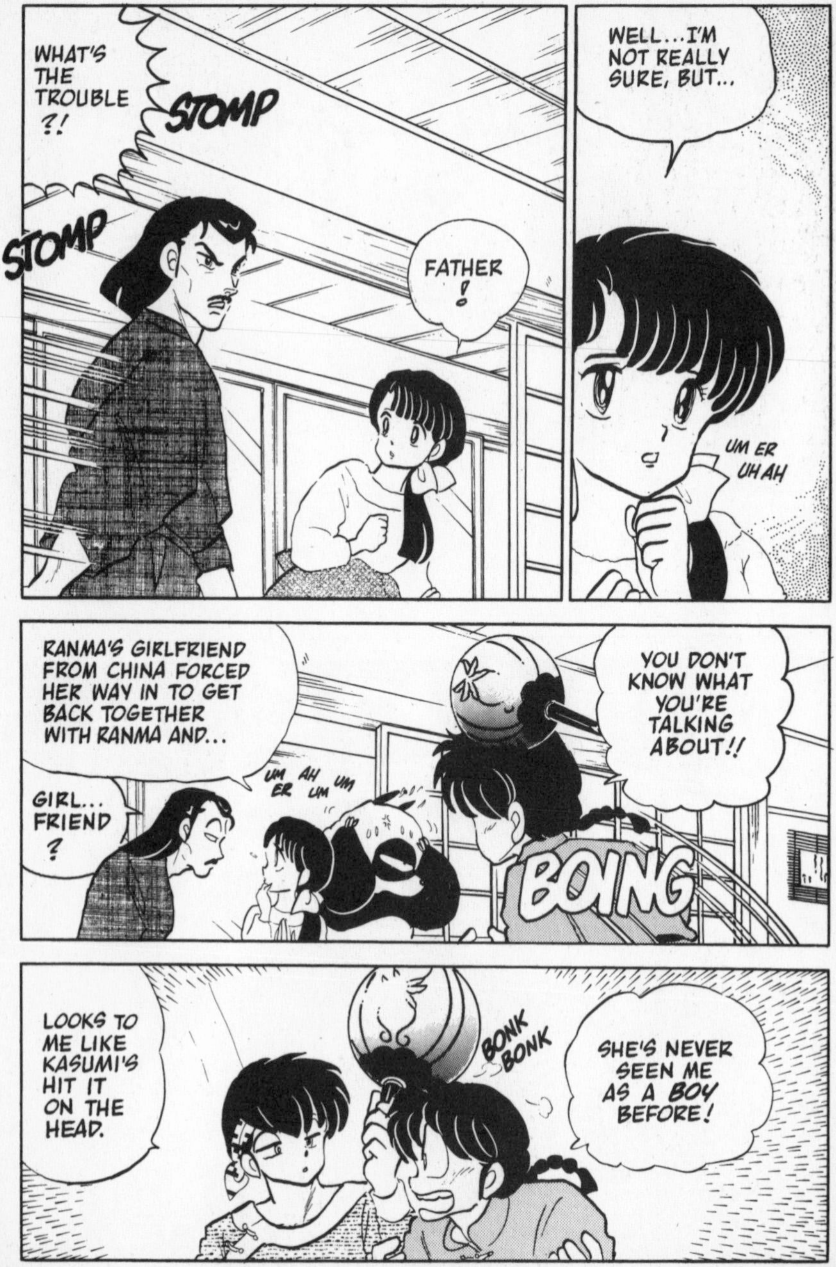
WHAT'S THE TROUBLE ?!
STOMP
STOMP
FATHER!
WELL...I'M NOT REALLY SURE, BUT...
UM ER UH AH
RANMA'S GIRLFRIEND FROM CHINA FORCED HER WAY IN TO GET BACK TOGETHER WITH RANMA AND...
GIRL... FRIEND?
UM AH UM ER UM
YOU DON'T KNOW WHAT YOU'RE TALKING ABOUT!!
BOING
LOOKS TO ME LIKE KASUMI'S HIT IT ON THE HEAD.
BONK BONK
SHE'S NEVER SEEN ME AS A *BOY* BEFORE!

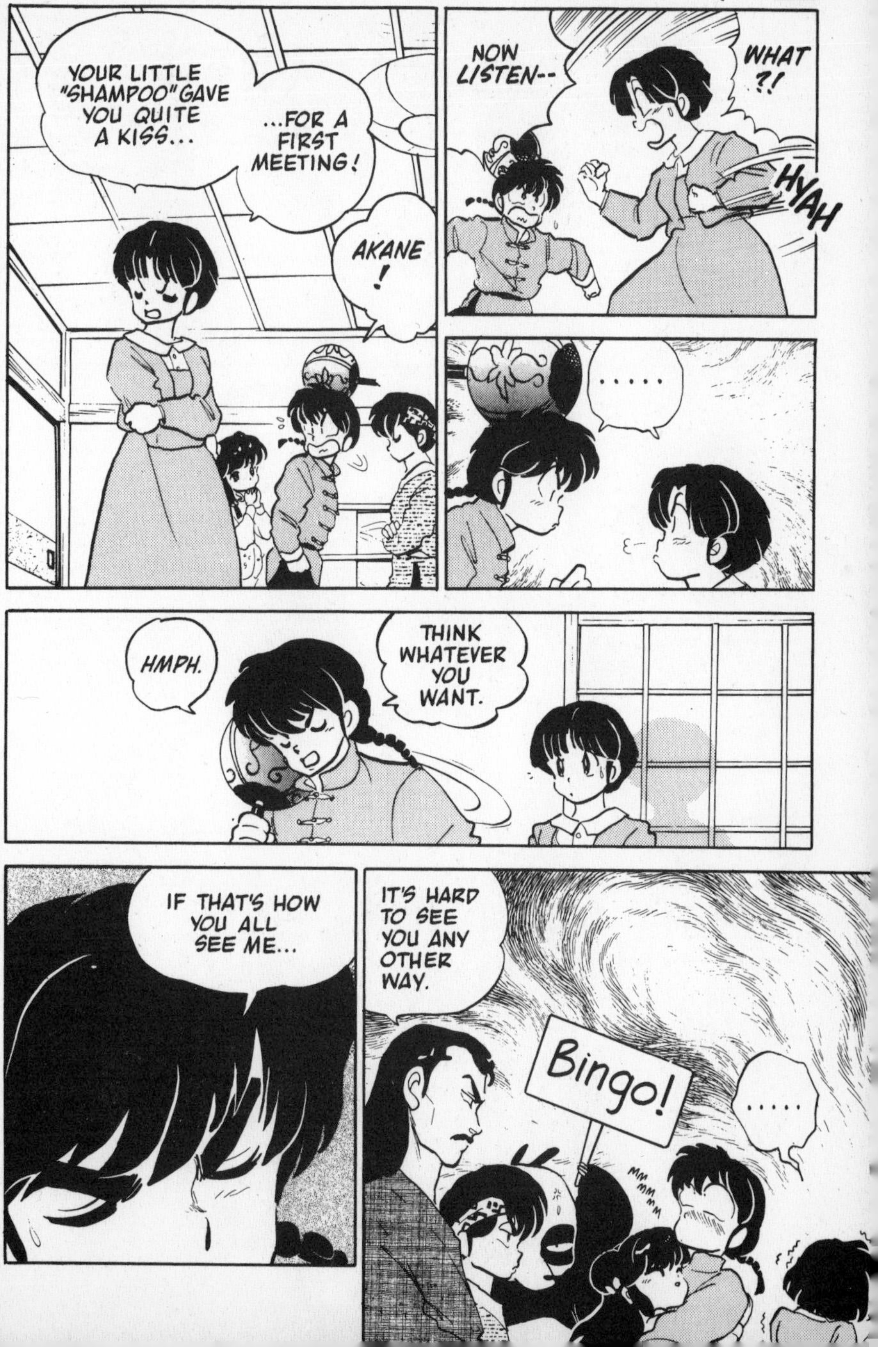
YOUR LITTLE "SHAMPOO" GAVE YOU QUITE A KISS...
...FOR A FIRST MEETING!
AKANE!
NOW LISTEN--
WHAT ?!
HYAH
......
HMPH.
THINK WHATEVER YOU WANT.
IF THAT'S HOW YOU ALL SEE ME...
IT'S HARD TO SEE YOU ANY OTHER WAY.
Bingo!
.....
MM MM MM

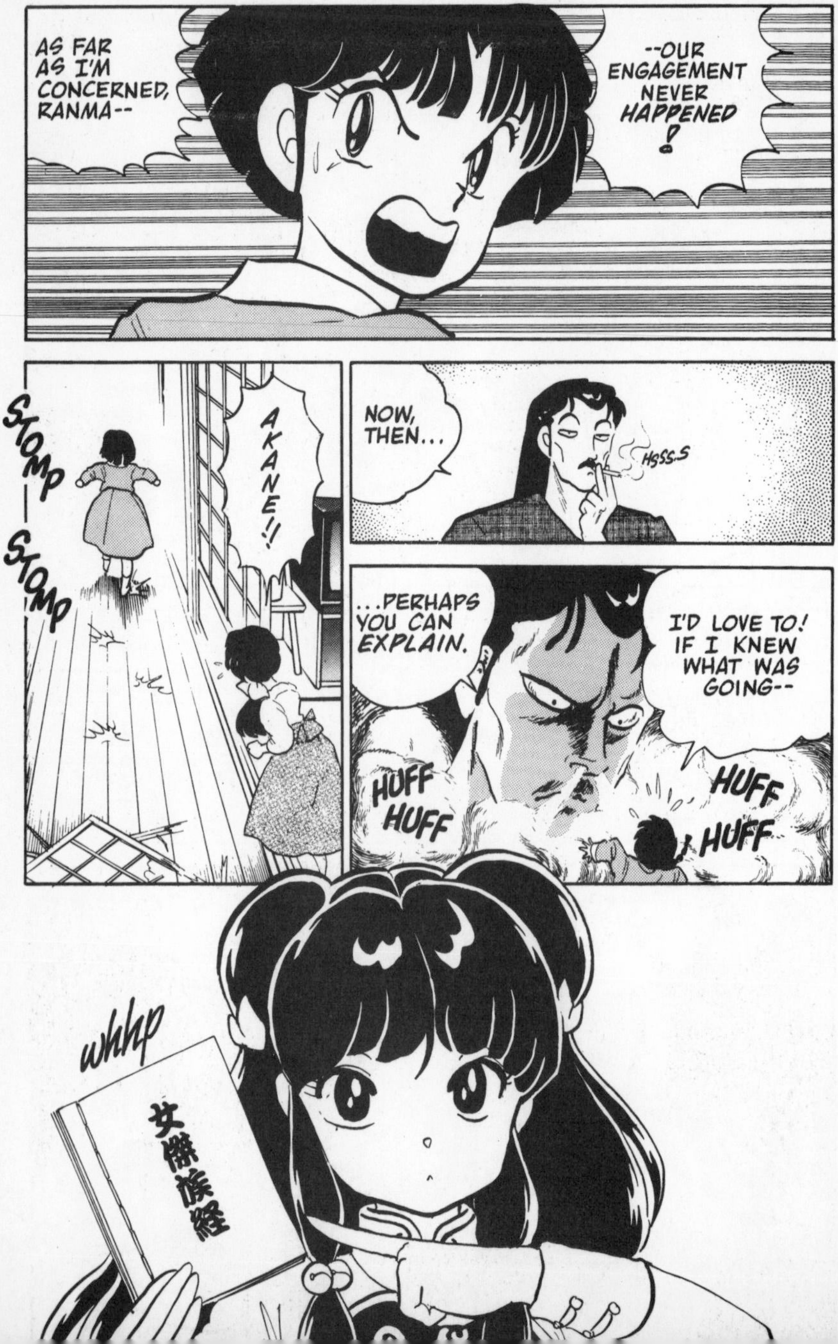
AS FAR AS I'M CONCERNED, RANMA--
--OUR ENGAGEMENT NEVER HAPPENED!
STOMP
STOMP
AKANE!!
NOW, THEN...
HSSS
...PERHAPS YOU CAN EXPLAIN.
I'D LOVE TO! IF I KNEW WHAT WAS GOING--
HUFF HUFF
HUFF HUFF
whhp
女傑族経

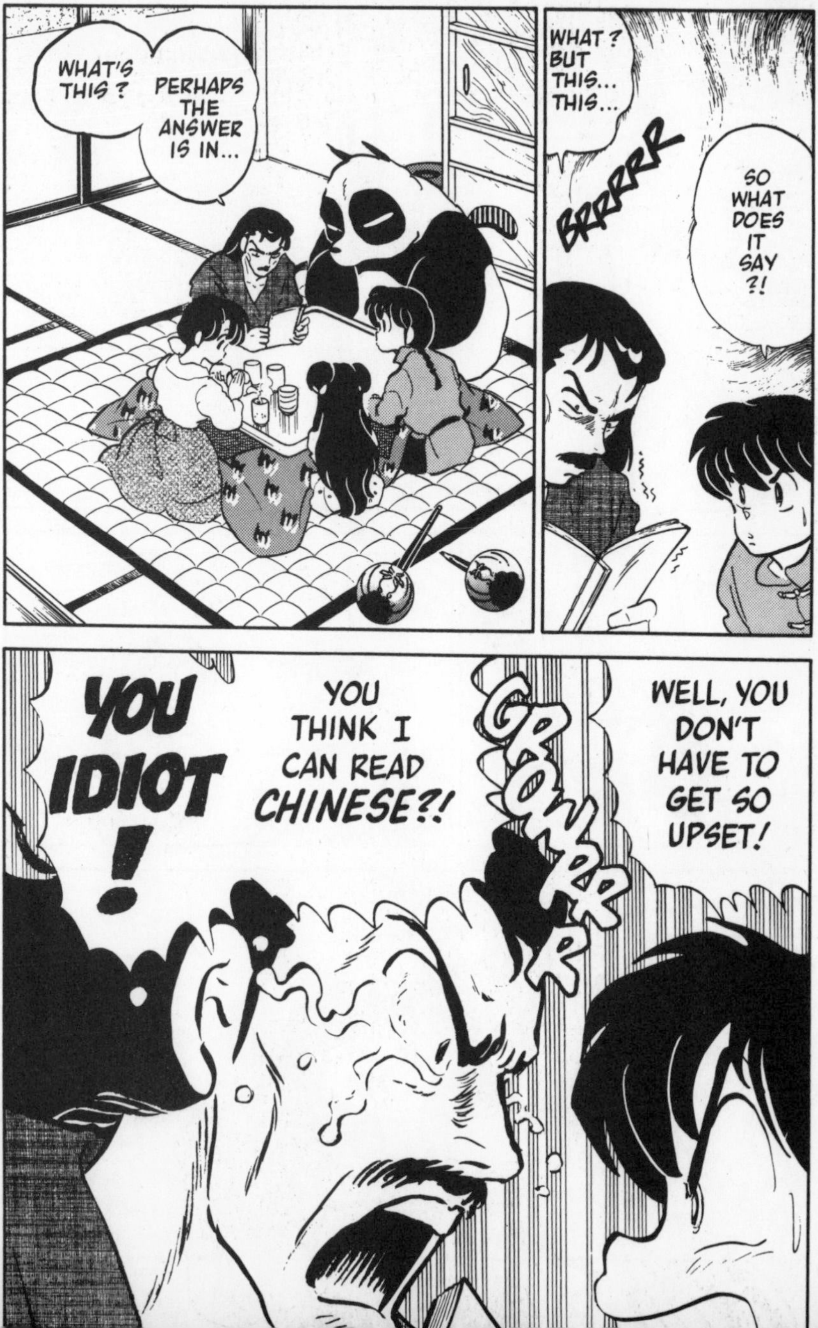
WHAT'S THIS?
PERHAPS THE ANSWER IS IN...
WHAT? BUT THIS... THIS...
BRRRRR
SO WHAT DOES IT SAY?!
YOU IDIOT!
YOU THINK I CAN READ CHINESE?!
GROWRRR
WELL, YOU DON'T HAVE TO GET SO UPSET!

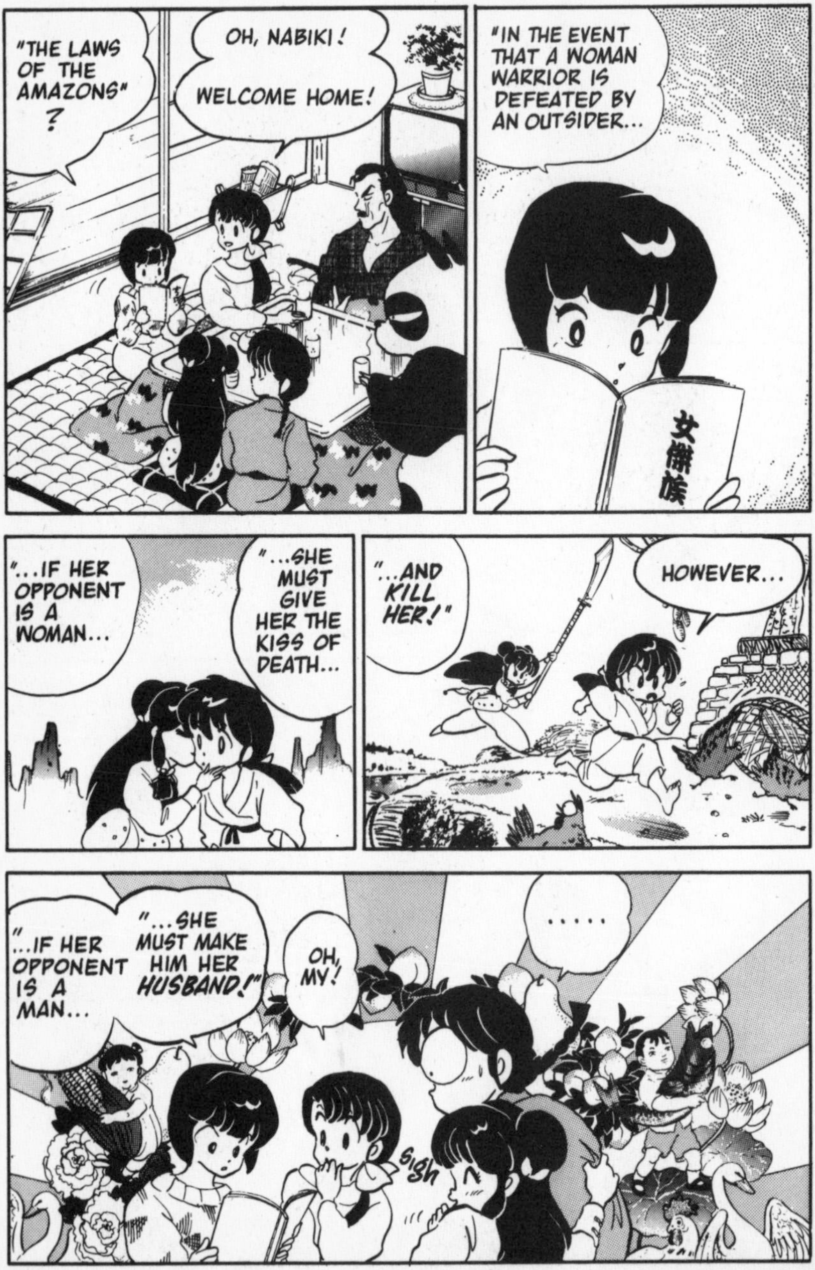
"THE LAWS OF THE AMAZONS" ?
OH, NABIKI!
WELCOME HOME!
"IN THE EVENT THAT A WOMAN WARRIOR IS DEFEATED BY AN OUTSIDER...
女傑族
"...IF HER OPPONENT IS A WOMAN...
"...SHE MUST GIVE HER THE KISS OF DEATH...
"...AND KILL HER!"
HOWEVER...
"...IF HER OPPONENT IS A MAN...
"...SHE MUST MAKE HIM HER HUSBAND!"
OH, MY!
.....
Sigh

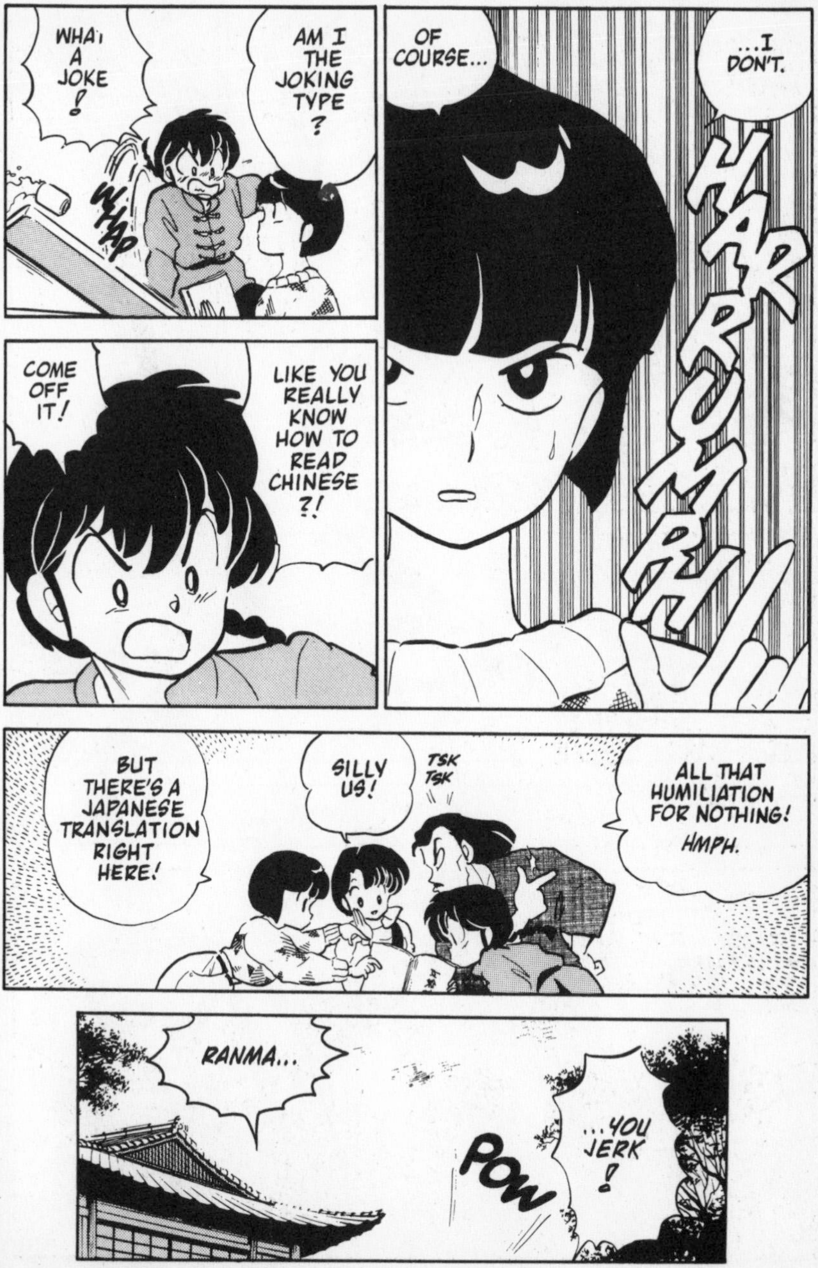
WHAT A JOKE!
WHAP
AM I THE JOKING TYPE?
COME OFF IT!
LIKE YOU REALLY KNOW HOW TO READ CHINESE?!
OF COURSE...
...I DON'T.
HARRUMPH!
BUT THERE'S A JAPANESE TRANSLATION RIGHT HERE!
SILLY US!
TSK TSK
ALL THAT HUMILIATION FOR NOTHING!
HMPH.
RANMA...
POW
...YOU JERK!

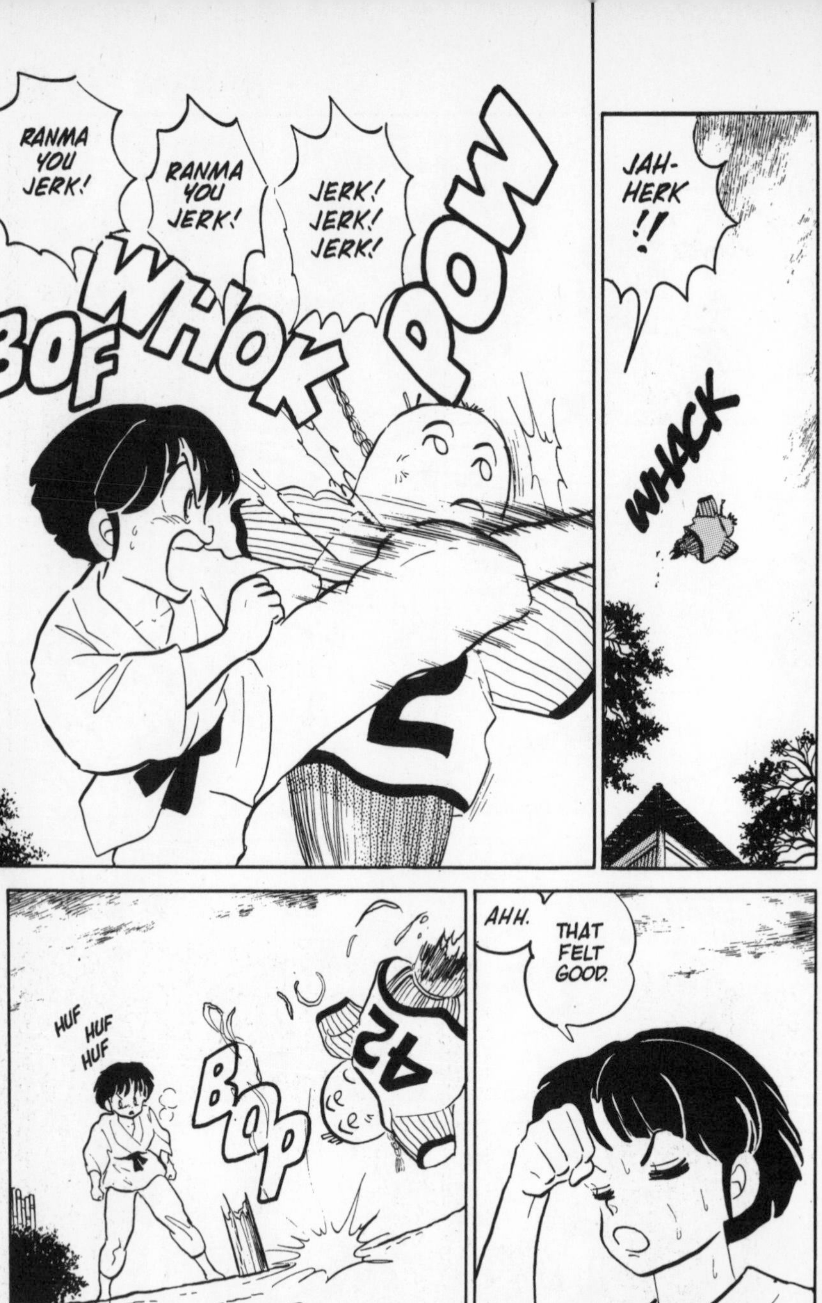
RANMA YOU JERK!
RANMA YOU JERK!
JERK! JERK! JERK!
BOF
WHOK
POW
JAH-HERK!!
WHACK
HUF HUF HUF
BOP
AHH.
THAT FELT GOOD.

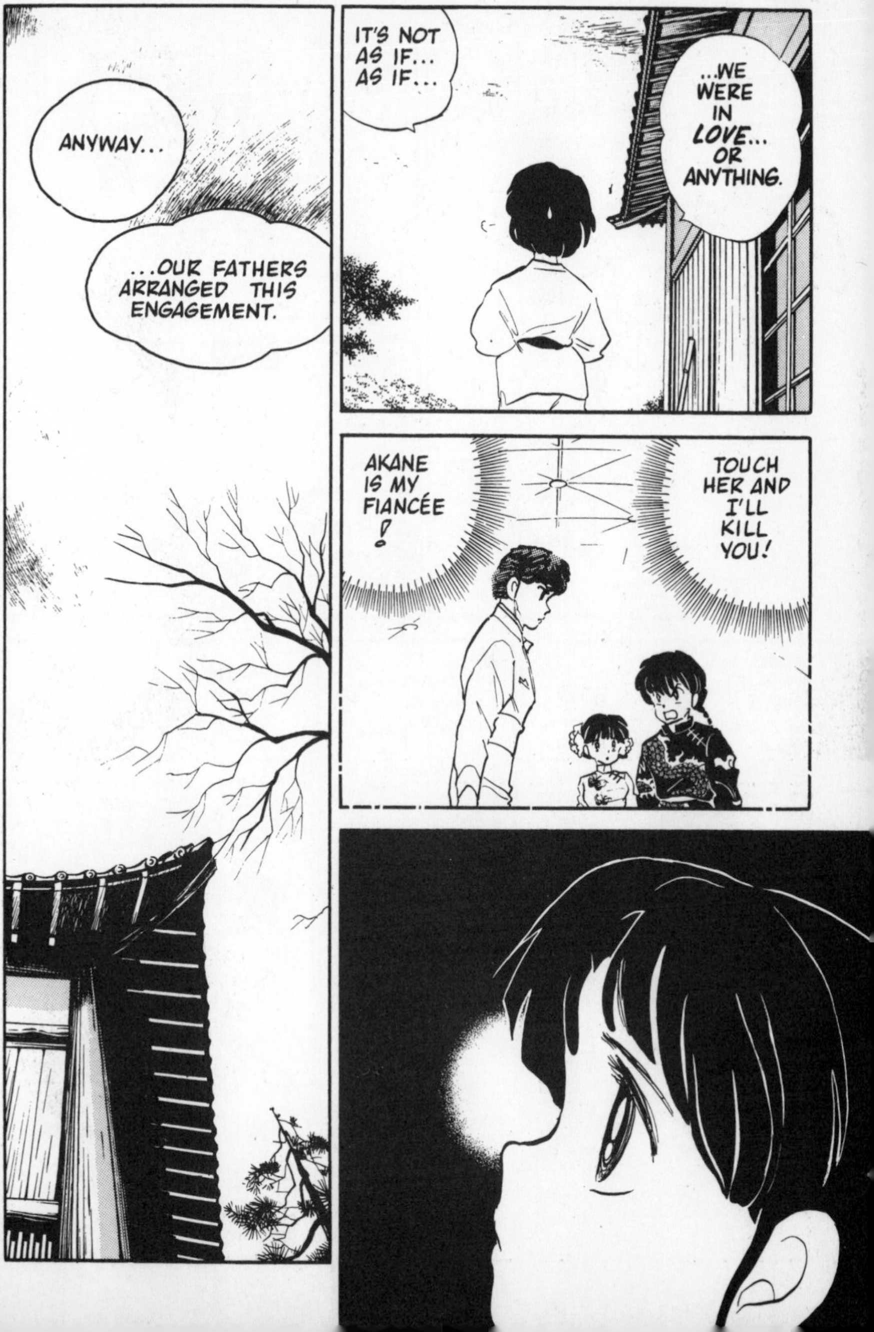
ANYWAY...
...OUR FATHERS ARRANGED THIS ENGAGEMENT.
IT'S NOT AS IF... AS IF...
...WE WERE IN LOVE... OR ANYTHING.
AKANE IS MY FIANCÉE!
TOUCH HER AND I'LL KILL YOU!

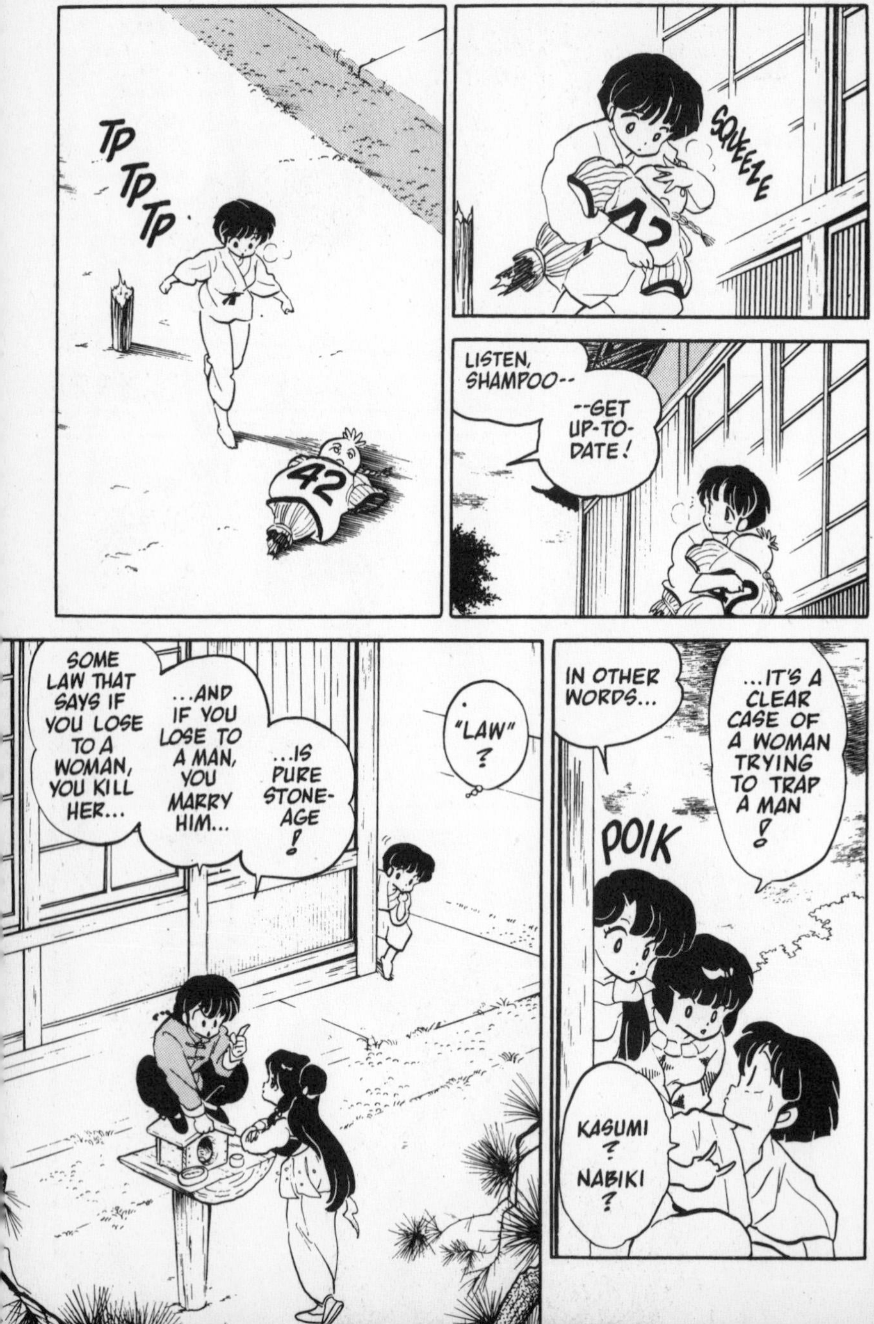
TP TP TP TP
SQUEEZE
LISTEN, SHAMPOO--
--GET UP-TO-DATE!
SOME LAW THAT SAYS IF YOU LOSE TO A WOMAN, YOU KILL HER...
...AND IF YOU LOSE TO A MAN, YOU MARRY HIM...
...IS PURE STONE-AGE!
"LAW"?
IN OTHER WORDS...
...IT'S A CLEAR CASE OF A WOMAN TRYING TO TRAP A MAN!
POIK
KASUMI? NABIKI?

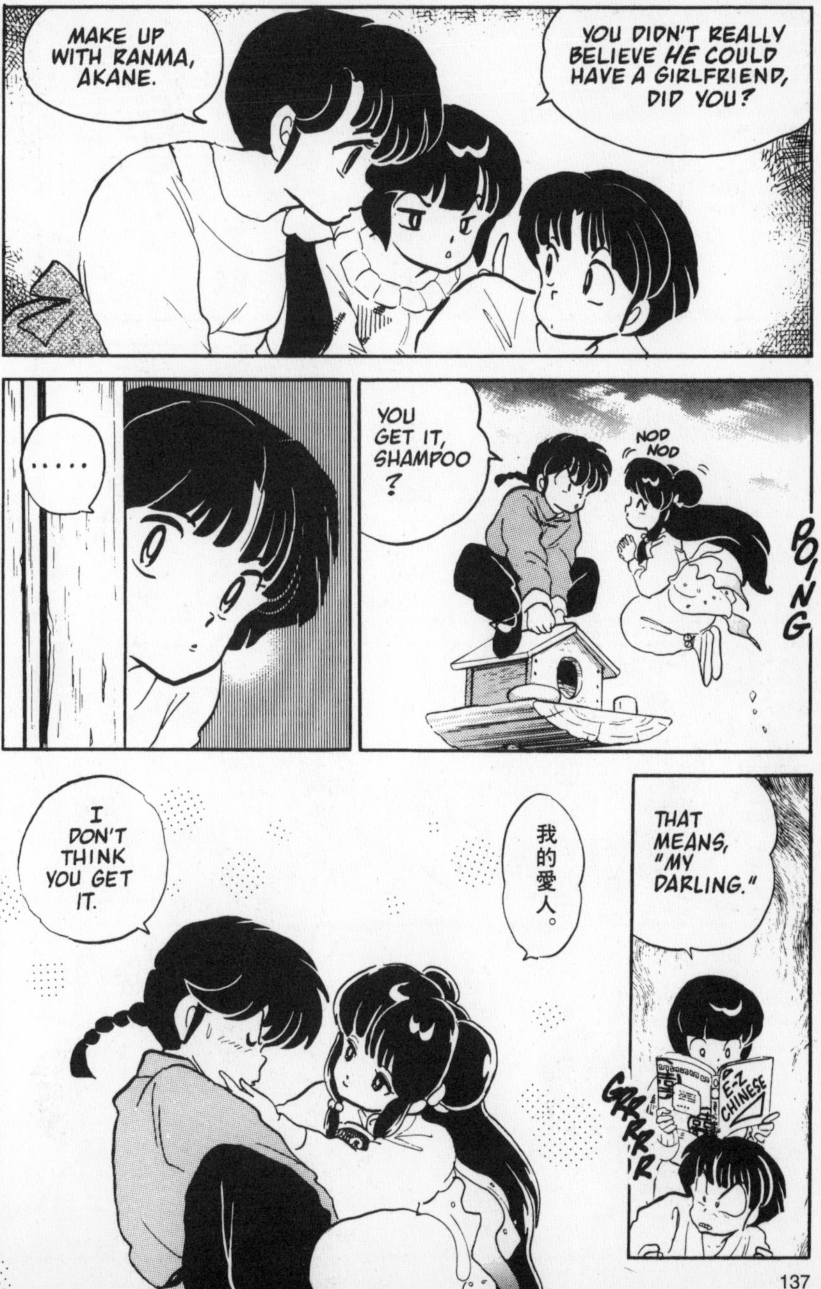
MAKE UP WITH RANMA, AKANE.
YOU DIDN'T REALLY BELIEVE HE COULD HAVE A GIRLFRIEND, DID YOU?
.....
YOU GET IT, SHAMPOO?
NOD NOD
POING
I DON'T THINK YOU GET IT.
我的愛人。
THAT MEANS, "MY DARLING."
GRRRRR
E-Z CHINESE

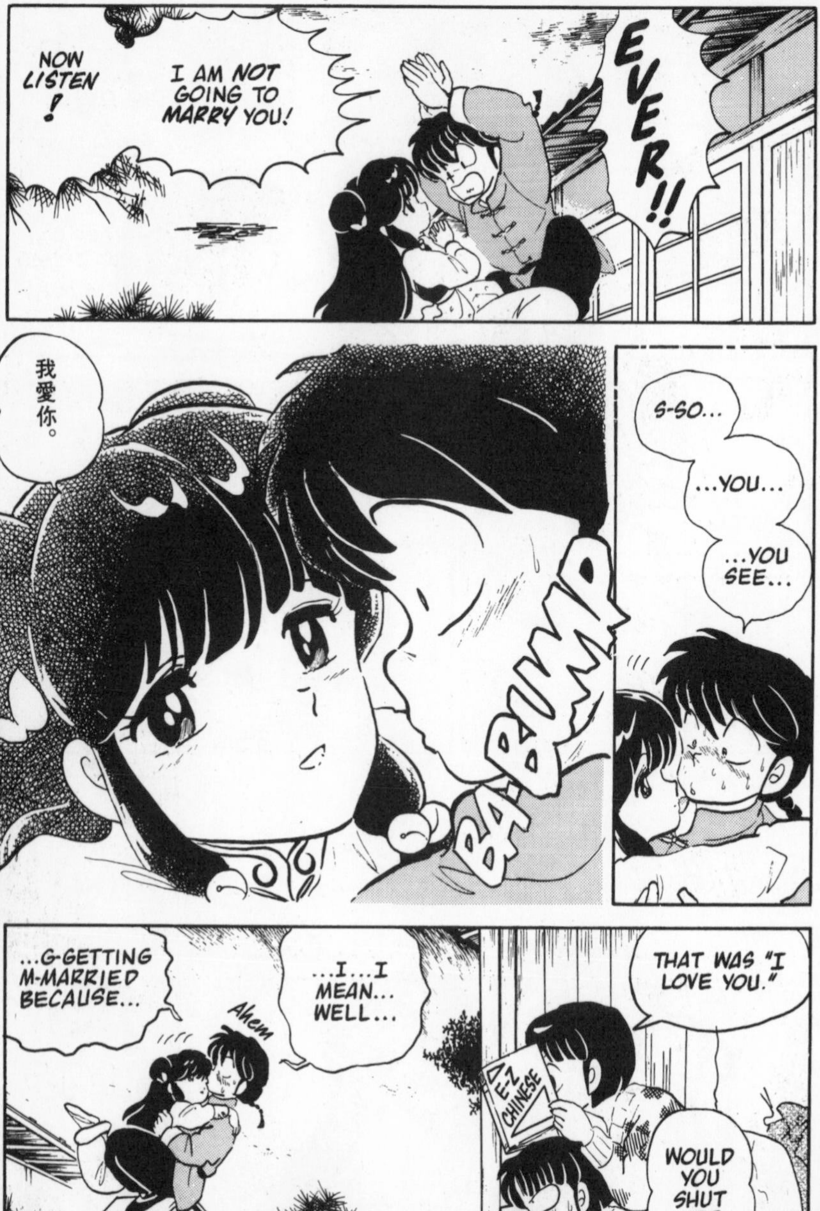
NOW LISTEN!
I AM NOT GOING TO MARRY YOU!
EVER!!
我愛你。
BA-BUMP
S-SO...
...YOU...
...YOU SEE...
...G-GETTING M-MARRIED BECAUSE...
Ahem
...I...I MEAN... WELL...
THAT WAS "I LOVE YOU."
E-Z CHINESE
WOULD YOU SHUT UP?

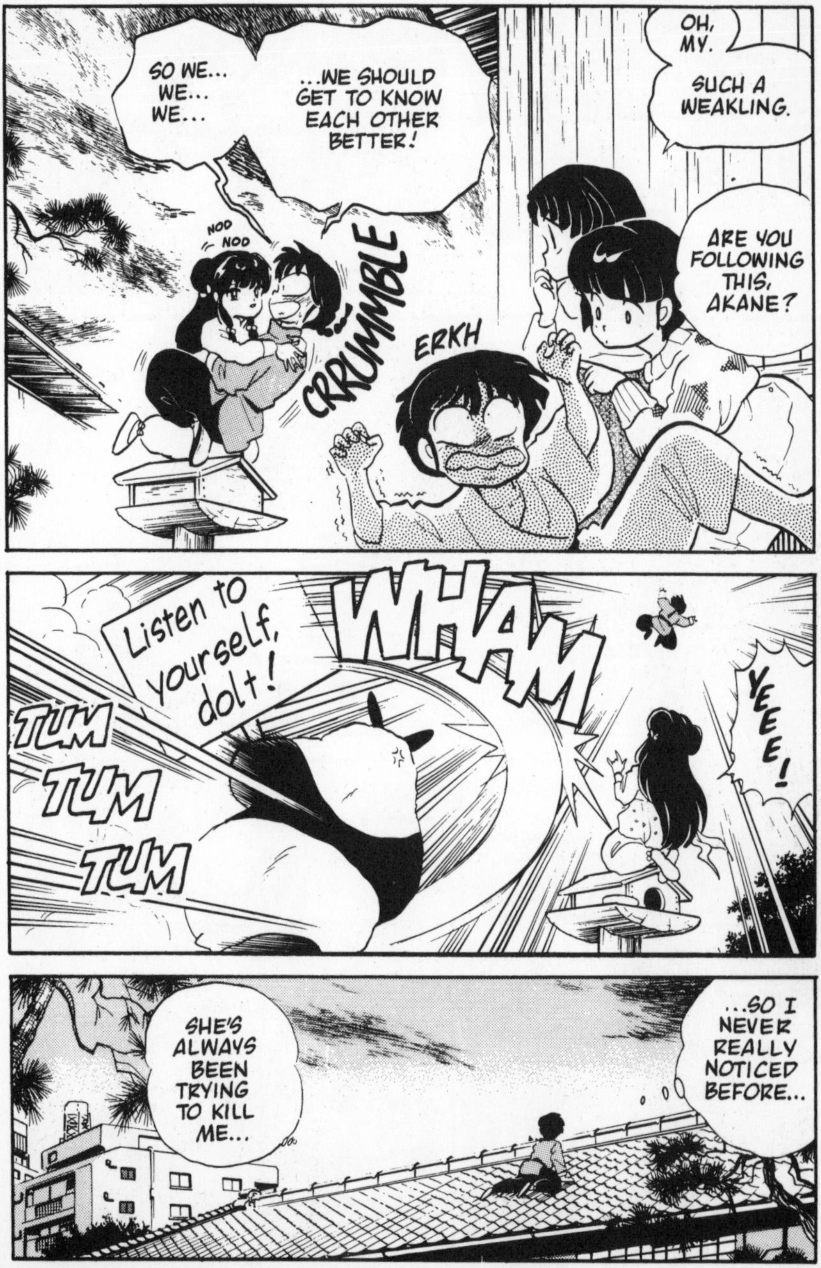
SO WE... WE... WE...
...WE SHOULD GET TO KNOW EACH OTHER BETTER!
NOD NOD
CRRUMMBLE
OH, MY. SUCH A WEAKLING.
ERKH
ARE YOU FOLLOWING THIS, AKANE?
Listen to yourself, dolt!
WHAM
TUM TUM TUM
YEEEE!
SHE'S ALWAYS BEEN TRYING TO KILL ME...
...SO I NEVER REALLY NOTICED BEFORE...

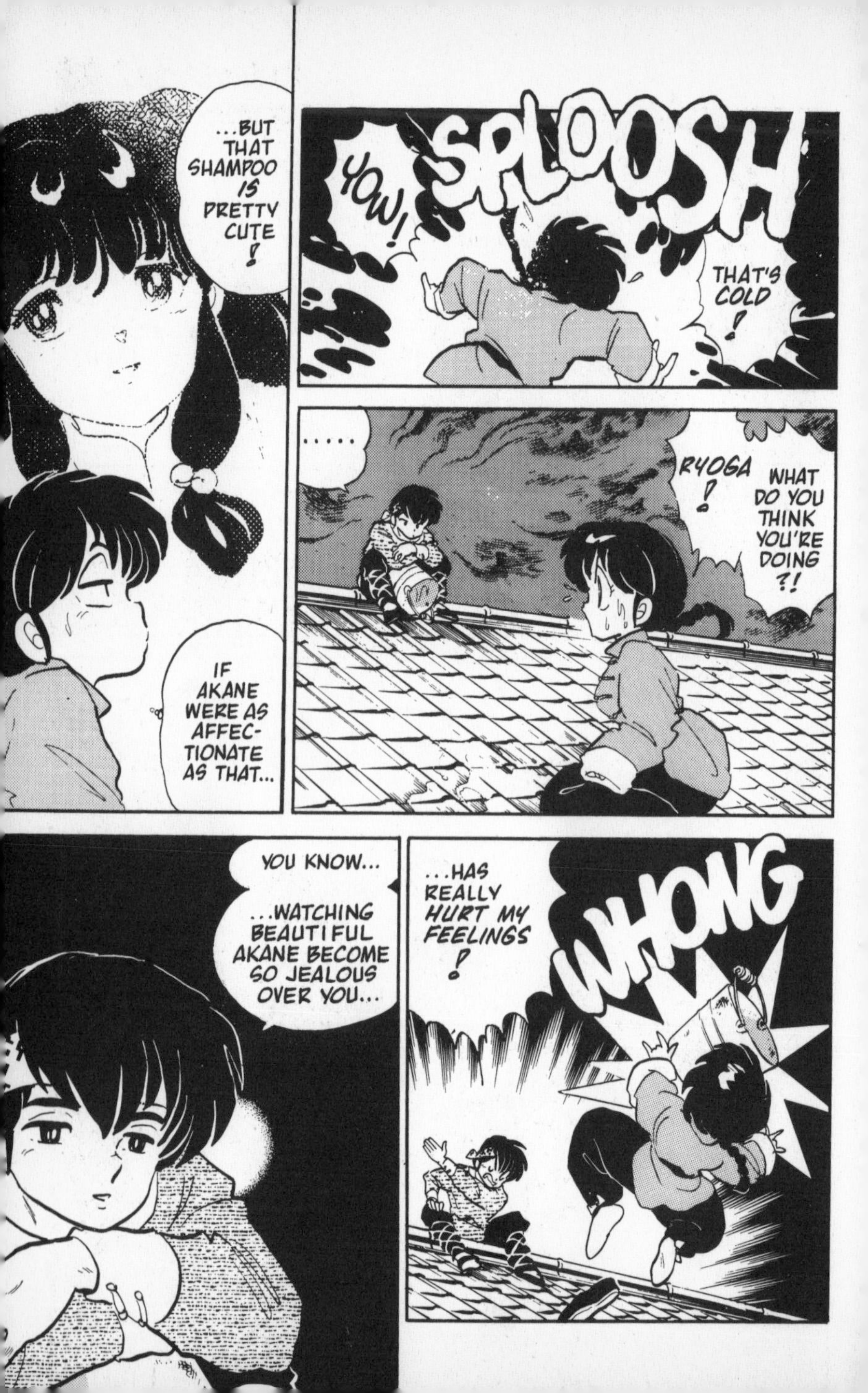
...BUT THAT SHAMPOO IS PRETTY CUTE!
IF AKANE WERE AS AFFECTIONATE AS THAT...
YOW!
SPLOOSH
THAT'S COLD!
......
RYOGA!
WHAT DO YOU THINK YOU'RE DOING?!
YOU KNOW...
...WATCHING BEAUTIFUL AKANE BECOME SO JEALOUS OVER YOU...
...HAS REALLY HURT MY FEELINGS!
WHONG

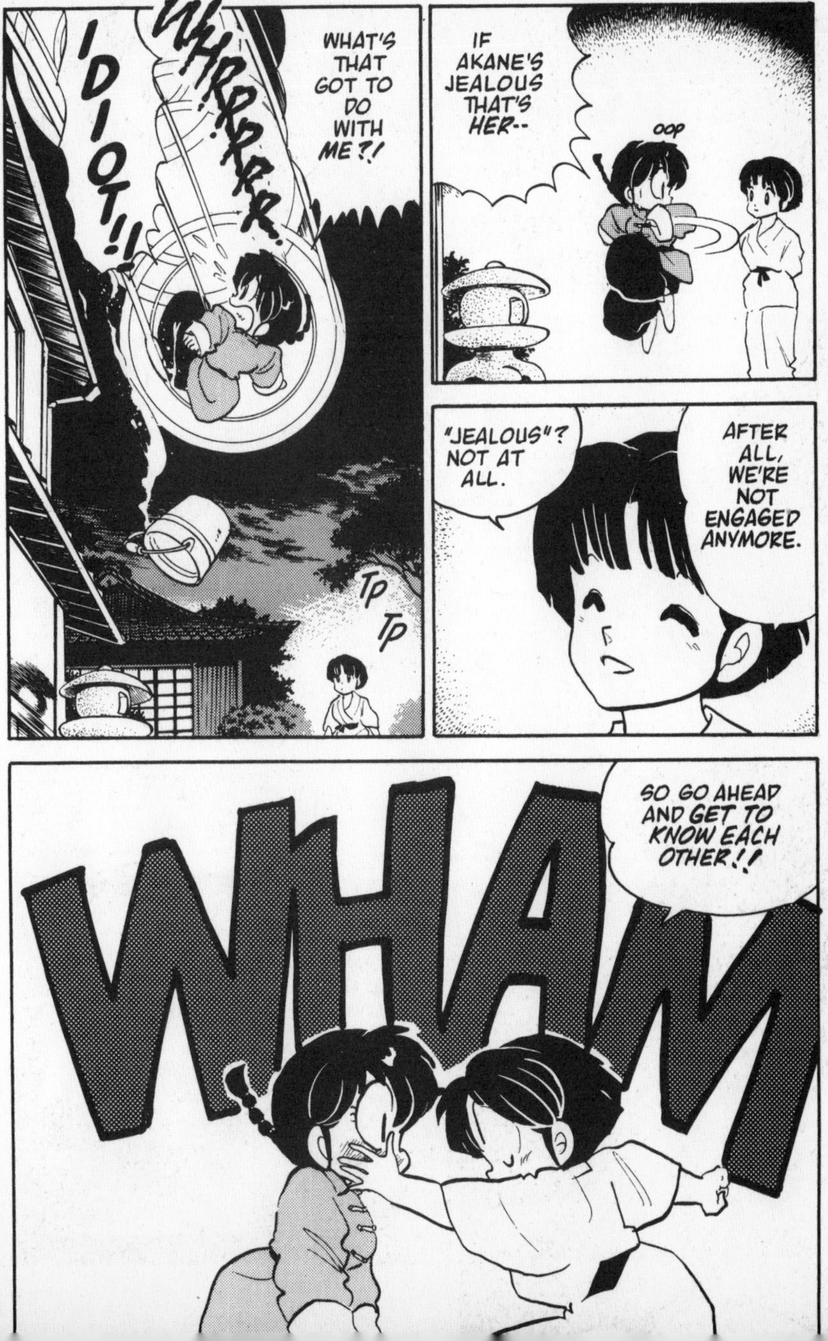
IDIOT!!
WHRRRRRRR
WHAT'S THAT GOT TO DO WITH ME?!
TP TP
IF AKANE'S JEALOUS THAT'S HER--
OOP
"JEALOUS"? NOT AT ALL.
AFTER ALL, WE'RE NOT ENGAGED ANYMORE.
WHAM
SO GO AHEAD AND GET TO KNOW EACH OTHER!!

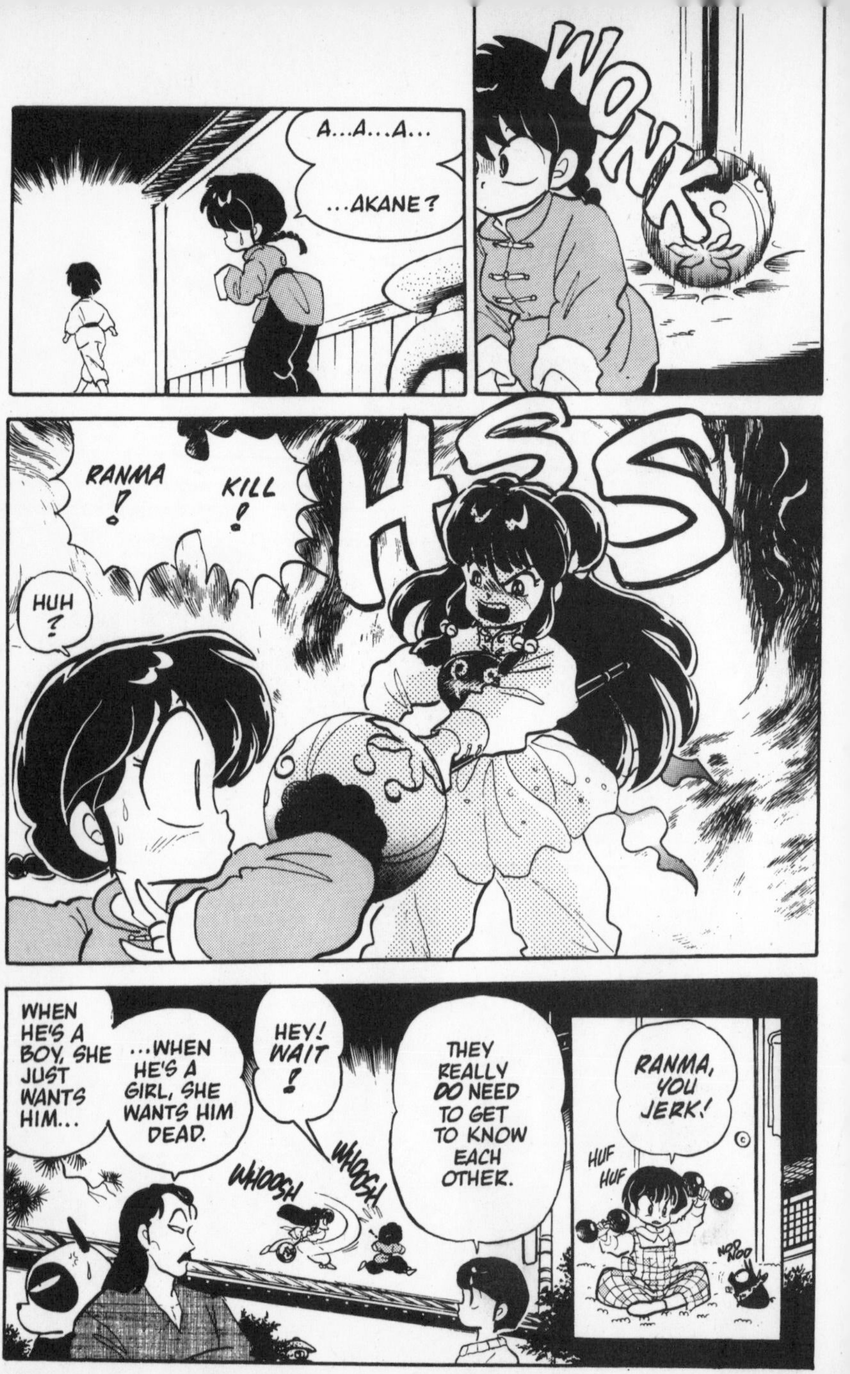
A...A...A...
...AKANE?
WONK
HSS
RANMA!
KILL!
HUH?
WHEN HE'S A BOY, SHE JUST WANTS HIM...
...WHEN HE'S A GIRL, SHE WANTS HIM DEAD.
HEY! WAIT!
WHOOSH
WHOOSH
THEY REALLY DO NEED TO GET TO KNOW EACH OTHER.
RANMA, YOU JERK!
HUF HUF
NOD NOD

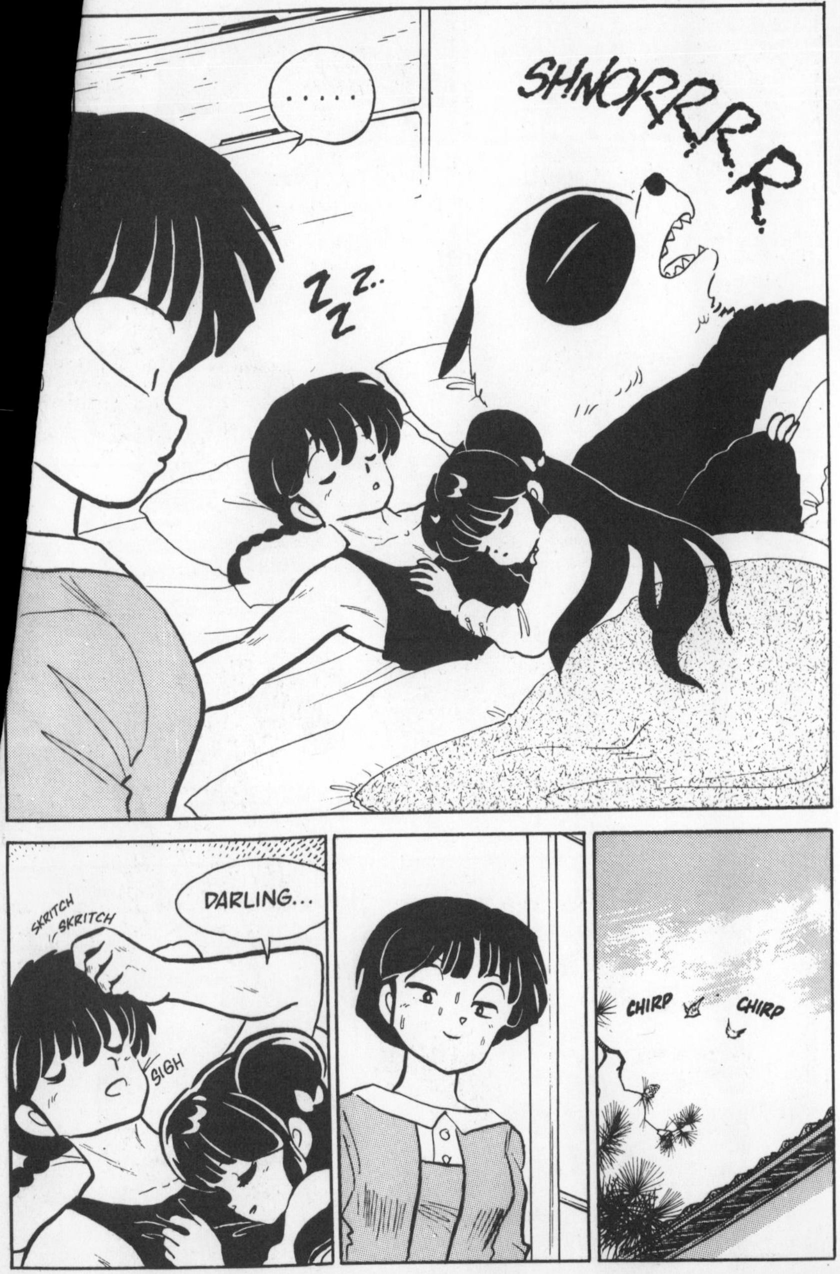
......
SHNORRR.R.R
Z Z Z..
SKRITCH SKRITCH
DARLING...
SIGH
CHIRP CHIRP

Part 8

AKANE GETS SHAMPOOED

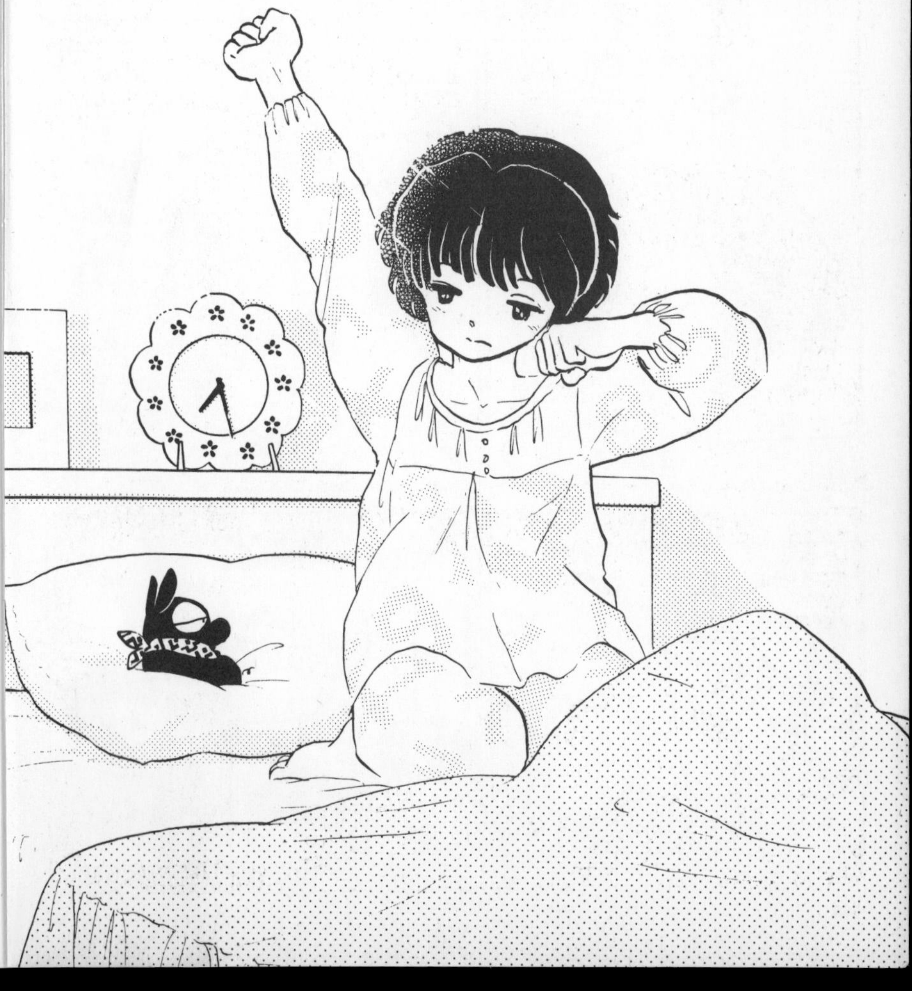

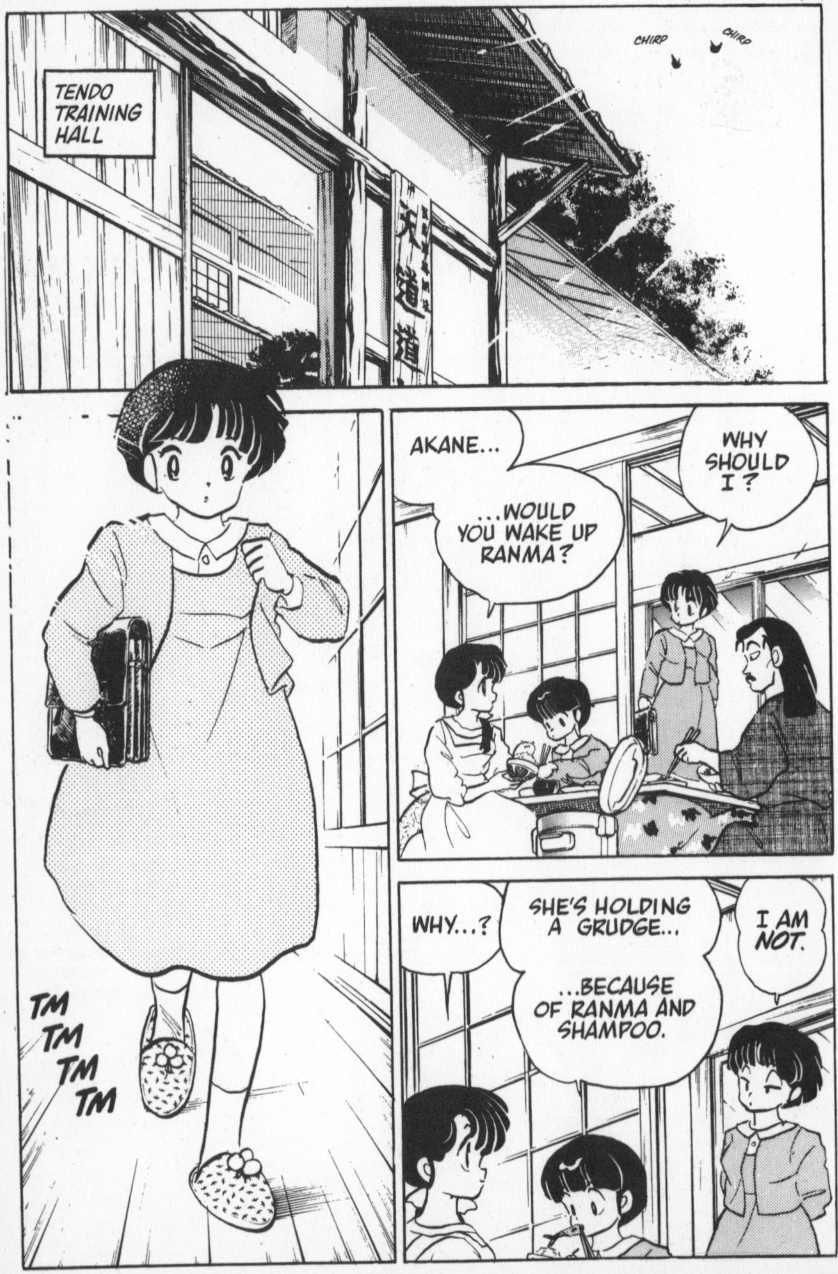

TENDO TRAINING HALL
CHIRP
CHIRP
TM TM TM TM
AKANE...
...WOULD YOU WAKE UP RANMA?
WHY SHOULD I?
WHY...?
SHE'S HOLDING A GRUDGE...
...BECAUSE OF RANMA AND SHAMPOO.
I AM NOT.

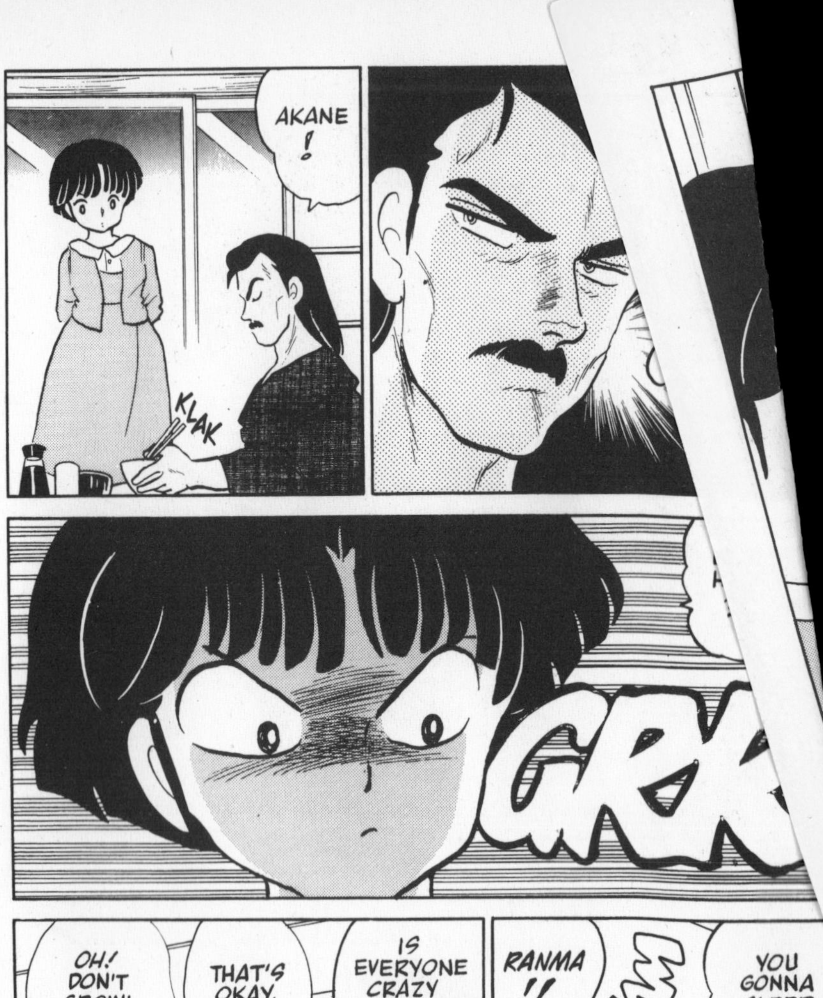

AKANE!
KLAK
GRR
OH! DON'T GROWL AT ME LIKE THAT!
THAT'S OKAY, DADDY, THAT'S OKAY.
IS EVERYONE CRAZY HERE BUT ME?
BOO HOO
BOO HOO HOO
RANMA!!
WHAM
YOU GONNA SLEEP ALL DAY?!

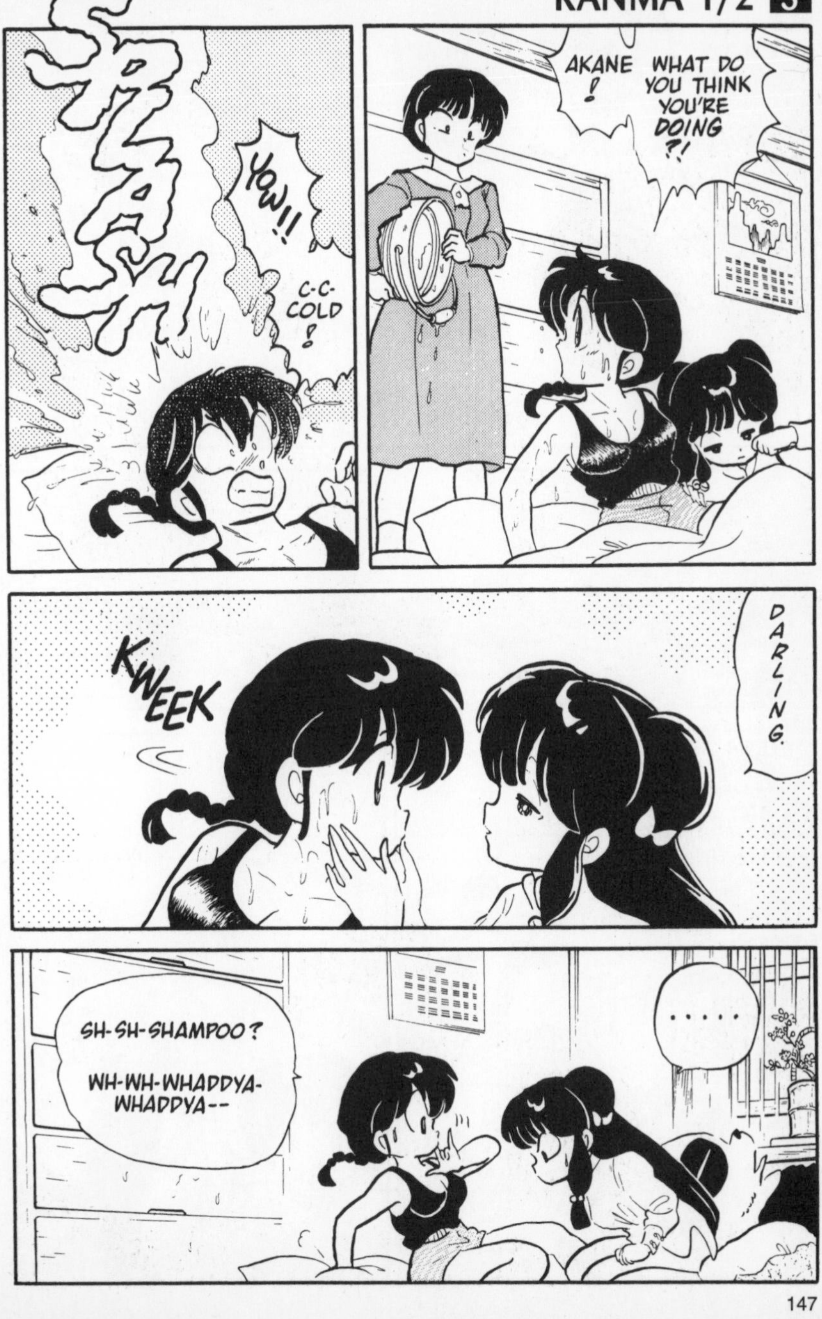
SPLASH
YOW!!
C-C-COLD!
AKANE!
WHAT DO YOU THINK YOU'RE DOING?!
KWEEK
DARLING.
SH-SH-SHAMPOO?
WH-WH-WHADDYA-WHADDYA--
.....

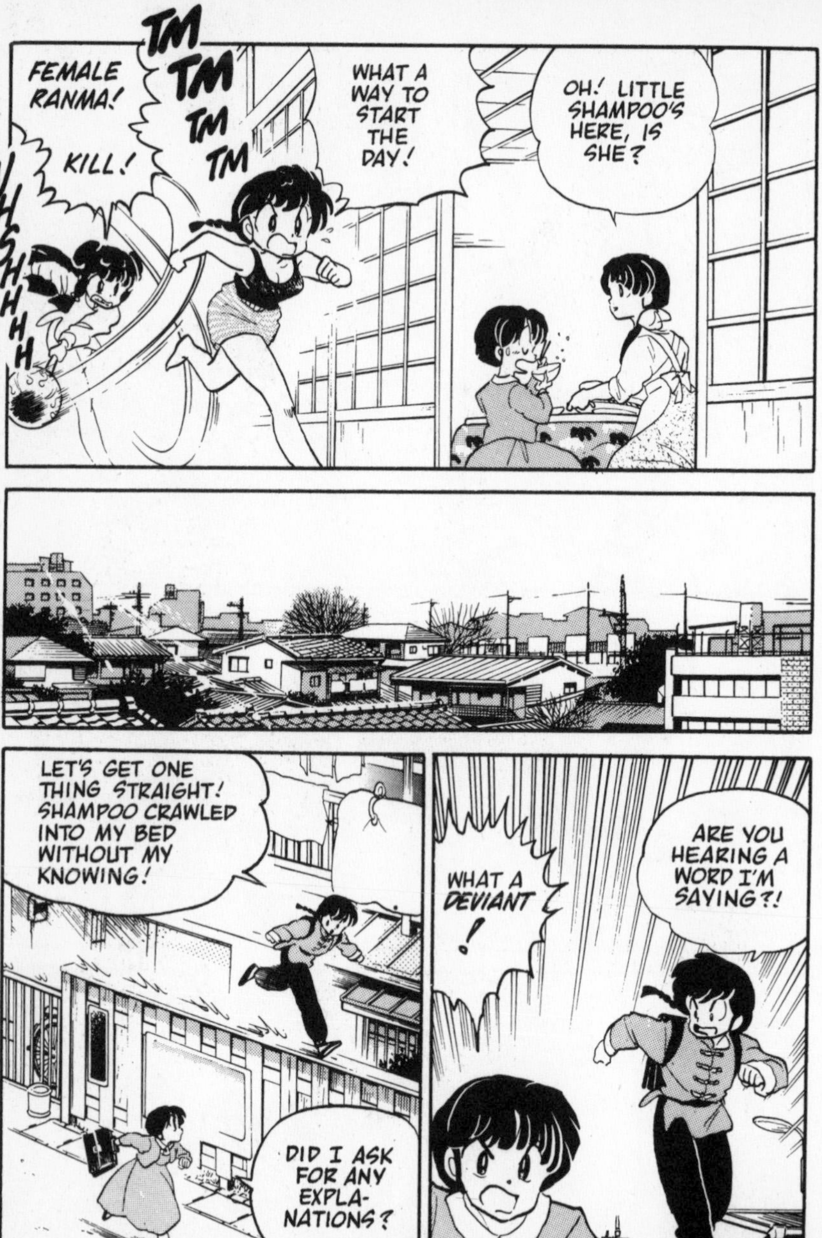
FEMALE RANMA!
KILL!
TM TM TM TM
WHSHHHHH
WHAT A WAY TO START THE DAY!
OH! LITTLE SHAMPOO'S HERE, IS SHE?
LET'S GET ONE THING STRAIGHT! SHAMPOO CRAWLED INTO MY BED WITHOUT MY KNOWING!
DID I ASK FOR ANY EXPLA-NATIONS?
WHAT A DEVIANT!
ARE YOU HEARING A WORD I'M SAYING?!

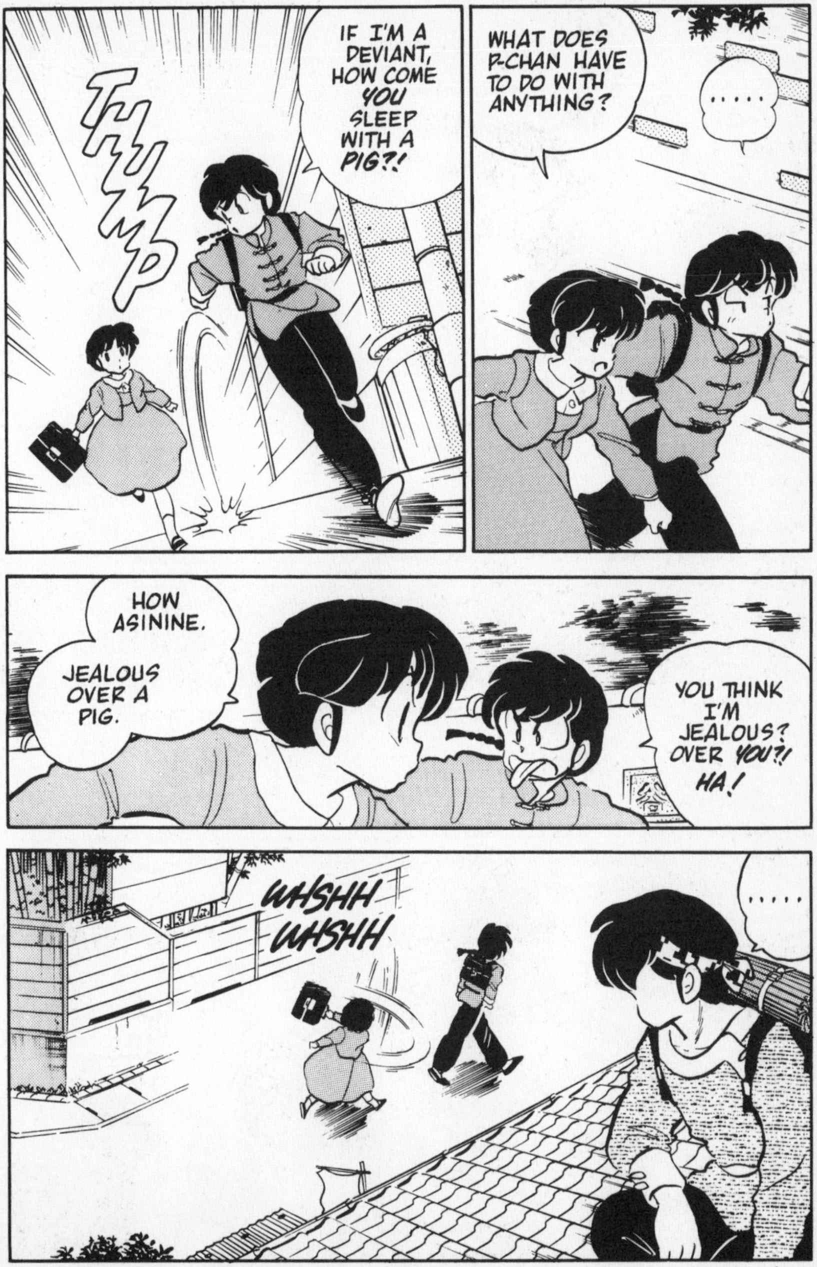
THUMP
IF I'M A DEVIANT, HOW COME YOU SLEEP WITH A PIG?!
WHAT DOES P-CHAN HAVE TO DO WITH ANYTHING?
.....
HOW ASININE.
JEALOUS OVER A PIG.
YOU THINK I'M JEALOUS? OVER YOU?! HA!
WHSHH WHSHH
.....

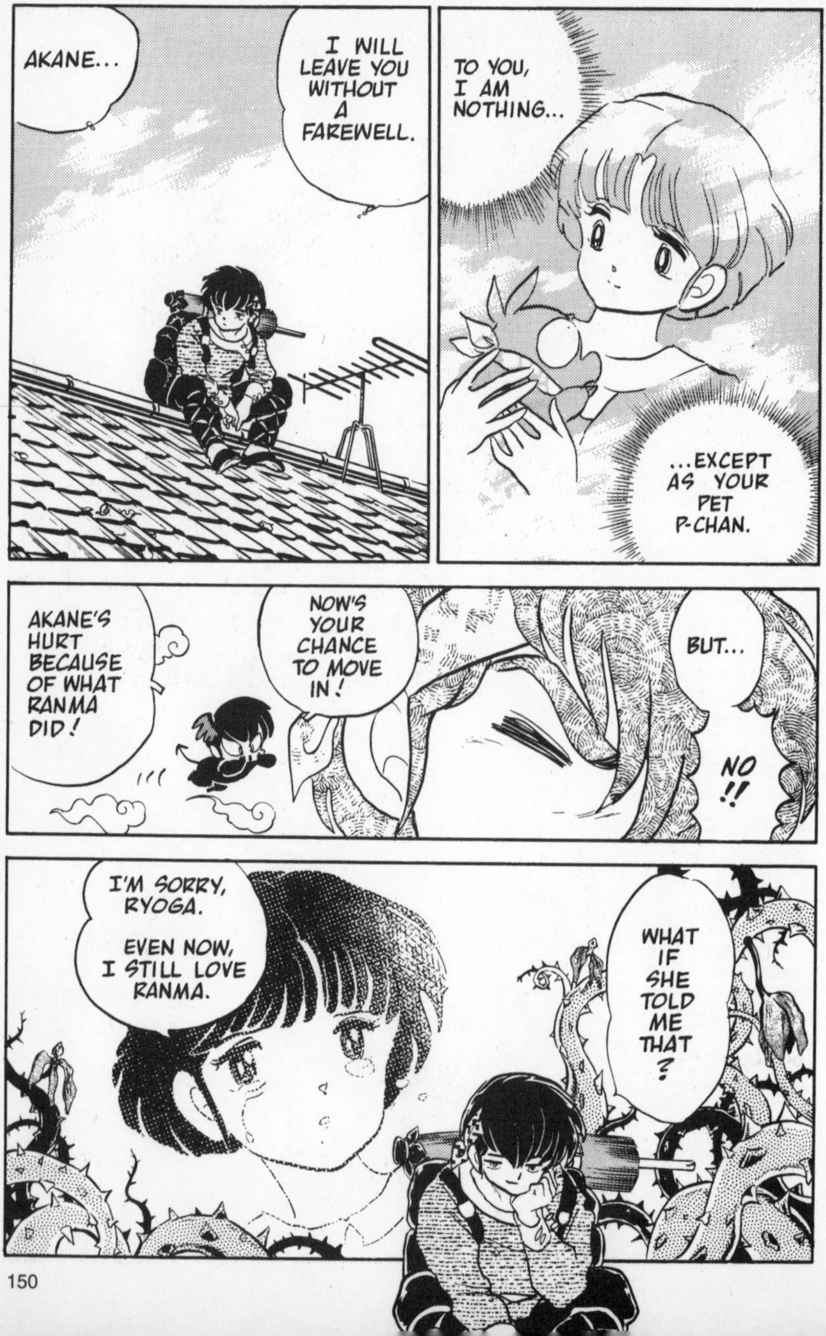
AKANE...
I WILL LEAVE YOU WITHOUT A FAREWELL.
TO YOU, I AM NOTHING...
...EXCEPT AS YOUR PET P-CHAN.
AKANE'S HURT BECAUSE OF WHAT RANMA DID!
NOW'S YOUR CHANCE TO MOVE IN!
BUT...
NO!!
I'M SORRY, RYOGA.
EVEN NOW, I STILL LOVE RANMA.
WHAT IF SHE TOLD ME THAT?

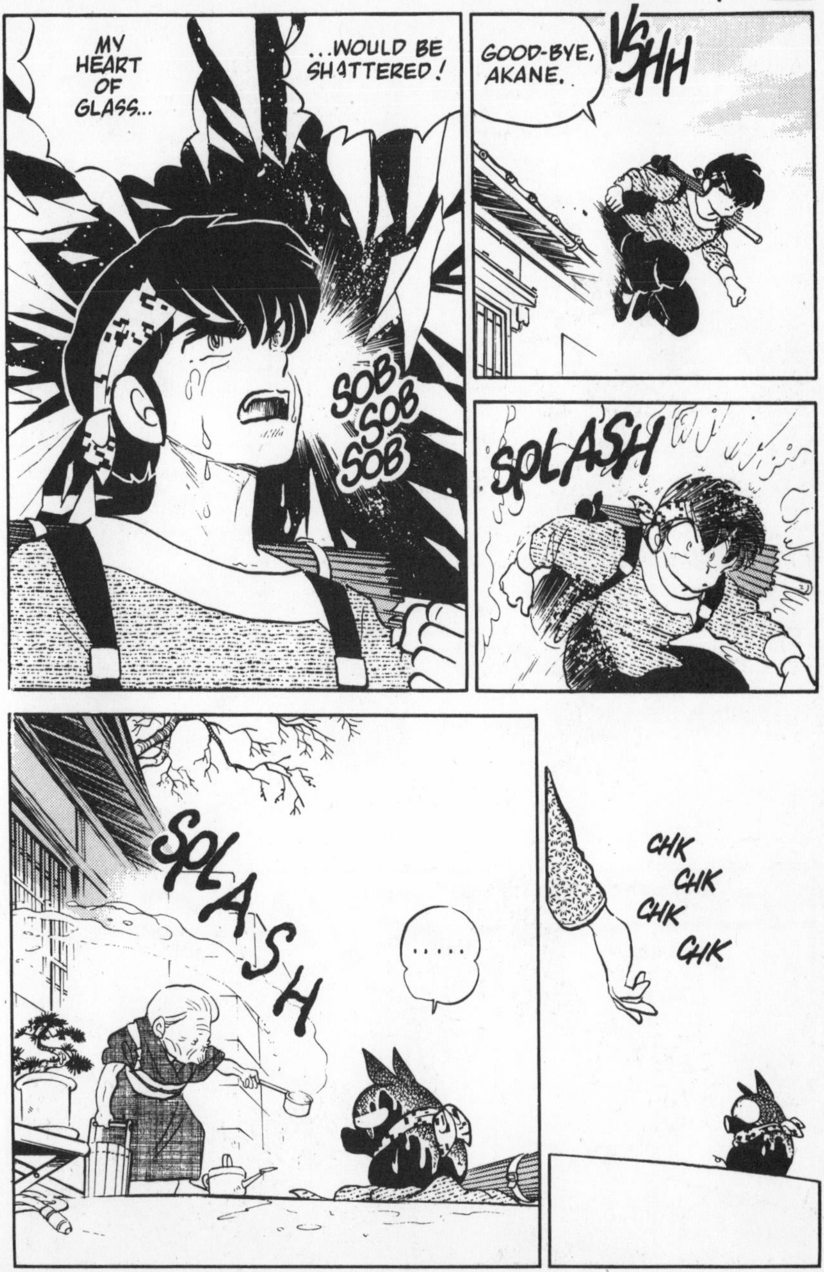
MY HEART OF GLASS...
...WOULD BE SHATTERED!
SOB SOB SOB
GOOD-BYE, AKANE.
VSHH
SPLASH
SPLASH
.....
CHK CHK CHK CHK

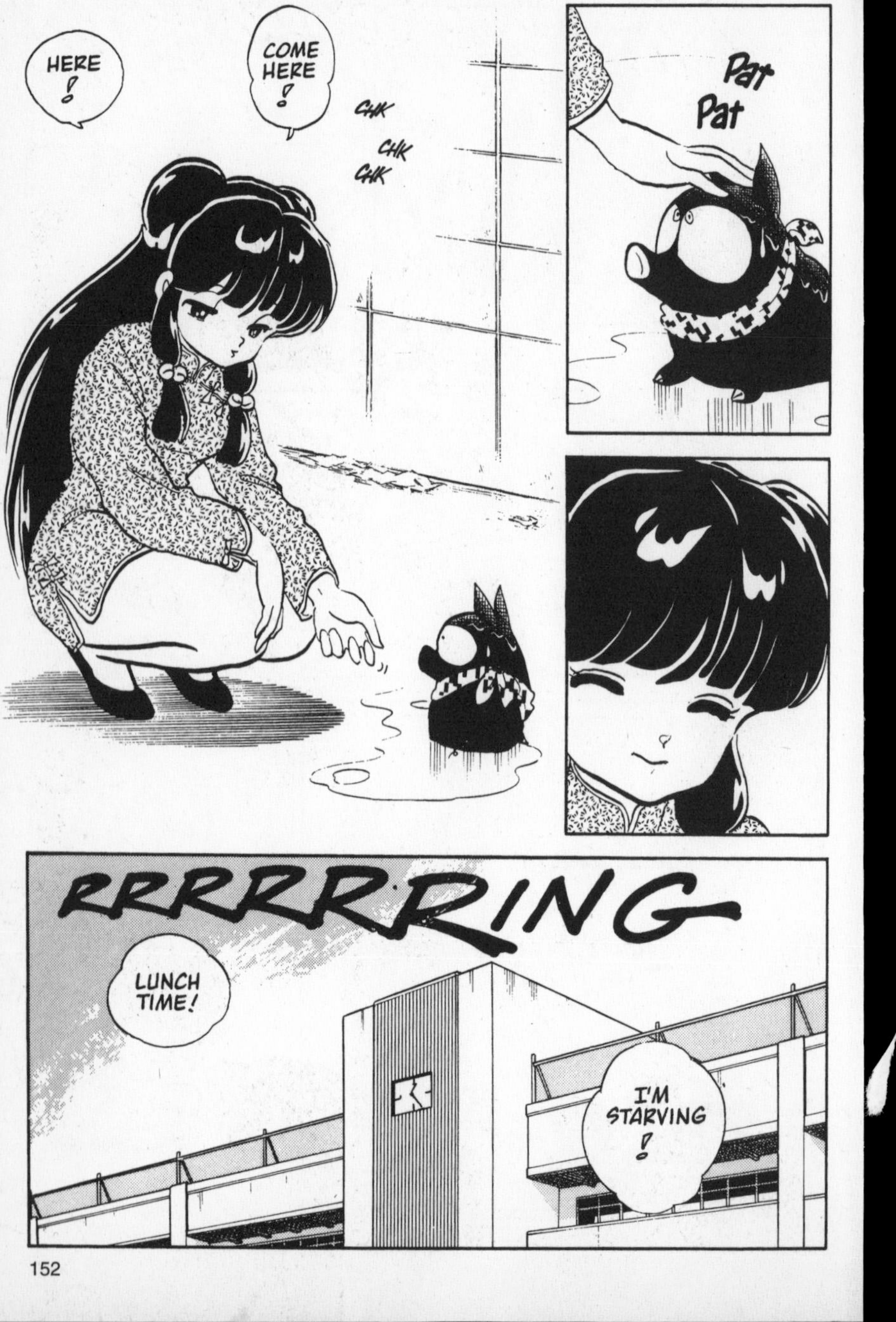
HERE!
COME HERE!
CHK
CHK
CHK
Pat
Pat
RRRRRRING
LUNCH TIME!
I'M STARVING!

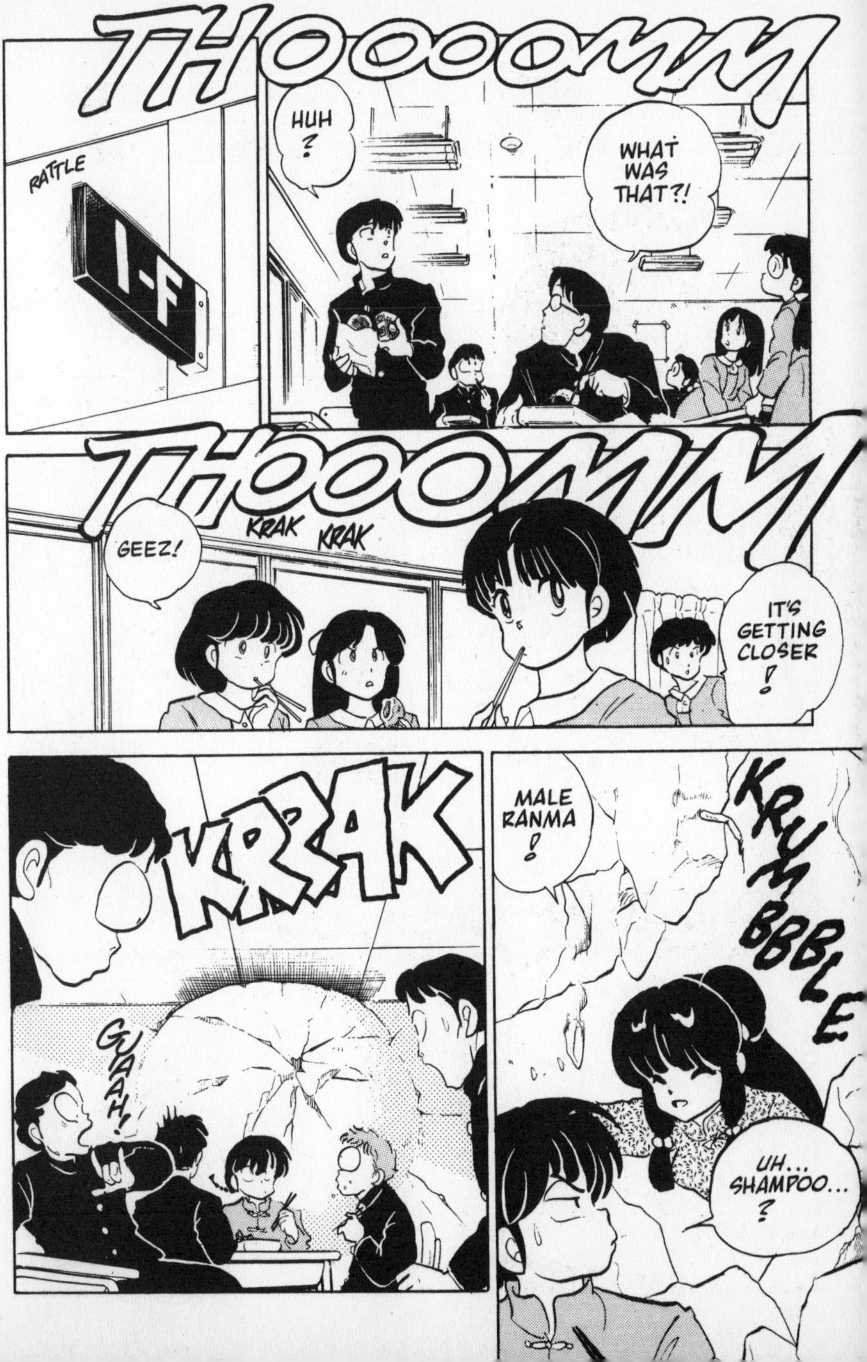
THOOOOMM
RATTLE
I-F
HUH?
WHAT WAS THAT?!
THOOOMM
GEEZ!
KRAK KRAK
IT'S GETTING CLOSER!
KRAK
GUAAAH!
MALE RANMA!
KRUMBBBLE
UH... SHAMPOO...?

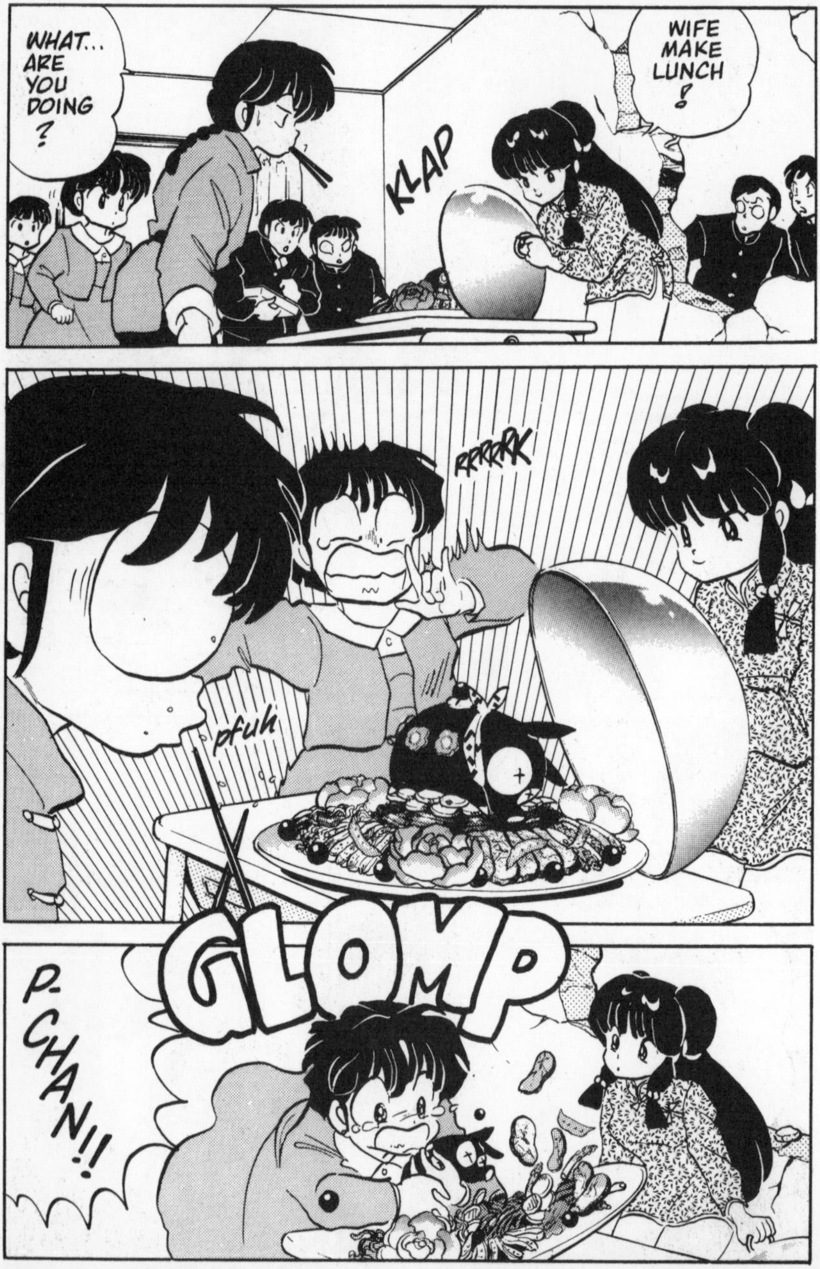
WHAT... ARE YOU DOING?
WIFE MAKE LUNCH!
KLAP
RRRRRK
pfuh
GLOMP
P-CHAN!!

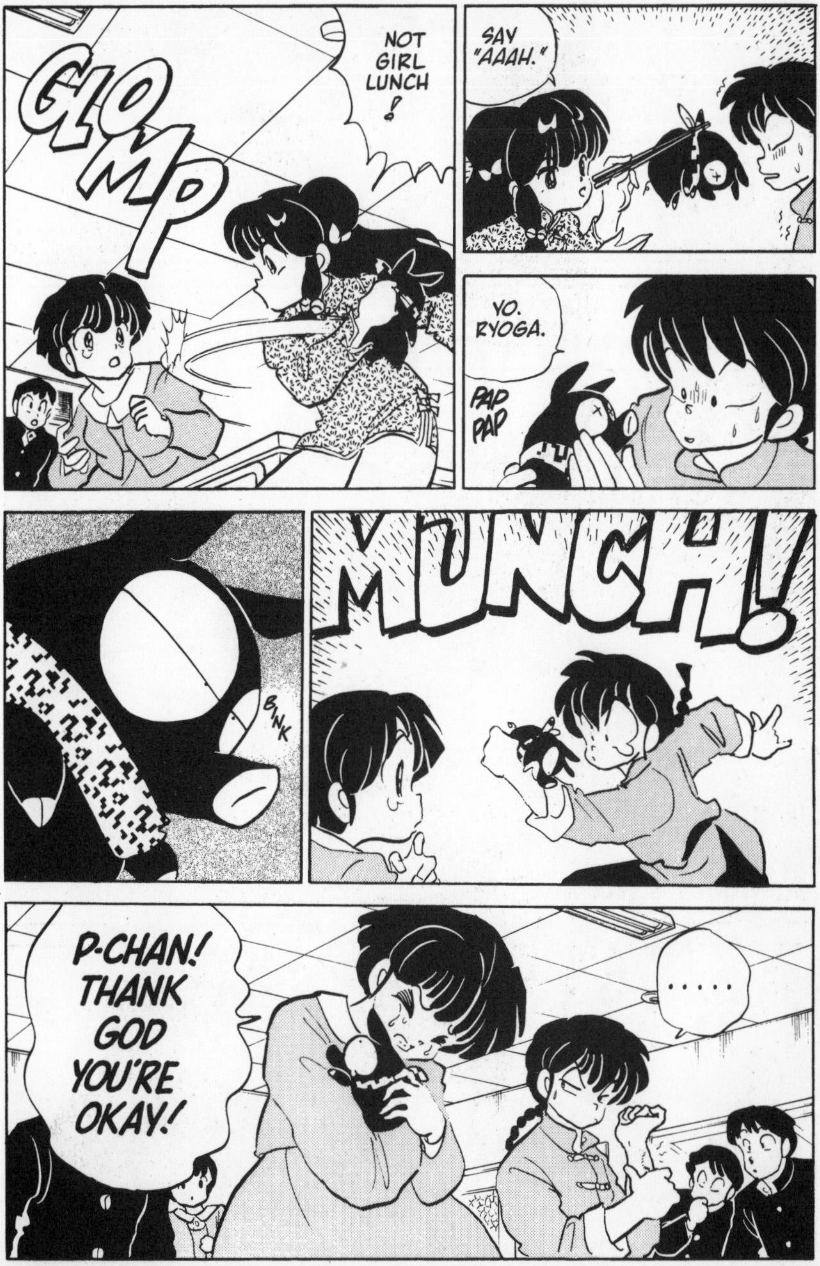
GLOMP
NOT GIRL LUNCH!
SAY "AAAH."
YO. RYOGA.
PAP PAP
BINK
MUNCH!
P-CHAN! THANK GOD YOU'RE OKAY!
. . . . .

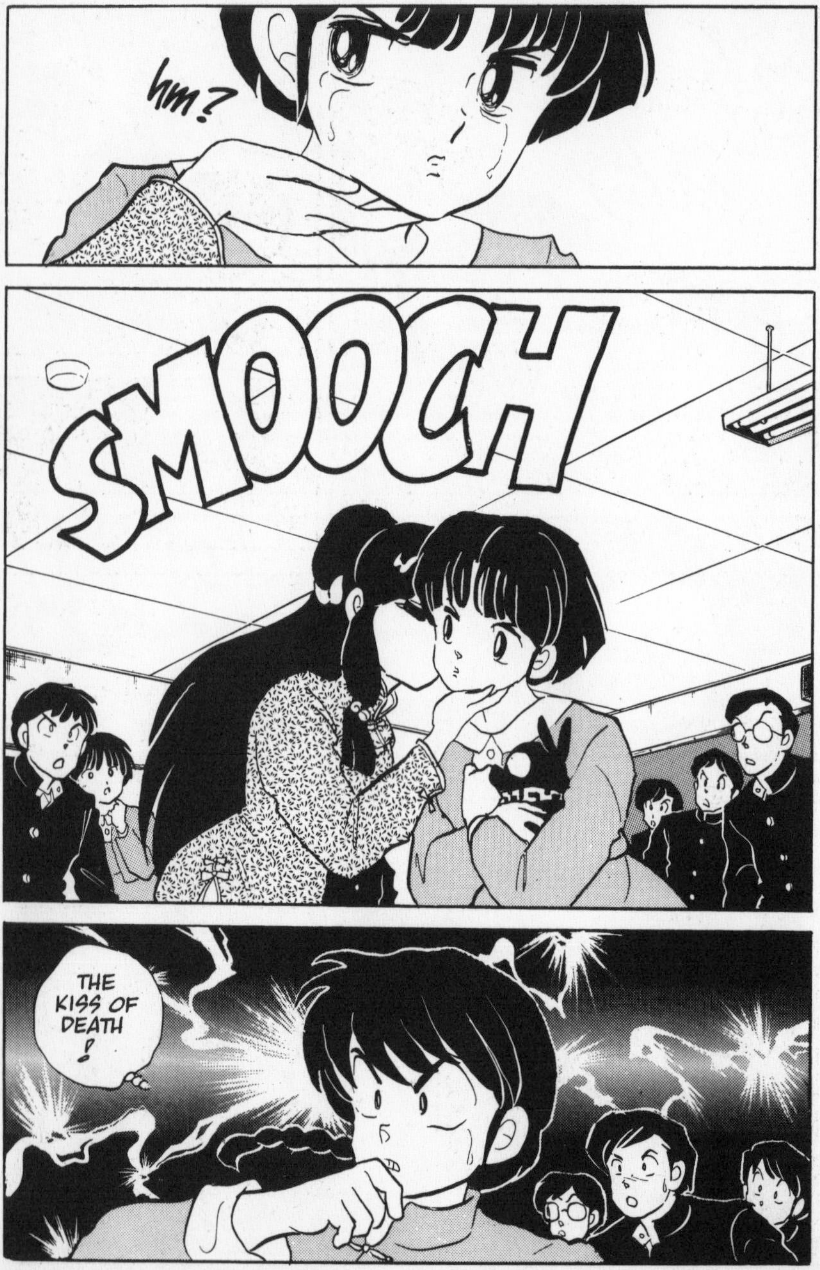
hm?
SMOOCH
THE KISS OF DEATH!

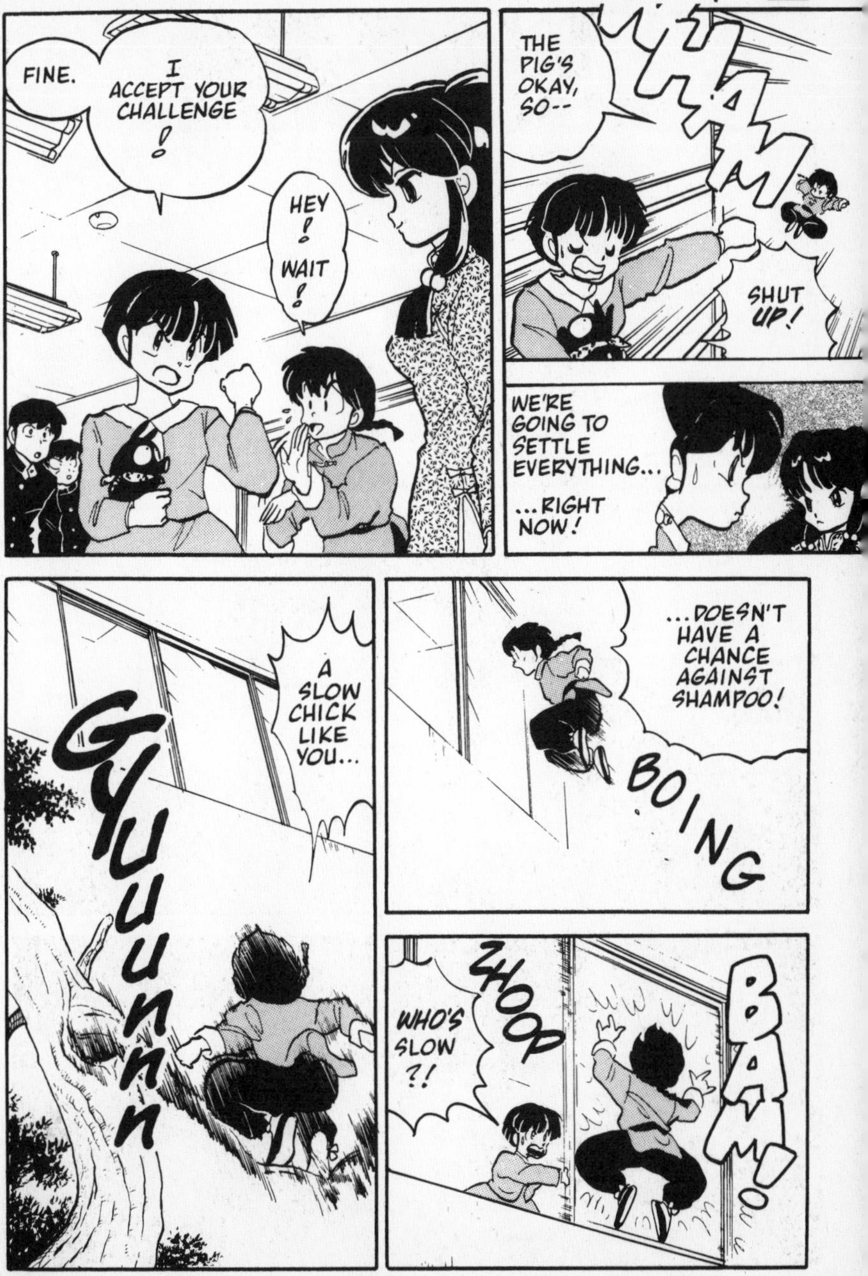
FINE.
I ACCEPT YOUR CHALLENGE!
HEY! WAIT!
THE PIG'S OKAY, SO--
WHAM
SHUT UP!
WE'RE GOING TO SETTLE EVERYTHING...
...RIGHT NOW!
A SLOW CHICK LIKE YOU...
GYUUUNNN
...DOESN'T HAVE A CHANCE AGAINST SHAMPOO!
BOING
WHO'S SLOW?!
ZHOOP
BAMOOOM

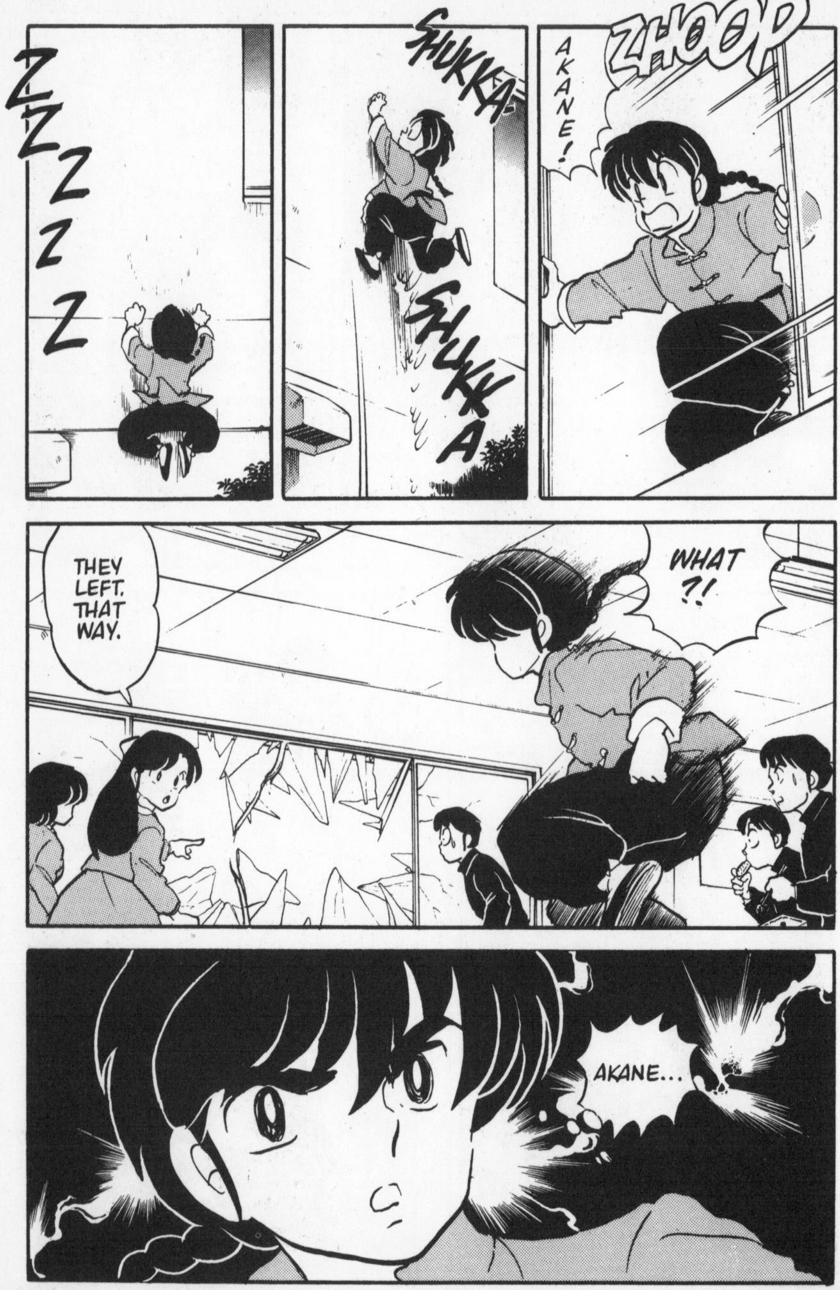
ZZZZZZ
SHUKKA
SHUKKA
AKANE!
ZHOOP
THEY LEFT. THAT WAY.
WHAT ?!
AKANE...

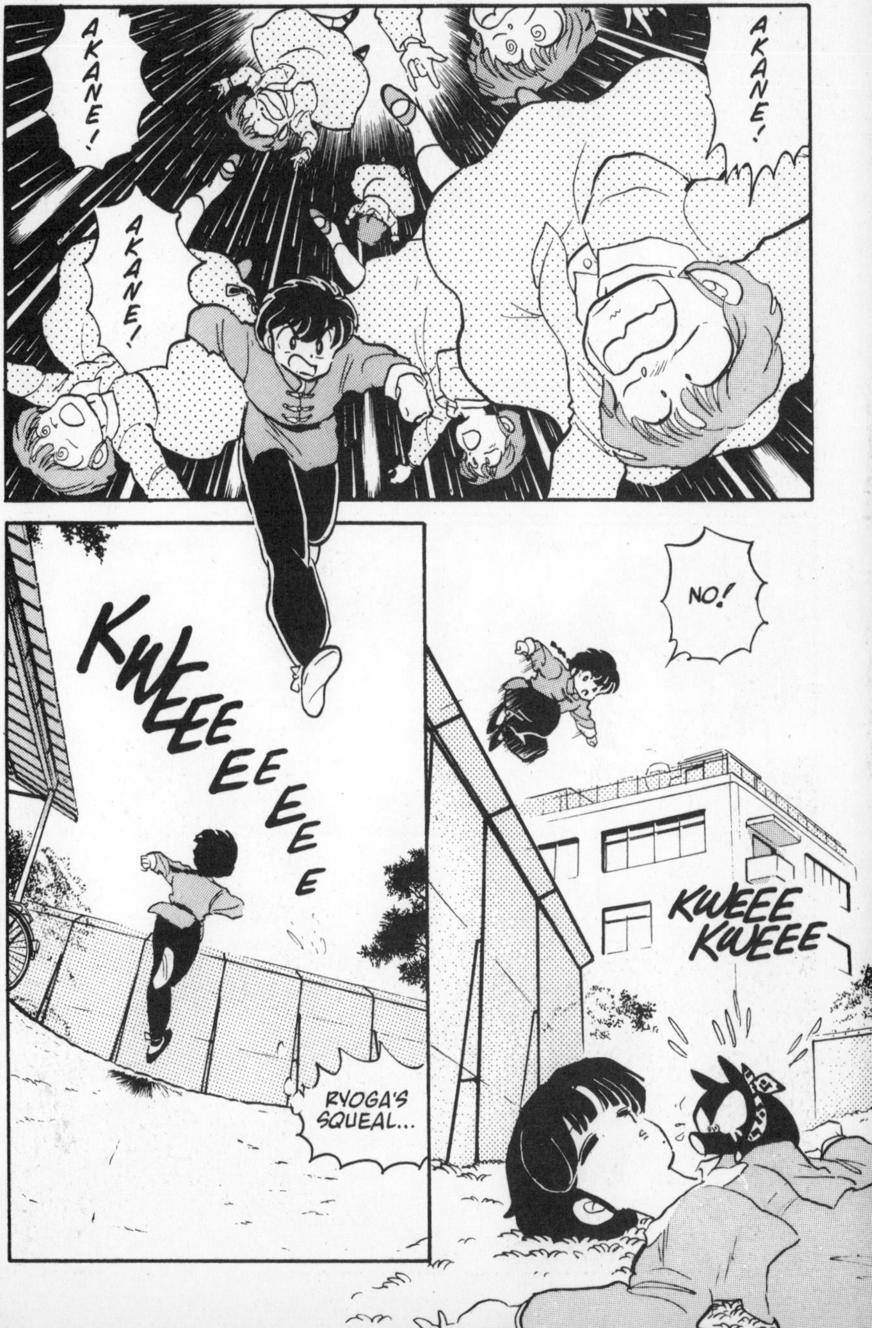
AKANE!
AKANE!
AKANE!
KWEEEEEEEEE
RYOGA'S SQUEAL...
NO!
KWEEEE KWEEEE

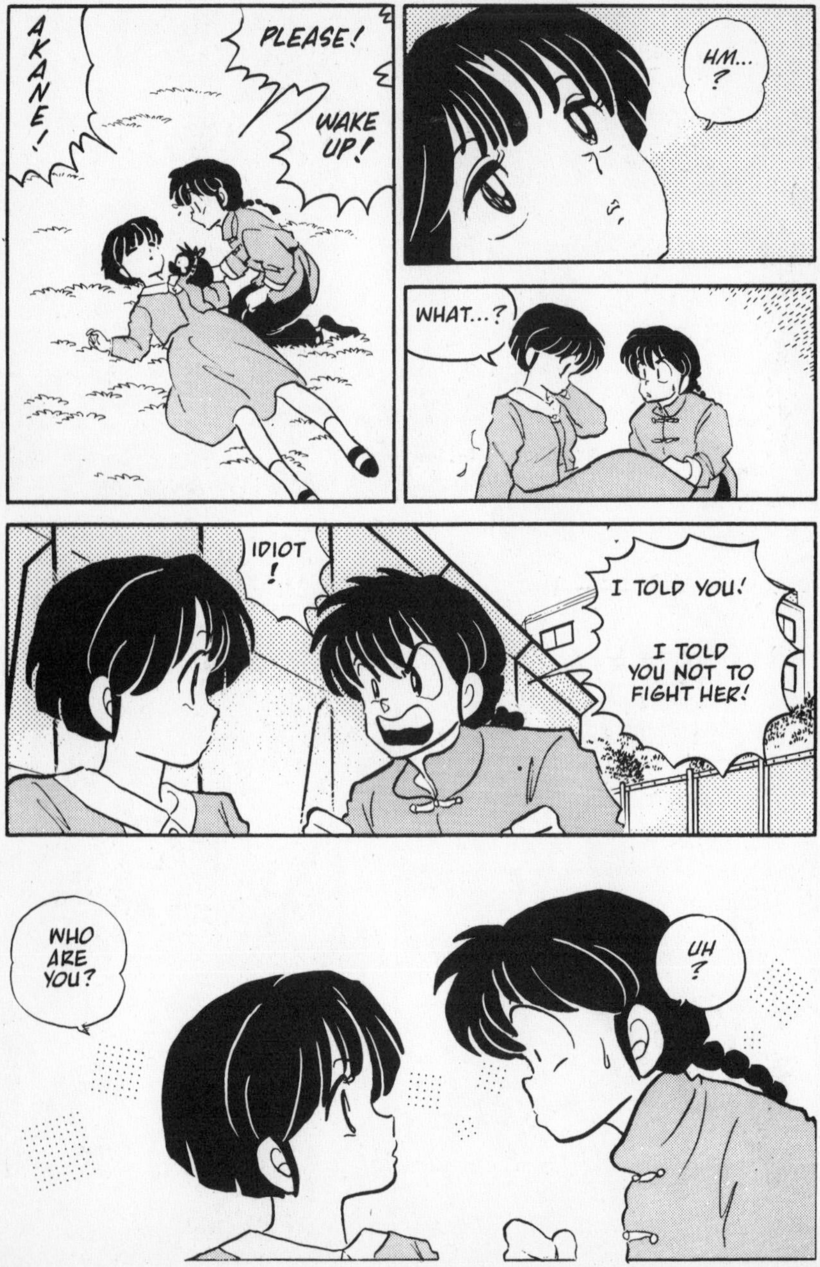
AKANE!
PLEASE!
WAKE UP!
HM...?
WHAT...?
IDIOT!
I TOLD YOU!
I TOLD YOU NOT TO FIGHT HER!
WHO ARE YOU?
UH?

Part 9

SHAMPOO CLEANS UP

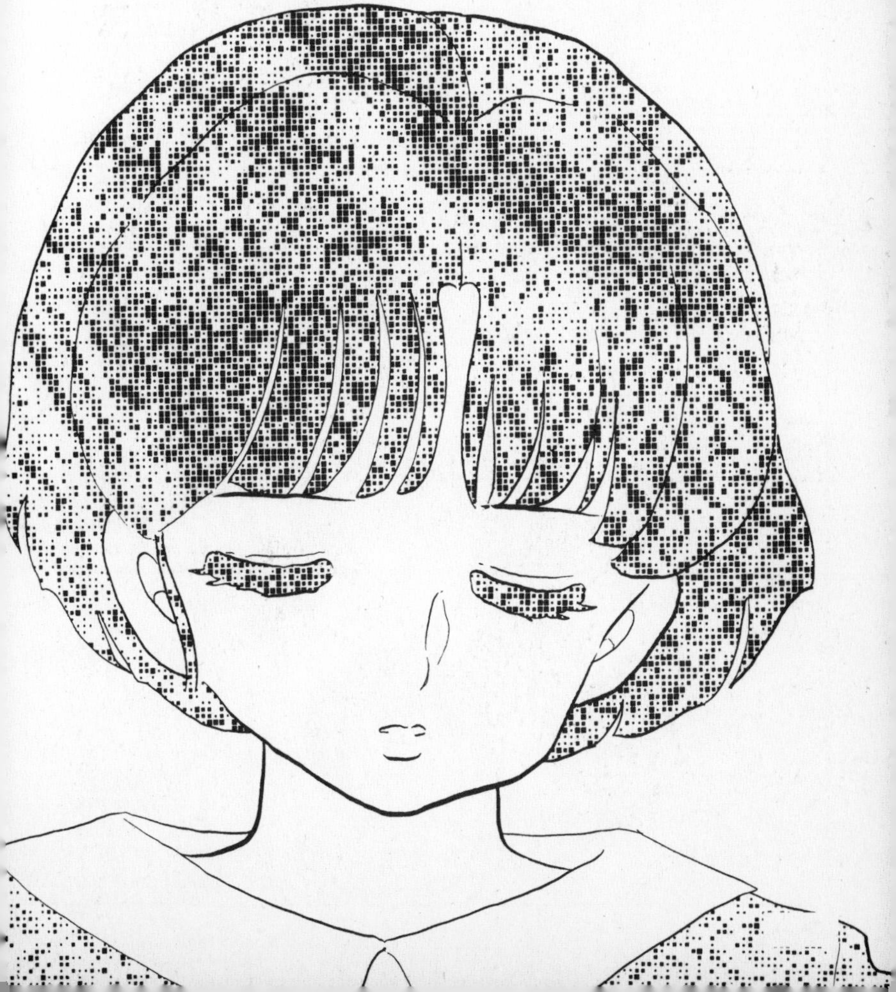

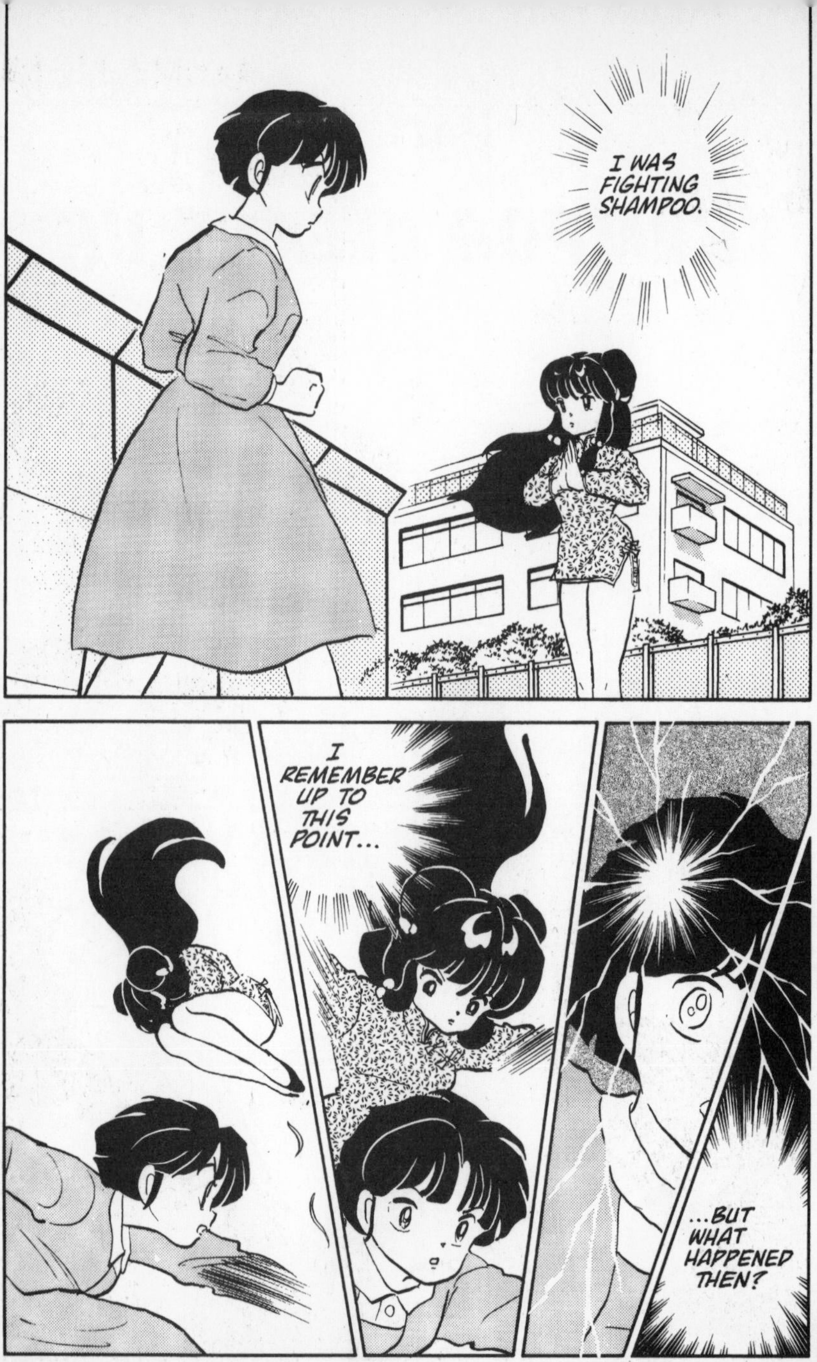
I WAS FIGHTING SHAMPOO.
I REMEMBER UP TO THIS POINT...
...BUT WHAT HAPPENED THEN?

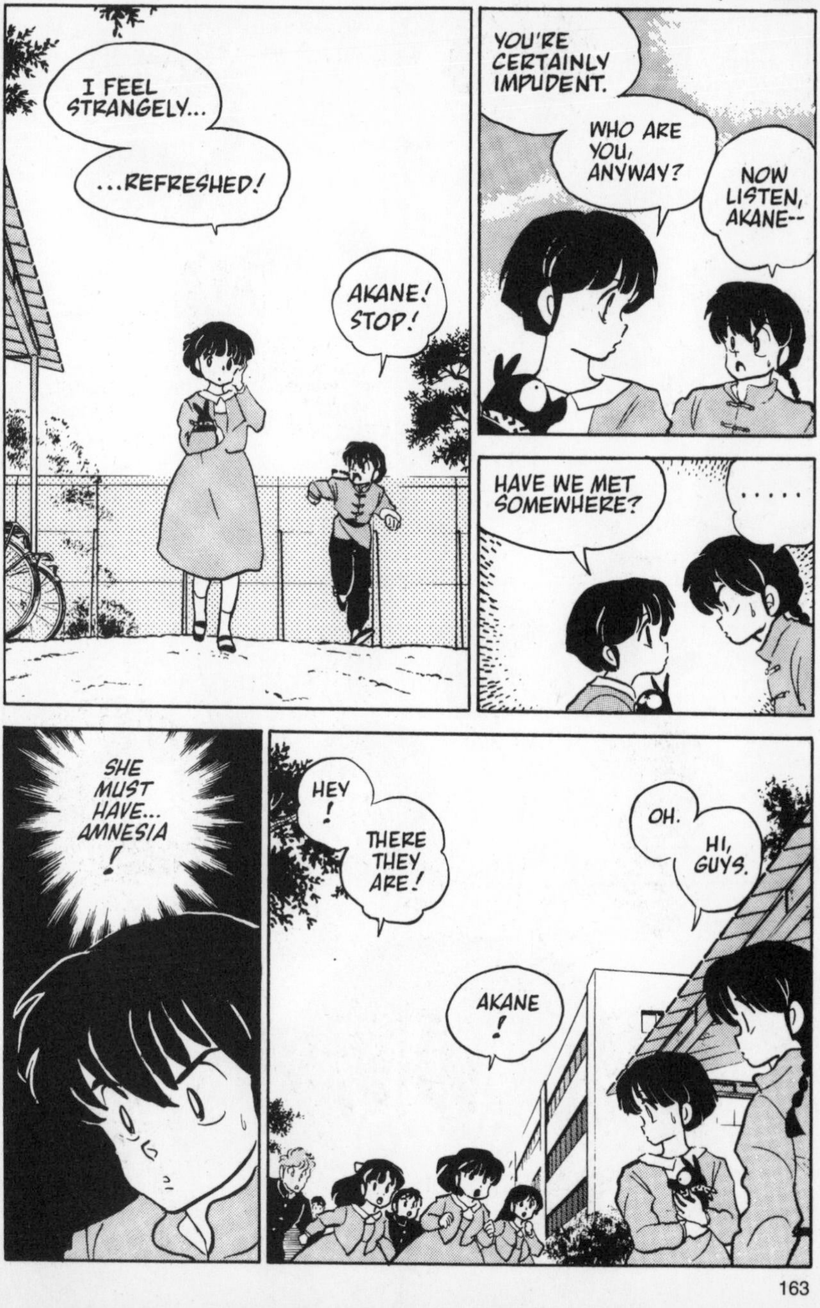
I FEEL STRANGELY...
...REFRESHED!
AKANE! STOP!
YOU'RE CERTAINLY IMPUDENT.
WHO ARE YOU, ANYWAY?
NOW LISTEN, AKANE--
HAVE WE MET SOMEWHERE?
.....
SHE MUST HAVE... AMNESIA!
HEY!
THERE THEY ARE!
AKANE!
OH.
HI, GUYS.

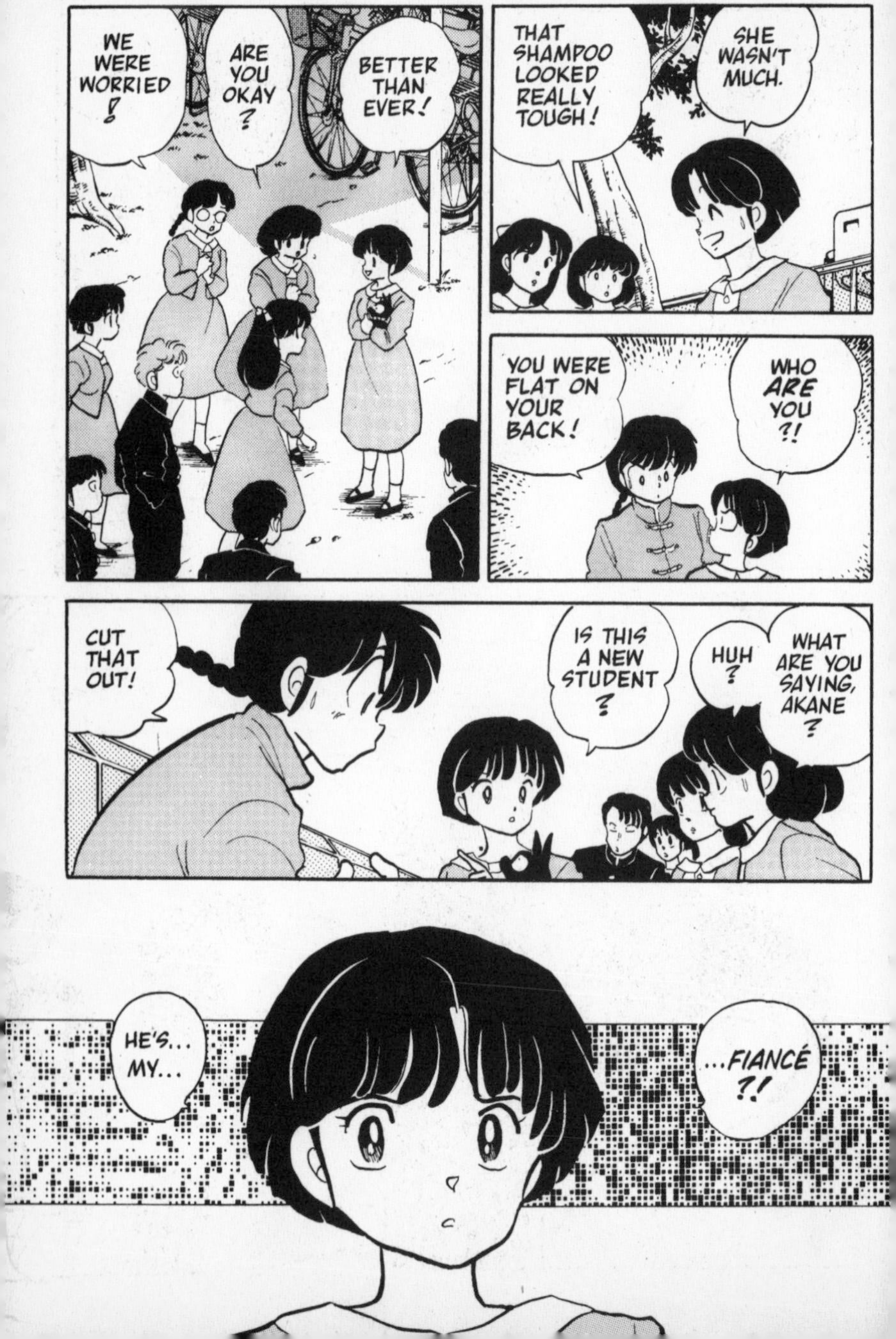
WE WERE WORRIED!
ARE YOU OKAY?
BETTER THAN EVER!
THAT SHAMPOO LOOKED REALLY TOUGH!
SHE WASN'T MUCH.
YOU WERE FLAT ON YOUR BACK!
WHO ARE YOU?!
CUT THAT OUT!
IS THIS A NEW STUDENT?
HUH?
WHAT ARE YOU SAYING, AKANE?
HE'S... MY...
...FIANCÉ?!

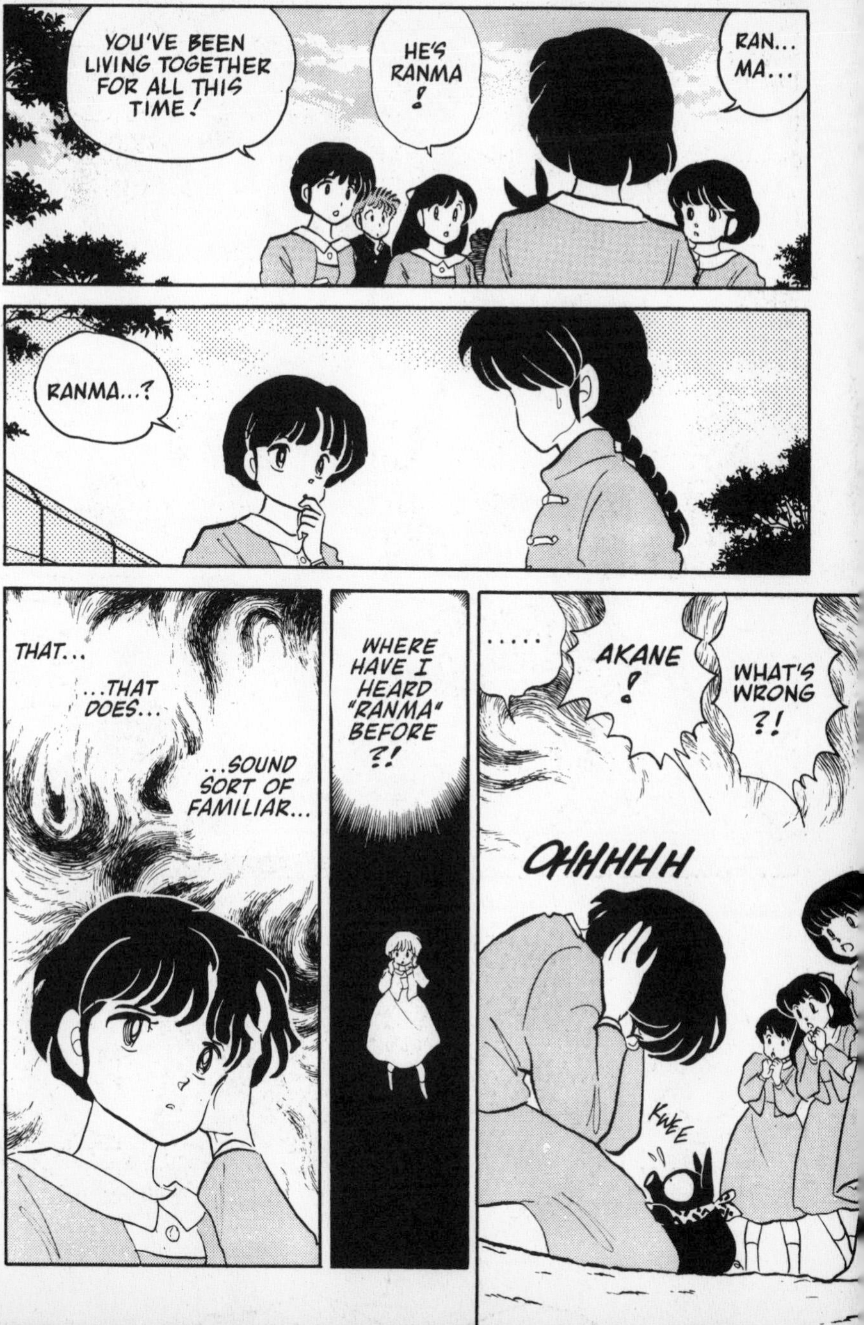
YOU'VE BEEN LIVING TOGETHER FOR ALL THIS TIME!
HE'S RANMA!
RAN... MA...
RANMA...?
THAT...
...THAT DOES...
...SOUND SORT OF FAMILIAR...
WHERE HAVE I HEARD "RANMA" BEFORE?!
.....
AKANE!
WHAT'S WRONG?!
OHHHHH
KWEE

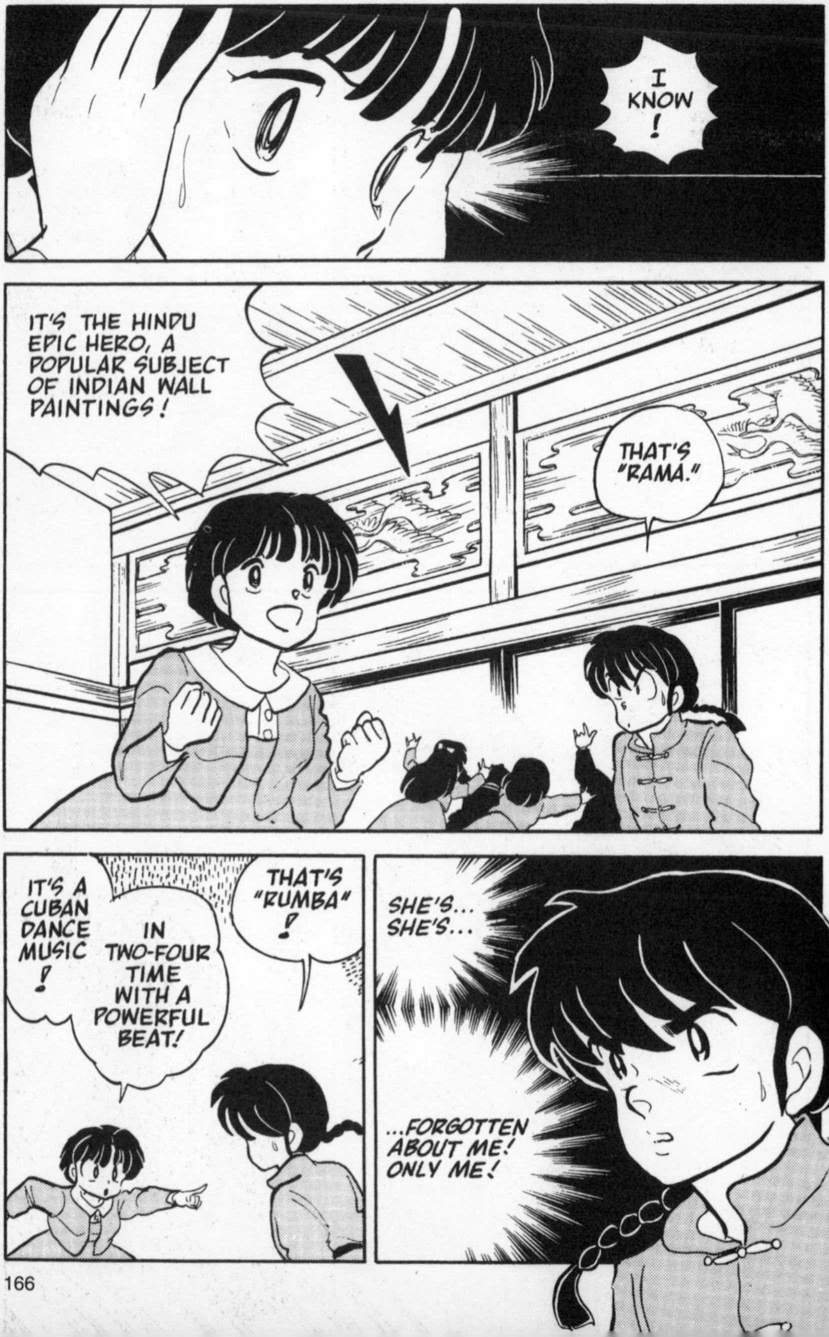
I KNOW !
IT'S THE HINDU EPIC HERO, A POPULAR SUBJECT OF INDIAN WALL PAINTINGS!
THAT'S "RAMA."
IT'S A CUBAN DANCE MUSIC ! IN TWO-FOUR TIME WITH A POWERFUL BEAT!
THAT'S "RUMBA" !
SHE'S... SHE'S...
...FORGOTTEN ABOUT ME! ONLY ME!

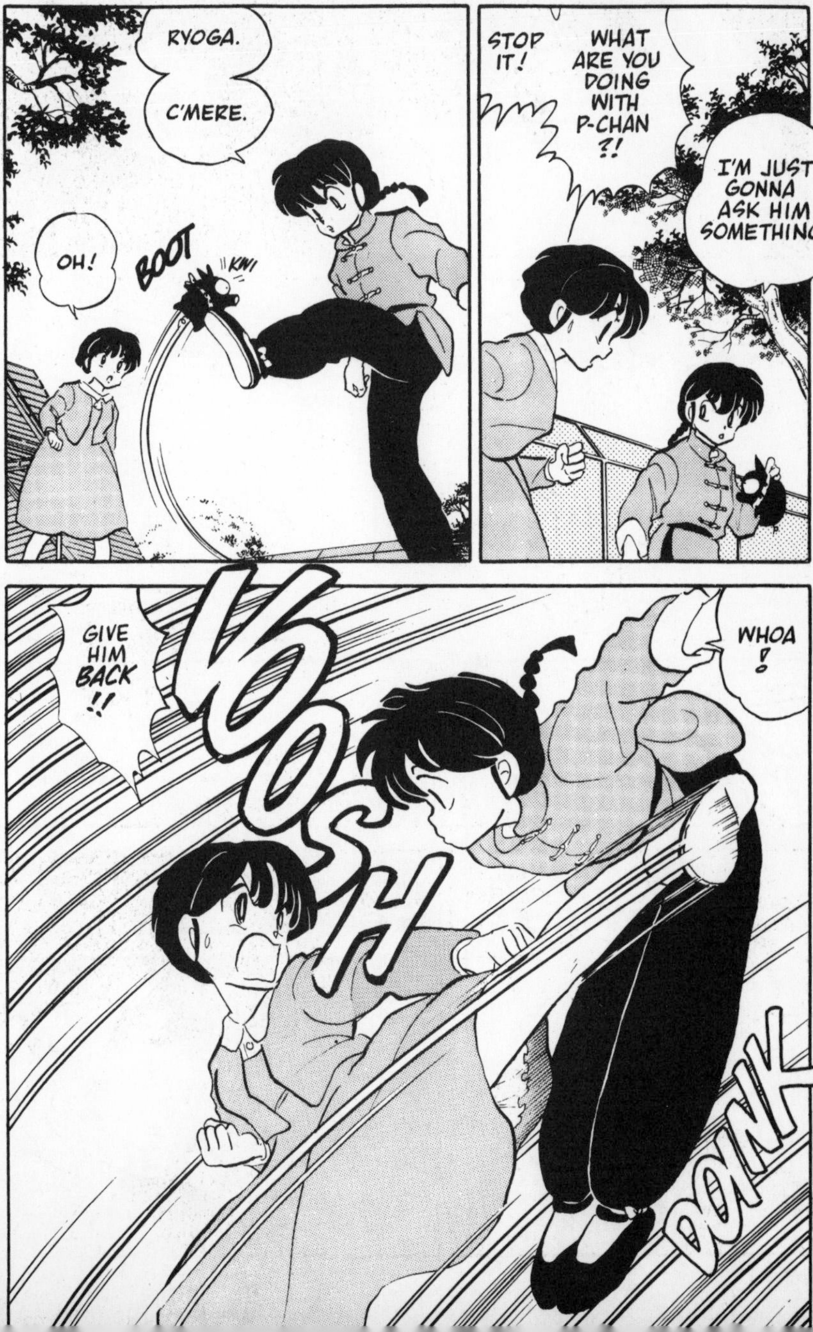
RYOGA.
C'MERE.
OH!
BOOT
KWI
STOP IT!
WHAT ARE YOU DOING WITH P-CHAN ?!
I'M JUST GONNA ASK HIM SOMETHING.
GIVE HIM BACK !!
WOOSH
WHOA !
DOINK

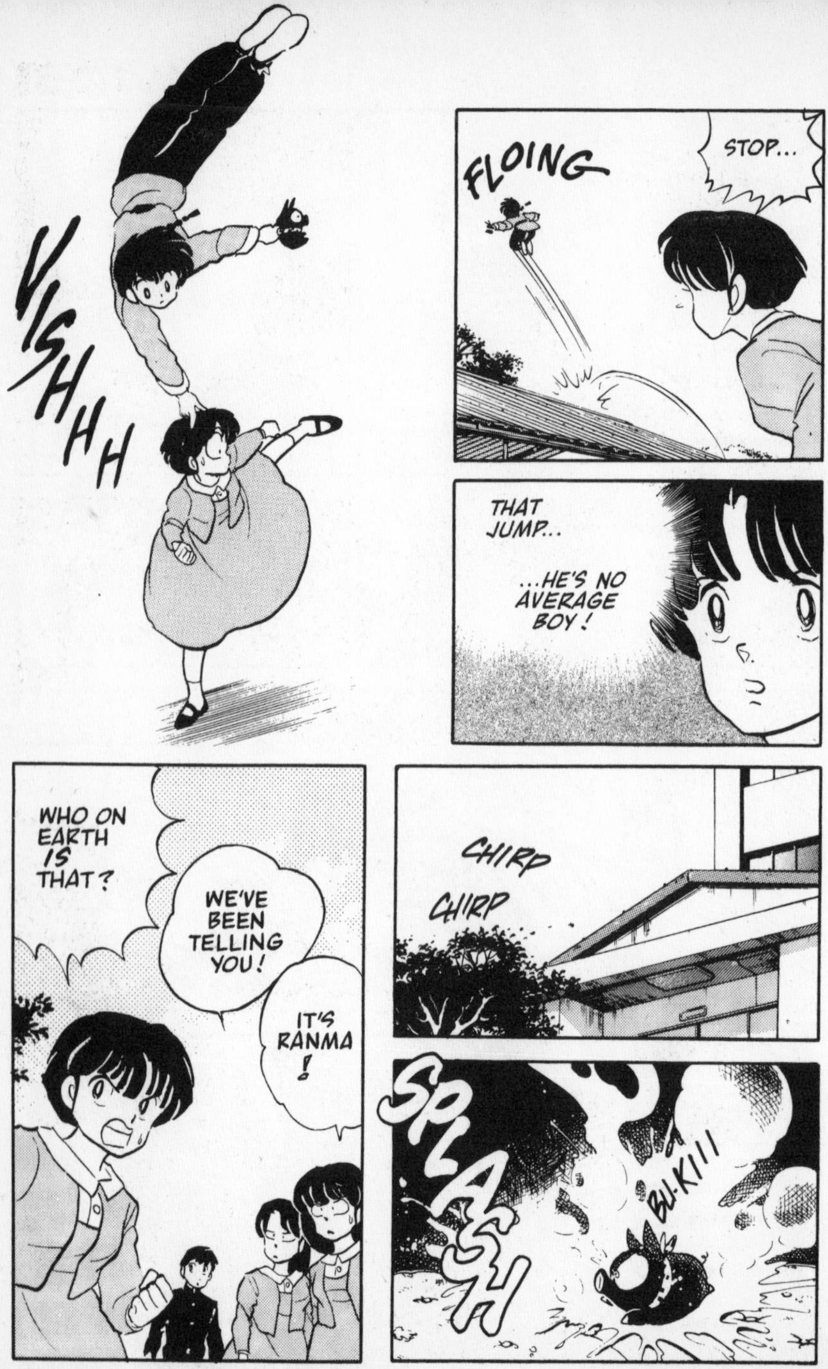
VISHHHH
FLOING
STOP...
THAT JUMP...
...HE'S NO AVERAGE BOY!
WHO ON EARTH IS THAT?
WE'VE BEEN TELLING YOU!
IT'S RANMA!
CHIRP
CHIRP
SPLASH
BU-KIII

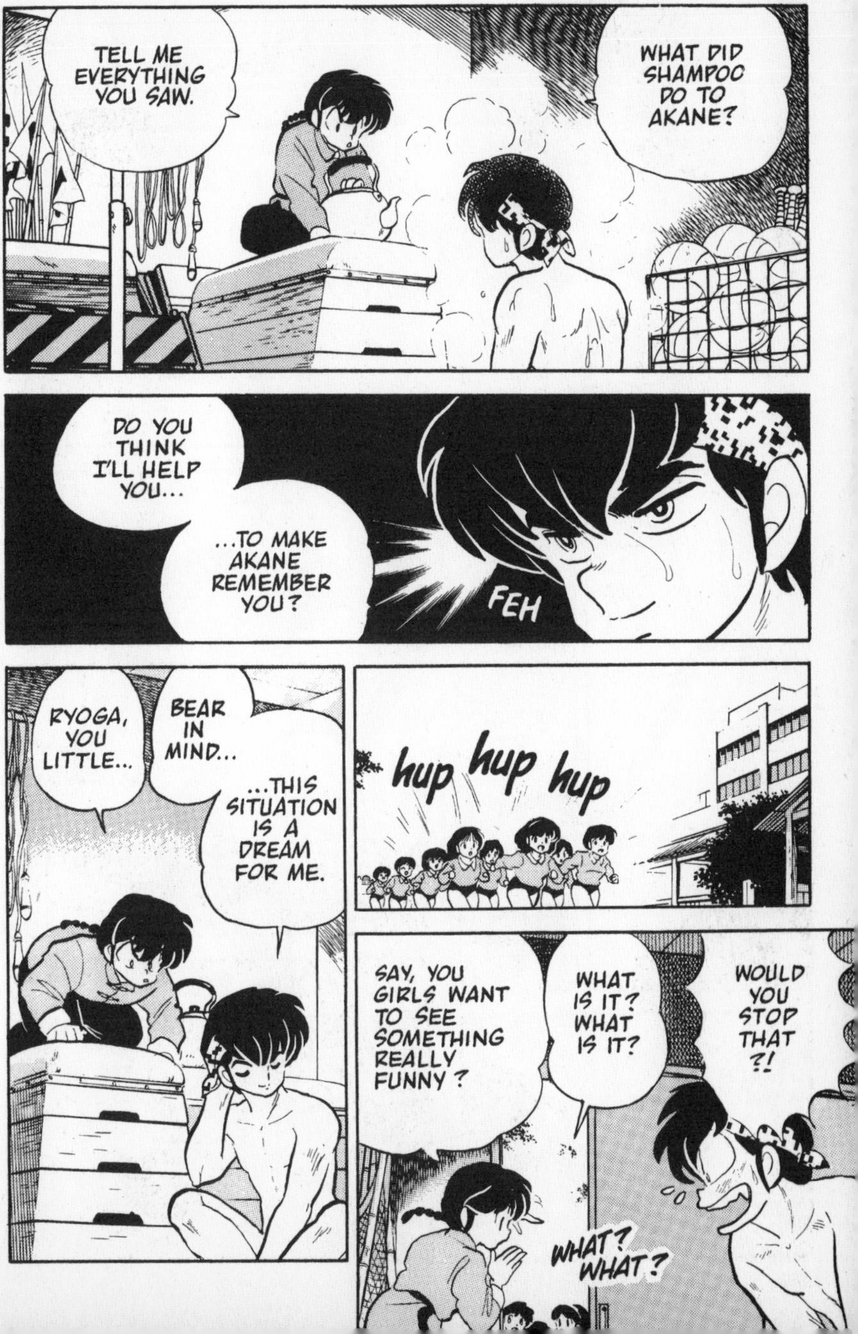
TELL ME EVERYTHING YOU SAW.
WHAT DID SHAMPOO DO TO AKANE?
DO YOU THINK I'LL HELP YOU...
...TO MAKE AKANE REMEMBER YOU?
FEH
RYOGA, YOU LITTLE...
BEAR IN MIND...
...THIS SITUATION IS A DREAM FOR ME.
hup hup hup
SAY, YOU GIRLS WANT TO SEE SOMETHING REALLY FUNNY?
WHAT IS IT? WHAT IS IT?
WOULD YOU STOP THAT?!
WHAT? WHAT?

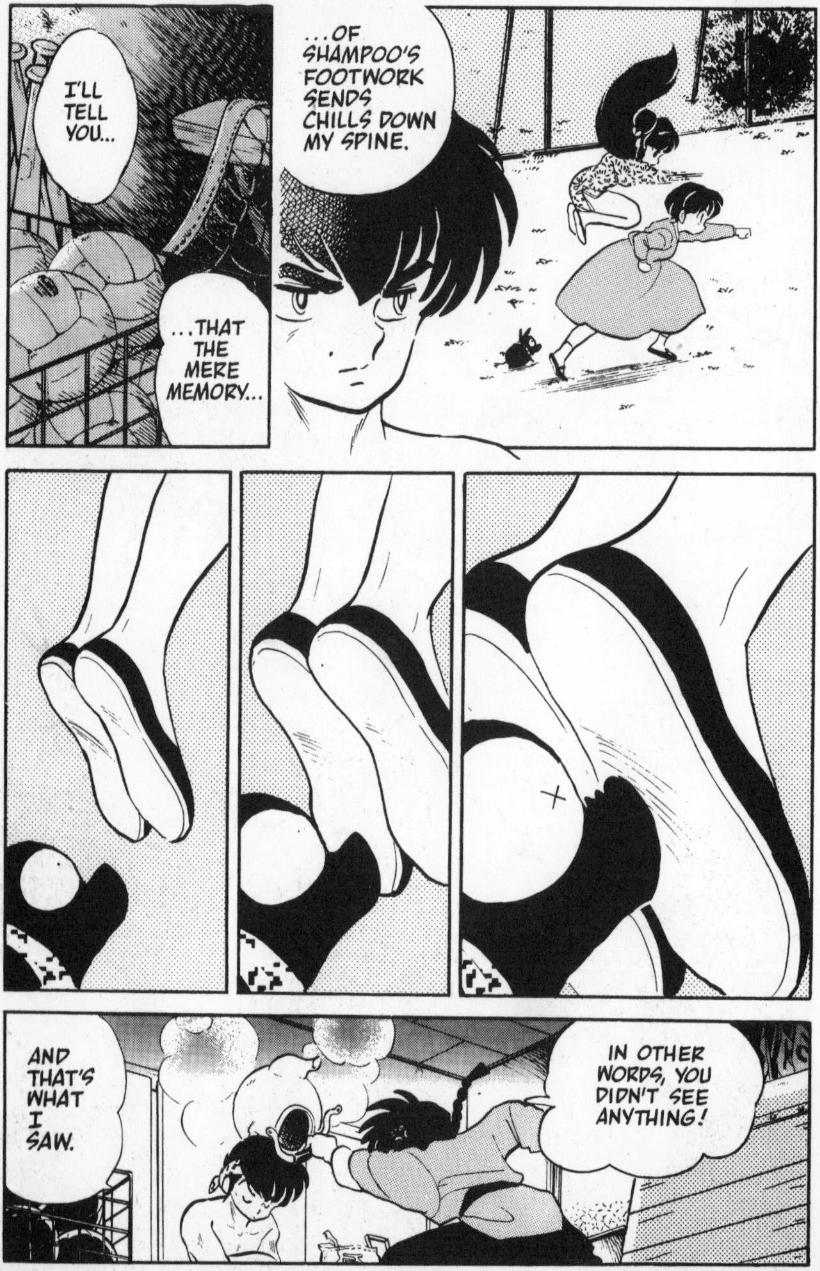
I'LL TELL YOU...
...THAT THE MERE MEMORY...
...OF SHAMPOO'S FOOTWORK SENDS CHILLS DOWN MY SPINE.
AND THAT'S WHAT I SAW.
IN OTHER WORDS, YOU DIDN'T SEE ANYTHING!

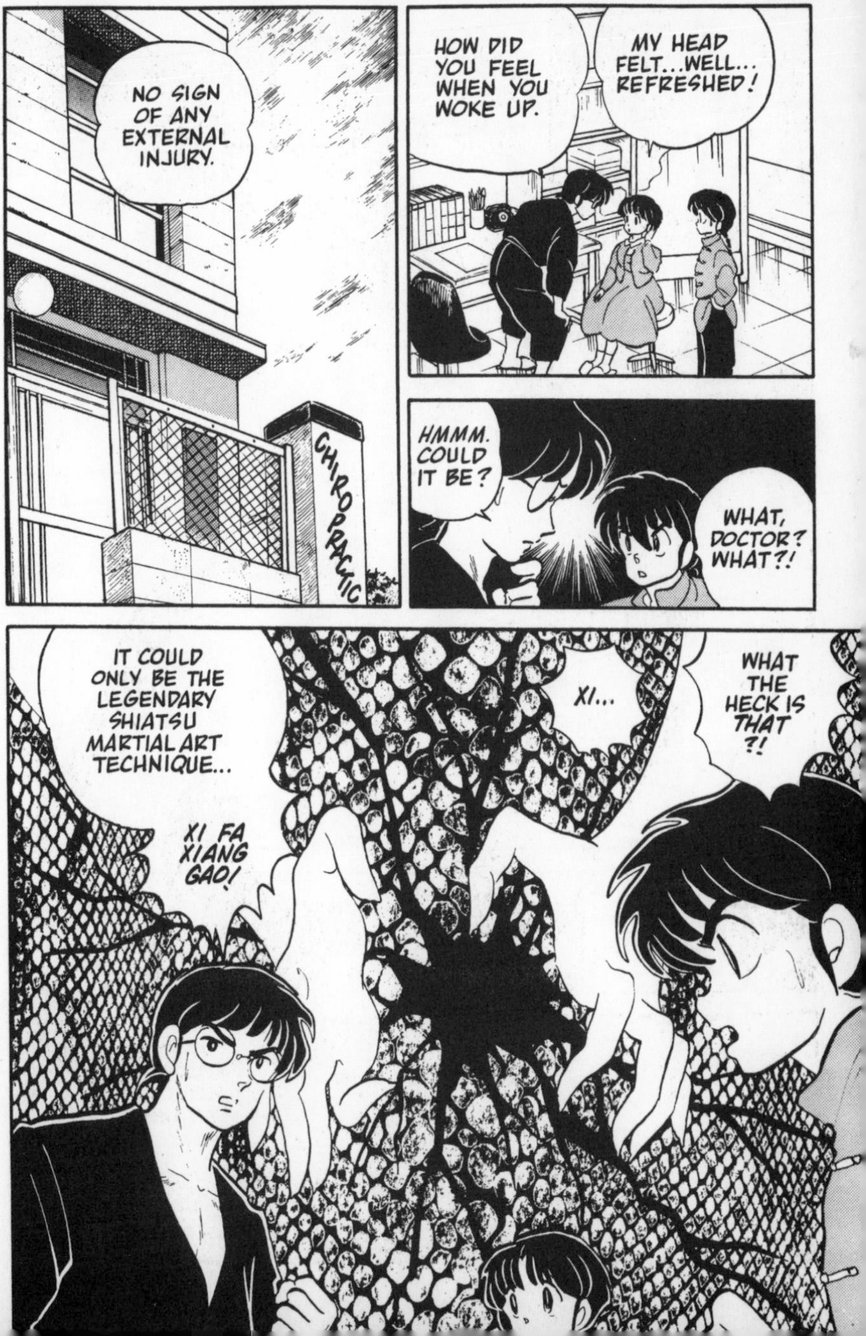
NO SIGN OF ANY EXTERNAL INJURY.
CHIROPRACTIC
HOW DID YOU FEEL WHEN YOU WOKE UP.
MY HEAD FELT...WELL... REFRESHED!
HMMM. COULD IT BE?
WHAT, DOCTOR? WHAT?!
IT COULD ONLY BE THE LEGENDARY SHIATSU MARTIAL ART TECHNIQUE...
XI FA XIANG GAO!
XI...
WHAT THE HECK IS THAT ?!

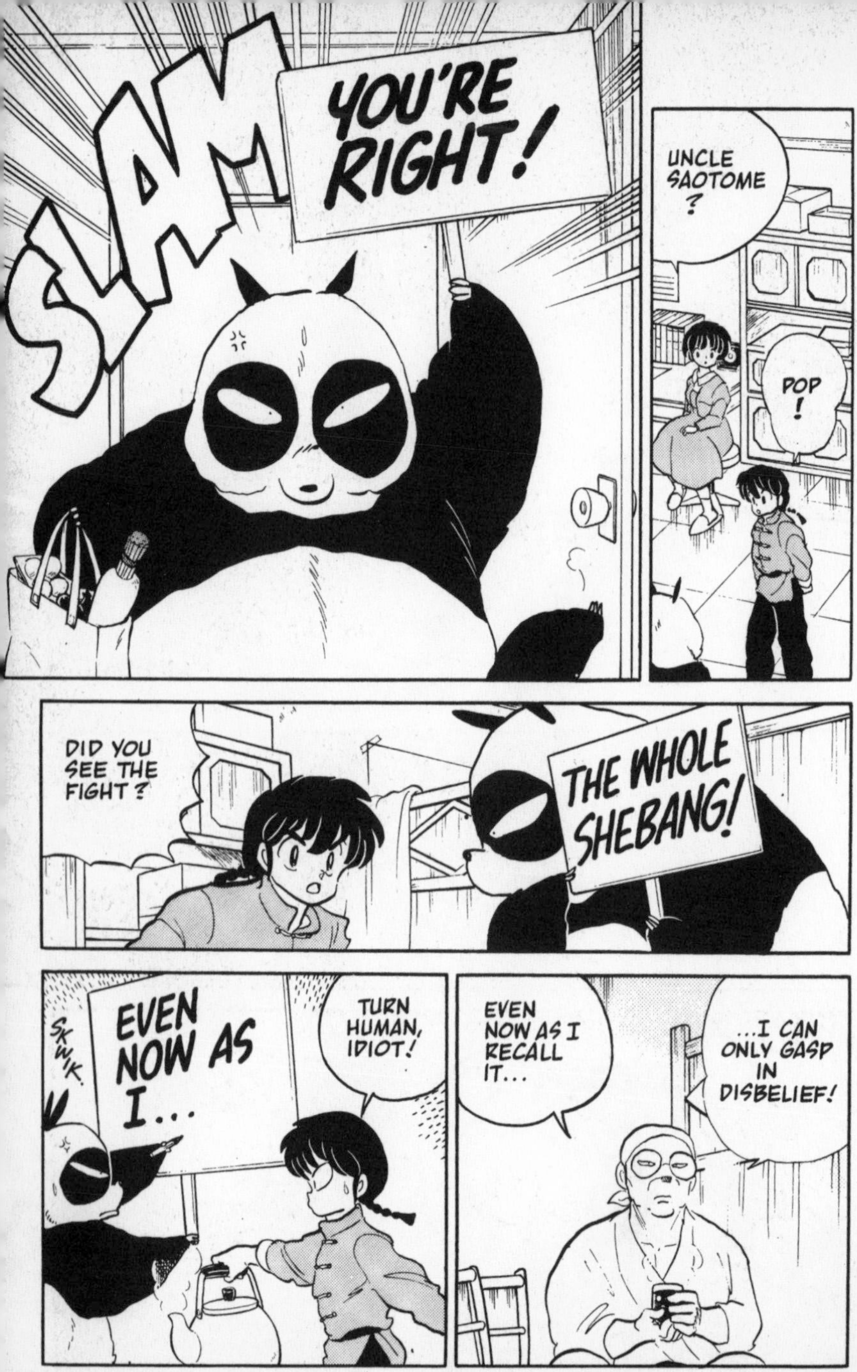
SLAM
YOU'RE RIGHT!
UNCLE SAOTOME?
POP!
DID YOU SEE THE FIGHT?
THE WHOLE SHEBANG!
SKWIK.
EVEN NOW AS I...
TURN HUMAN, IDIOT!
EVEN NOW AS I RECALL IT...
...I CAN ONLY GASP IN DISBELIEF!

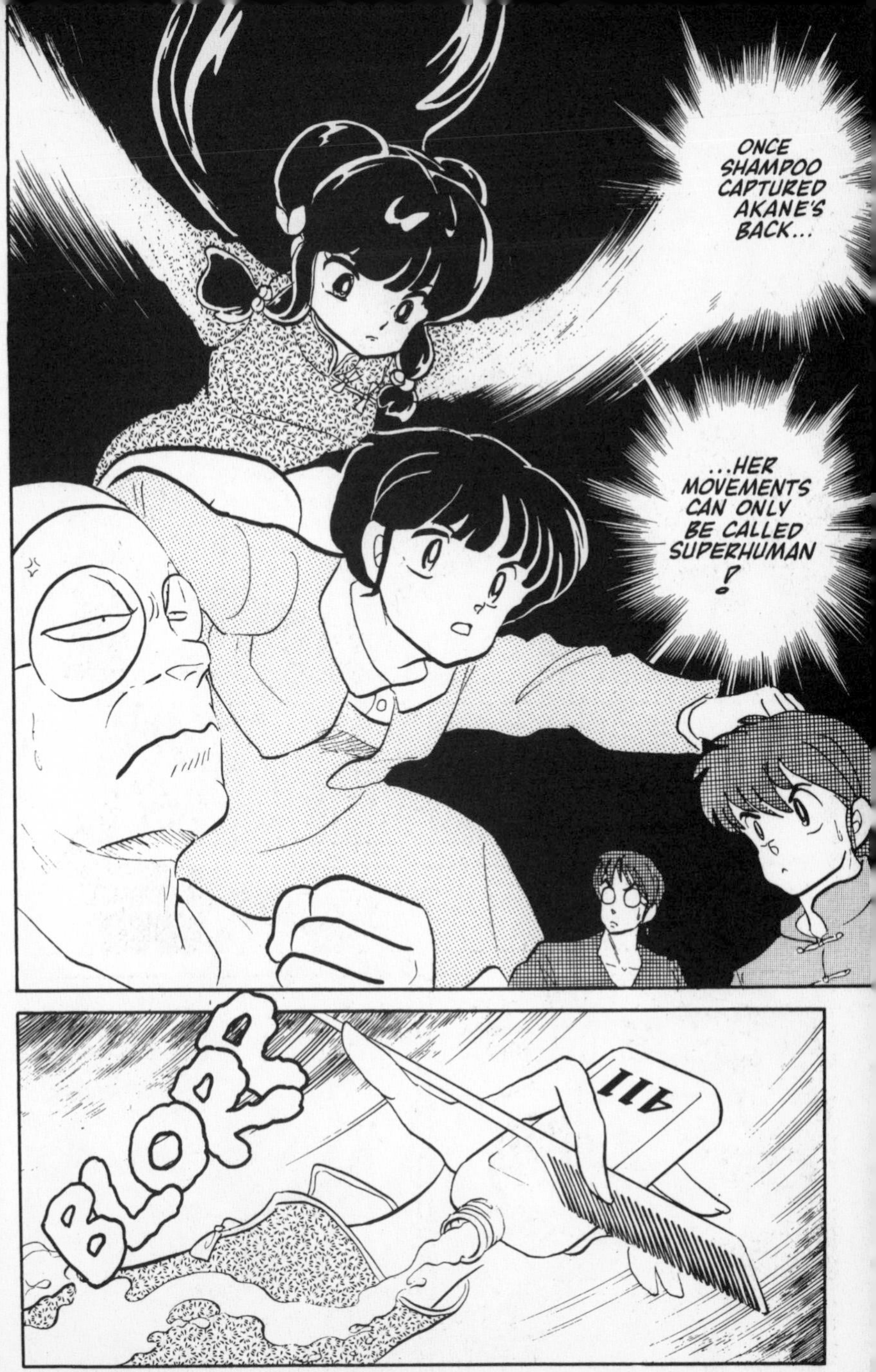
ONCE SHAMPOO CAPTURED AKANE'S BACK...
...HER MOVEMENTS CAN ONLY BE CALLED SUPERHUMAN!
BLOP

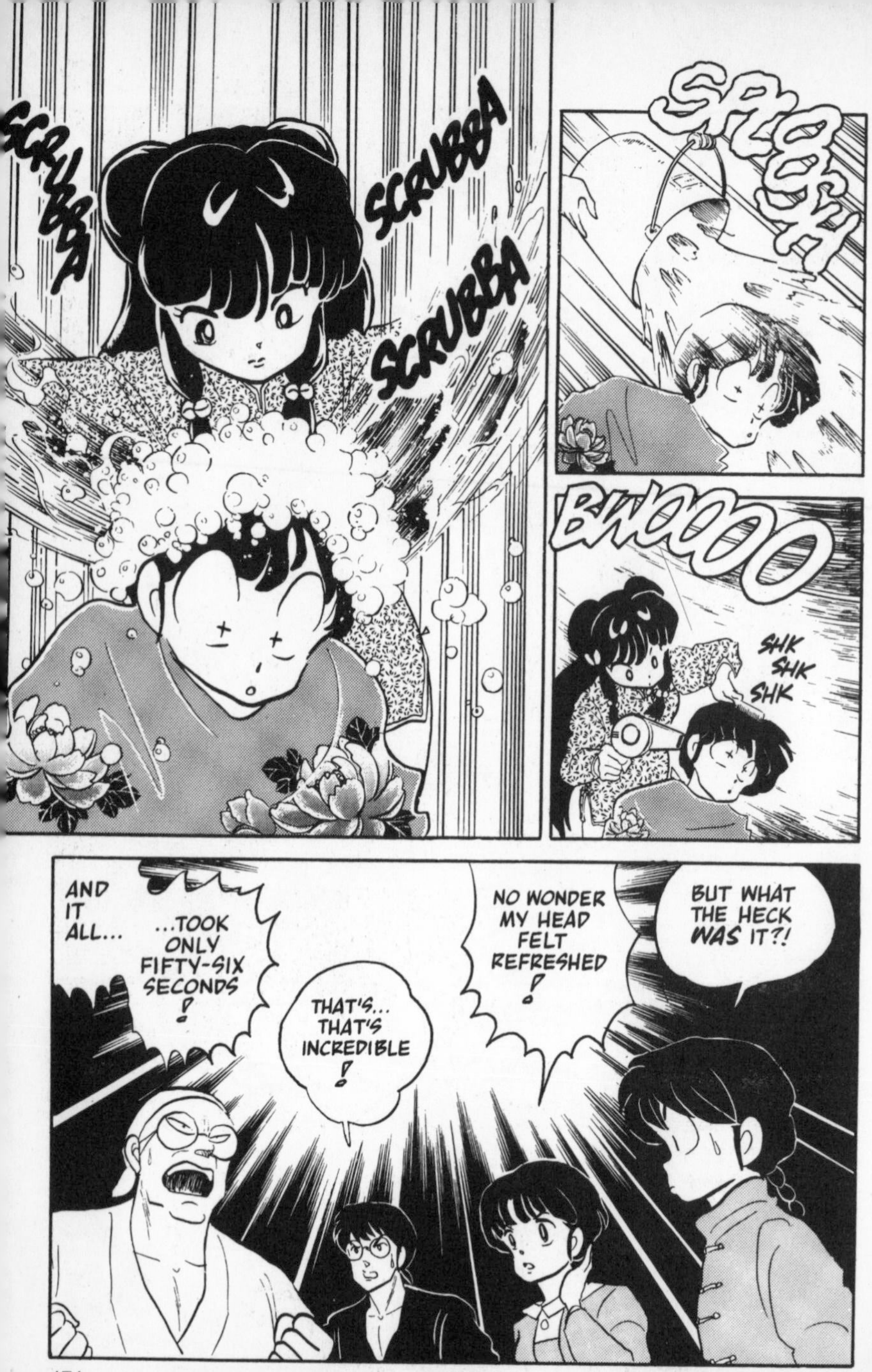
SCRUBBA
SCRUBBA
SCRUBBA
SPLOOSH
BWOOOOO
SHK SHK SHK
AND IT ALL...
...TOOK ONLY FIFTY-SIX SECONDS!
THAT'S... THAT'S INCREDIBLE!
NO WONDER MY HEAD FELT REFRESHED!
BUT WHAT THE HECK WAS IT?!

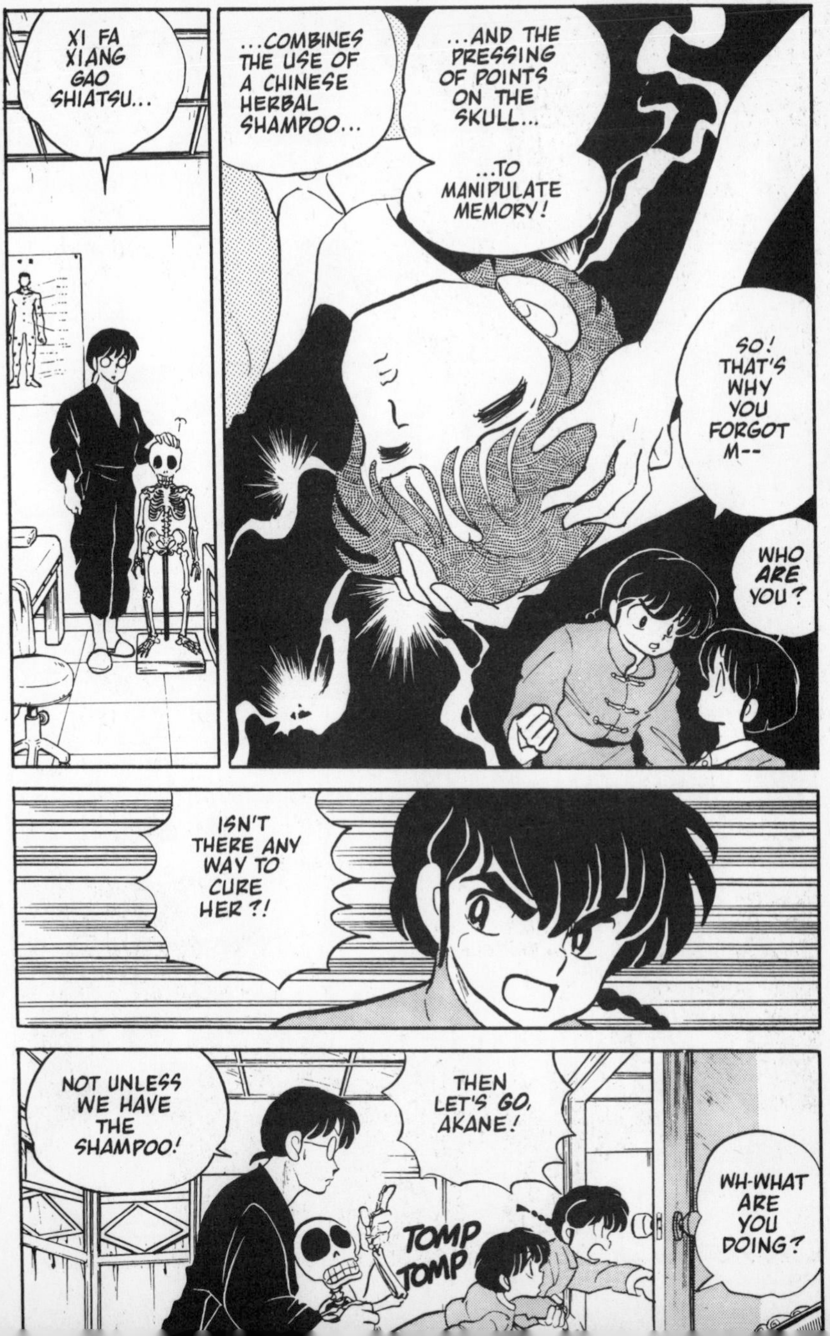
XI FA XIANG GAO SHIATSU...
...COMBINES THE USE OF A CHINESE HERBAL SHAMPOO...
...AND THE PRESSING OF POINTS ON THE SKULL...
...TO MANIPULATE MEMORY!
SO! THAT'S WHY YOU FORGOT M--
WHO ARE YOU?
ISN'T THERE ANY WAY TO CURE HER?!
NOT UNLESS WE HAVE THE SHAMPOO!
THEN LET'S GO, AKANE!
TOMP TOMP
WH-WHAT ARE YOU DOING?

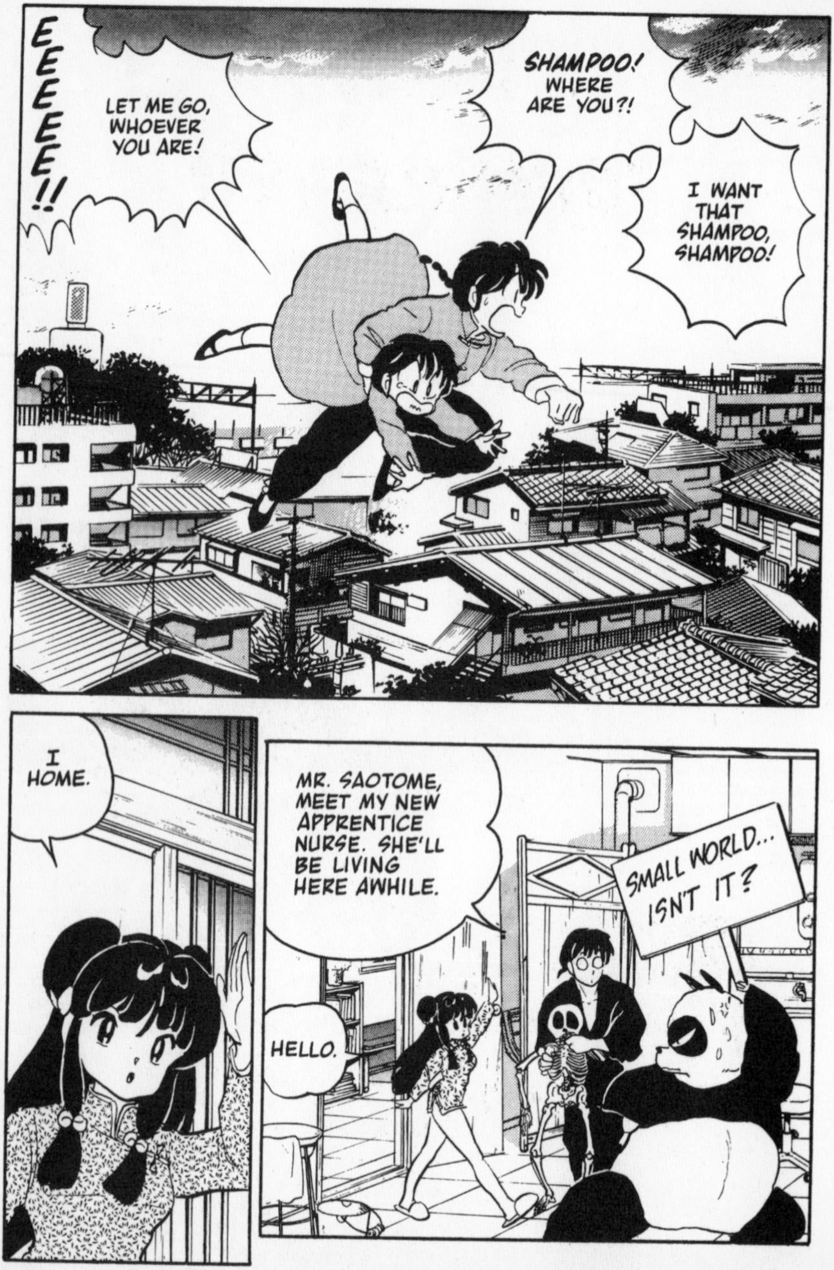
EEEEEE!!
LET ME GO, WHOEVER YOU ARE!
SHAMPOO! WHERE ARE YOU?!
I WANT THAT SHAMPOO, SHAMPOO!
I HOME.
MR. SAOTOME, MEET MY NEW APPRENTICE NURSE. SHE'LL BE LIVING HERE AWHILE.
SMALL WORLD... ISN'T IT?
HELLO.

Part 10
FORMULA #911

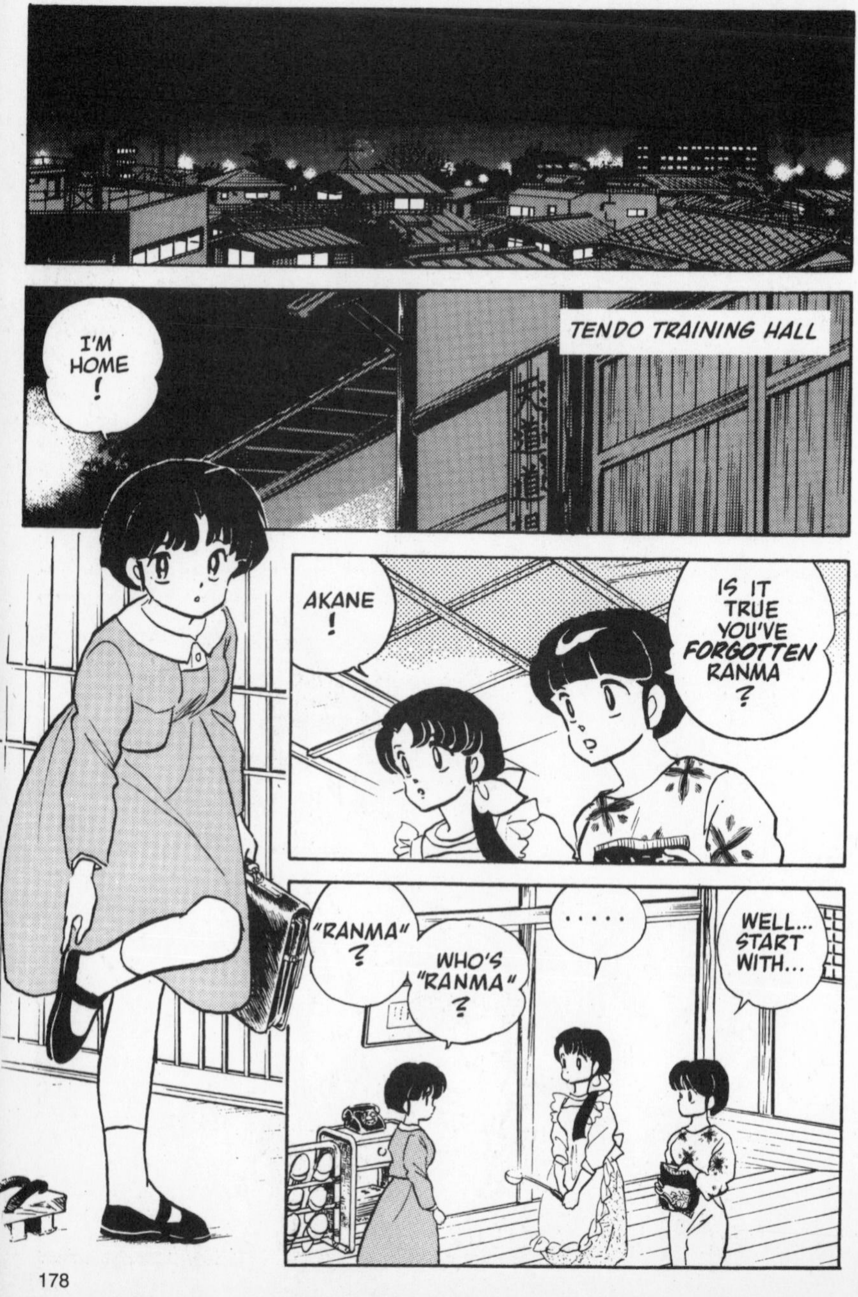
I'M HOME!
TENDO TRAINING HALL
AKANE!
IS IT TRUE YOU'VE FORGOTTEN RANMA?
"RANMA"?
WHO'S "RANMA"?
.....
WELL... START WITH...

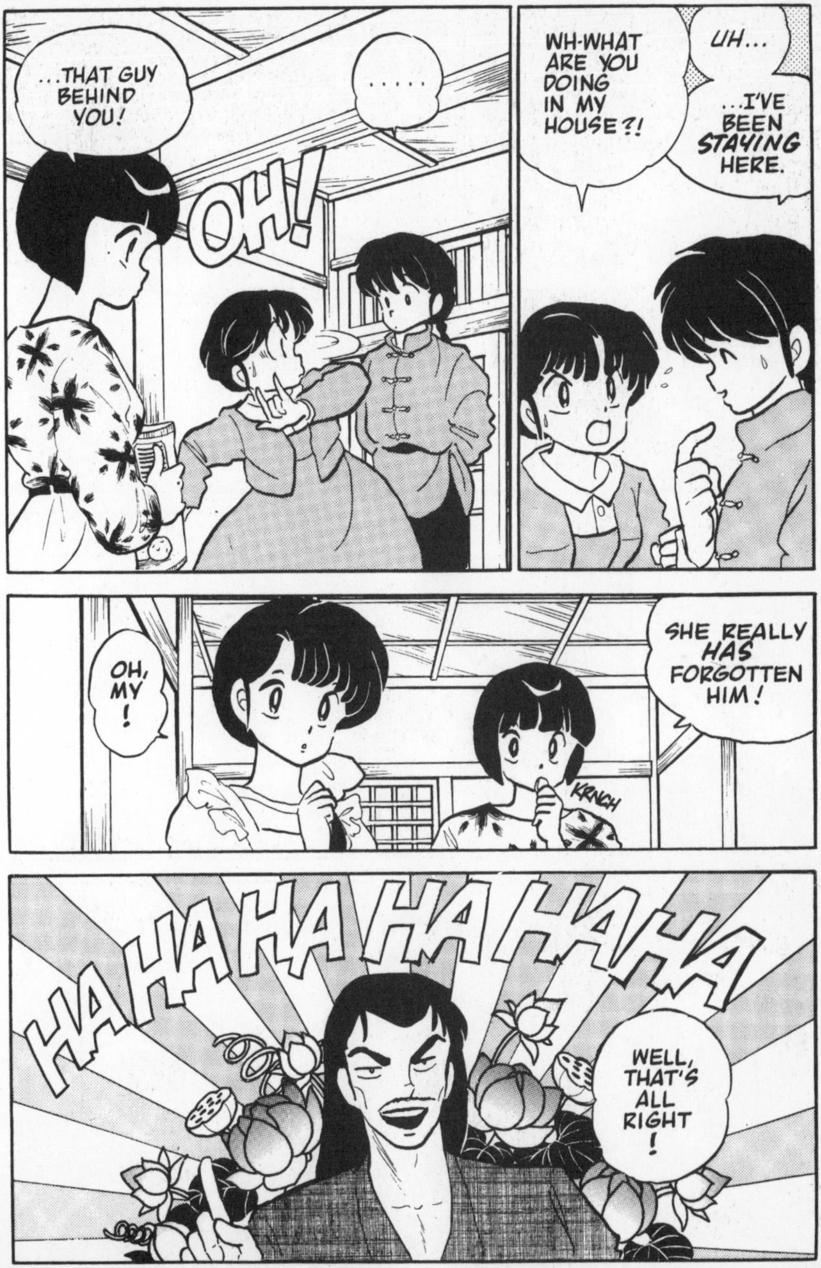
...THAT GUY BEHIND YOU!
......
OH!
WH-WHAT ARE YOU DOING IN MY HOUSE?!
UH...
...I'VE BEEN STAYING HERE.
OH, MY!
SHE REALLY HAS FORGOTTEN HIM!
KRNCH
HAHAHAHAHAHAHAHA
WELL, THAT'S ALL RIGHT!

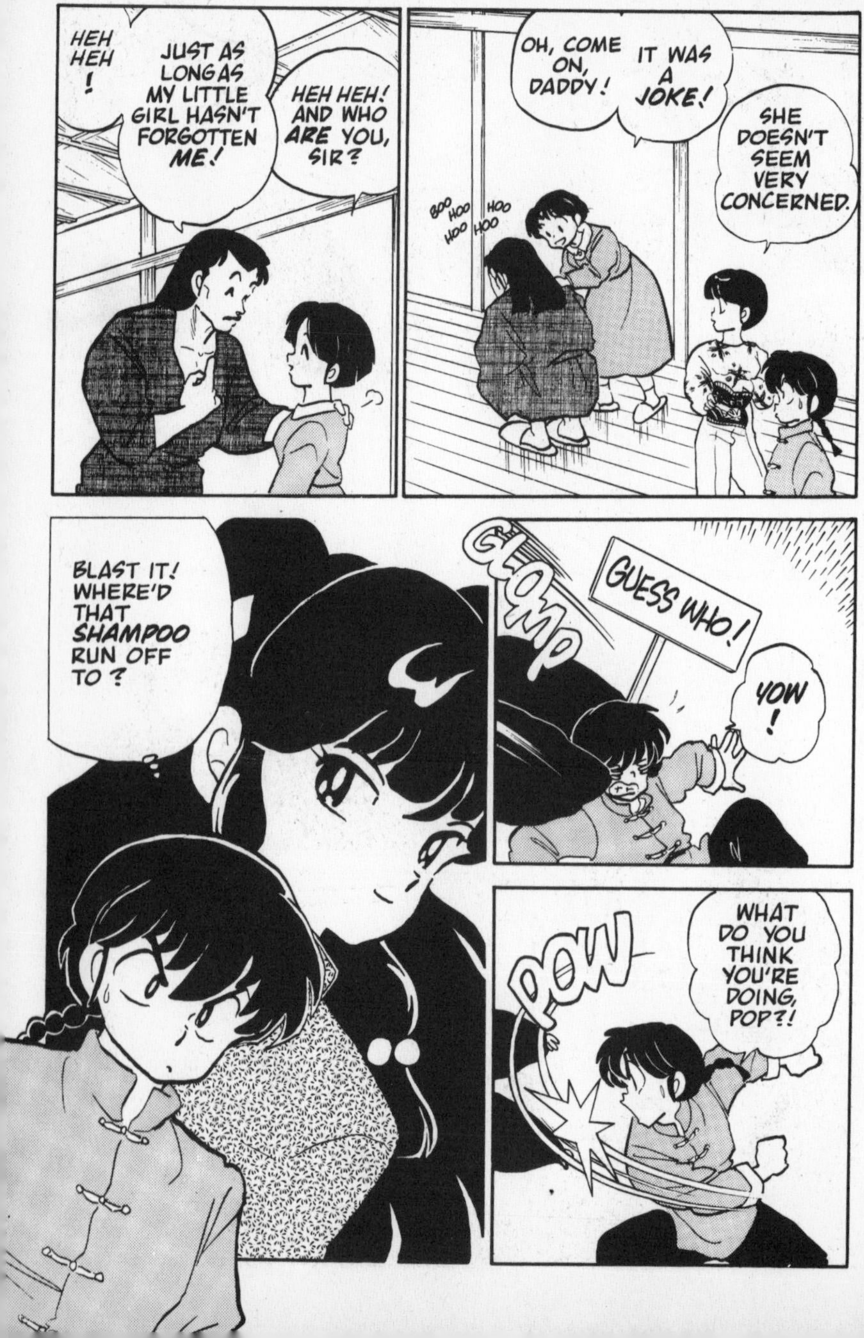
HEH HEH !
JUST AS LONG AS MY LITTLE GIRL HASN'T FORGOTTEN ME!
HEH HEH! AND WHO ARE YOU, SIR?
OH, COME ON, DADDY!
IT WAS A JOKE!
BOO HOO HOO HOO HOO
SHE DOESN'T SEEM VERY CONCERNED.
BLAST IT! WHERE'D THAT SHAMPOO RUN OFF TO?
GLOMP
GUESS WHO!
YOW !
POW
WHAT DO YOU THINK YOU'RE DOING, POP?!

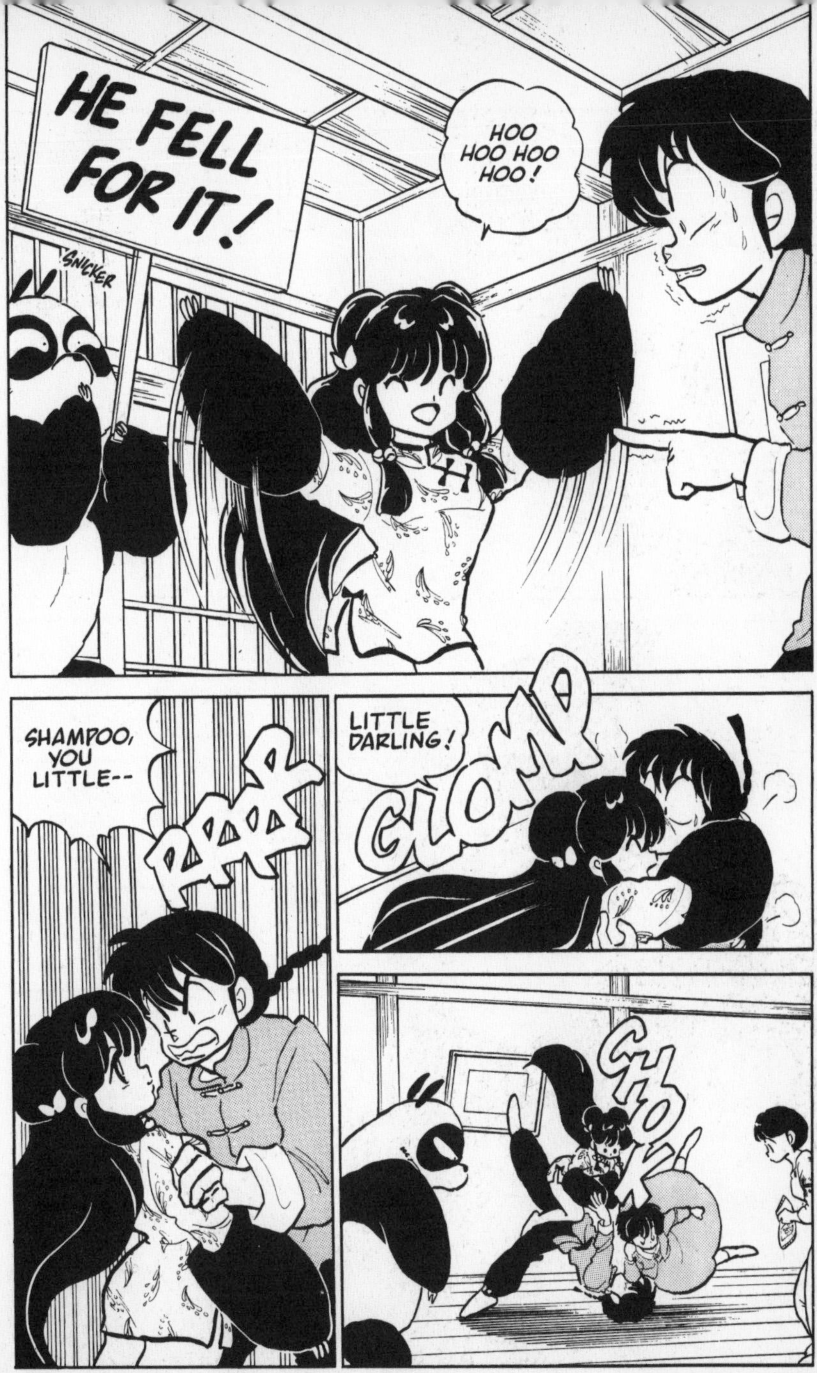
HE FELL FOR IT!
HOO HOO HOO HOO!
SNICKER
SHAMPOO, YOU LITTLE--
RRRR
LITTLE DARLING!
GLOMP
CHOY

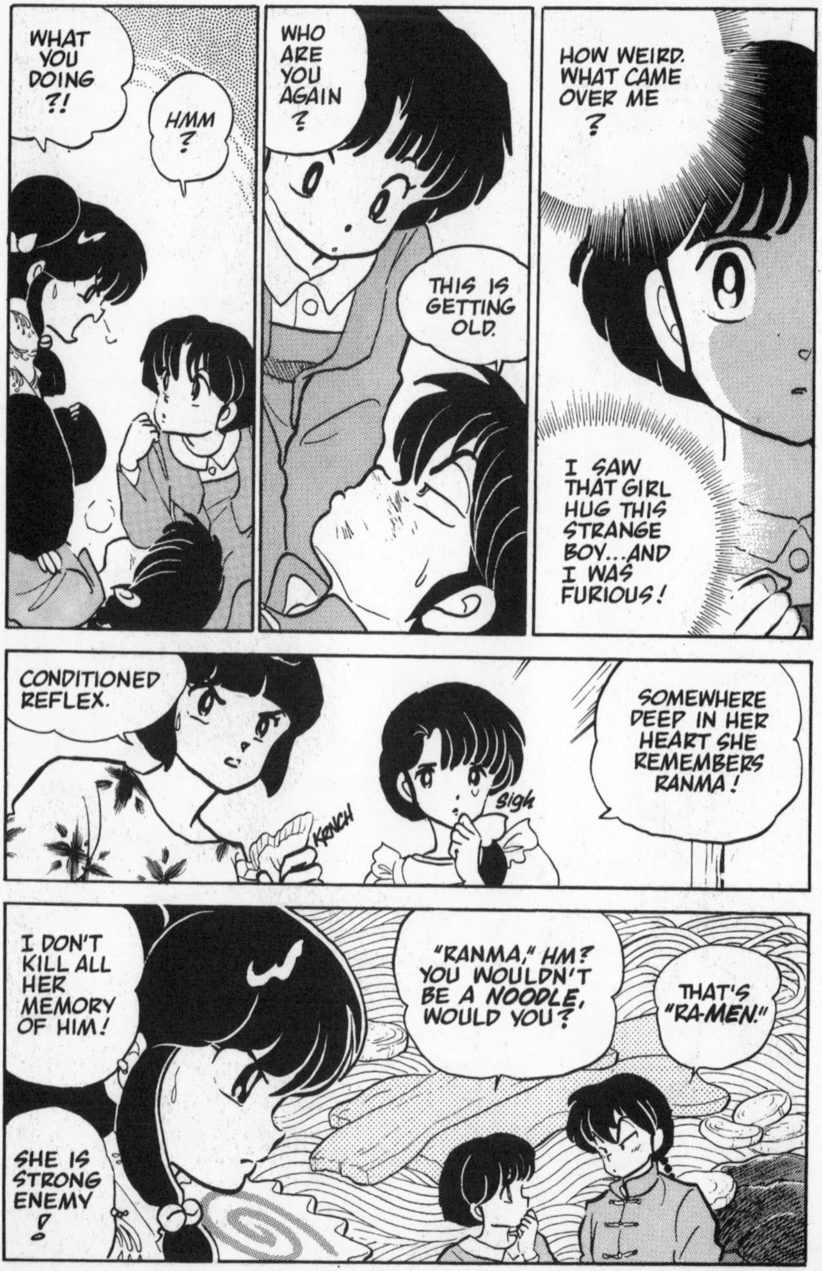
WHAT YOU DOING ?!
HMM ?
WHO ARE YOU AGAIN ?
THIS IS GETTING OLD.
HOW WEIRD. WHAT CAME OVER ME ?
I SAW THAT GIRL HUG THIS STRANGE BOY...AND I WAS FURIOUS!
CONDITIONED REFLEX.
KRNCH
Sigh
SOMEWHERE DEEP IN HER HEART SHE REMEMBERS RANMA!
I DON'T KILL ALL HER MEMORY OF HIM!
SHE IS STRONG ENEMY !
"RANMA," HM? YOU WOULDN'T BE A NOODLE, WOULD YOU?
THAT'S "RA-MEN."

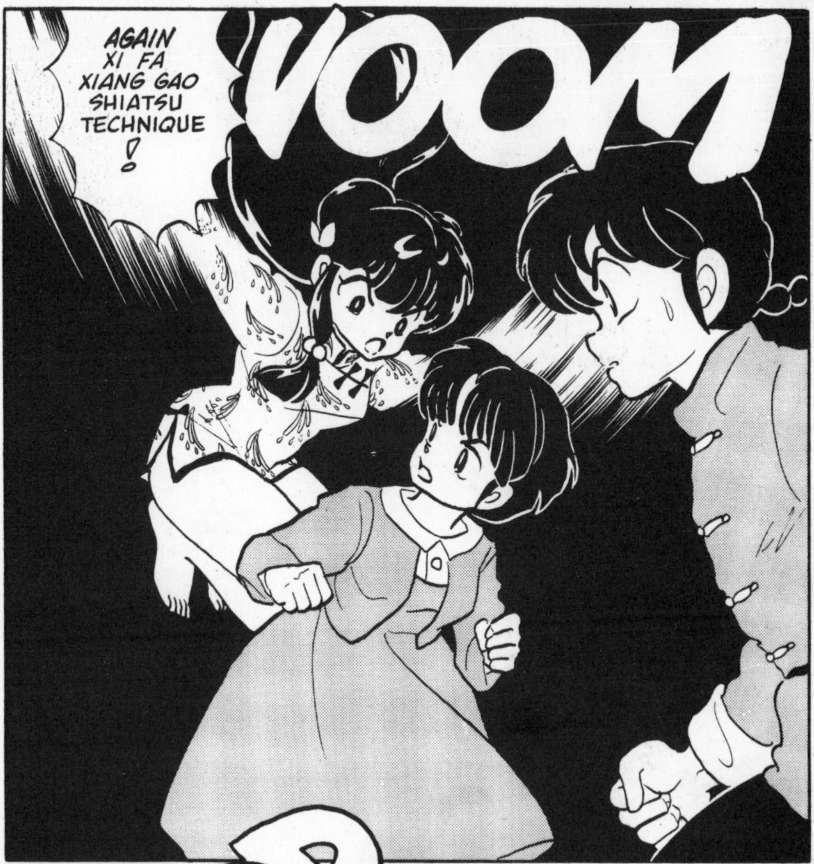
AGAIN XI FA XIANG GAO SHIATSU TECHNIQUE !
VOOM

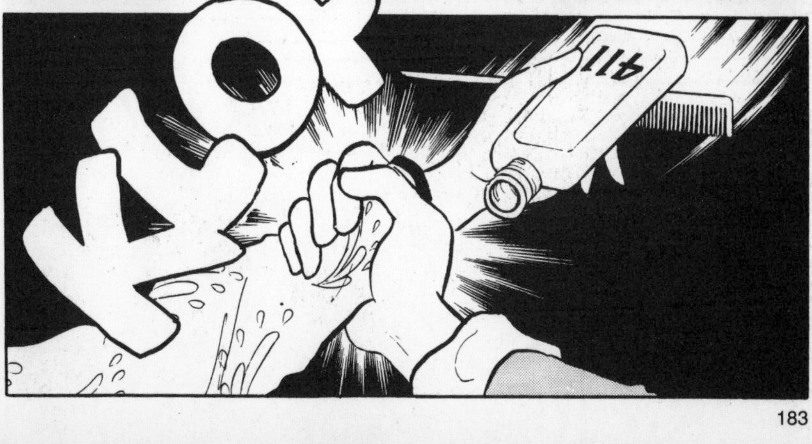
KLOP
411

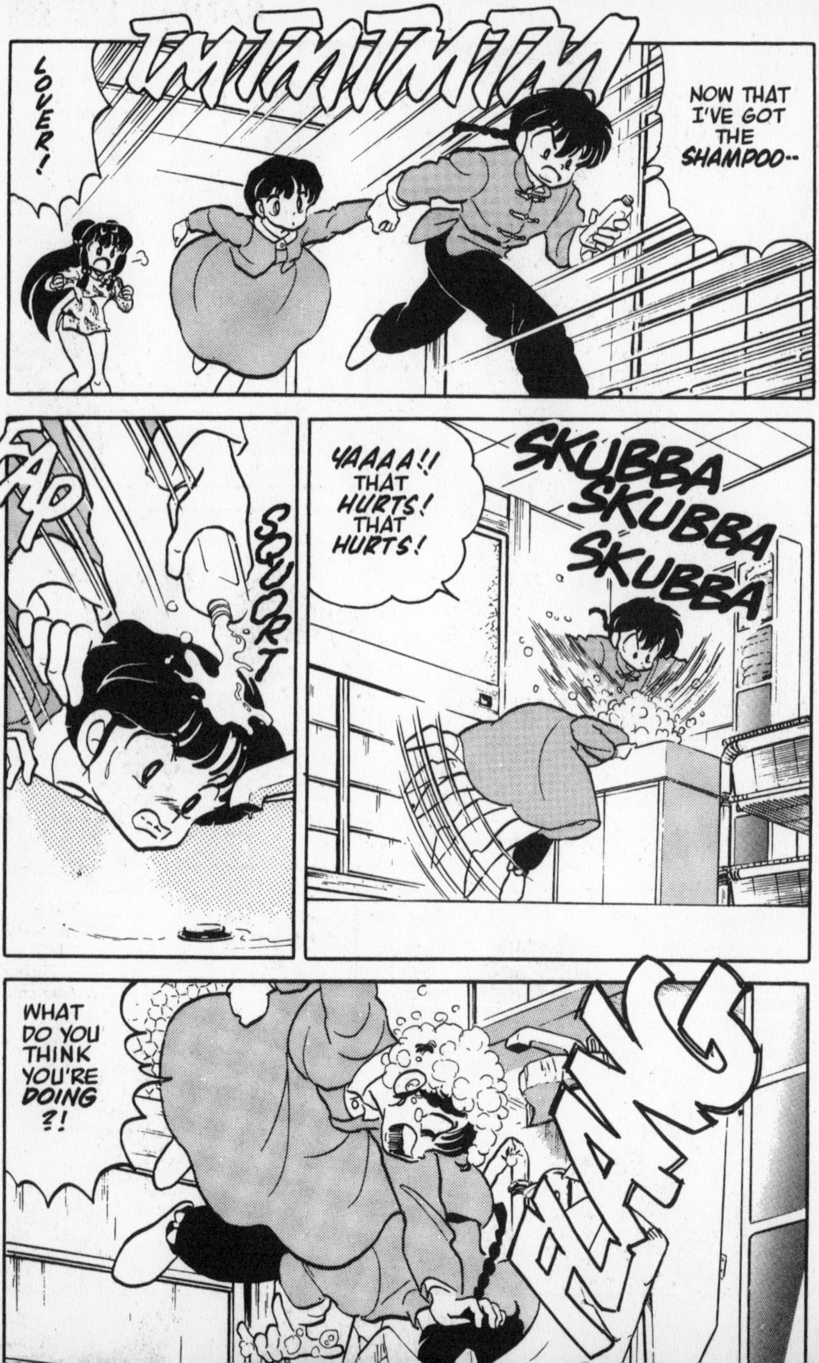
LOVER!
TMTMTMTMTM
NOW THAT I'VE GOT THE SHAMPOO--
FAP
SQUOORT
YAAAA!! THAT HURTS! THAT HURTS!
SKUBBA SKUBBA SKUBBA
WHAT DO YOU THINK YOU'RE DOING ?!
BAMG

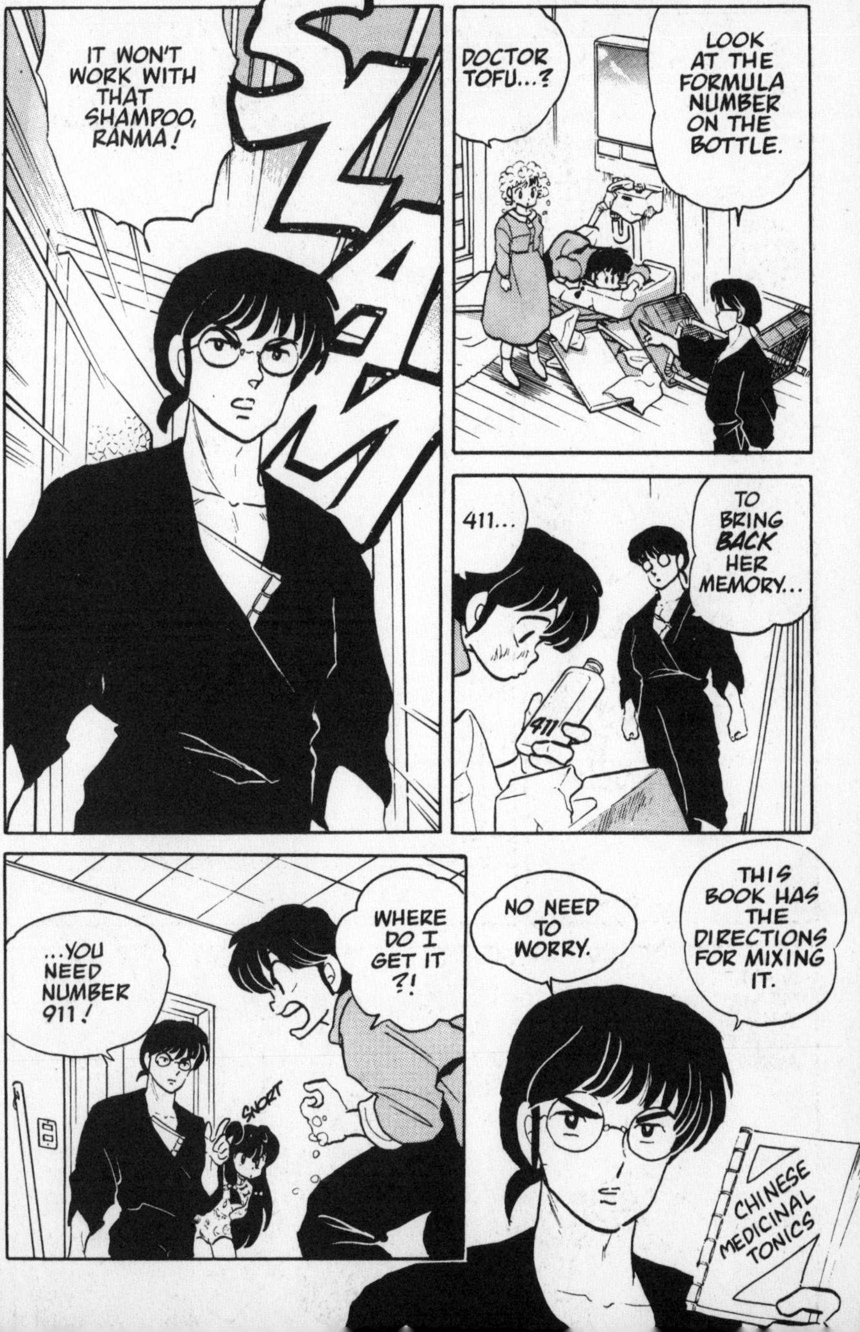
SLAM
IT WON'T WORK WITH THAT SHAMPOO, RANMA!
DOCTOR TOFU...?
LOOK AT THE FORMULA NUMBER ON THE BOTTLE.
411...
TO BRING BACK HER MEMORY...
...YOU NEED NUMBER 911!
WHERE DO I GET IT?!
SNORT
NO NEED TO WORRY.
THIS BOOK HAS THE DIRECTIONS FOR MIXING IT.
CHINESE MEDICINAL TONICS

OH, DR. TOFU!

YOU MEAN YOU CAN CURE AKANE?

KA-KA-KA-KASUMI!

WH-WHATEVER BR-BRINGS YOU HERE?

WELL... THIS IS MY HOUSE.

GYAAA!! LOOK WHAT YOU'RE DOING!!

BA-BUMP BA-BUMP BA-BUMP

RIP RIP RIP

HWOOOO OWF OWF

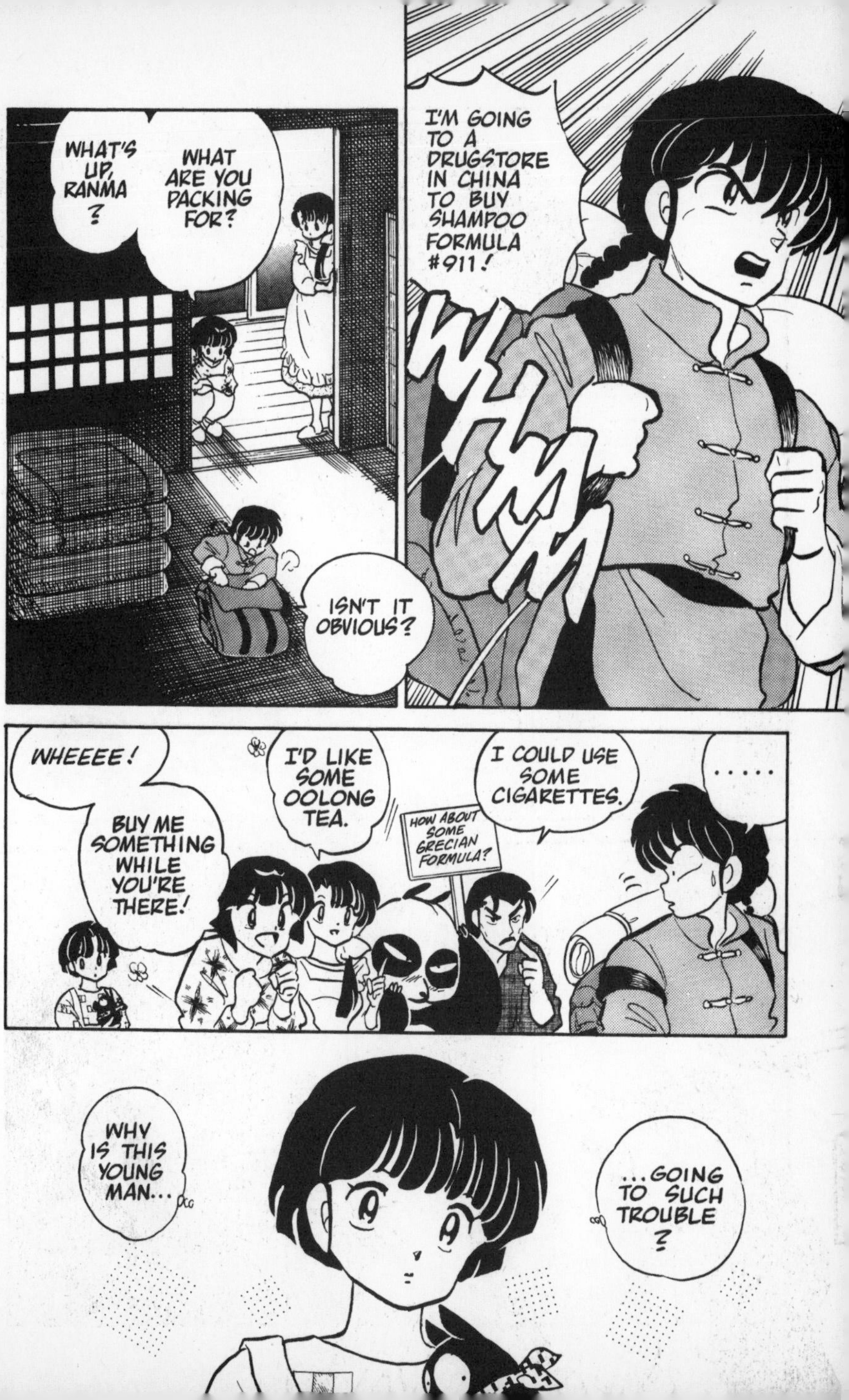
WHAT'S UP, RANMA?
WHAT ARE YOU PACKING FOR?
ISN'T IT OBVIOUS?
I'M GOING TO A DRUGSTORE IN CHINA TO BUY SHAMPOO FORMULA #911!
WHEEEE!
BUY ME SOMETHING WHILE YOU'RE THERE!
I'D LIKE SOME OOLONG TEA.
HOW ABOUT SOME GRECIAN FORMULA?
I COULD USE SOME CIGARETTES.
.....
WHY IS THIS YOUNG MAN...
...GOING TO SUCH TROUBLE?

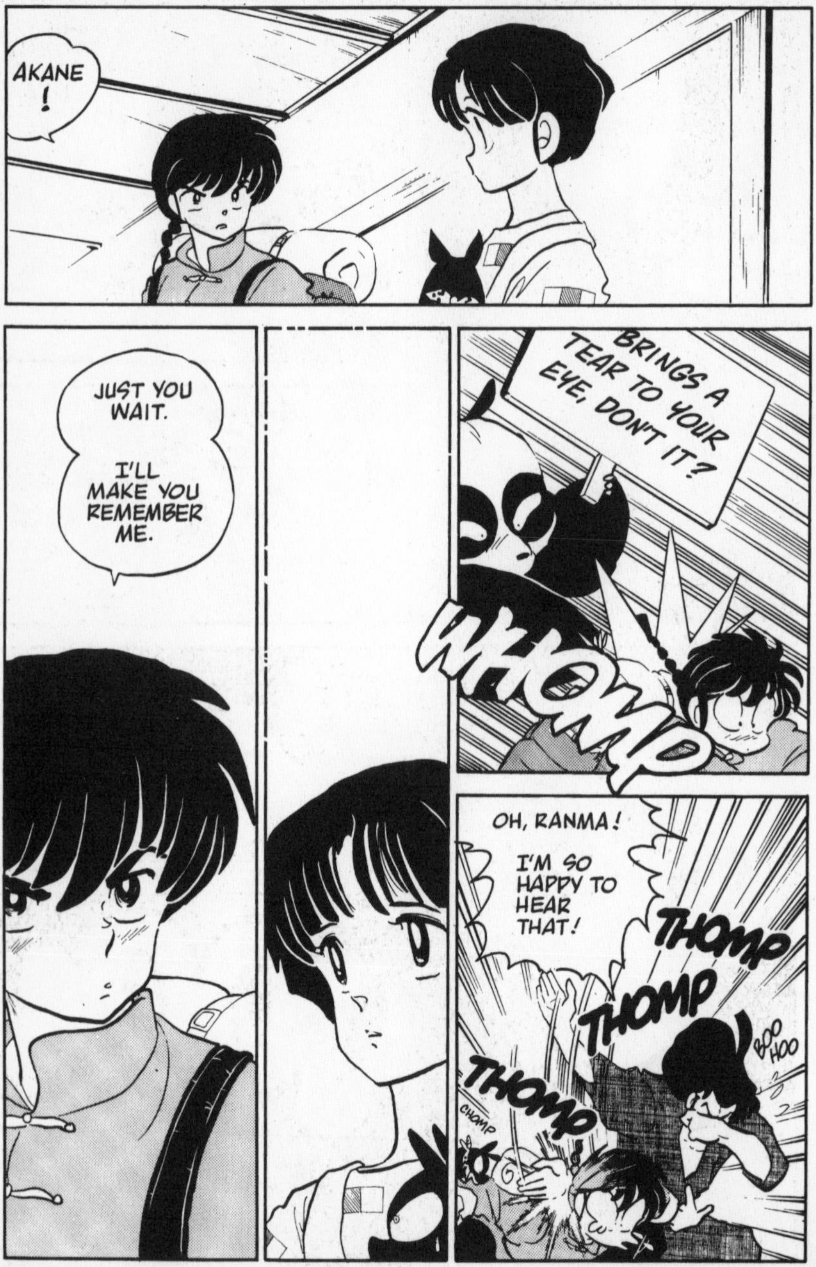
AKANE !
JUST YOU WAIT.
I'LL MAKE YOU REMEMBER ME.
BRINGS A TEAR TO YOUR EYE, DON'T IT?
WHOMP
OH, RANMA!
I'M SO HAPPY TO HEAR THAT!
THOMP
THOMP
THOMP
BOO HOO
CHOMP

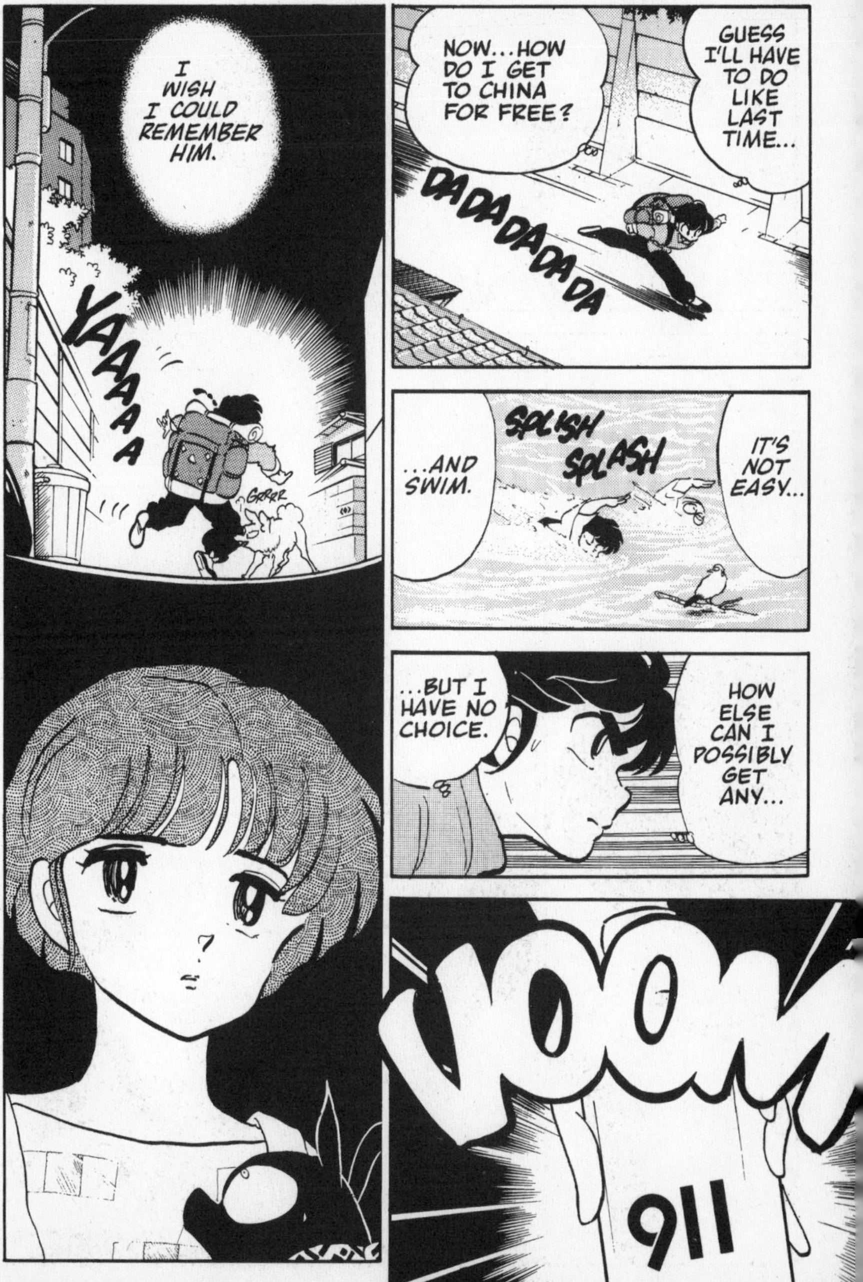
I WISH I COULD REMEMBER HIM.
YAAAAAA
GRRRR
NOW...HOW DO I GET TO CHINA FOR FREE?
GUESS I'LL HAVE TO DO LIKE LAST TIME...
DA DA DA DA DA DA
...AND SWIM.
SPLISH
SPLASH
IT'S NOT EASY...
...BUT I HAVE NO CHOICE.
HOW ELSE CAN I POSSIBLY GET ANY...
VOOM
911

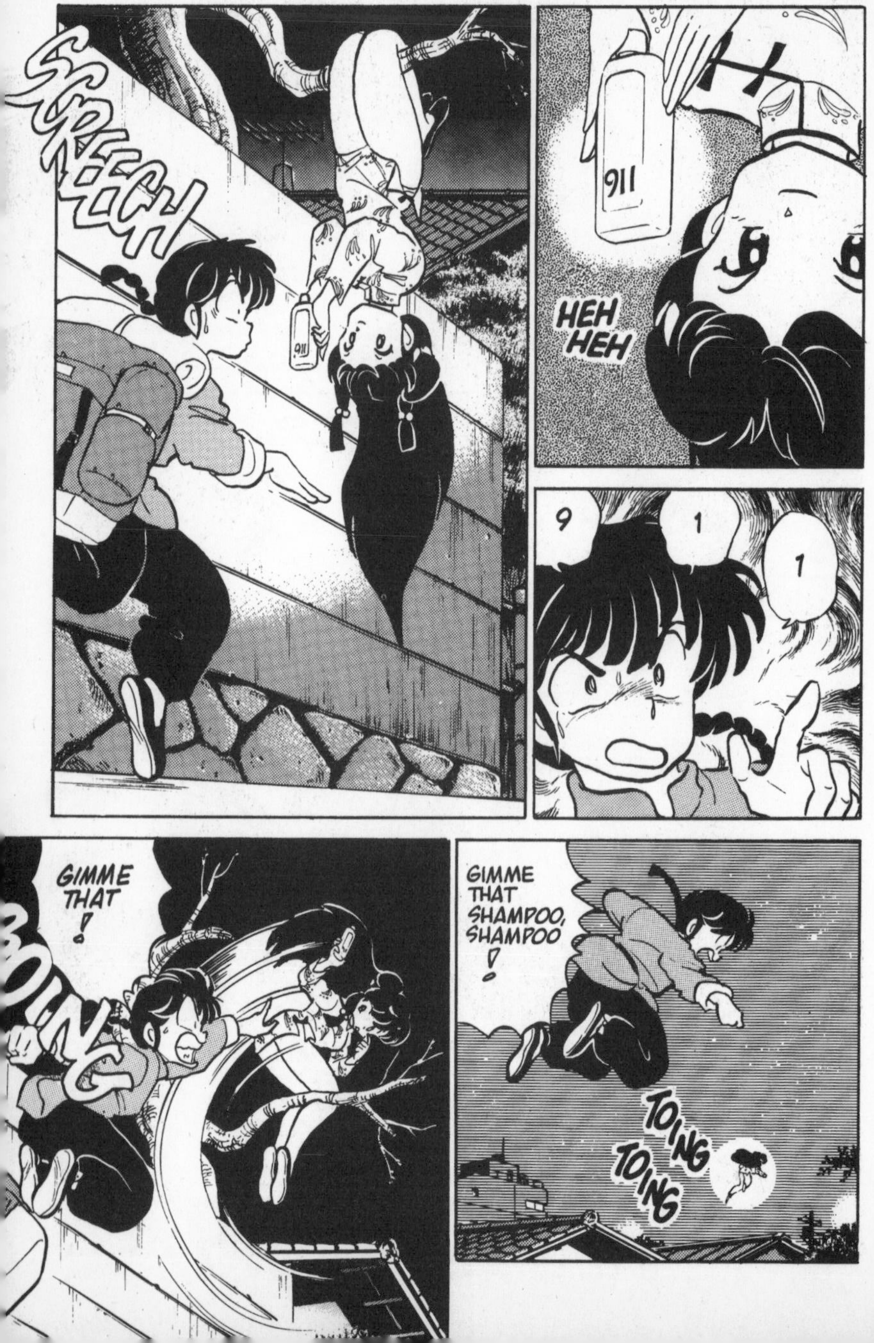
SCREECH
HEH HEH
9
1
1
GIMME THAT!
BOING
GIMME THAT SHAMPOO, SHAMPOO!
TOING TOING

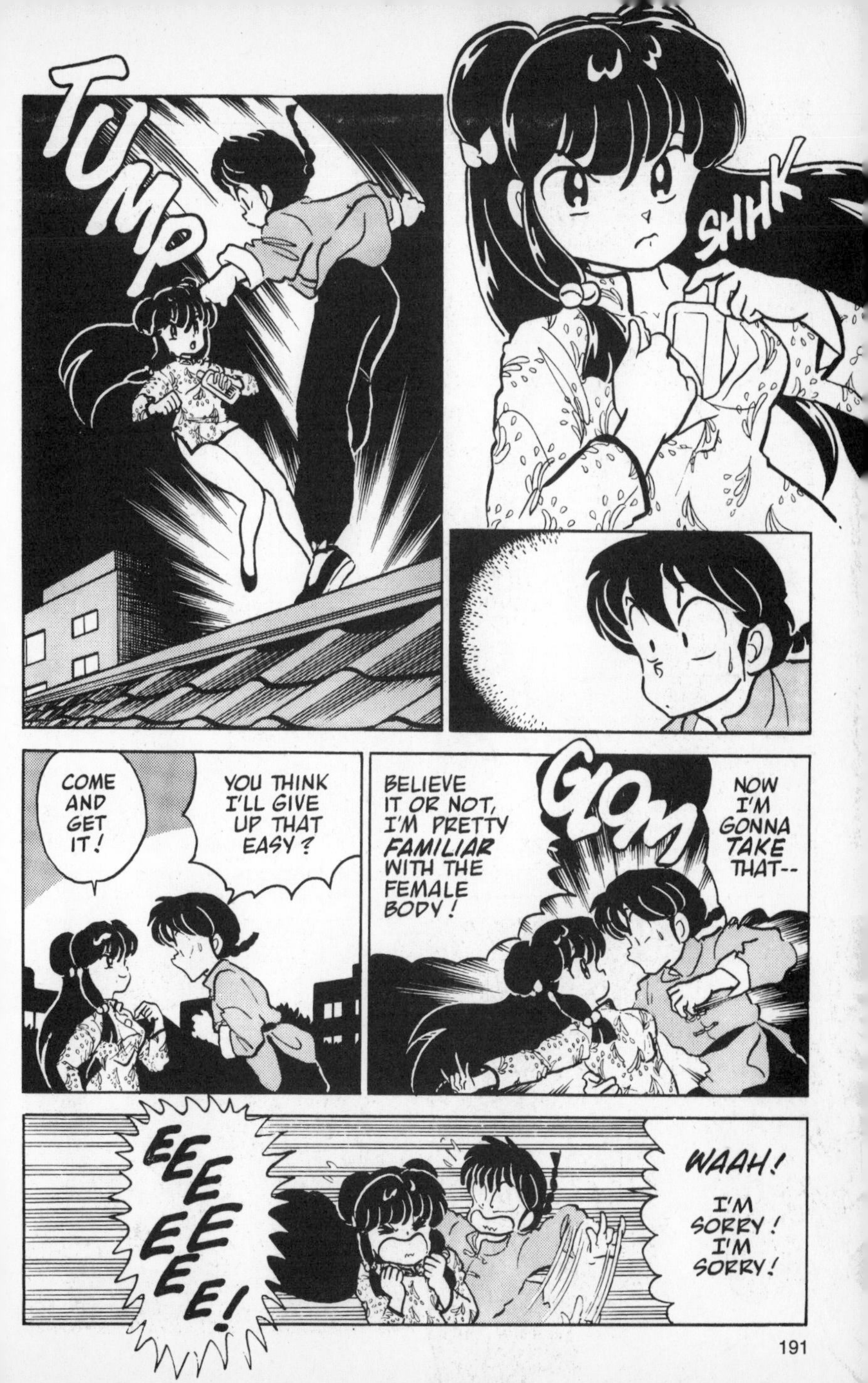
TUMP
SHHK
COME AND GET IT!
YOU THINK I'LL GIVE UP THAT EASY?
BELIEVE IT OR NOT, I'M PRETTY *FAMILIAR* WITH THE FEMALE BODY!
GLOM
NOW I'M GONNA TAKE THAT--
EEEEEEEEE!
WAAH!
I'M SORRY! I'M SORRY!

ALL RIGHT.

I'LL TELL YOU WHAT.

GIVE ME THE SHAMPOO AND I'LL DO WHATEVER YOU WANT.

SLAP

REALLY?

YOU HAVE MY WORD.

AS LONG AS YOU DON'T ASK ME TO MARRY YOU OR KILL AKANE.

GLINT

OKAY...

...KILL FEMALE RANMA!

HUH?

Part 11
BIE LIAO (GOODBYE)

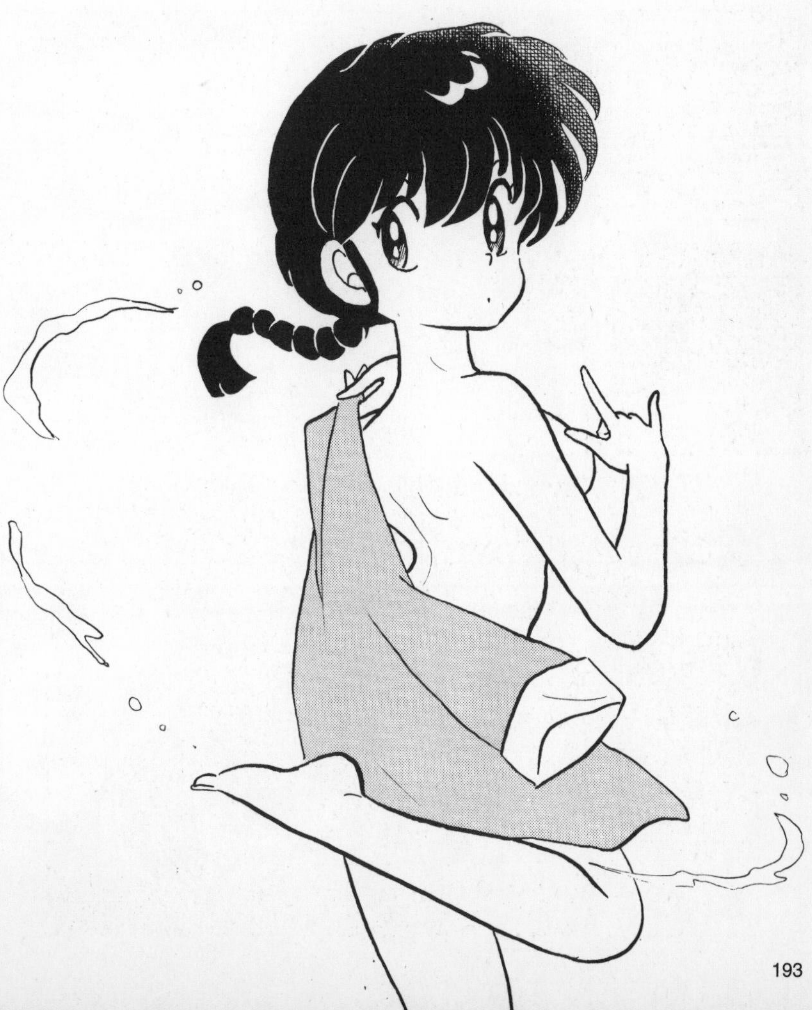

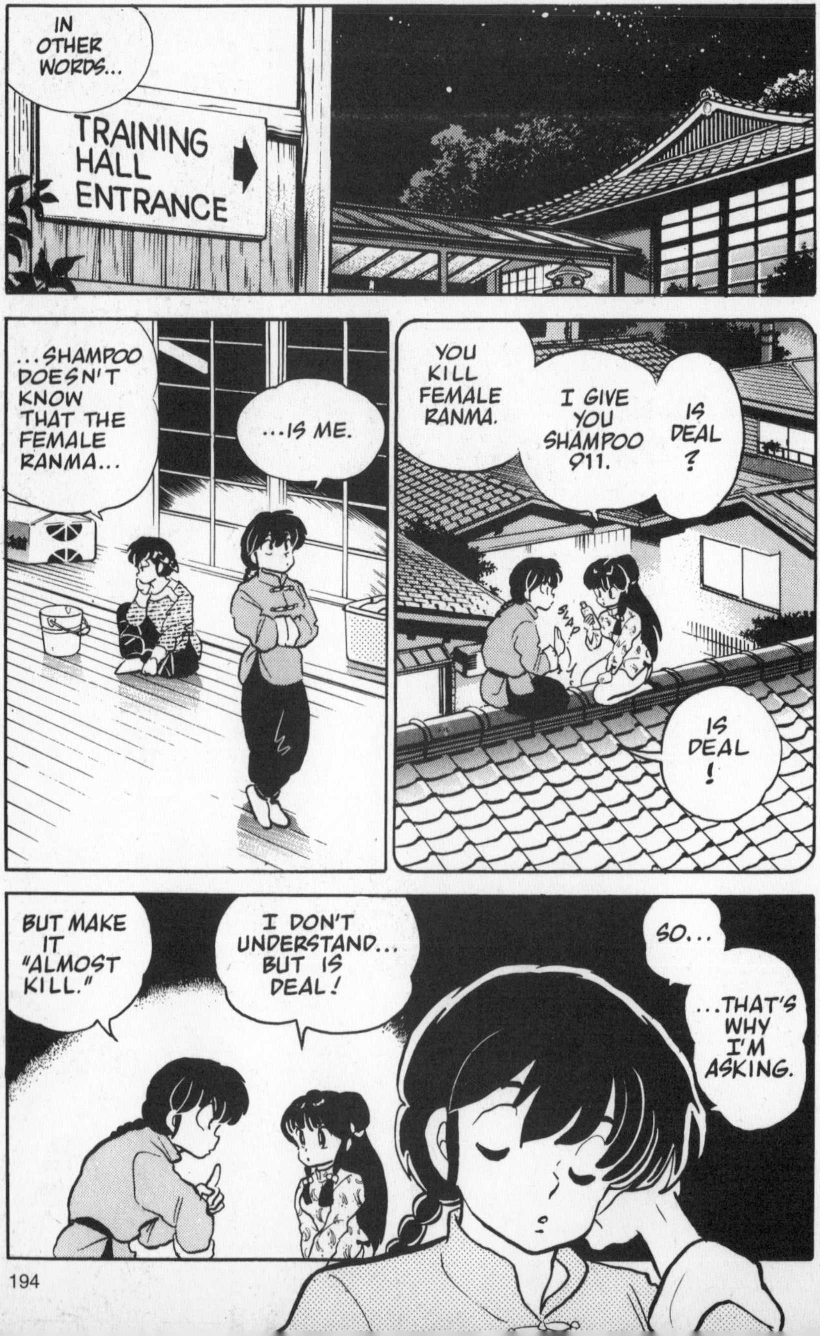
IN OTHER WORDS...
TRAINING HALL ENTRANCE
...SHAMPOO DOESN'T KNOW THAT THE FEMALE RANMA...
...IS ME.
YOU KILL FEMALE RANMA.
I GIVE YOU SHAMPOO 911.
IS DEAL?
SLAP
IS DEAL!
BUT MAKE IT "ALMOST KILL."
I DON'T UNDERSTAND... BUT IS DEAL!
SO...
...THAT'S WHY I'M ASKING.

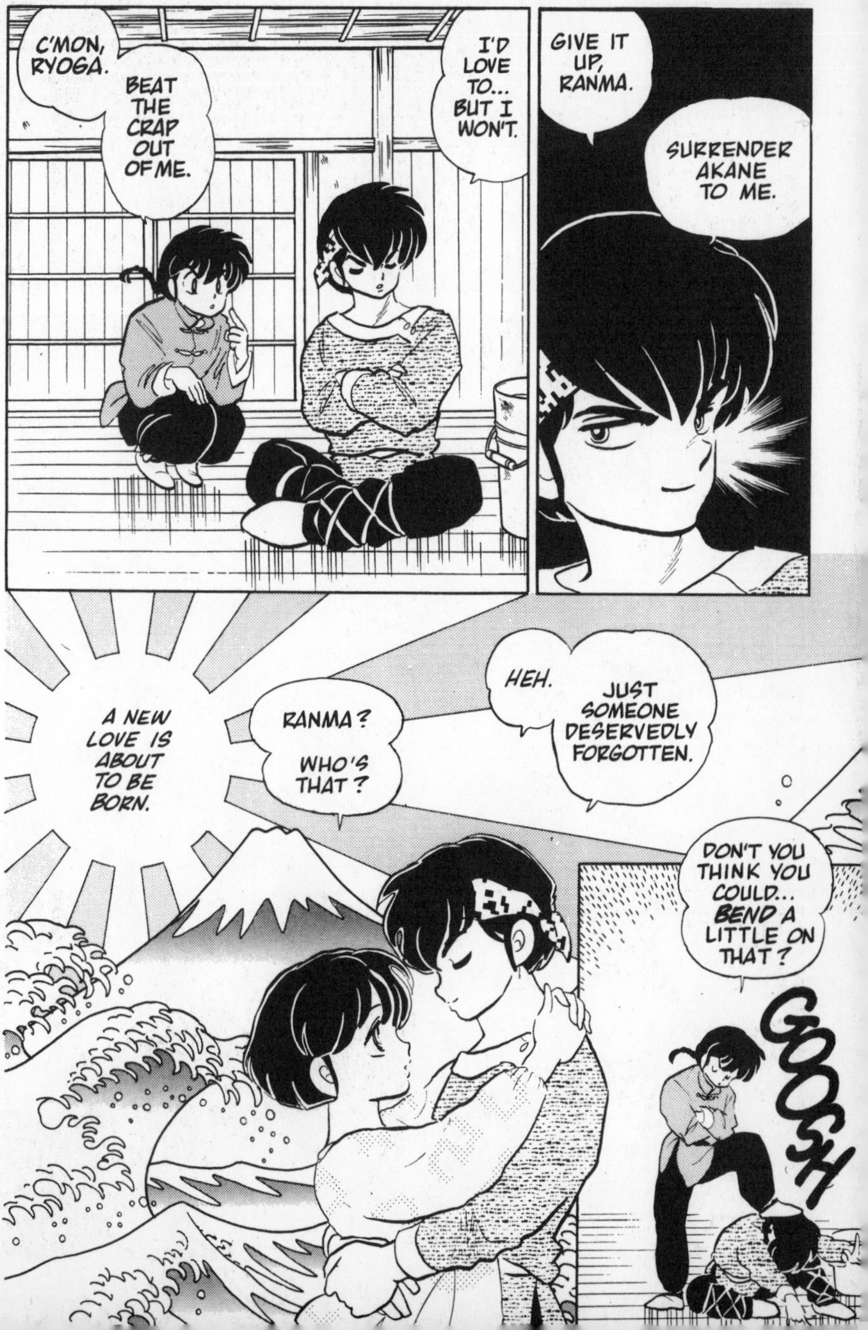
C'MON, RYOGA.
BEAT THE CRAP OUT OF ME.
I'D LOVE TO... BUT I WON'T.
GIVE IT UP, RANMA.
SURRENDER AKANE TO ME.
A NEW LOVE IS ABOUT TO BE BORN.
RANMA? WHO'S THAT?
HEH.
JUST SOMEONE DESERVEDLY FORGOTTEN.
DON'T YOU THINK YOU COULD... BEND A LITTLE ON THAT?
GOOSH

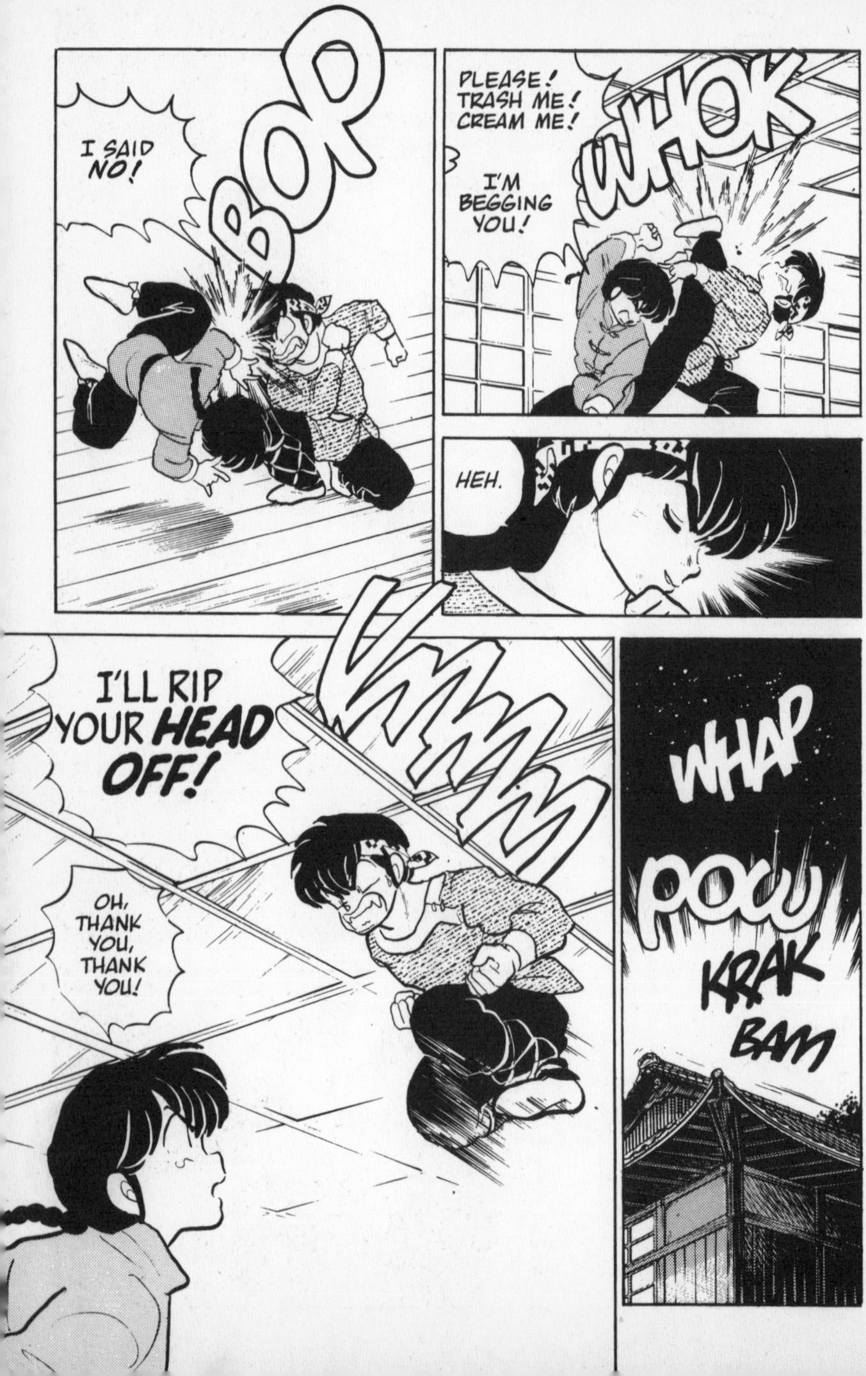
I SAID NO!
BOP
PLEASE! TRASH ME! CREAM ME!
I'M BEGGING YOU!
WHOK
HEH.
I'LL RIP YOUR HEAD OFF!
OH, THANK YOU, THANK YOU!
VMMM
WHAP
POW
KRAK
BAM

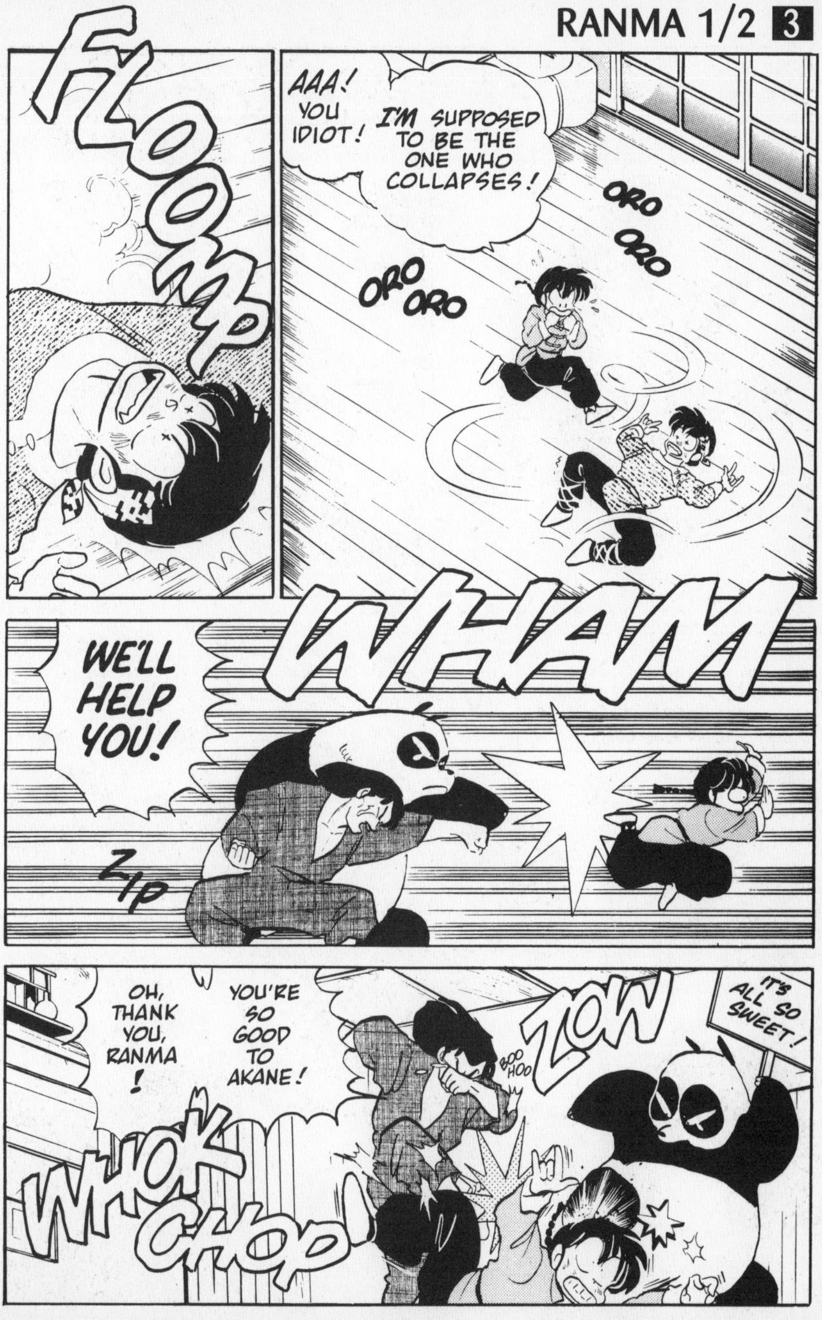
FLOOMP
AAA! YOU IDIOT!
I'M SUPPOSED TO BE THE ONE WHO COLLAPSES!
ORO
ORO
ORO
ORO
WHAM
WE'LL HELP YOU!
ZIP
OH, THANK YOU, RANMA!
YOU'RE SO GOOD TO AKANE!
BOO HOO
ZOW
IT'S ALL SO SWEET!
WHOK
CHOP

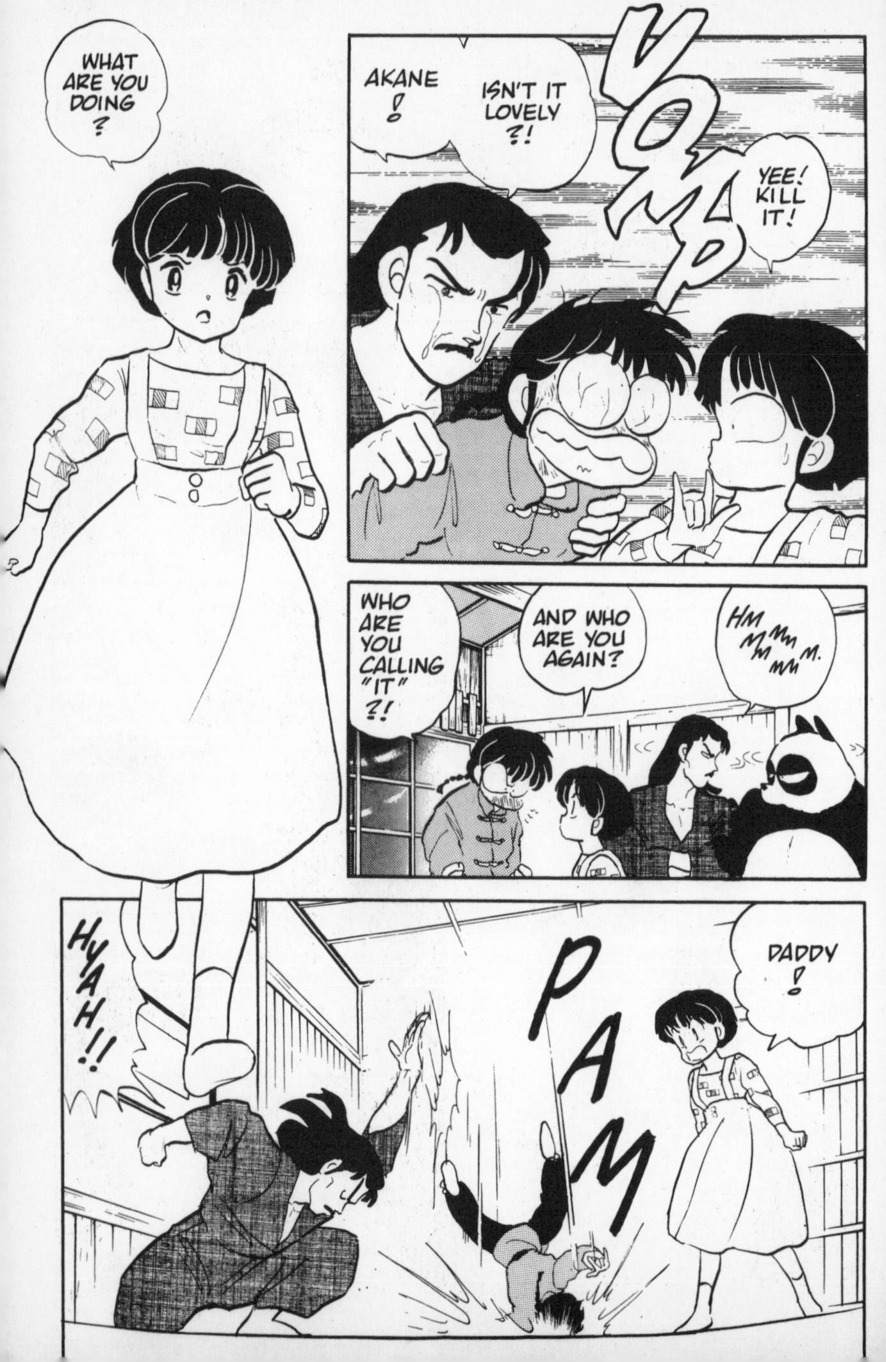
WHAT ARE YOU DOING?
AKANE!
ISN'T IT LOVELY?!
VOMP
YEE! KILL IT!
WHO ARE YOU CALLING "IT"?!
AND WHO ARE YOU AGAIN?
HMMMMMMMMM.
HYAH!!
PAM
DADDY!

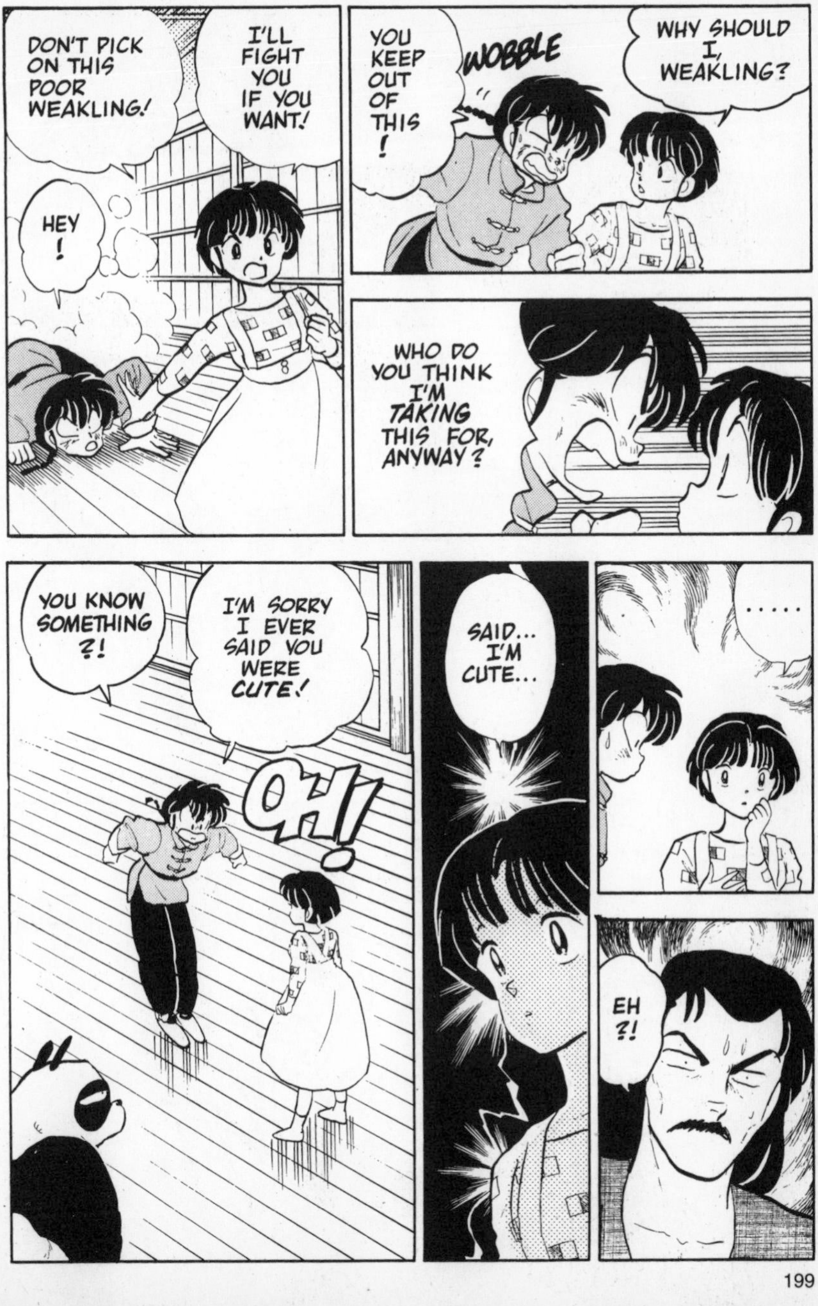
DON'T PICK ON THIS POOR WEAKLING!
I'LL FIGHT YOU IF YOU WANT!
HEY!
YOU KEEP OUT OF THIS!
WOBBLE
WHY SHOULD I, WEAKLING?
WHO DO YOU THINK I'M *TAKING* THIS FOR, ANYWAY?
YOU KNOW SOMETHING ?!
I'M SORRY I EVER SAID YOU WERE *CUTE!*
OH!
SAID... I'M CUTE...
......
EH ?!

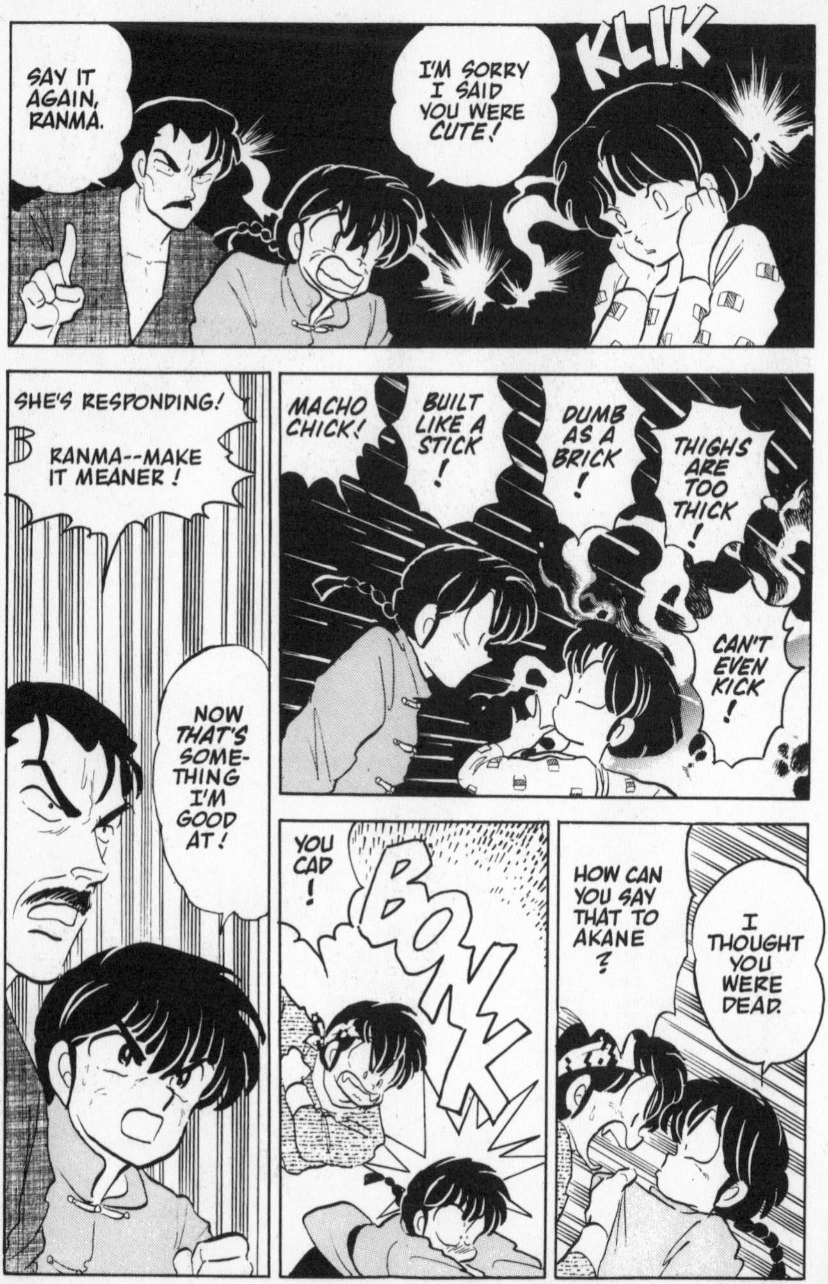
SAY IT AGAIN, RANMA.
I'M SORRY I SAID YOU WERE CUTE!
KLIK
SHE'S RESPONDING!
RANMA--MAKE IT MEANER!
NOW THAT'S SOMETHING I'M GOOD AT!
MACHO CHICK!
BUILT LIKE A STICK!
DUMB AS A BRICK!
THIGHS ARE TOO THICK!
CAN'T EVEN KICK!
YOU CAD!
BONK
HOW CAN YOU SAY THAT TO AKANE?
I THOUGHT YOU WERE DEAD.

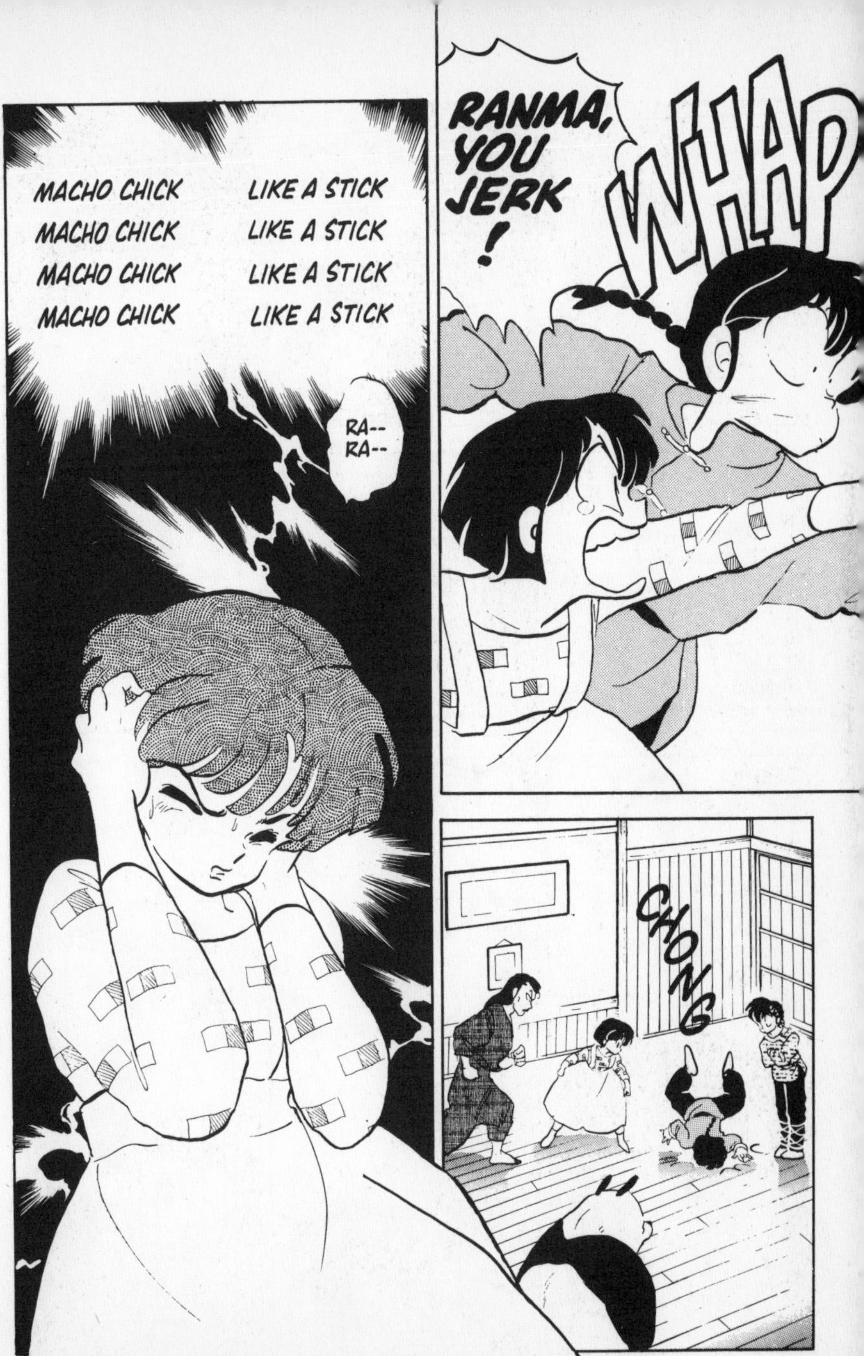
MACHO CHICK LIKE A STICK
MACHO CHICK LIKE A STICK
MACHO CHICK LIKE A STICK
MACHO CHICK LIKE A STICK
RA-- RA--
RANMA, YOU JERK!
WHAP
CHONG

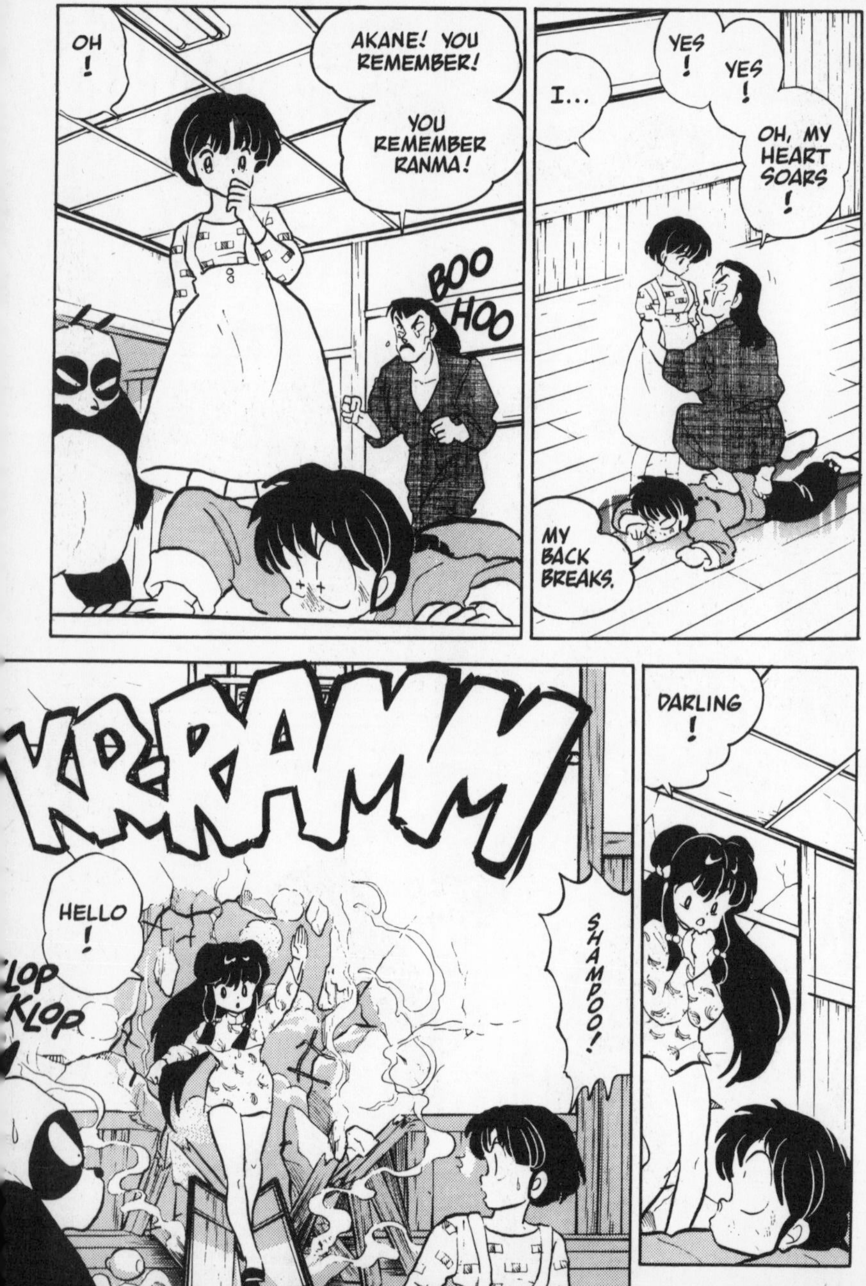
OH!
AKANE! YOU REMEMBER!
YOU REMEMBER RANMA!
BOO HOO
I...
YES! YES!
OH, MY HEART SOARS!
MY BACK BREAKS.
KRRAMM
HELLO!
KLOP KLOP
SHAMPOO!
DARLING!

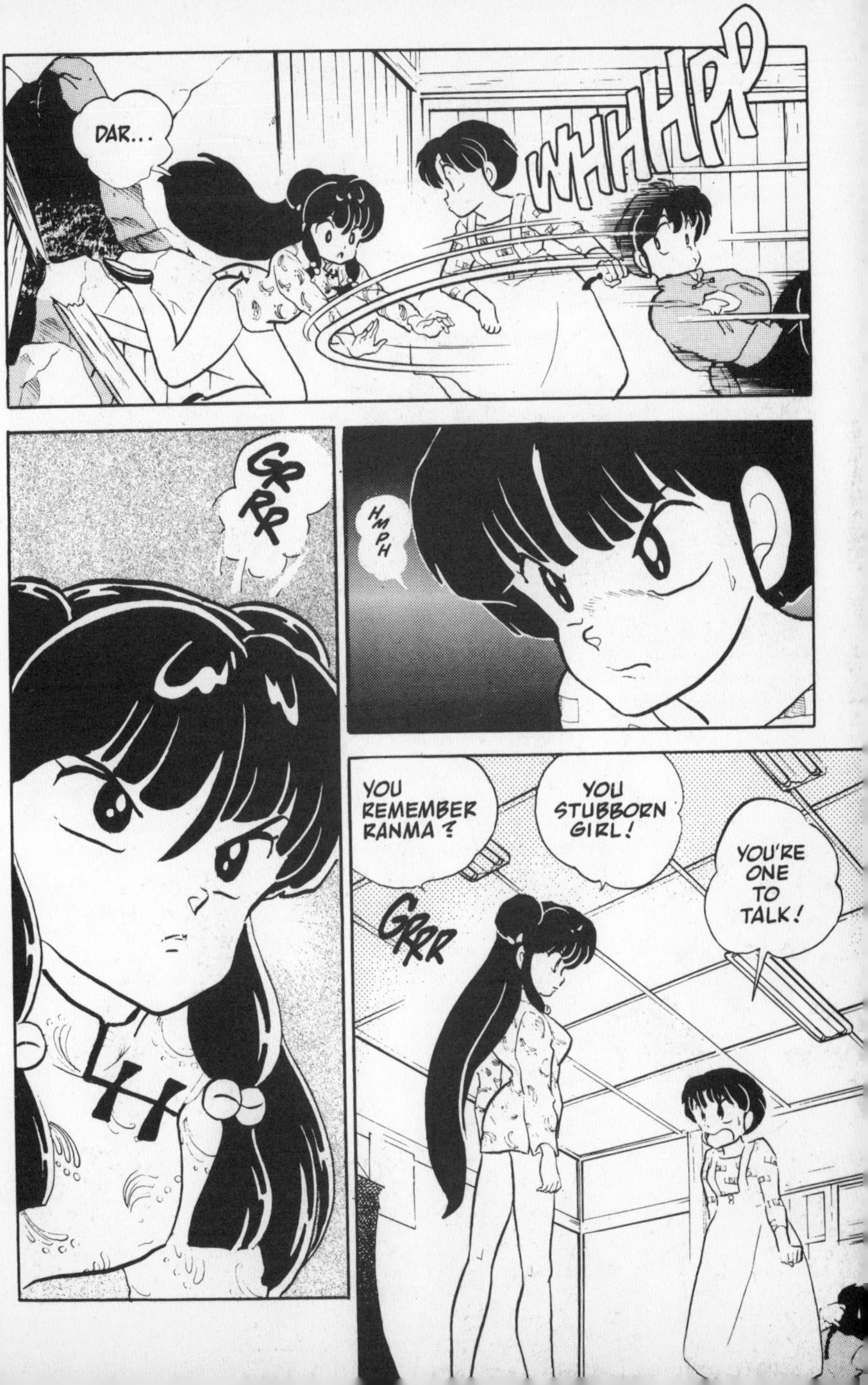
DAR...
WHHHPP
GRRR
HMPH
YOU REMEMBER RANMA?
YOU STUBBORN GIRL!
GRRR
YOU'RE ONE TO TALK!

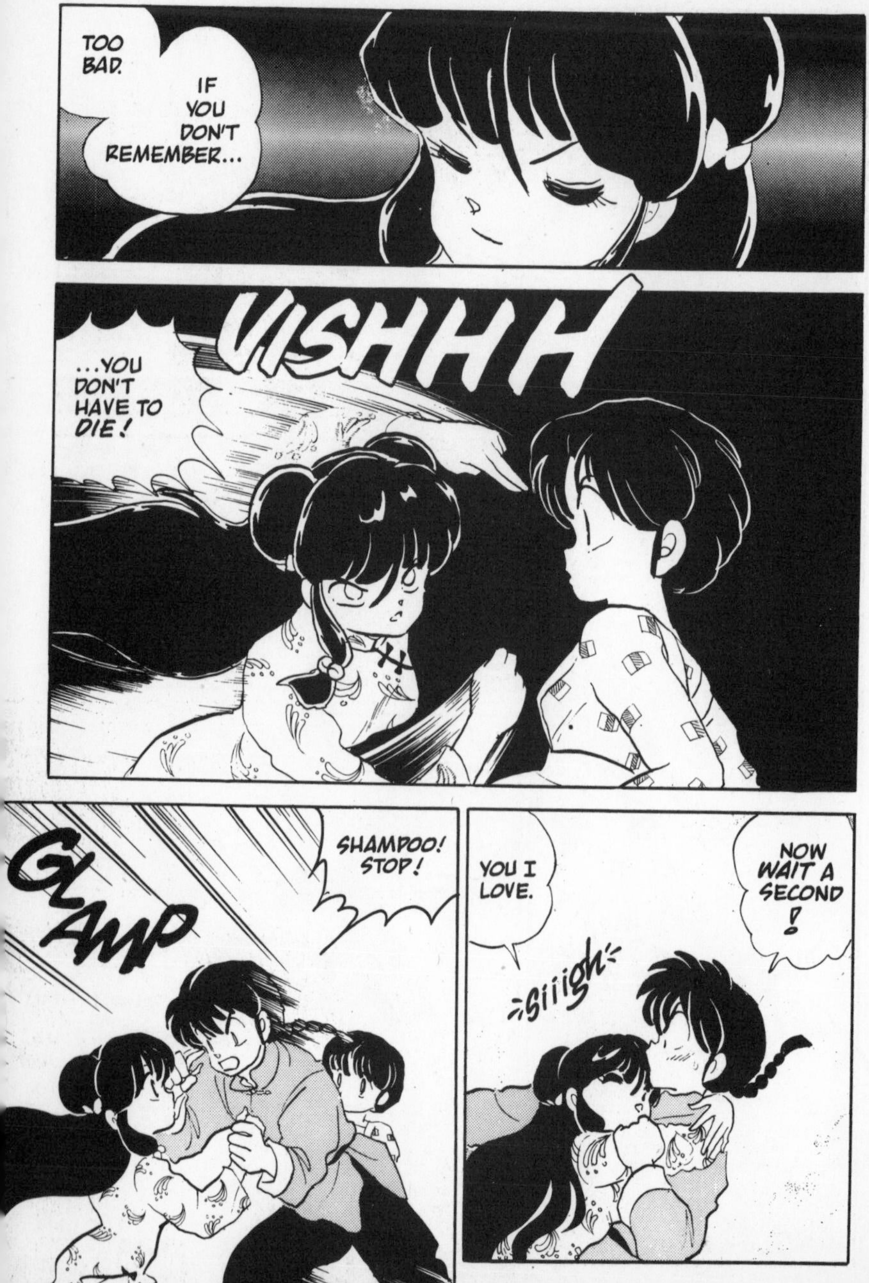
TOO BAD.
IF YOU DON'T REMEMBER...
VISHHH
...YOU DON'T HAVE TO DIE!
GLAMP
SHAMPOO! STOP!
YOU I LOVE.
NOW WAIT A SECOND!
SIIIGH

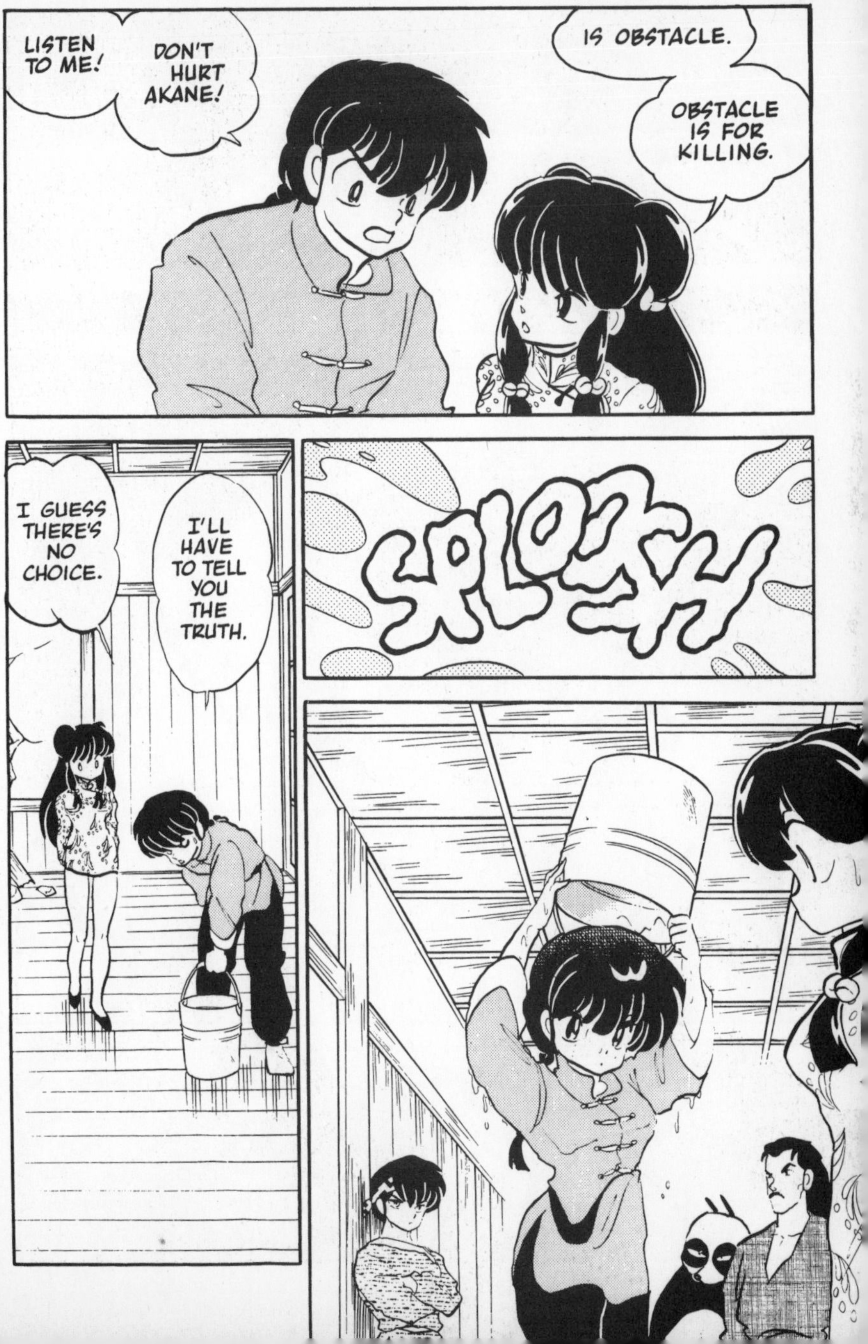
LISTEN TO ME!
DON'T HURT AKANE!
IS OBSTACLE.
OBSTACLE IS FOR KILLING.
I GUESS THERE'S NO CHOICE.
I'LL HAVE TO TELL YOU THE TRUTH.
SPLOOSH

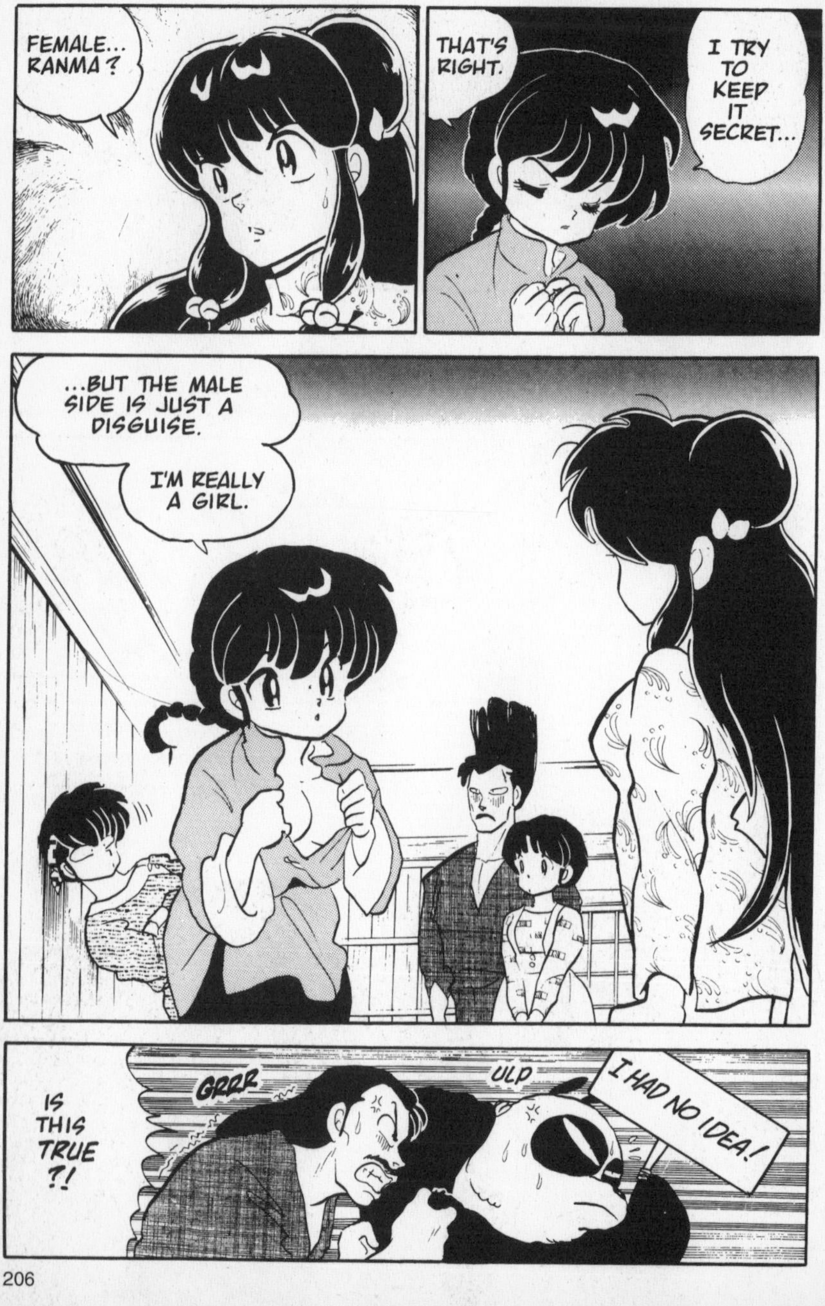
FEMALE... RANMA?
THAT'S RIGHT.
I TRY TO KEEP IT SECRET...
...BUT THE MALE SIDE IS JUST A DISGUISE.
I'M REALLY A GIRL.
IS THIS TRUE ?!
GRRR
ULP
I HAD NO IDEA!

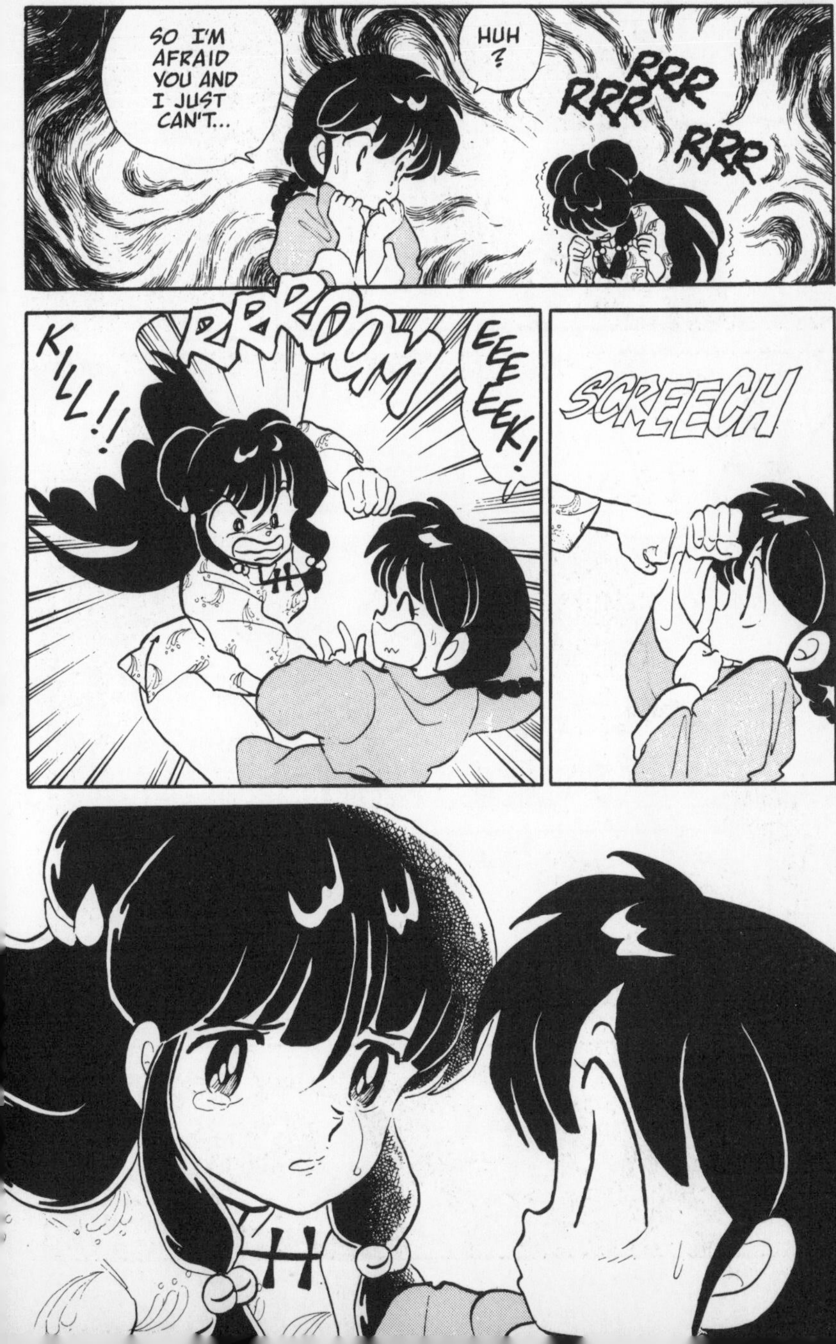
SO I'M AFRAID YOU AND I JUST CAN'T...
HUH ?
RRR RRR RRR
RRROOM
KILL!!
EEEEEEK!
SCREECH

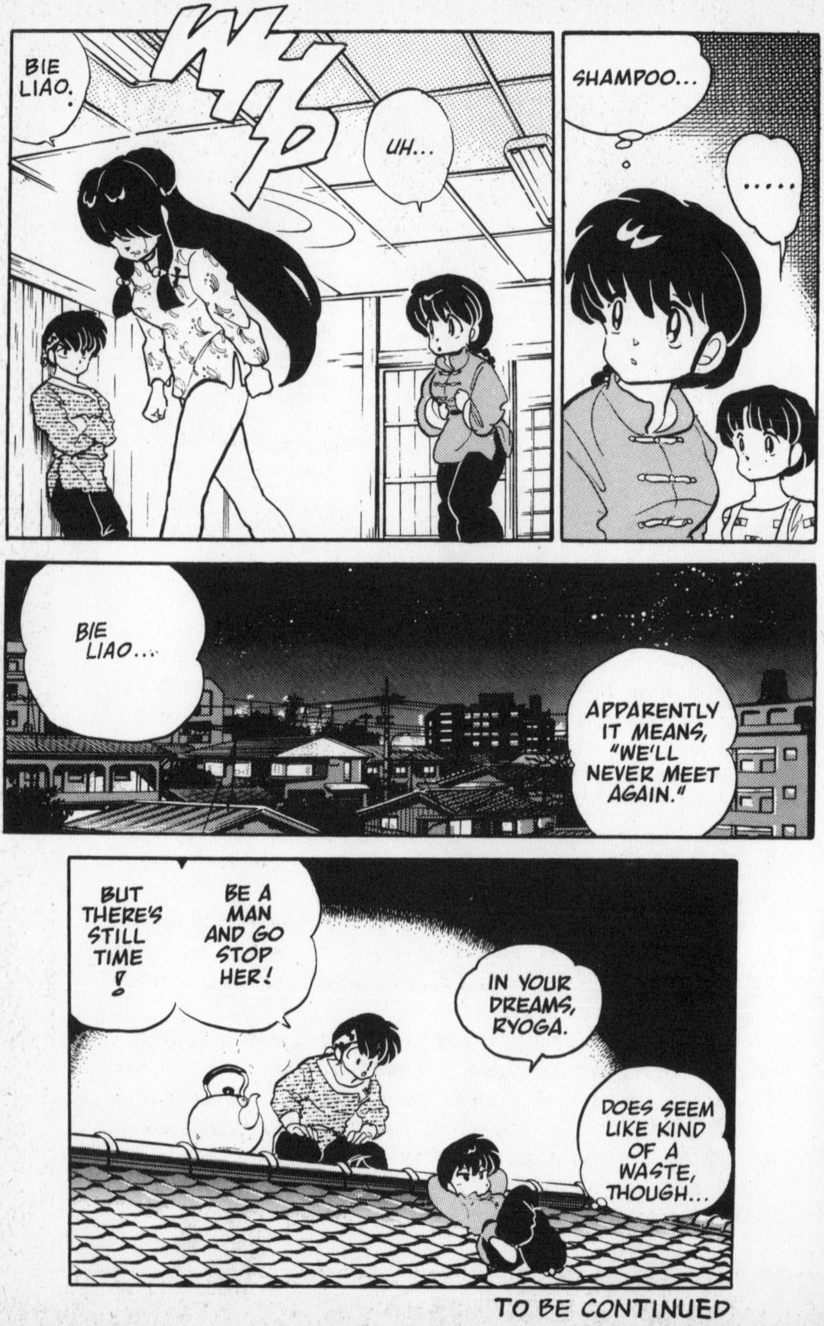
BIE LIAO.
WHIP
UH...
SHAMPOO...
.....
BIE LIAO...
APPARENTLY IT MEANS, "WE'LL NEVER MEET AGAIN."
BUT THERE'S STILL TIME!
BE A MAN AND GO STOP HER!
IN YOUR DREAMS, RYOGA.
DOES SEEM LIKE KIND OF A WASTE, THOUGH...

TO BE CONTINUED

About Rumiko Takahashi

Born in 1957 in Niigata, Japan, Rumiko Takahashi attended women's college in Tokyo, where she began studying comics with Kazuo Koike, author of *Crying Freeman*. She later became an assistant to horror-manga artist Kazuo Umezu (*Orochi*). In 1978, she won a prize in Shogakukan's annual "New Comic Artist Contest," and in that same year her boy-meets-alien comedy series *Urusei Yatsura* began appearing in the weekly manga magazine *Shônen Sunday*. This phenomenally successful series ran for nine years and sold over 22 million copies. Takahashi's later *Ranma 1/2* series enjoyed even greater popularity.

Takahashi is considered by many to be one of the world's most popular manga artists. With the publication of Volume 34 of her *Ranma 1/2* series in Japan, Takahashi's total sales passed *one hundred million* copies of her compiled works.

Takahashi's serial titles include *Urusei Yatsura, Ranma 1/2, One-Pound Gospel, Maison Ikkoku* and *InuYasha*. Additionally, Takahashi has drawn many short stories which have been published in America under the title "Rumic Theater," and several installments of a saga known as her "Mermaid" series. Most of Takahashi's major stories have also been animated, and are widely available in translation worldwide. *InuYasha* is her most recent serial story, first published in *Shônen Sunday* in 1996.

EDITOR'S RECOMMENDATIONS

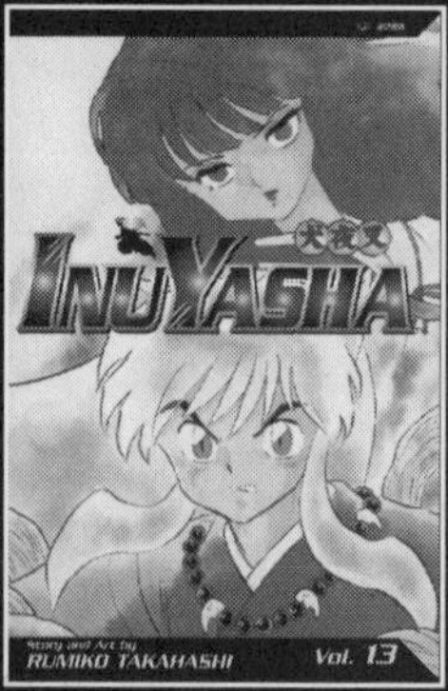

INUYASHA
Story and Art by
RUMIKO TAKAHASHI
Vol. 13

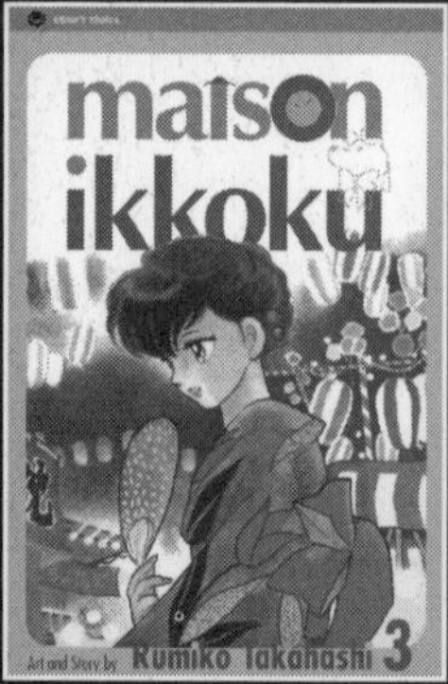

maison ikkoku
Art and Story by Rumiko Takahashi
3

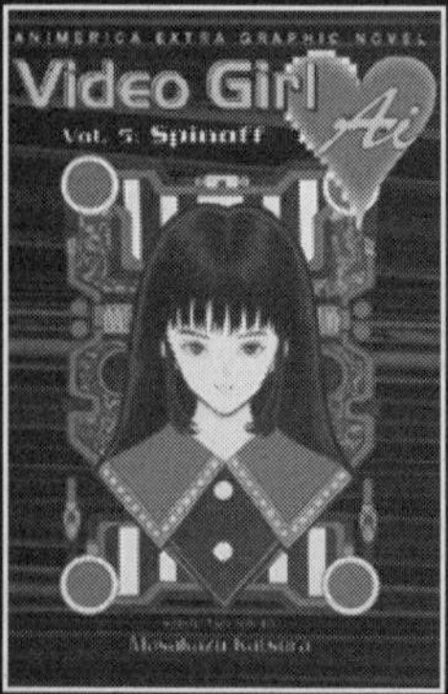

ANIMERICA EXTRA GRAPHIC NOVEL
Video Girl Ai
Vol. 5: Spinoff

Did you like *RANMA 1/2*? Here's what we recommend you try next:

INUYASHA is the manga serial Rumiko Takahashi began working on after she finished *RANMA 1/2*. It's a historical adventure set in ancient Japan, with romance, mystery, and horror elements.

MAISON IKKOKU is Takahashi's most romantic series. It's set in modern-day Japan, and traces the lives of the residents of a boarding house. It's intense, it's angsty, and it's one of the most absorbing manga romances ever written.

VIDEO GIRL AI, by Masakazu Katsura, is a romance set in modern day Japan. Whereas *RANMA 1/2* deals with teen romances in a comedic way, *VIDEO GIRL AI* goes for angst, and masterfully explores the feelings of first love and loss. Katsura also draws some of the most beautiful women in manga!

COMPLETE OUR SURVEY AND LET US KNOW WHAT YOU THINK!

☐ Please check here if you DO NOT wish to receive information or future offers from VIZ

Name: _____

Address: _____

City: _____ **State:** _____ **Zip:** _____

E-mail: _____

☐ Male   ☐ Female   **Date of Birth** (mm/dd/yyyy): ___ / ___ / ___   (Under 13? Parental consent required)

What race/ethnicity do you consider yourself? (please check one)

☐ Asian/Pacific Islander   ☐ Black/African American   ☐ Hispanic/Latino

☐ Native American/Alaskan Native ☐ White/Caucasian   ☐ Other: _____

What VIZ product did you purchase? (check all that apply and indicate title purchased)

☐ DVD/VHS _____

☐ Graphic Novel _____

☐ Magazines _____

☐ Merchandise _____

Reason for purchase: (check all that apply)

☐ Special offer   ☐ Favorite title   ☐ Gift

☐ Recommendation   ☐ Other _____

Where did you make your purchase? (please check one)

☐ Comic store   ☐ Bookstore   ☐ Mass/Grocery Store

☐ Newsstand   ☐ Video/Video Game Store   ☐ Other: _____

☐ Online (site: _____)

What other VIZ properties have you purchased/own? _____

_____

How many anime and/or manga titles have you purchased in the last year? How many were VIZ titles? **(please check one from each column)**

ANIME	MANGA	VIZ
☐ None	☐ None	☐ None
☐ 1-4	☐ 1-4	☐ 1-4
☐ 5-10	☐ 5-10	☐ 5-10
☐ 11+	☐ 11+	☐ 11+

I find the pricing of VIZ products to be: **(please check one)**

☐ Cheap ☐ Reasonable ☐ Expensive

What genre of manga and anime would you like to see from VIZ? **(please check two)**

☐ Adventure ☐ Comic Strip ☐ Detective ☐ Fighting

☐ Horror ☐ Romance ☐ Sci-Fi/Fantasy ☐ Sports

What do you think of VIZ's new look?

☐ Love It ☐ It's OK ☐ Hate It ☐ Didn't Notice ☐ No Opinion

THANK YOU! Please send the completed form to:

NJW Research
42 Catharine St.
Poughkeepsie, NY 12601

All information provided will be used for internal purposes only. We promise not to sell or otherwise divulge your information.